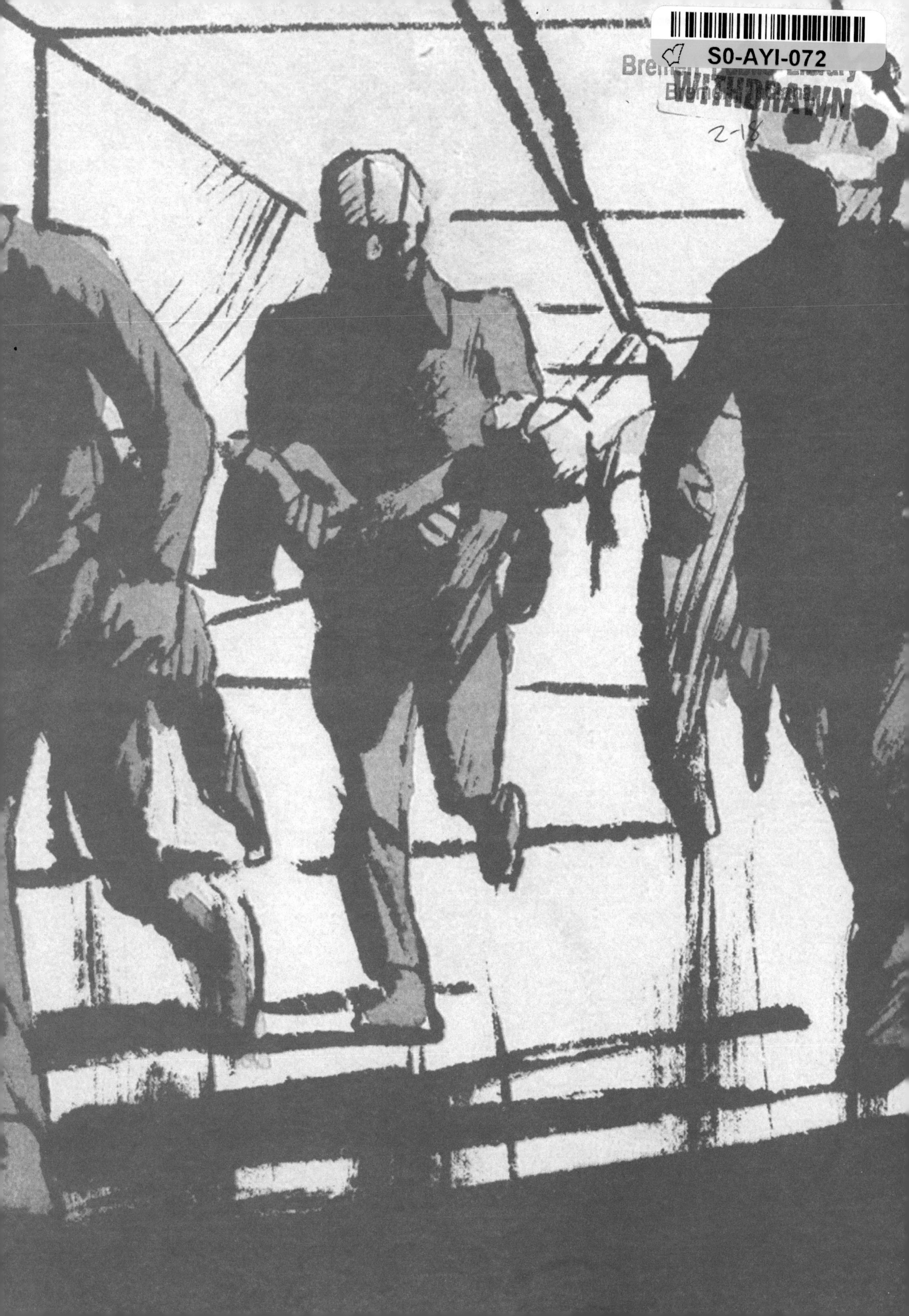

SNOW PIERCER

emic ublis
Bre en, Inc

3 : TERMINUS

SNOWPIERCER

3 : TERMINUS

WRITTEN BY

OLIVIER BOCQUET

ART BY

JEAN-MARC ROCHETTE

LETTERING BY JESSICA BURTON

TITAN
COMICS

Editor
Lizzie Kaye
Collection Designer
Dan Bura
Senior Editor
Steve White
Titan Comics Editorial
Andrew James, Tom William
Jess Burton
Production Supervisors
Kelly Fenlon, Jackie Floo
Production Assistant
Peter James
Art Director
Oz Browne
Studio Manager
Selina Juneja
Senior Sales Manager
Steve Tothill
Senior Marketing and Press Execut
Owen Johnson
Direct Sales & Marketing Manage
Ricky Claydon
Commercial Manager
Michelle Fairlamb
Publishing Manager
Darryl Tothill
Publishing Director
Chris Teather
Operations Director
Leigh Baulch
Executive Director
Vivian Cheung
Publisher
Nick Landau

SNOWPIERCER VOLUME 3: TERMIN

ISBN: 9781782767152

Published by Titan Comics
A division of Titan Publishing Group
144 Southwark St.
London
SE1 0UP

A CIP catalogue record for this title is av
from the British Library.

First edition: February 2016

Originally published in French as
Transperceneige: Terminus (2015

10 9 8 7 6 5 4 3 2 1

Printed in China.
Titan Comics. TC0910

SNOWPIERCER

3 : TERMINUS

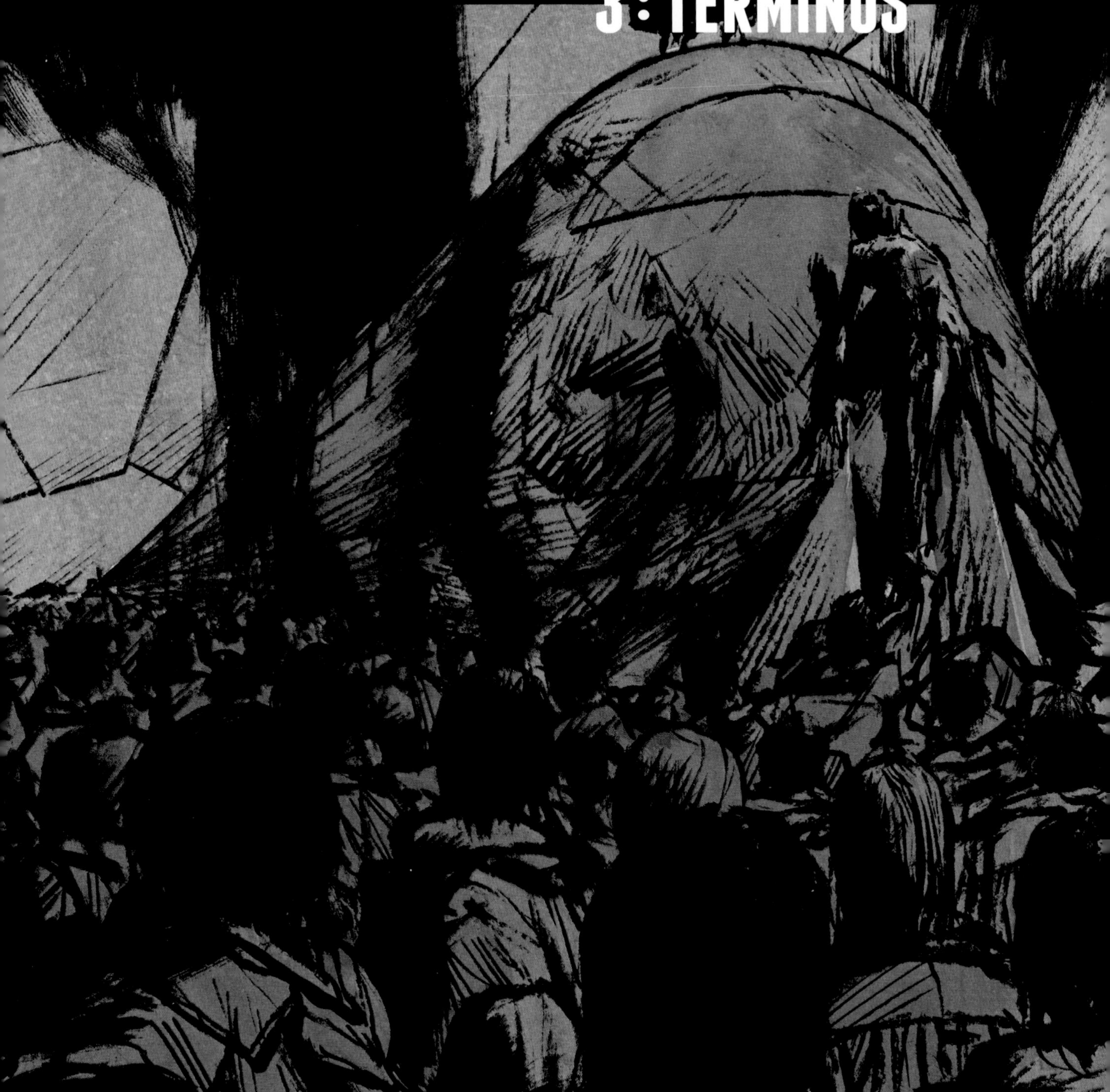

A climatic cataclysm has plunged our planet into a sudden glaciation.

The luckiest people died immediately.

The few remaining ones embarked on a train that never stops: the Snowpiercer.

After decades of wandering, violence and political struggles, the train picks up a radio signal from across the ocean.

Mounted on makeshift caterpillars, it crosses the frozen area, sacrificing on the way most of its cars and passengers.

At the end of the journey, four Explorers – people trained and equipped to survive in the cold – climb a mountain to the very source of the music, in the hope of finding survivors.

They only find frozen corpses. And a transmitter, playing a tune that never stops…

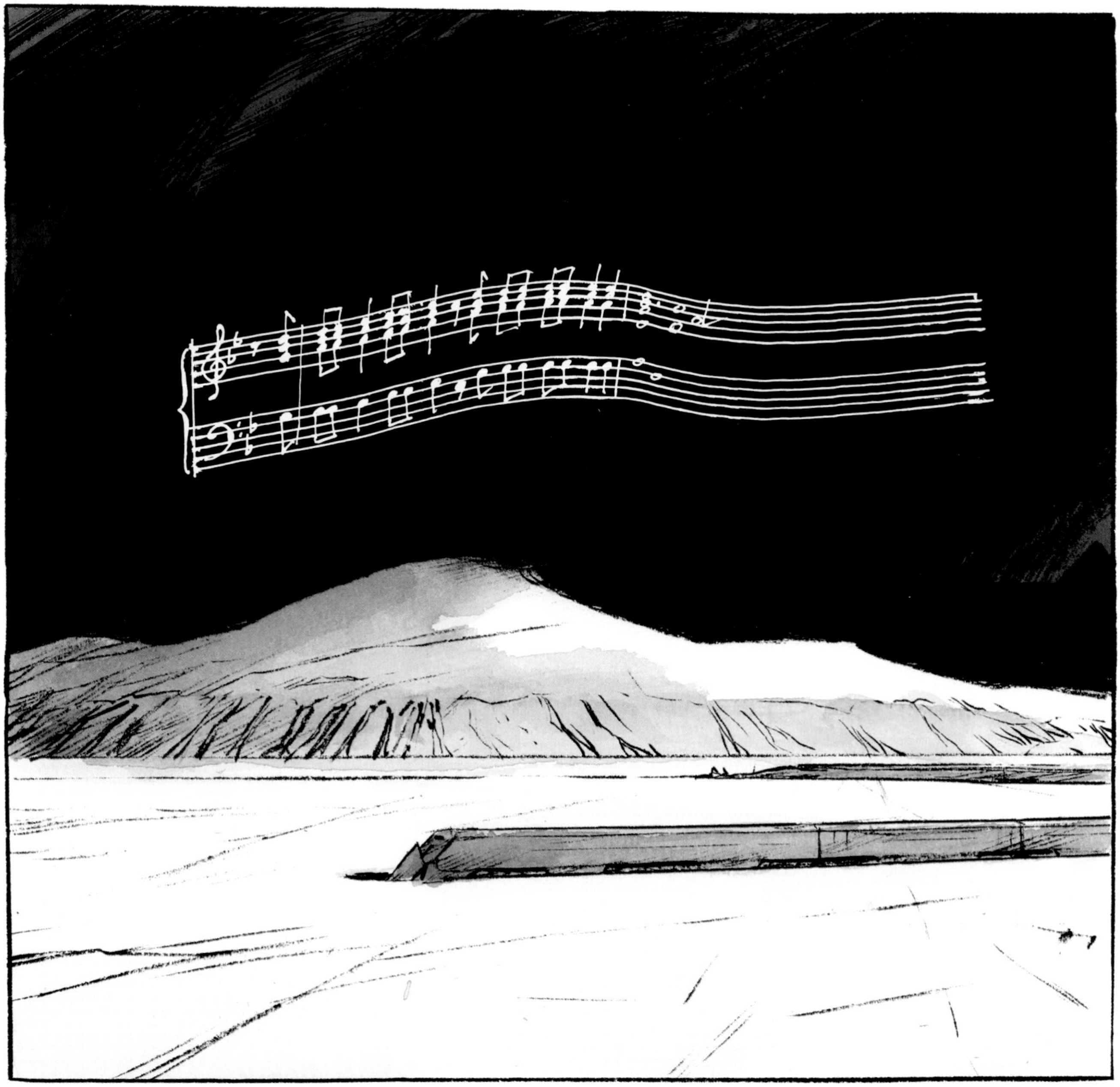

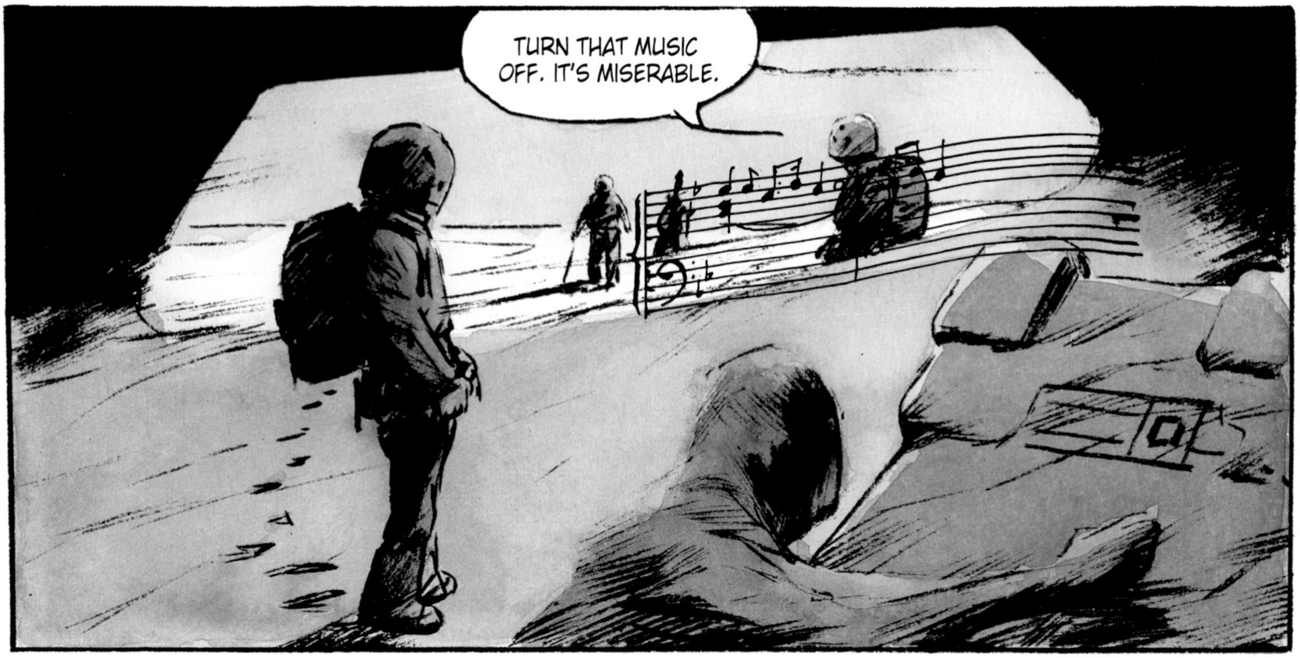
TURN THAT MUSIC OFF. IT'S MISERABLE.

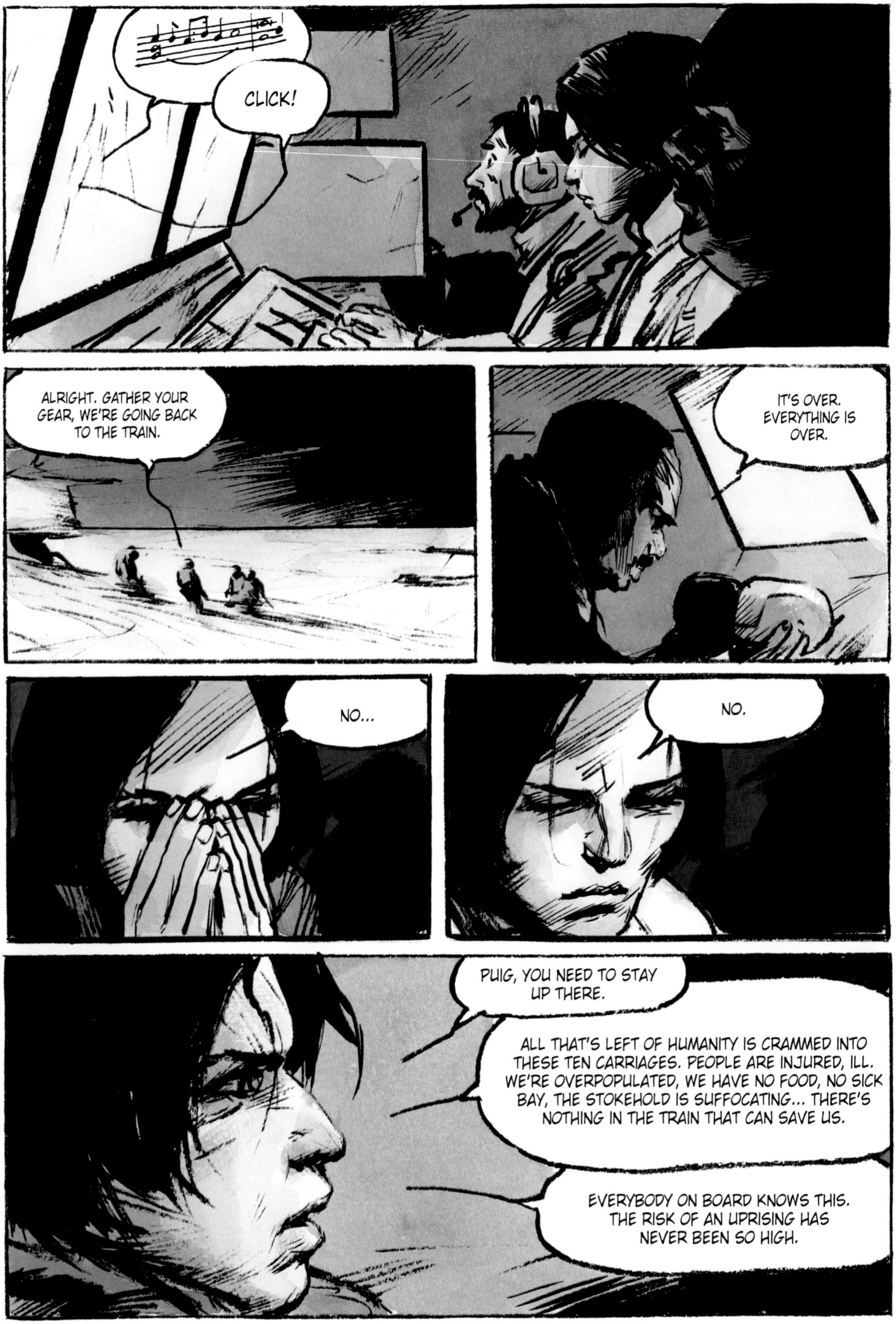
CLICK!
ALRIGHT. GATHER YOUR GEAR, WE'RE GOING BACK TO THE TRAIN.
IT'S OVER. EVERYTHING IS OVER.
NO...
NO.
PUIG, YOU NEED TO STAY UP THERE.
ALL THAT'S LEFT OF HUMANITY IS CRAMMED INTO THESE TEN CARRIAGES. PEOPLE ARE INJURED, ILL. WE'RE OVERPOPULATED, WE HAVE NO FOOD, NO SICK BAY, THE STOKEHOLD IS SUFFOCATING... THERE'S NOTHING IN THE TRAIN THAT CAN SAVE US.
EVERYBODY ON BOARD KNOWS THIS. THE RISK OF AN UPRISING HAS NEVER BEEN SO HIGH.

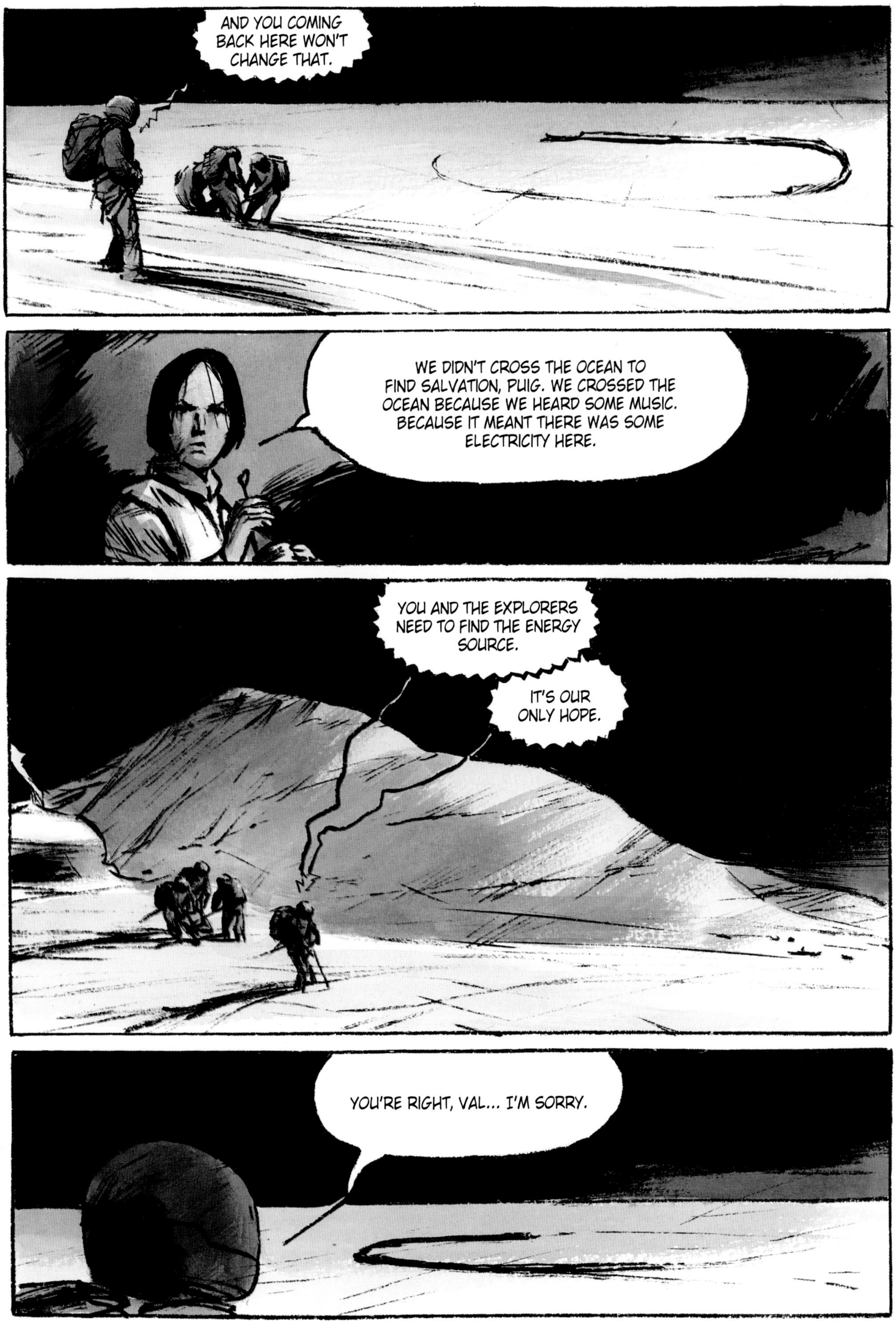
AND YOU COMING BACK HERE WON'T CHANGE THAT.
WE DIDN'T CROSS THE OCEAN TO FIND SALVATION, PUIG. WE CROSSED THE OCEAN BECAUSE WE HEARD SOME MUSIC. BECAUSE IT MEANT THERE WAS SOME ELECTRICITY HERE.
YOU AND THE EXPLORERS NEED TO FIND THE ENERGY SOURCE.
IT'S OUR ONLY HOPE.
YOU'RE RIGHT, VAL... I'M SORRY.

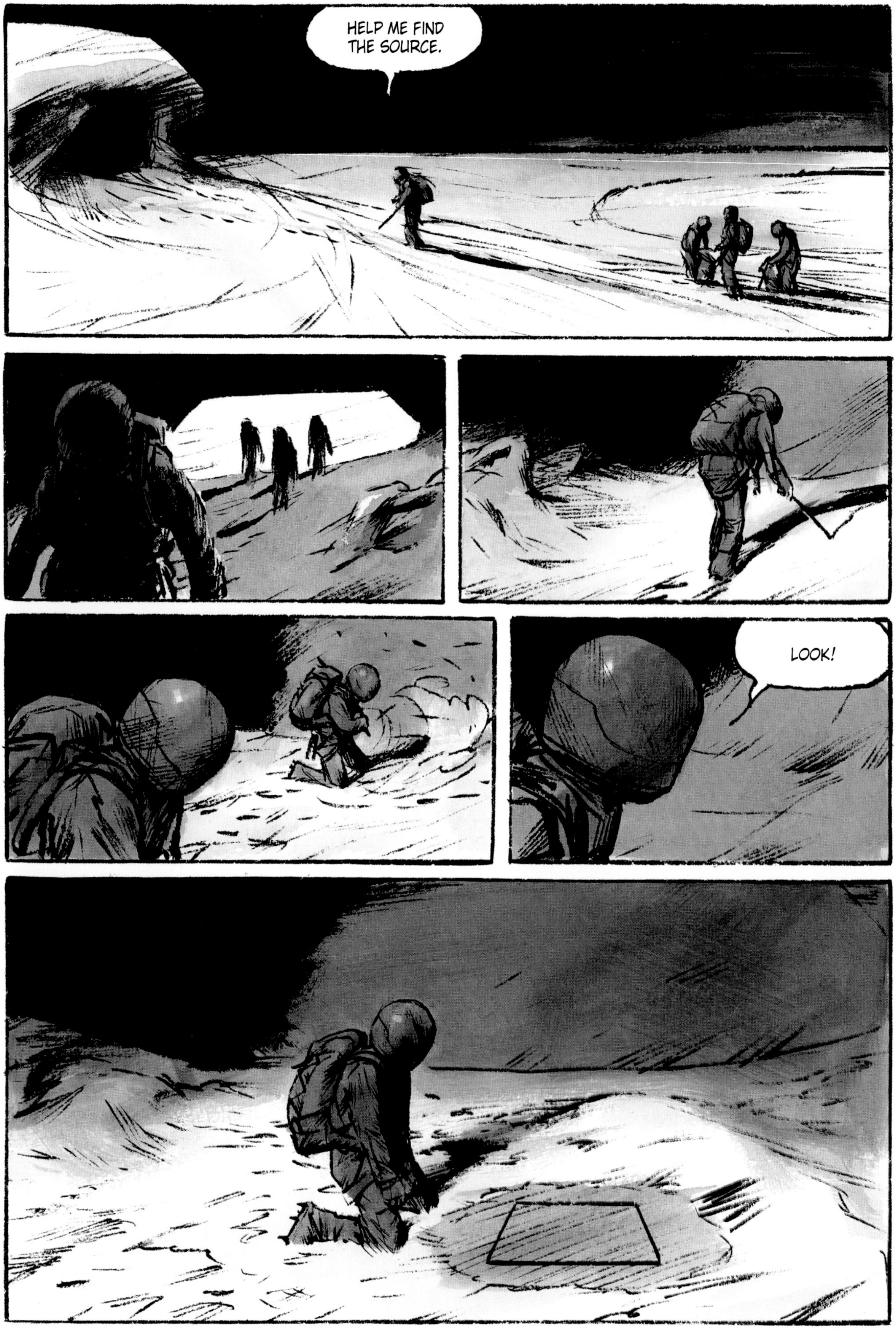
HELP ME FIND THE SOURCE.
LOOK!

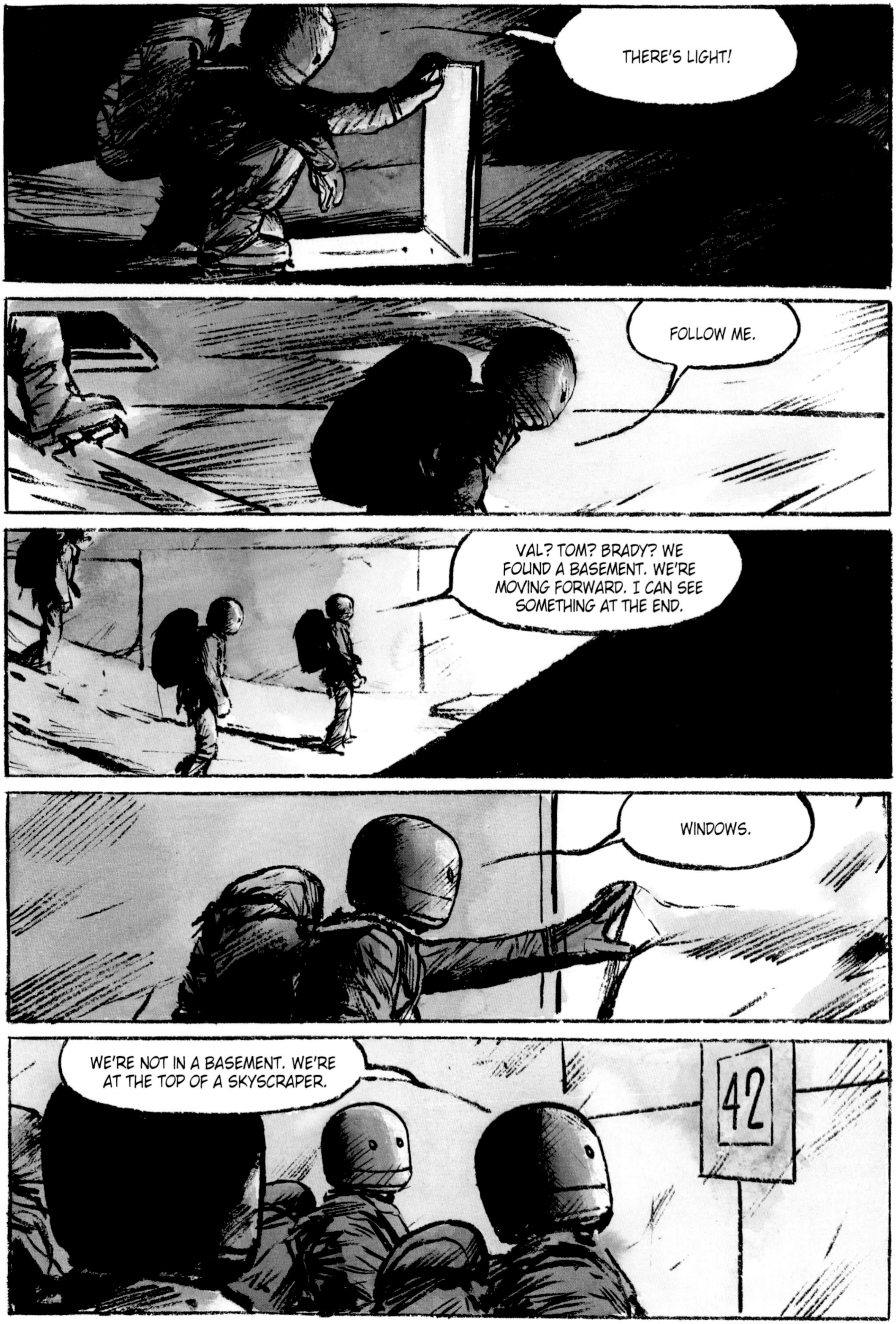
THERE'S LIGHT!
FOLLOW ME.
VAL? TOM? BRADY? WE FOUND A BASEMENT. WE'RE MOVING FORWARD. I CAN SEE SOMETHING AT THE END.
WINDOWS.
WE'RE NOT IN A BASEMENT. WE'RE AT THE TOP OF A SKYSCRAPER.
42

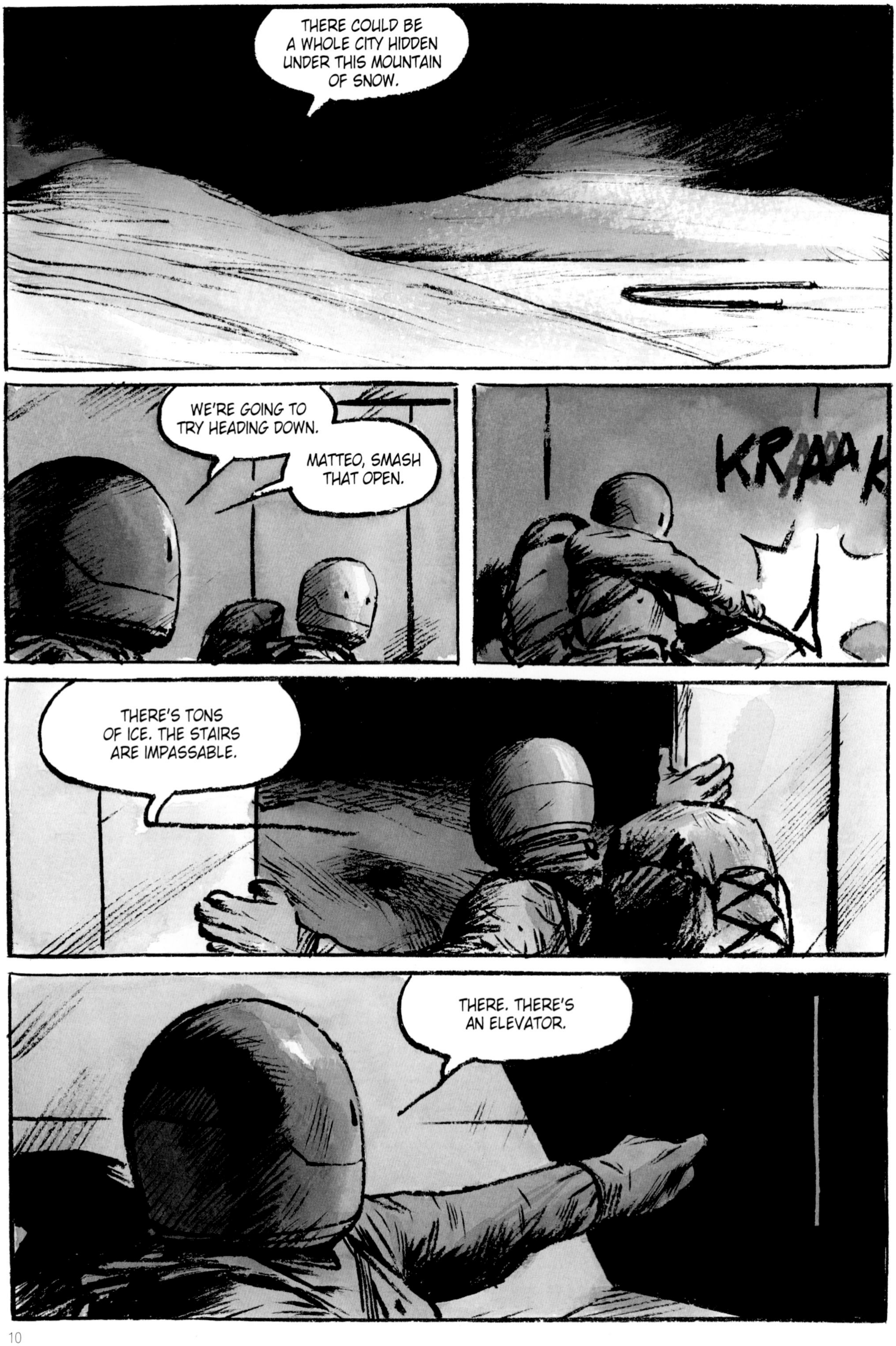
THERE COULD BE A WHOLE CITY HIDDEN UNDER THIS MOUNTAIN OF SNOW.
WE'RE GOING TO TRY HEADING DOWN.
MATTEO, SMASH THAT OPEN.
KRAAAK
THERE'S TONS OF ICE. THE STAIRS ARE IMPASSABLE.
THERE. THERE'S AN ELEVATOR.

WE'RE GONNA NEED TO HANG ON, GUYS.

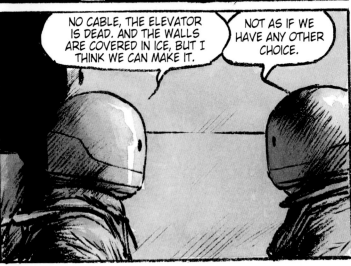

NO CABLE, THE ELEVATOR IS DEAD. AND THE WALLS ARE COVERED IN ICE, BUT I THINK WE CAN MAKE IT.

NOT AS IF WE HAVE ANY OTHER CHOICE.

HAVE ANY OF YOU EVER DONE ANYTHING LIKE THIS BEFORE?

I KNOW HOW IT WORKS IN THEORY...

OK, LET'S GET READY. AT LEAST WE DIDN'T BRING THE LAST ROPE ON EARTH FOR NOTHING.

YOU JUST HAVE TO PRETEND IT'S LIKE THE TRAIN, BUT VERTICAL.

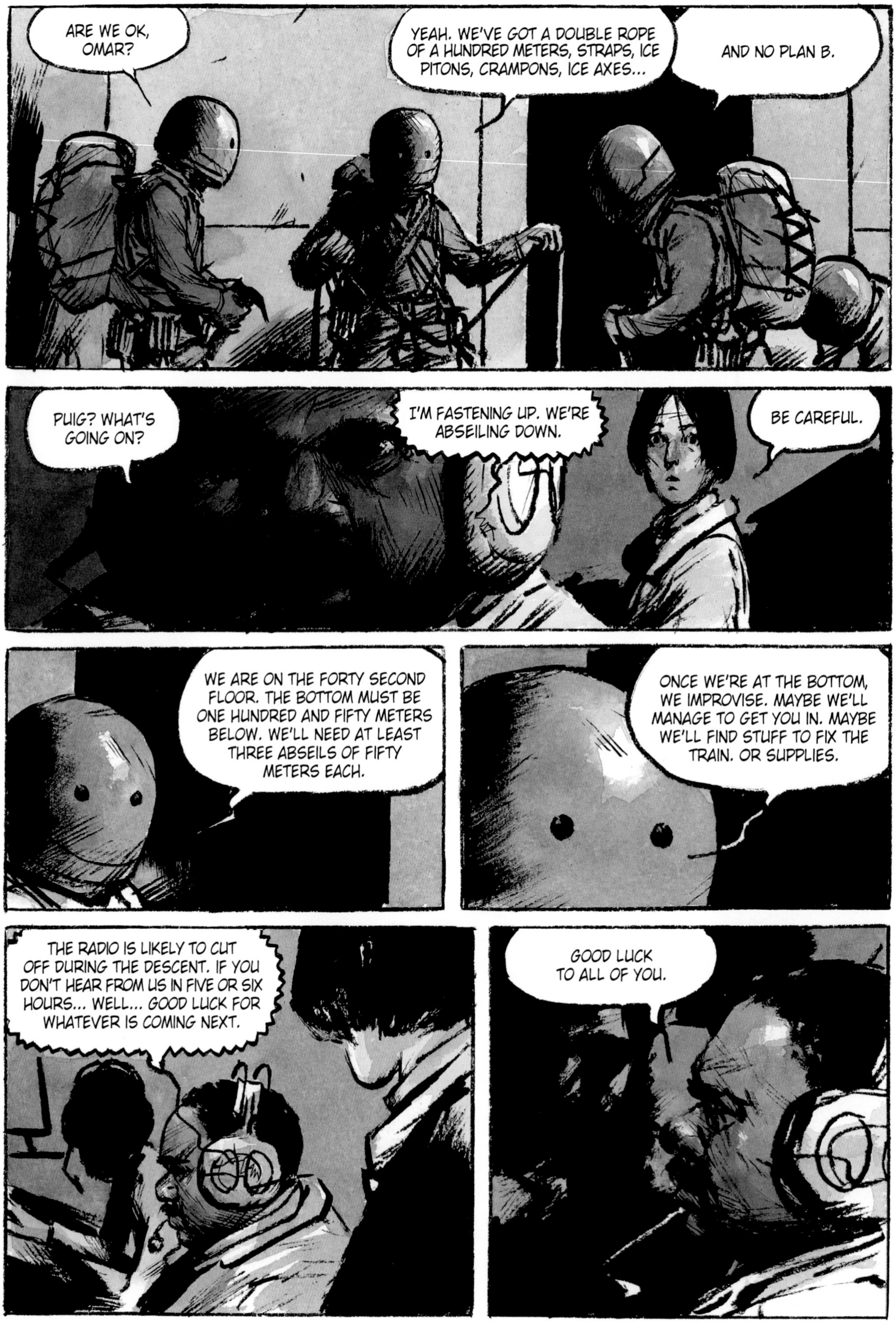
ARE WE OK, OMAR?
YEAH. WE'VE GOT A DOUBLE ROPE OF A HUNDRED METERS, STRAPS, ICE PITONS, CRAMPONS, ICE AXES...
AND NO PLAN B.
PUIG? WHAT'S GOING ON?
I'M FASTENING UP. WE'RE ABSEILING DOWN.
BE CAREFUL.
WE ARE ON THE FORTY SECOND FLOOR. THE BOTTOM MUST BE ONE HUNDRED AND FIFTY METERS BELOW. WE'LL NEED AT LEAST THREE ABSEILS OF FIFTY METERS EACH.
ONCE WE'RE AT THE BOTTOM, WE IMPROVISE. MAYBE WE'LL MANAGE TO GET YOU IN. MAYBE WE'LL FIND STUFF TO FIX THE TRAIN. OR SUPPLIES.
THE RADIO IS LIKELY TO CUT OFF DURING THE DESCENT. IF YOU DON'T HEAR FROM US IN FIVE OR SIX HOURS... WELL... GOOD LUCK FOR WHATEVER IS COMING NEXT.
GOOD LUCK TO ALL OF YOU.

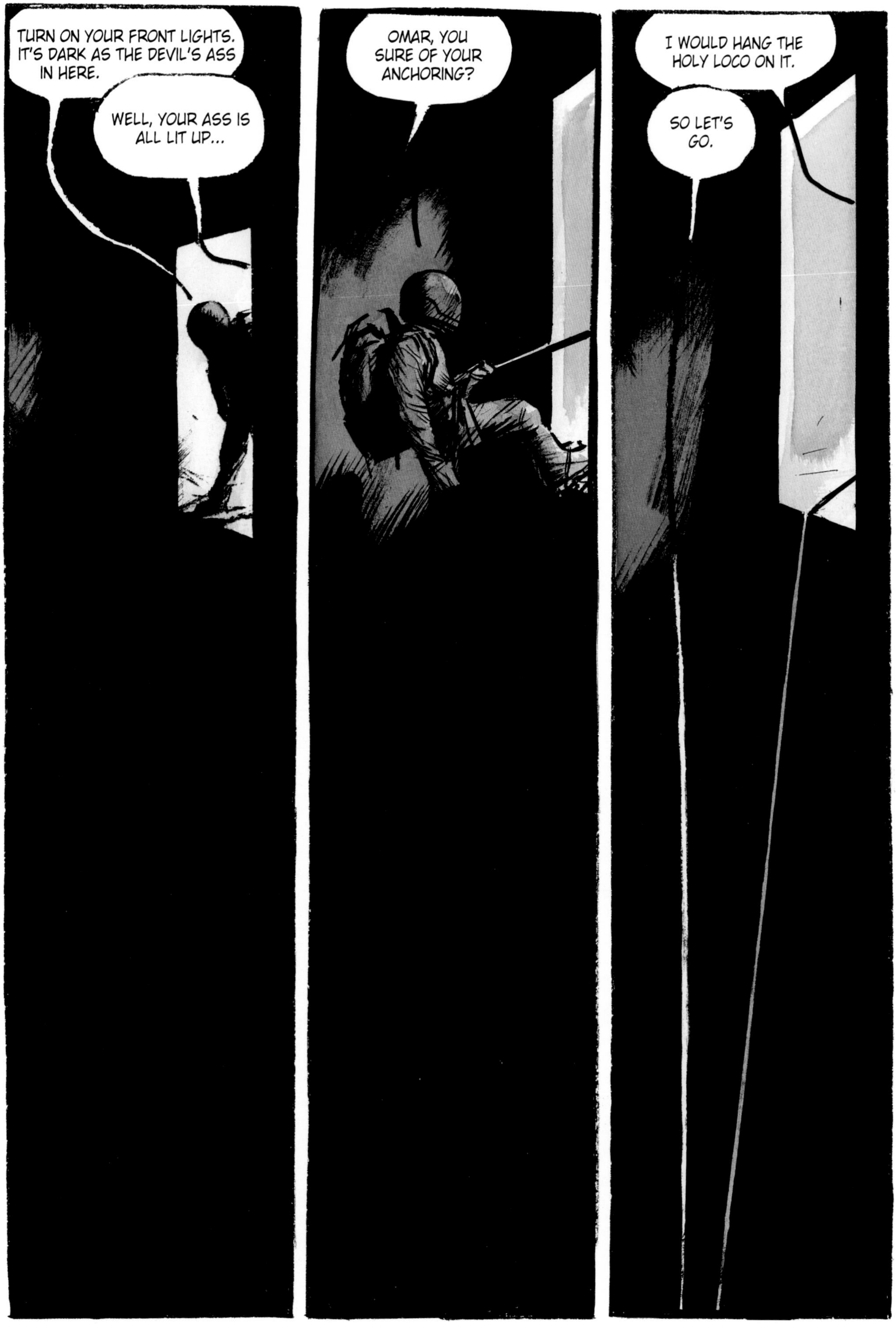
TURN ON YOUR FRONT LIGHTS. IT'S DARK AS THE DEVIL'S ASS IN HERE.
WELL, YOUR ASS IS ALL LIT UP...
OMAR, YOU SURE OF YOUR ANCHORING?
I WOULD HANG THE HOLY LOCO ON IT.
SO LET'S GO.

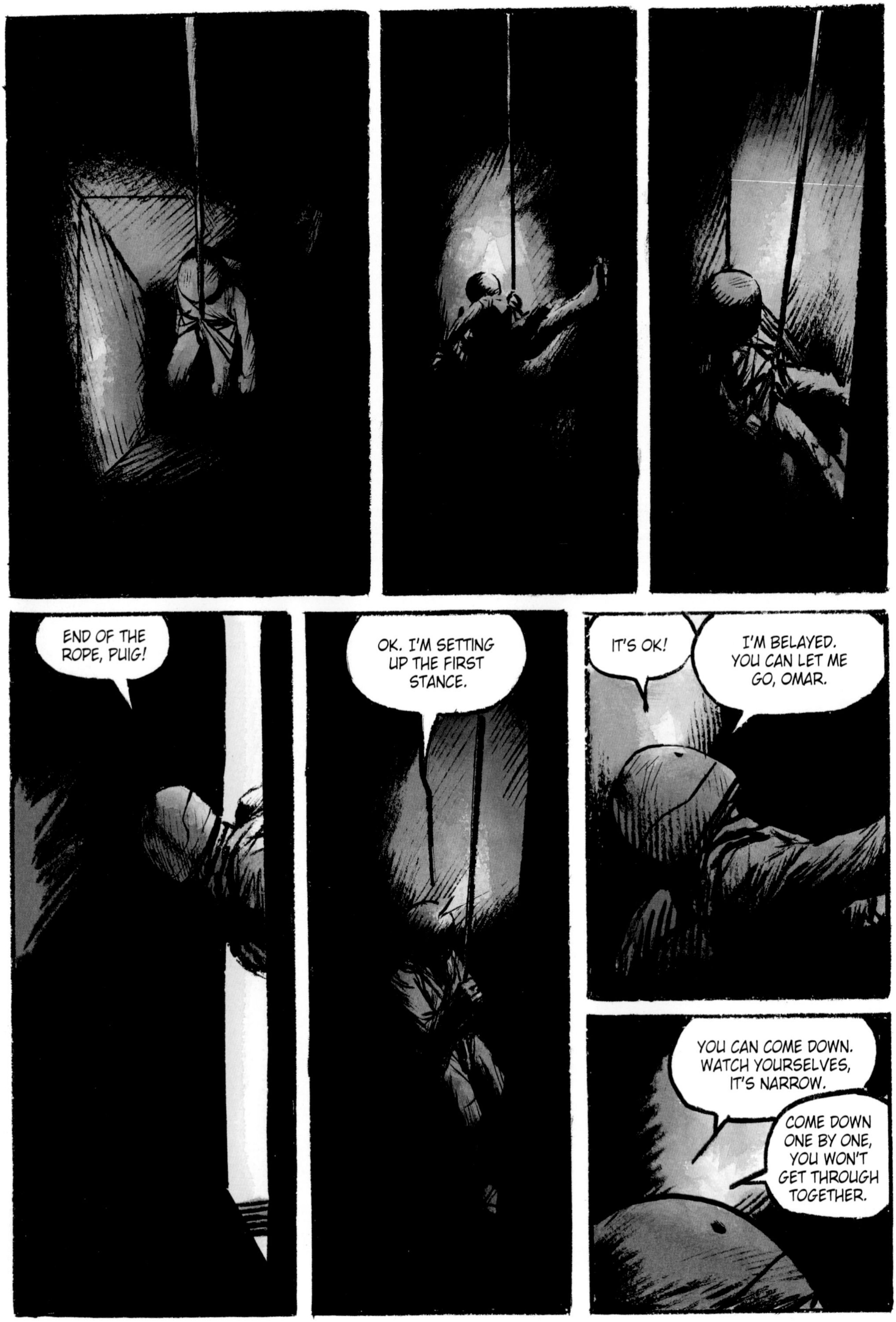
END OF THE ROPE, PUIG!
OK. I'M SETTING UP THE FIRST STANCE.
IT'S OK!
I'M BELAYED. YOU CAN LET ME GO, OMAR.
YOU CAN COME DOWN. WATCH YOURSELVES, IT'S NARROW.
COME DOWN ONE BY ONE, YOU WON'T GET THROUGH TOGETHER.

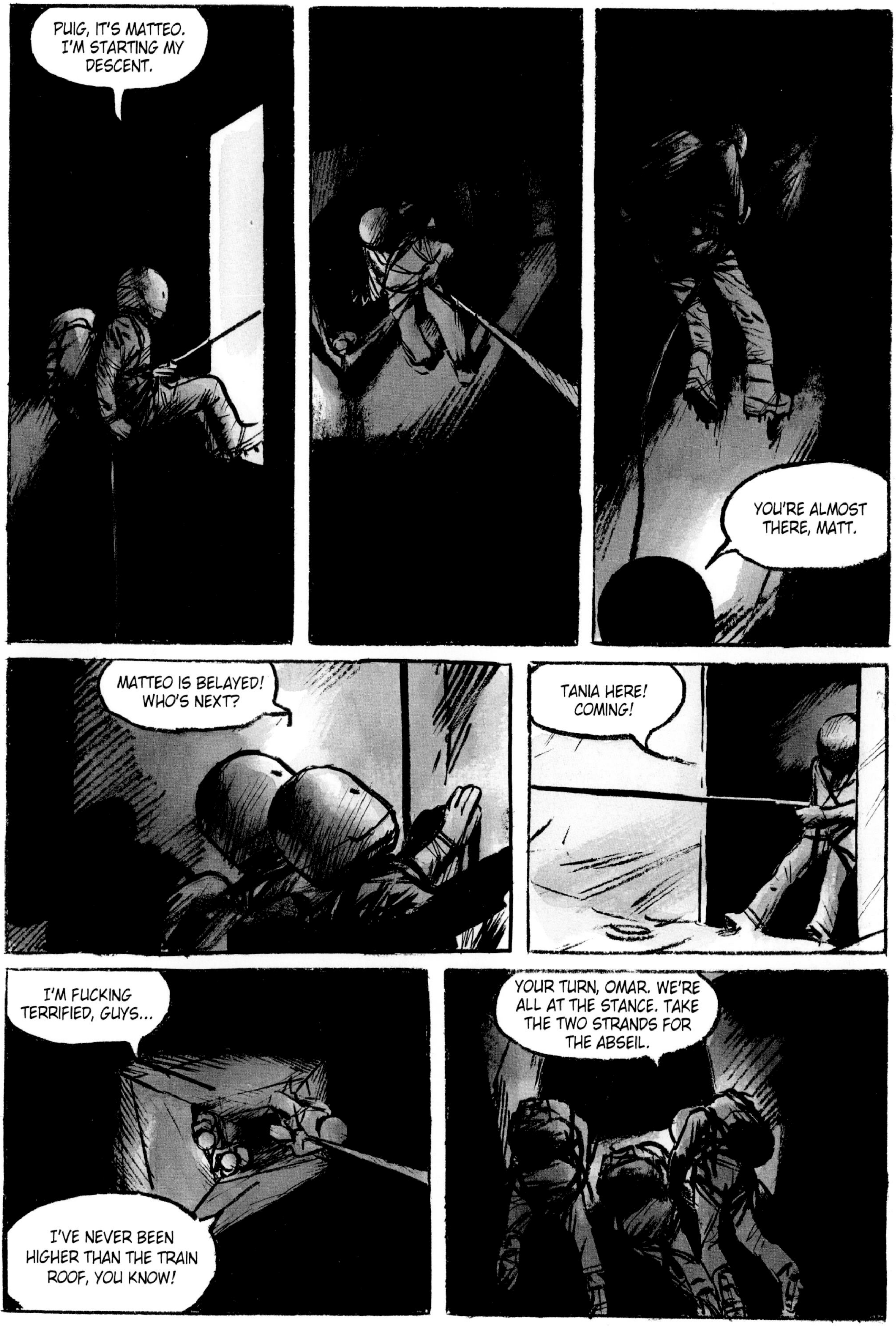

PUIG, IT'S MATTEO. I'M STARTING MY DESCENT.
YOU'RE ALMOST THERE, MATT.
MATTEO IS BELAYED! WHO'S NEXT?
TANIA HERE! COMING!
I'M FUCKING TERRIFIED, GUYS...
I'VE NEVER BEEN HIGHER THAN THE TRAIN ROOF, YOU KNOW!
YOUR TURN, OMAR. WE'RE ALL AT THE STANCE. TAKE THE TWO STRANDS FOR THE ABSEIL.

CRAP... I'VE HEARD OF VERTIGO, BUT I HAD NO IDEA WHAT IT REALLY FELT LIKE!

OK, WE'VE GOT YOU...

TOM? CAN YOU STILL HEAR ME?

WHAT?

ARE YOU RECEIVING ME?

VERY BADLY. IT'S GETTING WORSE AND WORSE.

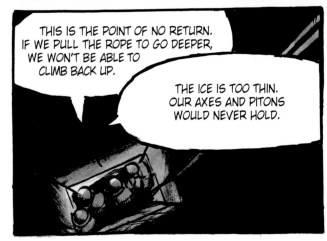

THIS IS THE POINT OF NO RETURN. IF WE PULL THE ROPE TO GO DEEPER, WE WON'T BE ABLE TO CLIMB BACK UP.

THE ICE IS TOO THIN. OUR AXES AND PITONS WOULD NEVER HOLD.

IF WE GO ON, EITHER WE FIND A WAY OUT FROM THE BOTTOM, OR WE DIE THERE.

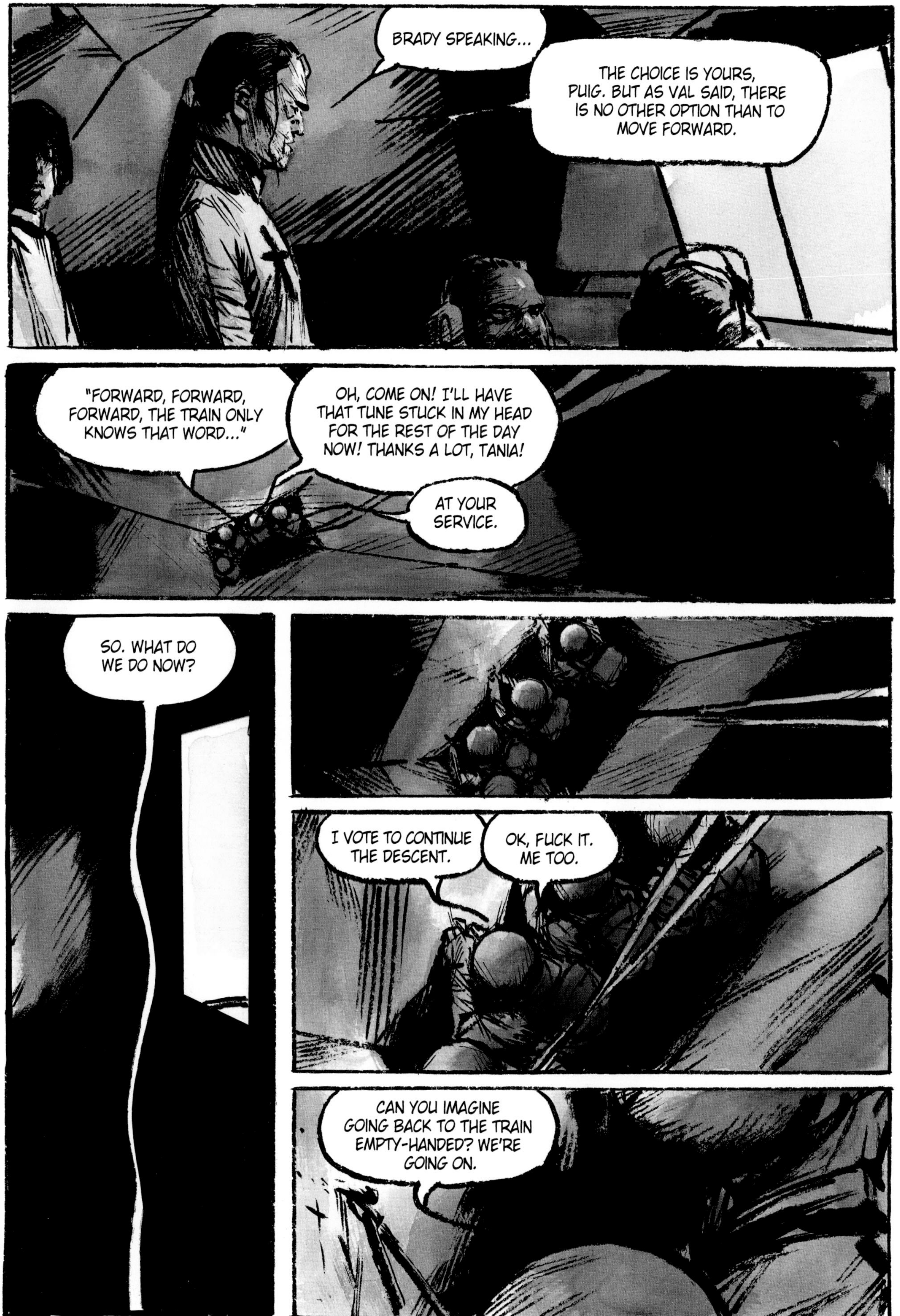
BRADY SPEAKING...
THE CHOICE IS YOURS, PUIG. BUT AS VAL SAID, THERE IS NO OTHER OPTION THAN TO MOVE FORWARD.
"FORWARD, FORWARD, FORWARD, THE TRAIN ONLY KNOWS THAT WORD..."
OH, COME ON! I'LL HAVE THAT TUNE STUCK IN MY HEAD FOR THE REST OF THE DAY NOW! THANKS A LOT, TANIA!
AT YOUR SERVICE.
SO. WHAT DO WE DO NOW?
I VOTE TO CONTINUE THE DESCENT.
OK, FUCK IT. ME TOO.
CAN YOU IMAGINE GOING BACK TO THE TRAIN EMPTY-HANDED? WE'RE GOING ON.

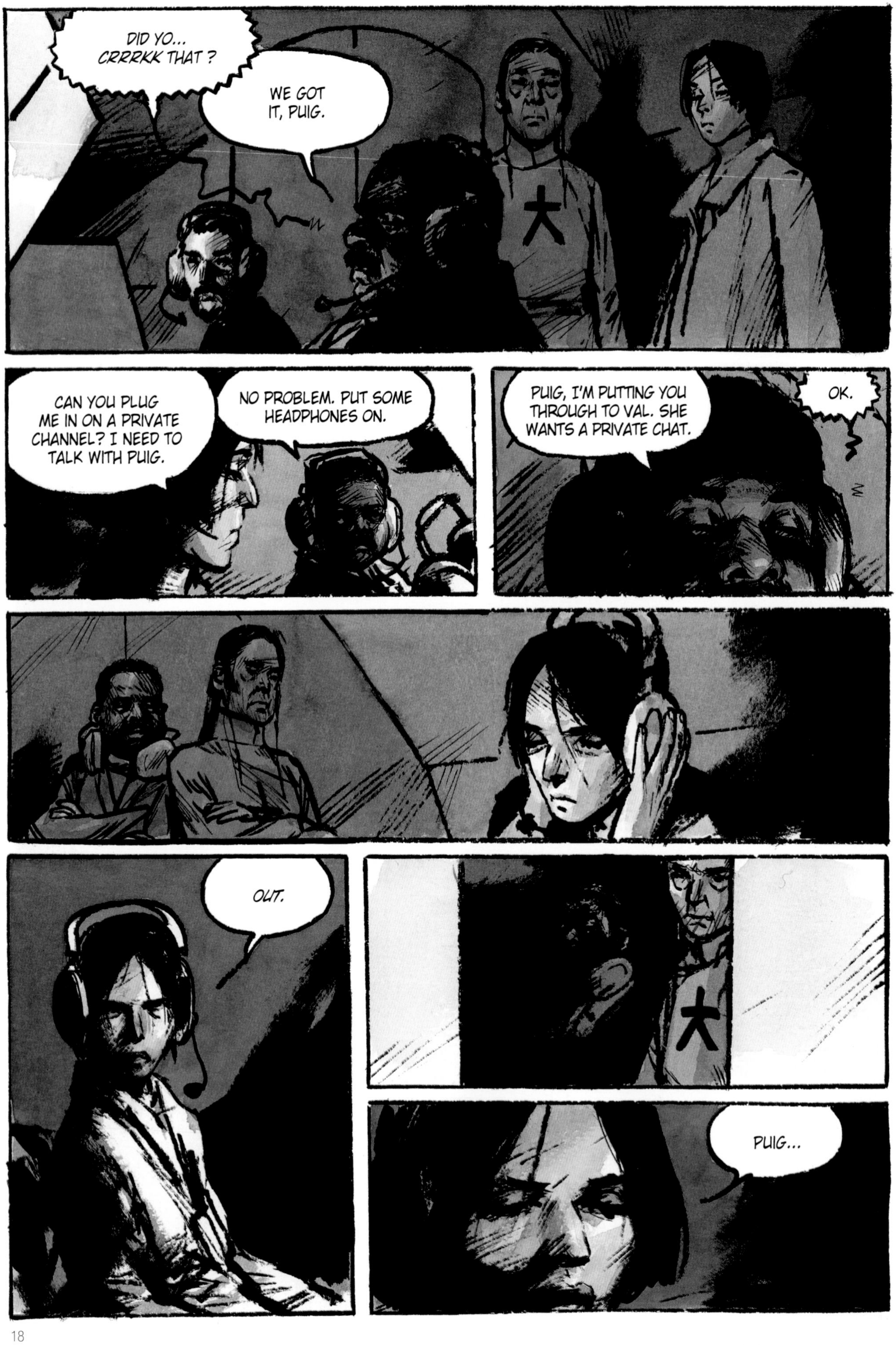
DID YO... CRRRKK THAT ?
WE GOT IT, PUIG.
CAN YOU PLUG ME IN ON A PRIVATE CHANNEL? I NEED TO TALK WITH PUIG.
NO PROBLEM. PUT SOME HEADPHONES ON.
PUIG, I'M PUTTING YOU THROUGH TO VAL. SHE WANTS A PRIVATE CHAT.
OK.
OUT.
PUIG...

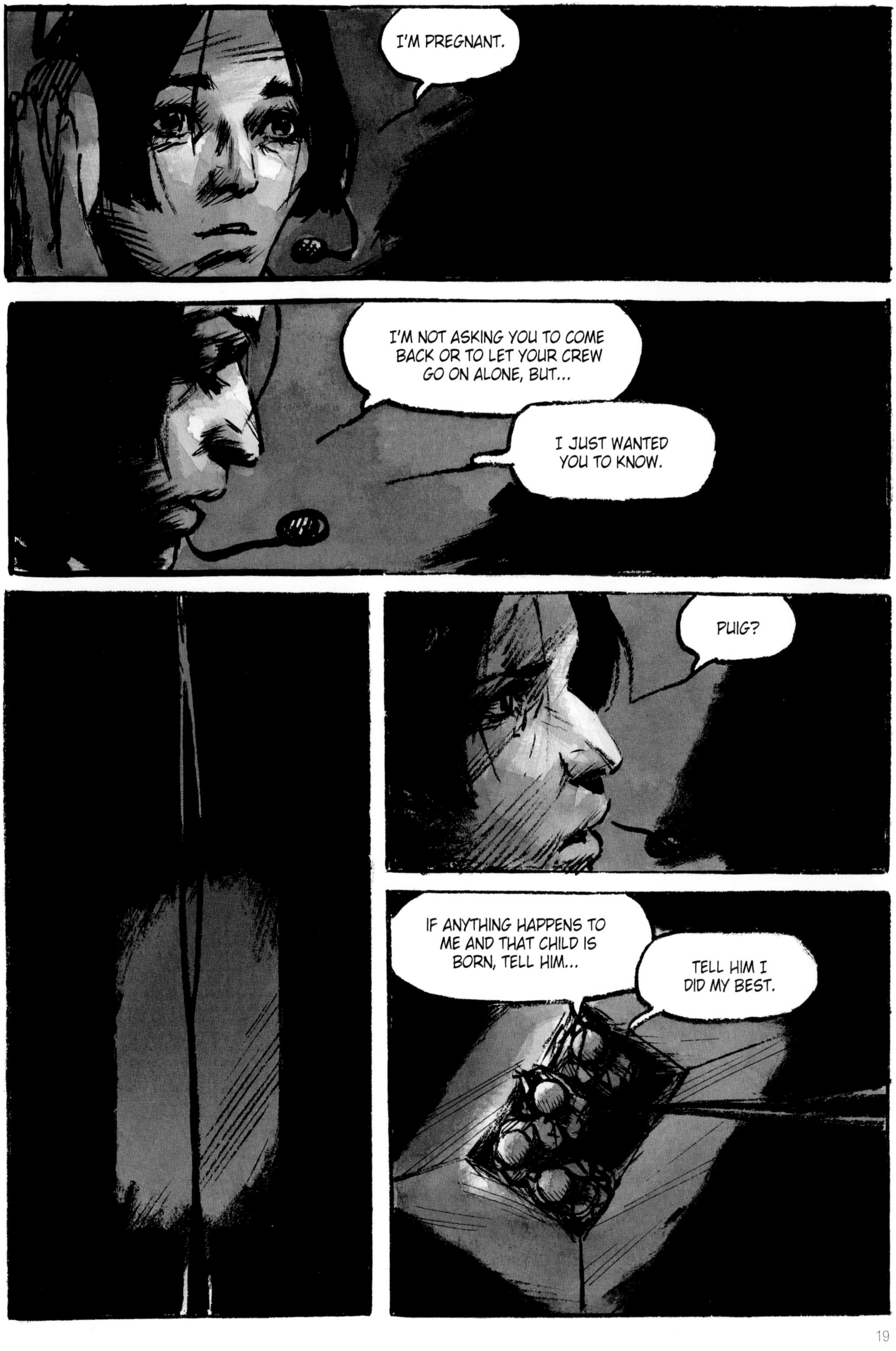
I'M PREGNANT.
I'M NOT ASKING YOU TO COME BACK OR TO LET YOUR CREW GO ON ALONE, BUT...
I JUST WANTED YOU TO KNOW.
PUIG?
IF ANYTHING HAPPENS TO ME AND THAT CHILD IS BORN, TELL HIM...
TELL HIM I DID MY BEST.

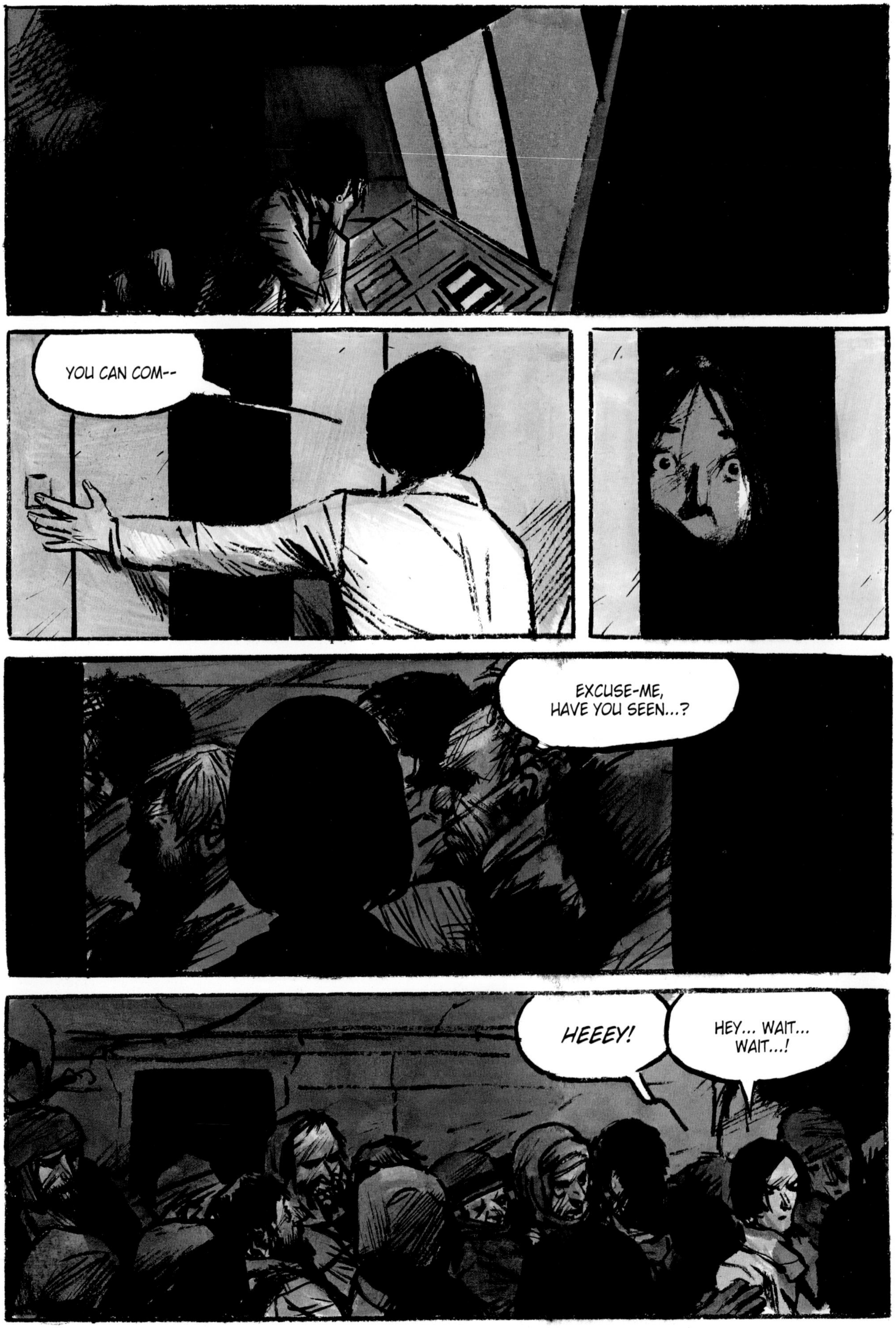

YOU CAN COM--
EXCUSE-ME, HAVE YOU SEEN...?
HEEEY!
HEY... WAIT... WAIT...!

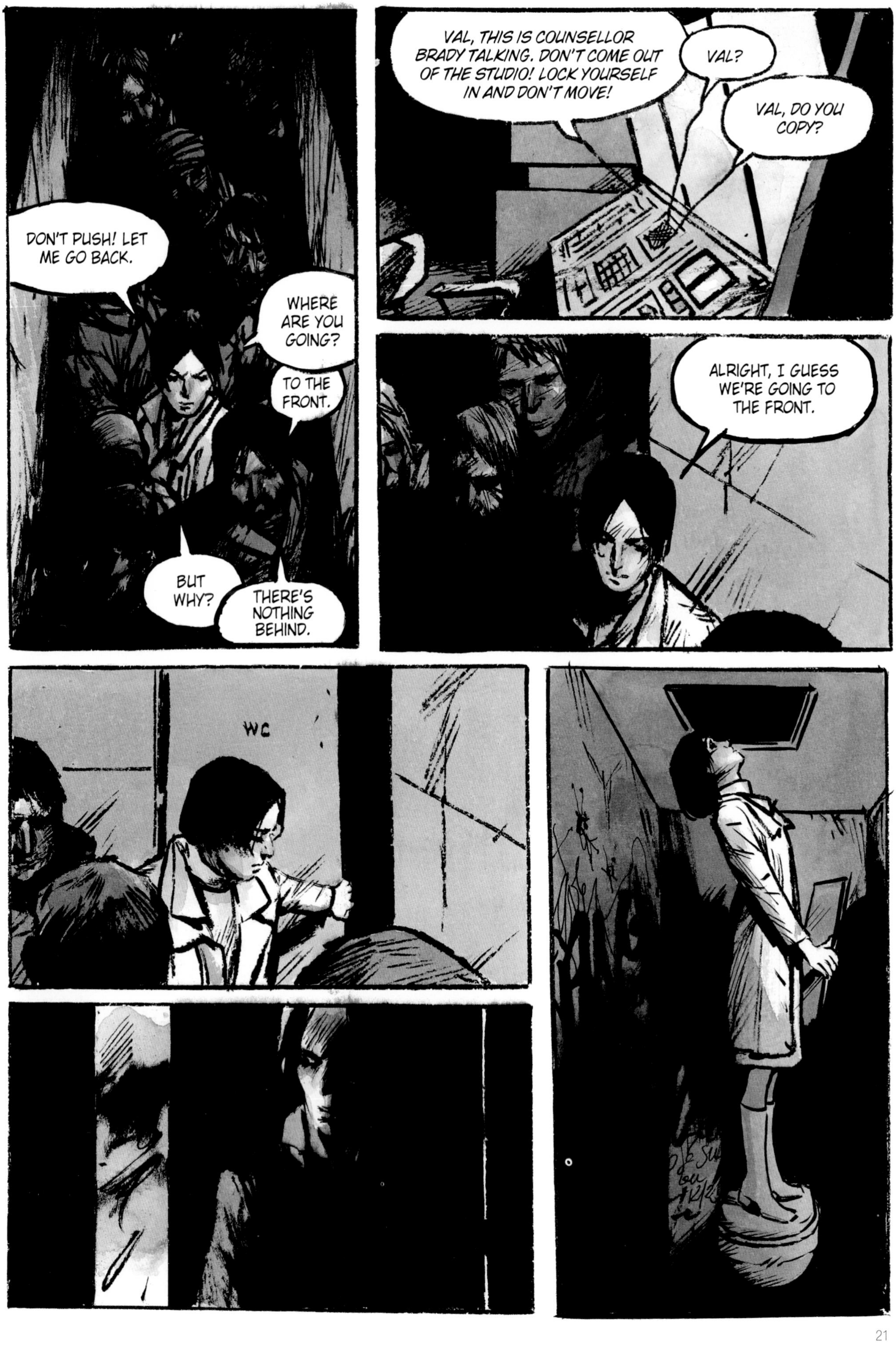
DON'T PUSH! LET ME GO BACK.
WHERE ARE YOU GOING?
TO THE FRONT.
BUT WHY?
THERE'S NOTHING BEHIND.
VAL, THIS IS COUNSELLOR BRADY TALKING. DON'T COME OUT OF THE STUDIO! LOCK YOURSELF IN AND DON'T MOVE!
VAL?
VAL, DO YOU COPY?
ALRIGHT, I GUESS WE'RE GOING TO THE FRONT.
WC

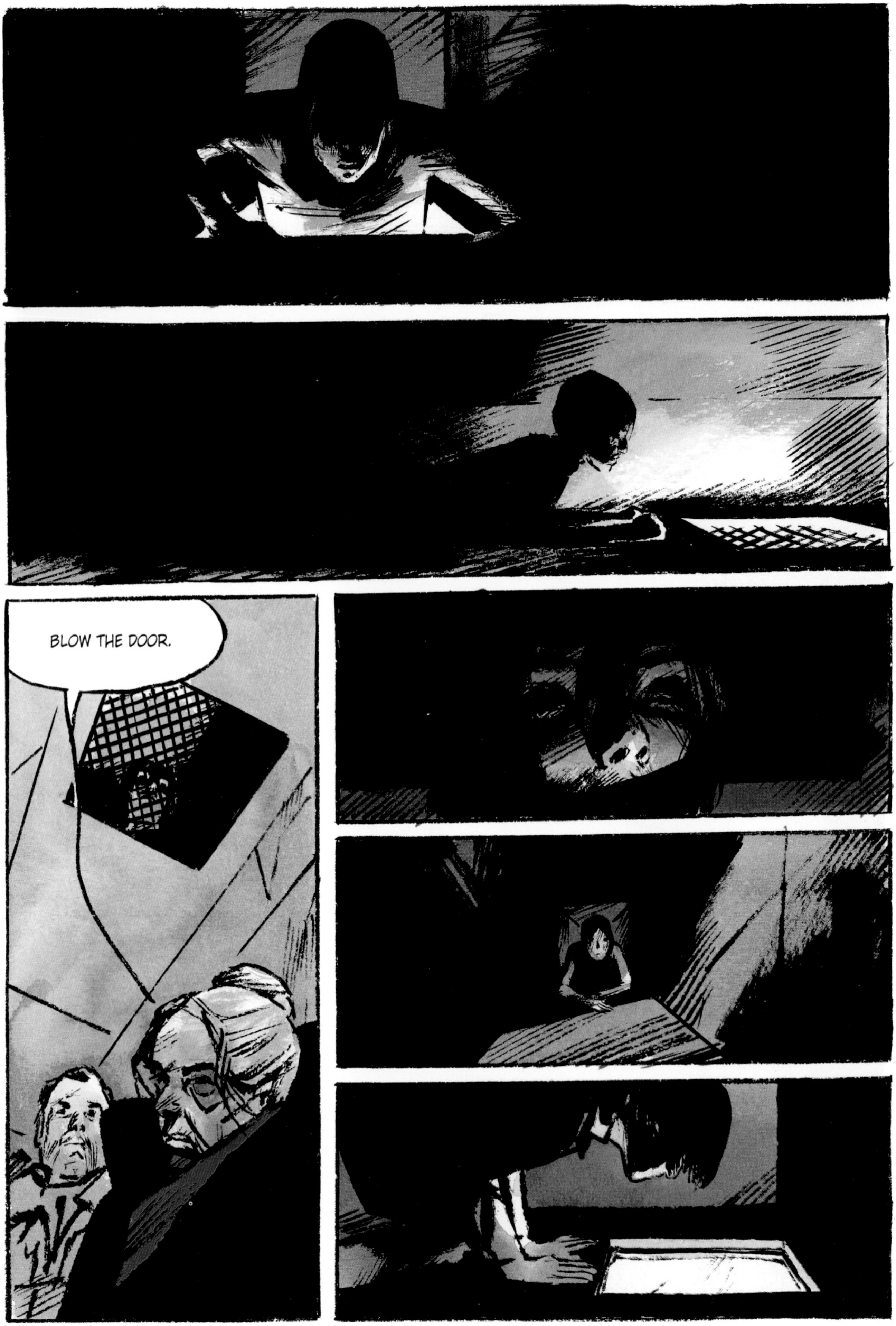
BLOW THE DOOR.

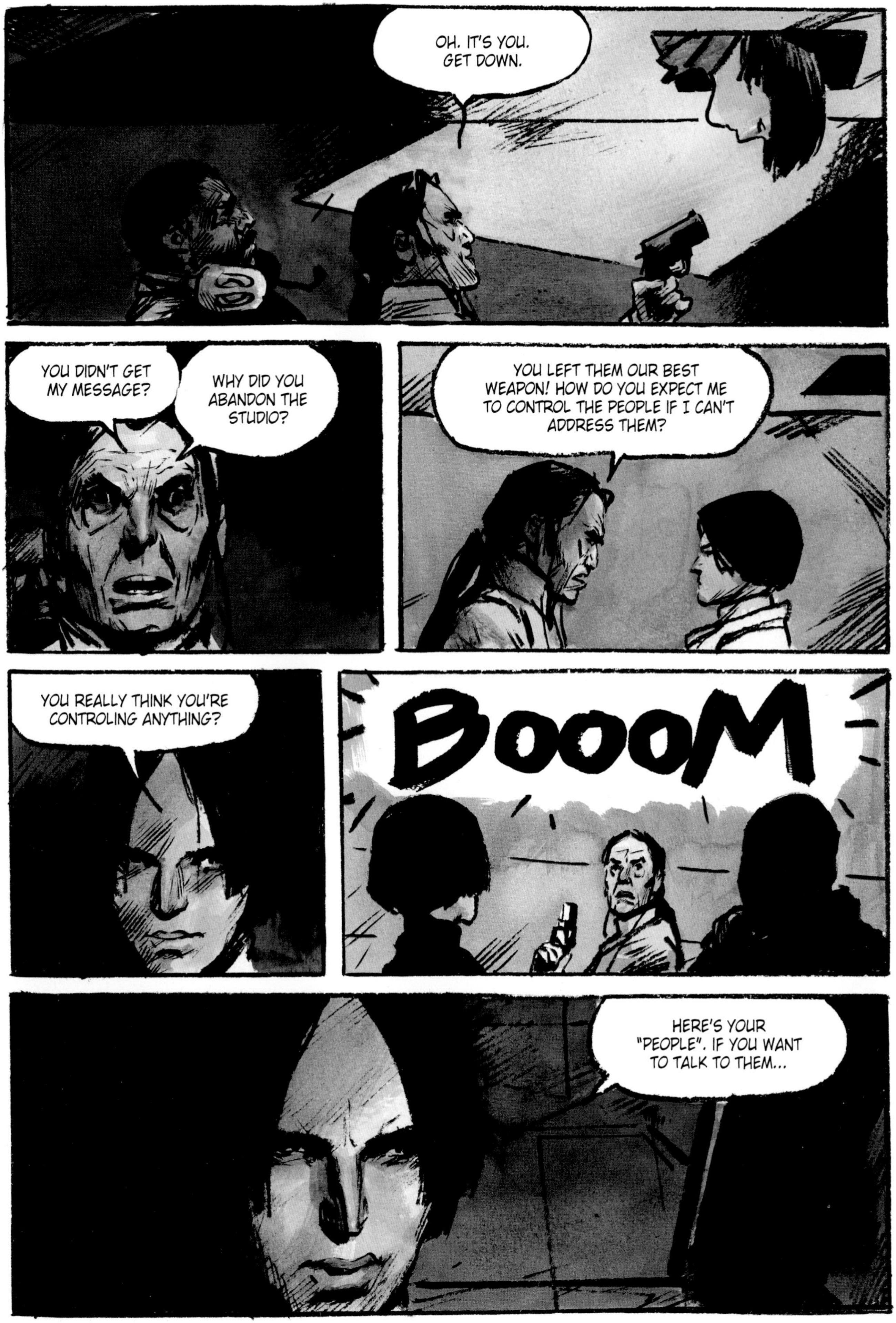
OH. IT'S YOU. GET DOWN.
YOU DIDN'T GET MY MESSAGE?
WHY DID YOU ABANDON THE STUDIO?
YOU LEFT THEM OUR BEST WEAPON! HOW DO YOU EXPECT ME TO CONTROL THE PEOPLE IF I CAN'T ADDRESS THEM?
YOU REALLY THINK YOU'RE CONTROLING ANYTHING?
BOOOM
HERE'S YOUR "PEOPLE". IF YOU WANT TO TALK TO THEM...

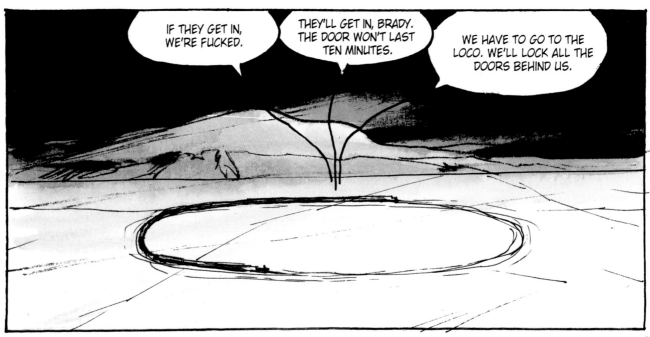

IF THEY GET IN, WE'RE FUCKED.

THEY'LL GET IN, BRADY. THE DOOR WON'T LAST TEN MINUTES.

WE HAVE TO GO TO THE LOCO. WE'LL LOCK ALL THE DOORS BEHIND US.

WHY GO UP THERE? FOR THE MIC? YOU STILL THINK THAT YET ANOTHER SPEECH IS GOING TO SAVE YOU?

STAY HERE IF YOU WANT. I'M GOING.

AND YOU REALLY EXPECT US TO QUIETLY AWAIT YOUR RETURN,?

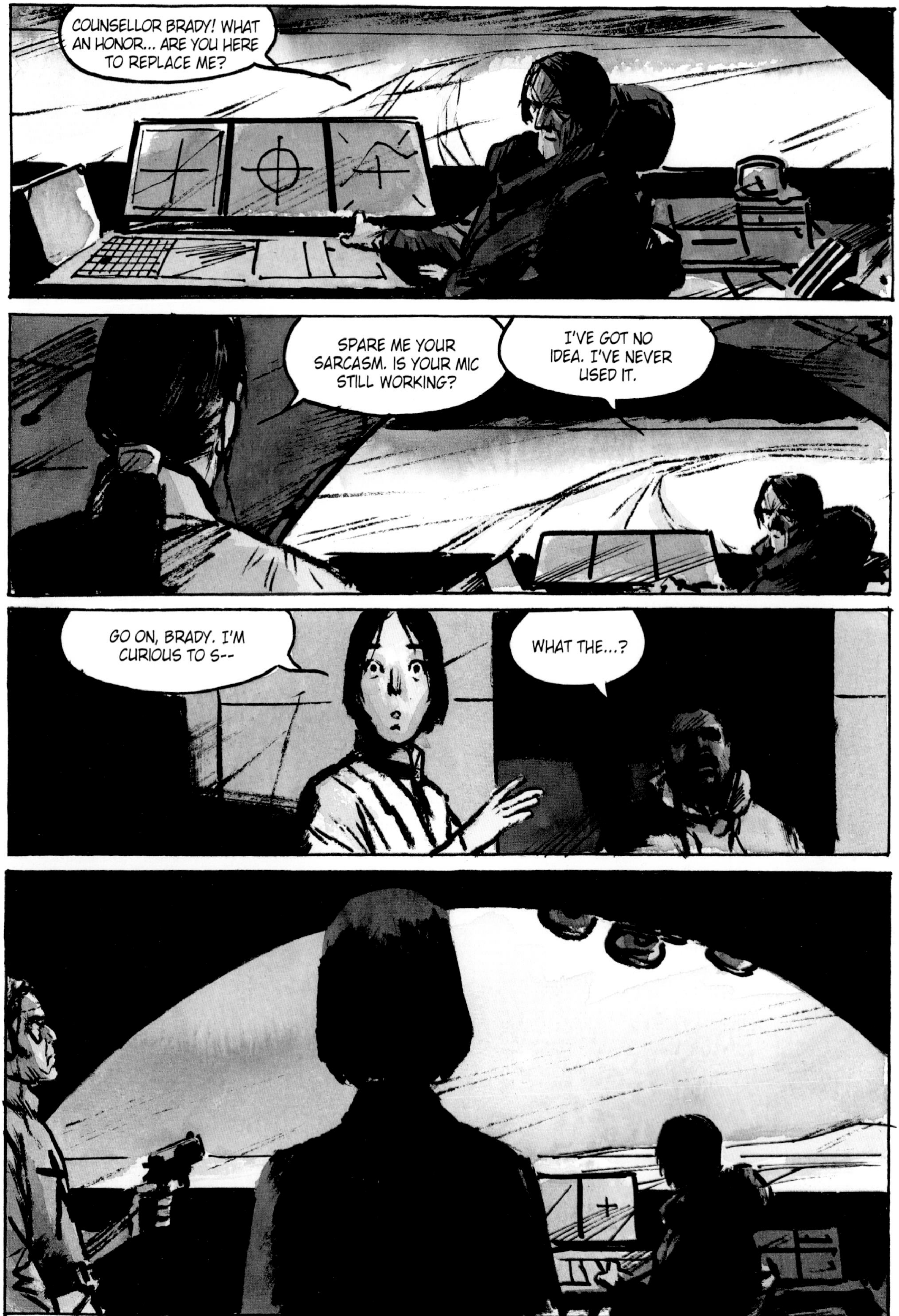
COUNSELLOR BRADY! WHAT AN HONOR... ARE YOU HERE TO REPLACE ME?
SPARE ME YOUR SARCASM. IS YOUR MIC STILL WORKING?
I'VE GOT NO IDEA. I'VE NEVER USED IT.
GO ON, BRADY. I'M CURIOUS TO S--
WHAT THE...?

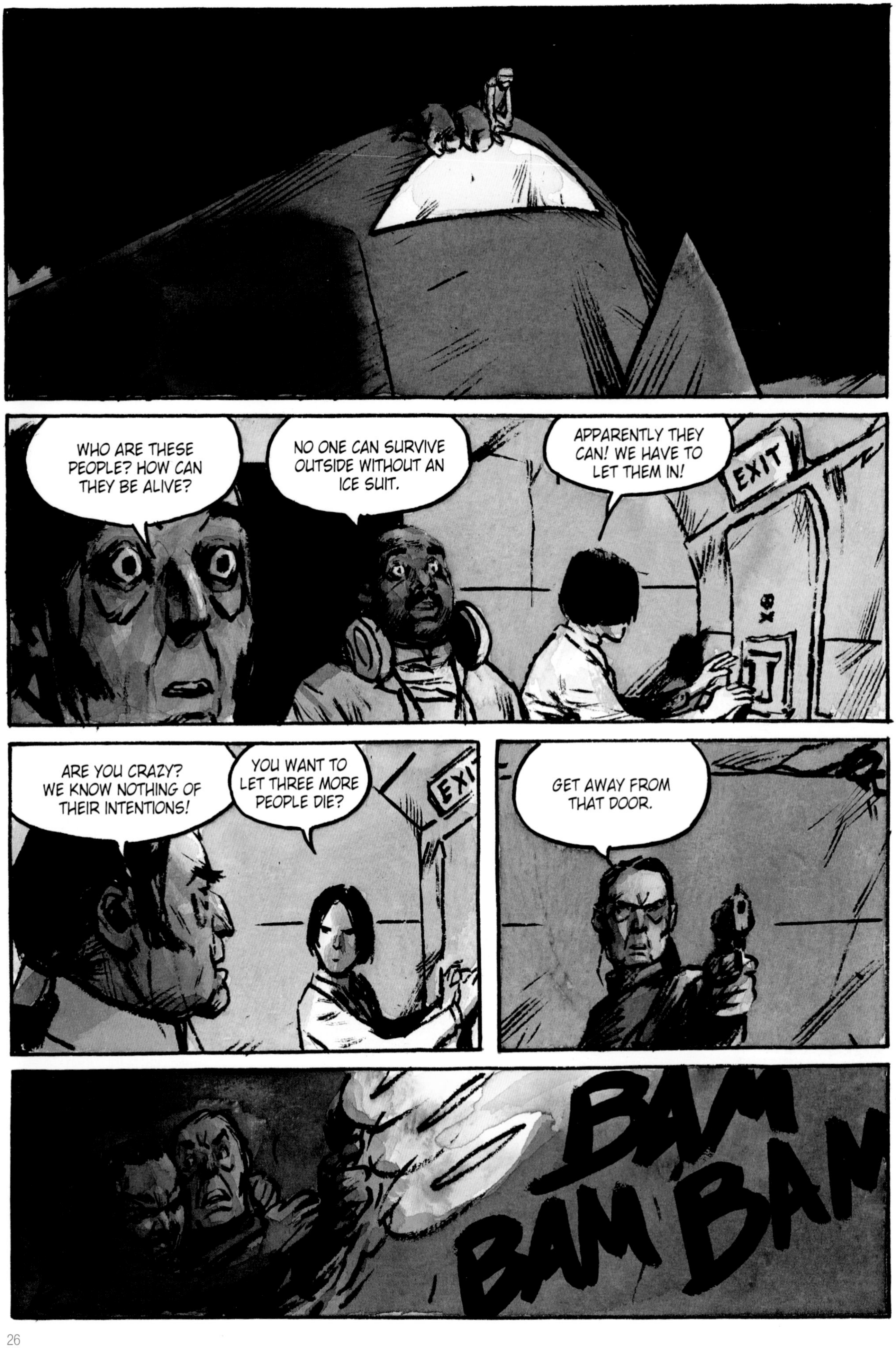
WHO ARE THESE PEOPLE? HOW CAN THEY BE ALIVE?
NO ONE CAN SURVIVE OUTSIDE WITHOUT AN ICE SUIT.
APPARENTLY THEY CAN! WE HAVE TO LET THEM IN!
EXIT
ARE YOU CRAZY? WE KNOW NOTHING OF THEIR INTENTIONS!
YOU WANT TO LET THREE MORE PEOPLE DIE?
GET AWAY FROM THAT DOOR.
BAM
BAM BA

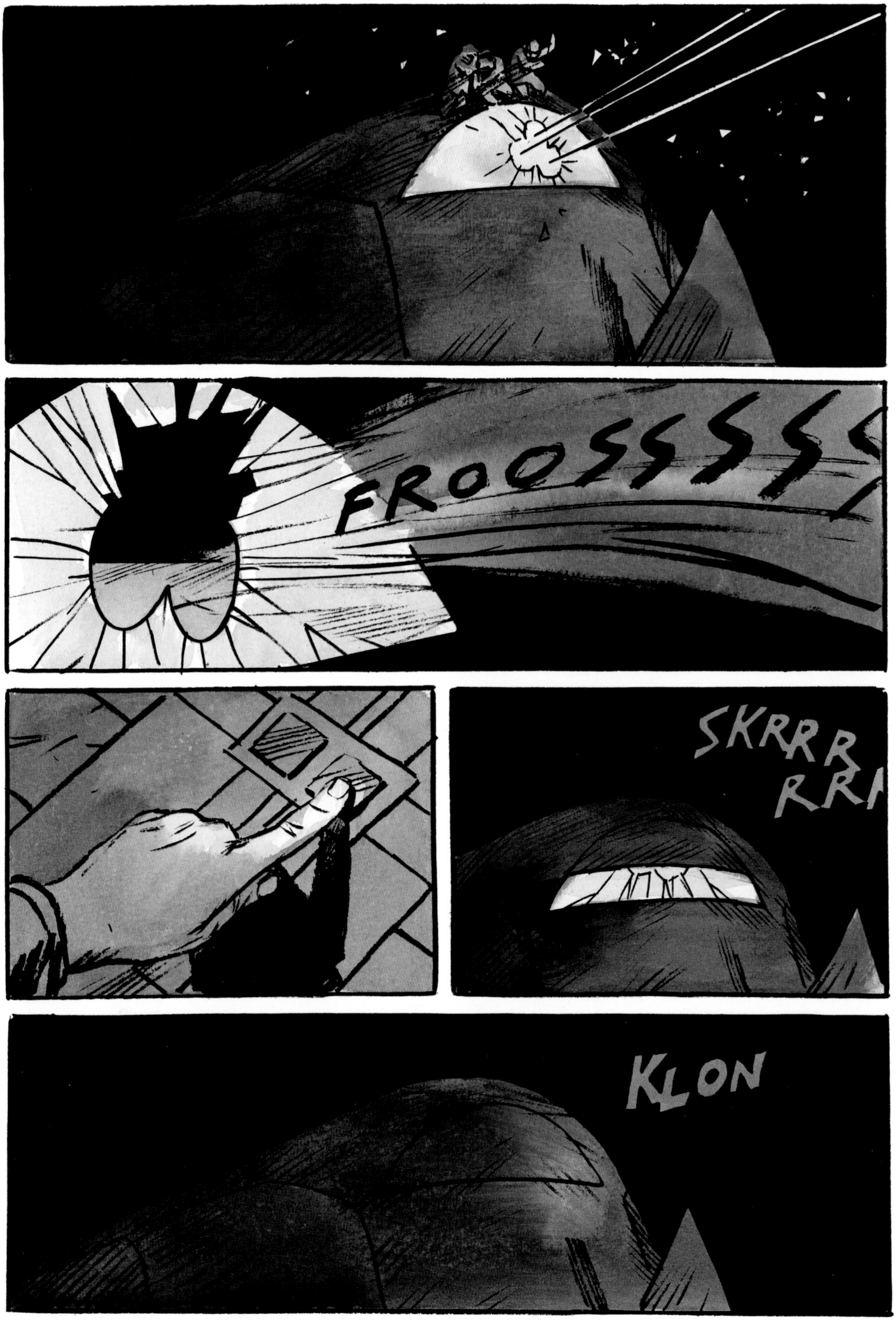
FROOSSSSS
SKRRR RRI
KLON

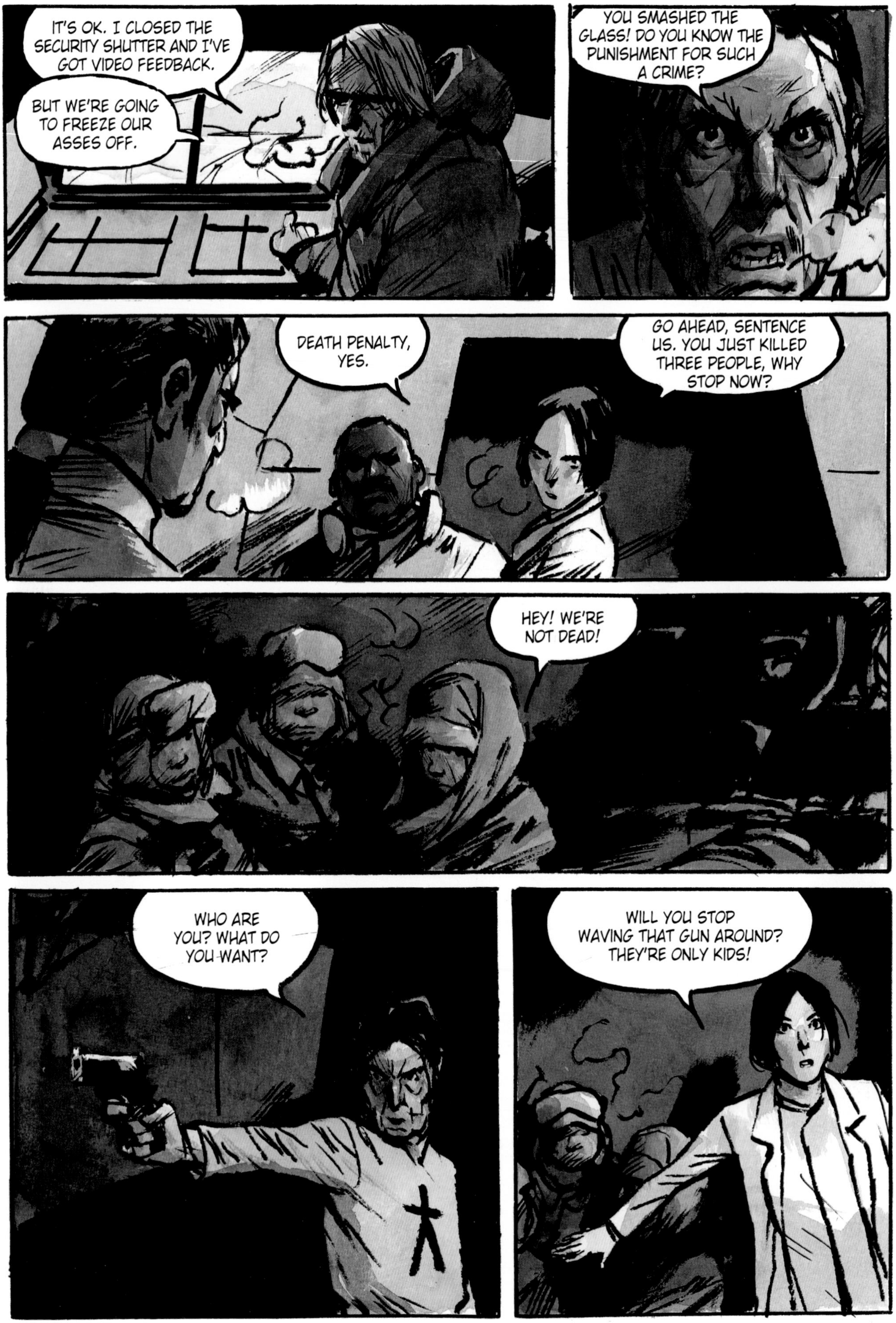
IT'S OK. I CLOSED THE SECURITY SHUTTER AND I'VE GOT VIDEO FEEDBACK.
BUT WE'RE GOING TO FREEZE OUR ASSES OFF.
YOU SMASHED THE GLASS! DO YOU KNOW THE PUNISHMENT FOR SUCH A CRIME?
DEATH PENALTY, YES.
GO AHEAD, SENTENCE US. YOU JUST KILLED THREE PEOPLE, WHY STOP NOW?
HEY! WE'RE NOT DEAD!
WHO ARE YOU? WHAT DO YOU WANT?
WILL YOU STOP WAVING THAT GUN AROUND? THEY'RE ONLY KIDS!

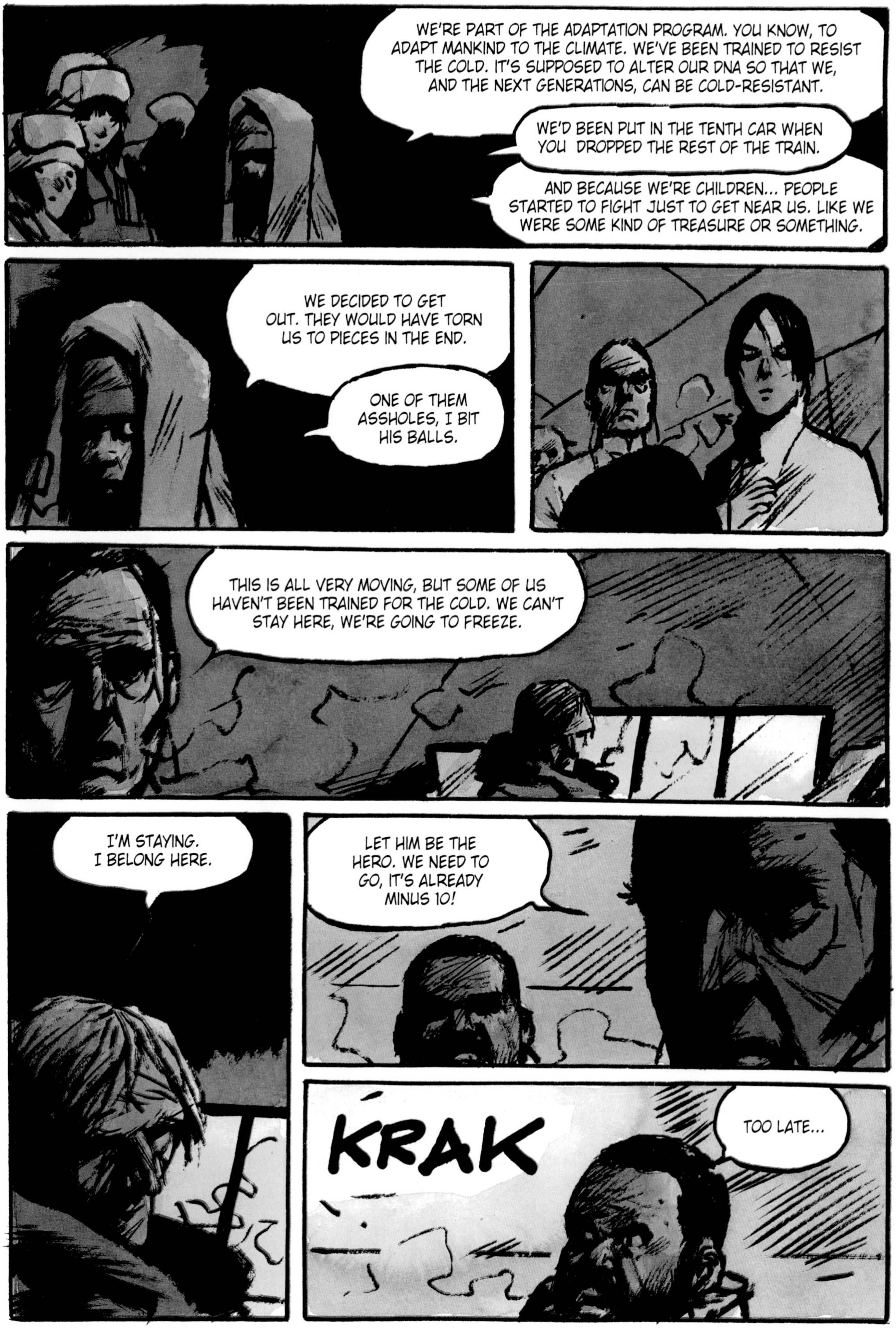
WE'RE PART OF THE ADAPTATION PROGRAM. YOU KNOW, TO ADAPT MANKIND TO THE CLIMATE. WE'VE BEEN TRAINED TO RESIST THE COLD. IT'S SUPPOSED TO ALTER OUR DNA SO THAT WE, AND THE NEXT GENERATIONS, CAN BE COLD-RESISTANT.
WE'D BEEN PUT IN THE TENTH CAR WHEN YOU DROPPED THE REST OF THE TRAIN.
AND BECAUSE WE'RE CHILDREN... PEOPLE STARTED TO FIGHT JUST TO GET NEAR US. LIKE WE WERE SOME KIND OF TREASURE OR SOMETHING.
WE DECIDED TO GET OUT. THEY WOULD HAVE TORN US TO PIECES IN THE END.
ONE OF THEM ASSHOLES, I BIT HIS BALLS.
THIS IS ALL VERY MOVING, BUT SOME OF US HAVEN'T BEEN TRAINED FOR THE COLD. WE CAN'T STAY HERE, WE'RE GOING TO FREEZE.
I'M STAYING. I BELONG HERE.
LET HIM BE THE HERO. WE NEED TO GO, IT'S ALREADY MINUS 10!
KRAK
TOO LATE...

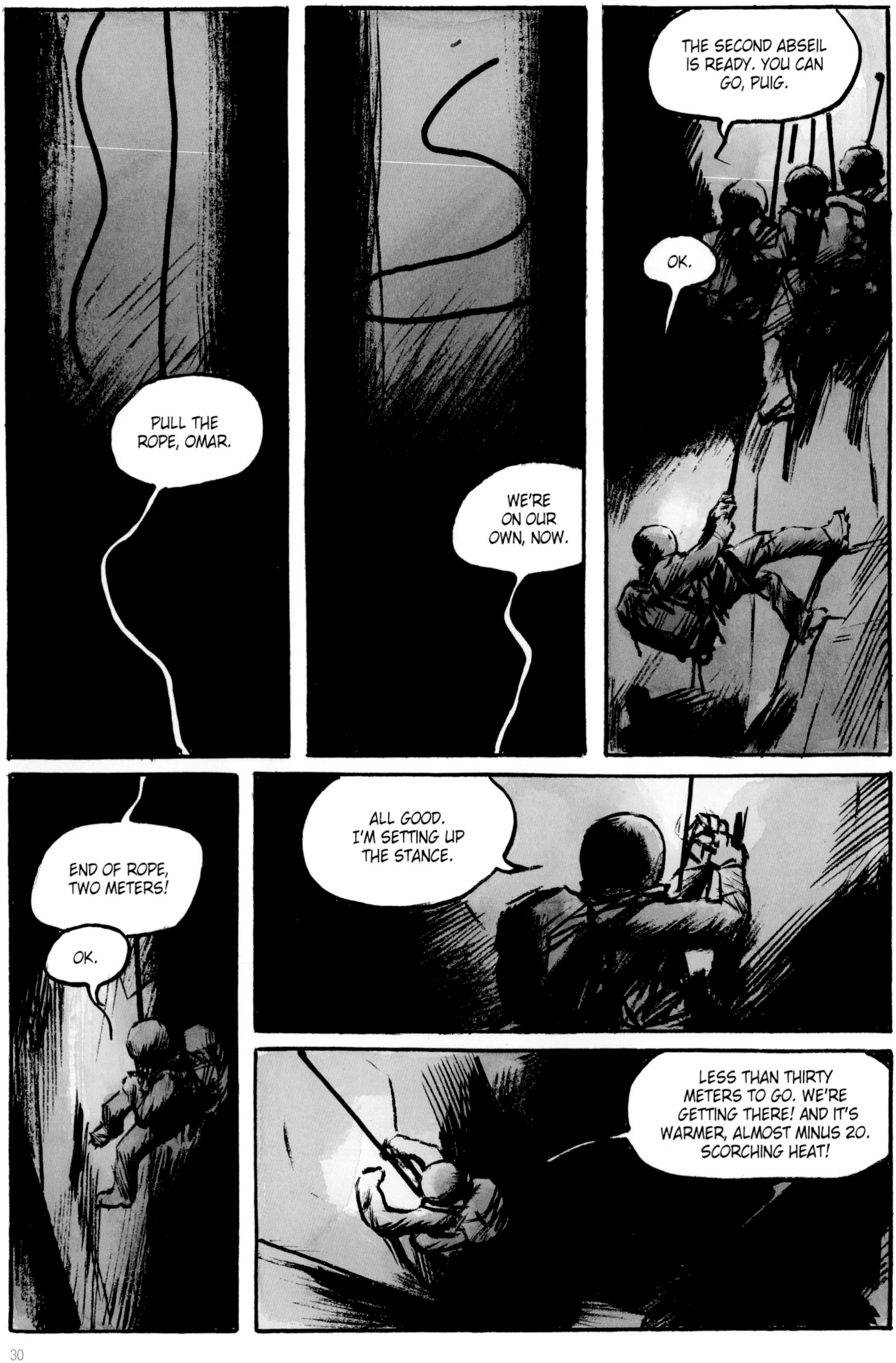
PULL THE ROPE, OMAR.
WE'RE ON OUR OWN, NOW.
THE SECOND ABSEIL IS READY. YOU CAN GO, PUIG.
OK.
END OF ROPE, TWO METERS!
OK.
ALL GOOD. I'M SETTING UP THE STANCE.
LESS THAN THIRTY METERS TO GO. WE'RE GETTING THERE! AND IT'S WARMER, ALMOST MINUS 20. SCORCHING HEAT!

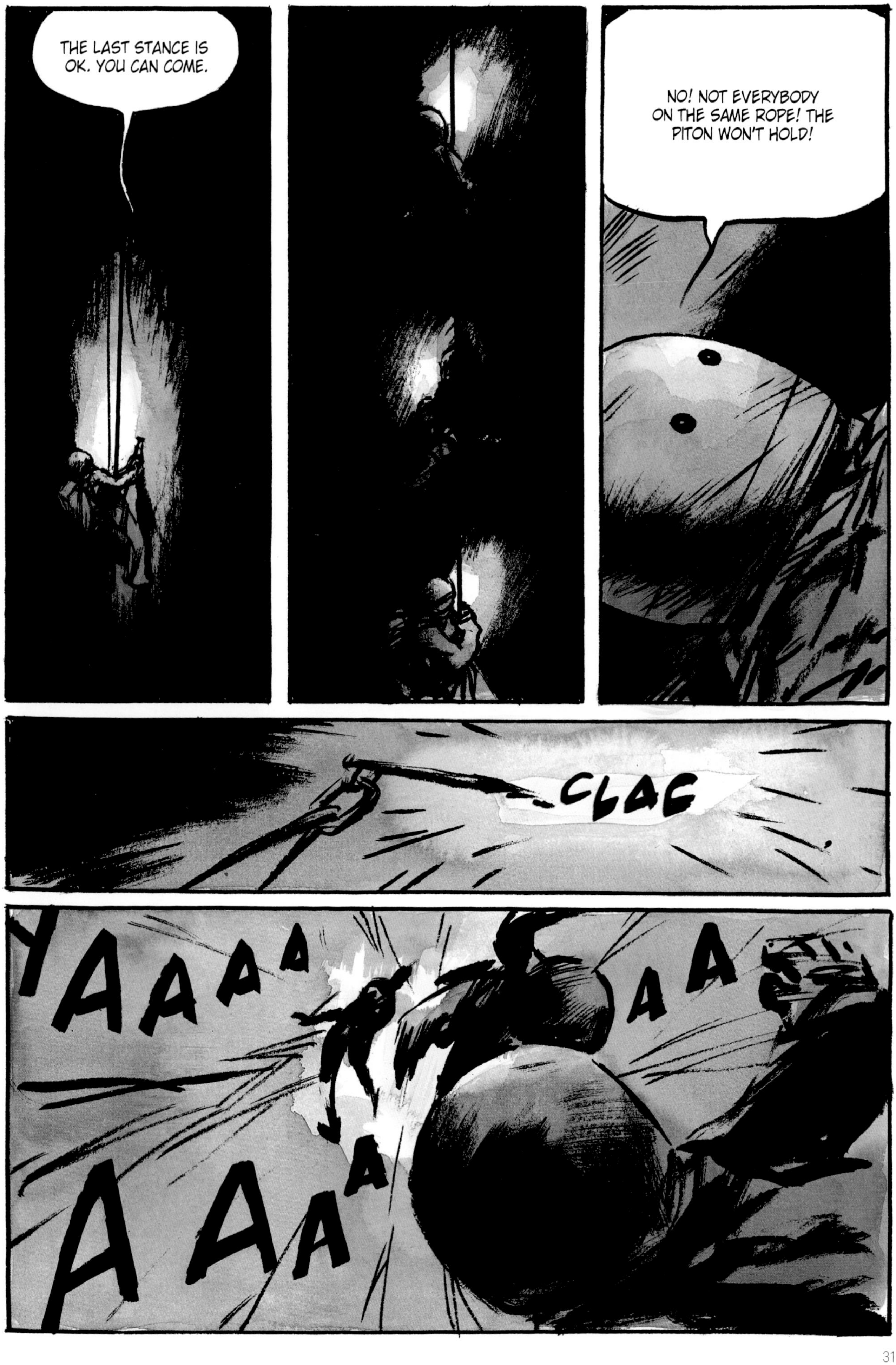
THE LAST STANCE IS OK. YOU CAN COME.
NO! NOT EVERYBODY ON THE SAME ROPE! THE PITON WON'T HOLD!
CLAC
YAAAAAAAAAAA

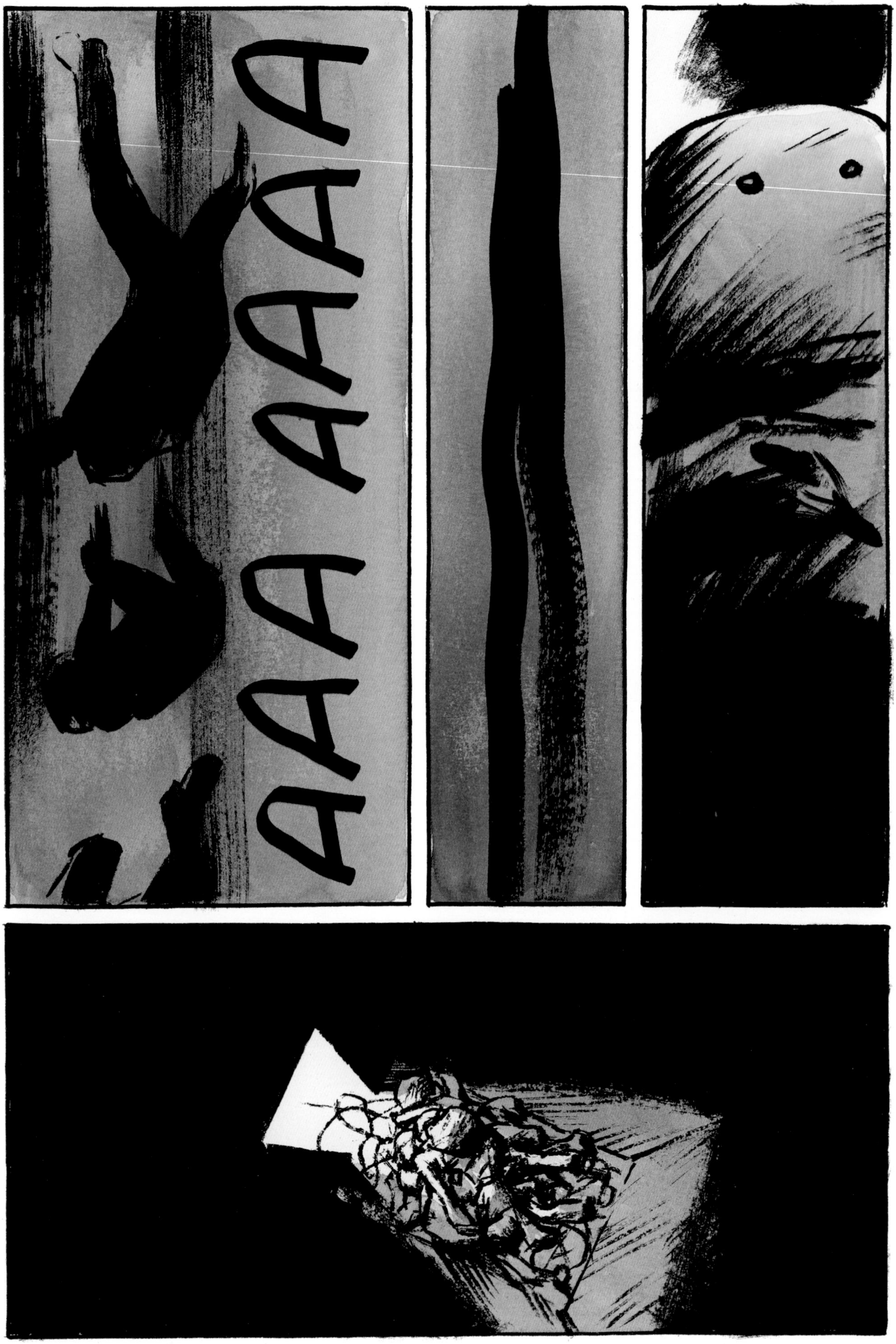
AAAAAAA

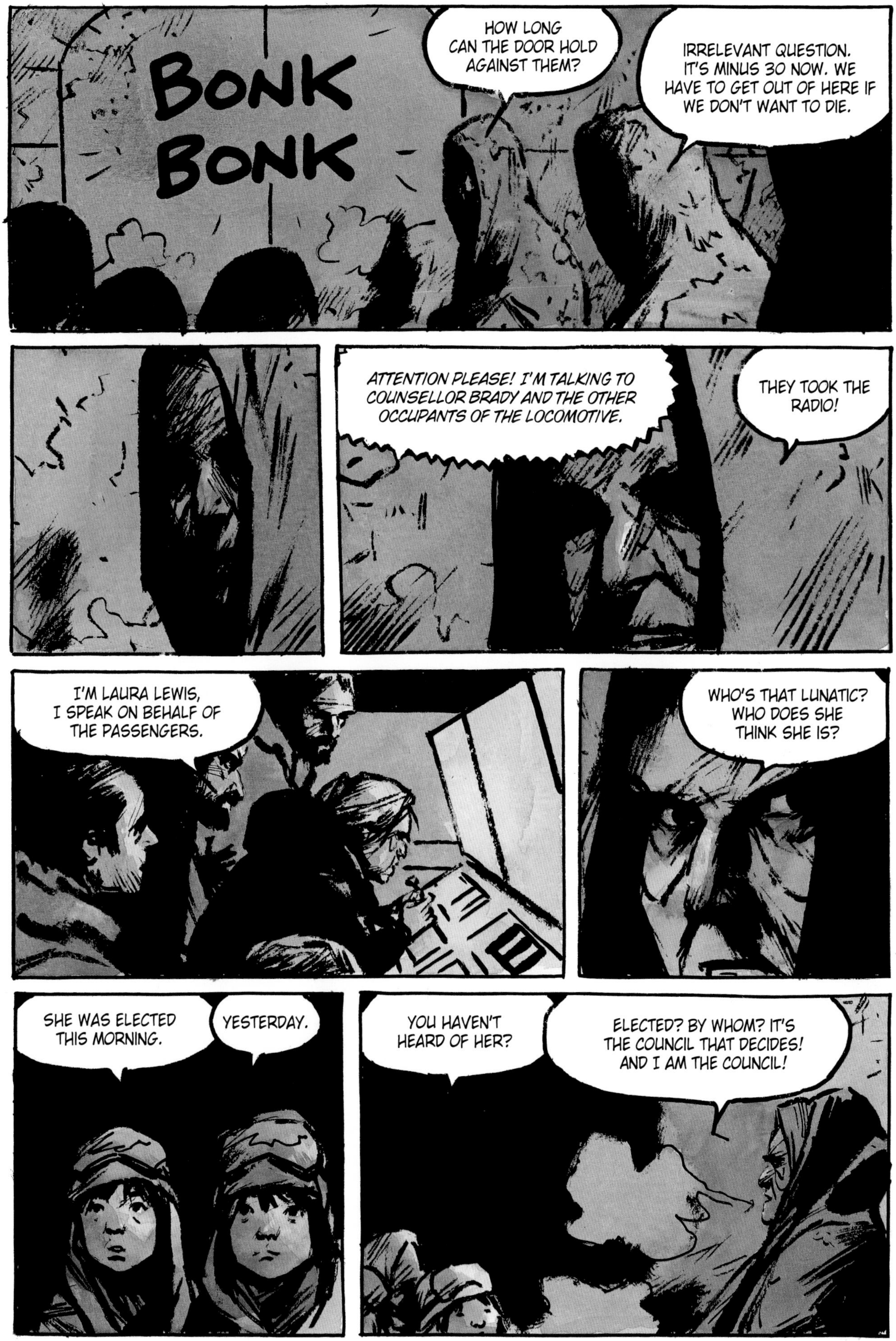

BONK
BONK
HOW LONG CAN THE DOOR HOLD AGAINST THEM?
IRRELEVANT QUESTION. IT'S MINUS 30 NOW. WE HAVE TO GET OUT OF HERE IF WE DON'T WANT TO DIE.
ATTENTION PLEASE! I'M TALKING TO COUNSELLOR BRADY AND THE OTHER OCCUPANTS OF THE LOCOMOTIVE.
THEY TOOK THE RADIO!
I'M LAURA LEWIS, I SPEAK ON BEHALF OF THE PASSENGERS.
WHO'S THAT LUNATIC? WHO DOES SHE THINK SHE IS?
SHE WAS ELECTED THIS MORNING.
YESTERDAY.
YOU HAVEN'T HEARD OF HER?
ELECTED? BY WHOM? IT'S THE COUNCIL THAT DECIDES! AND I AM THE COUNCIL!

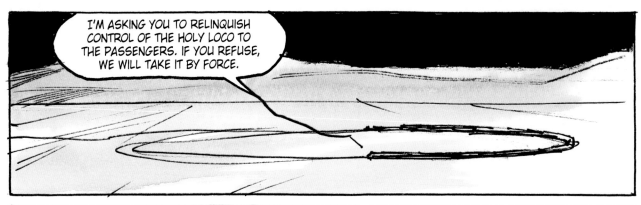

I'M ASKING YOU TO RELINQUISH CONTROL OF THE HOLY LOCO TO THE PASSENGERS. IF YOU REFUSE, WE WILL TAKE IT BY FORCE.

THEY CAN'T DO THAT! THEY DON'T HAVE THE RIGHT!

RIGHT IS A VERY CHANGEABLE NOTION ABOARD THIS TRAIN. YOU'D BETTER LET HER IN.

I AM THE GUARANTOR FOR THE RUNNING OF THIS TRAIN! I HAVE DOZENS OF ARMED MEN WITH ME! IF YOU GET IN, THEY WILL FIRE!

ZZZZT

ZZZT

AH. THEY HAVE A BLOWTORCH.

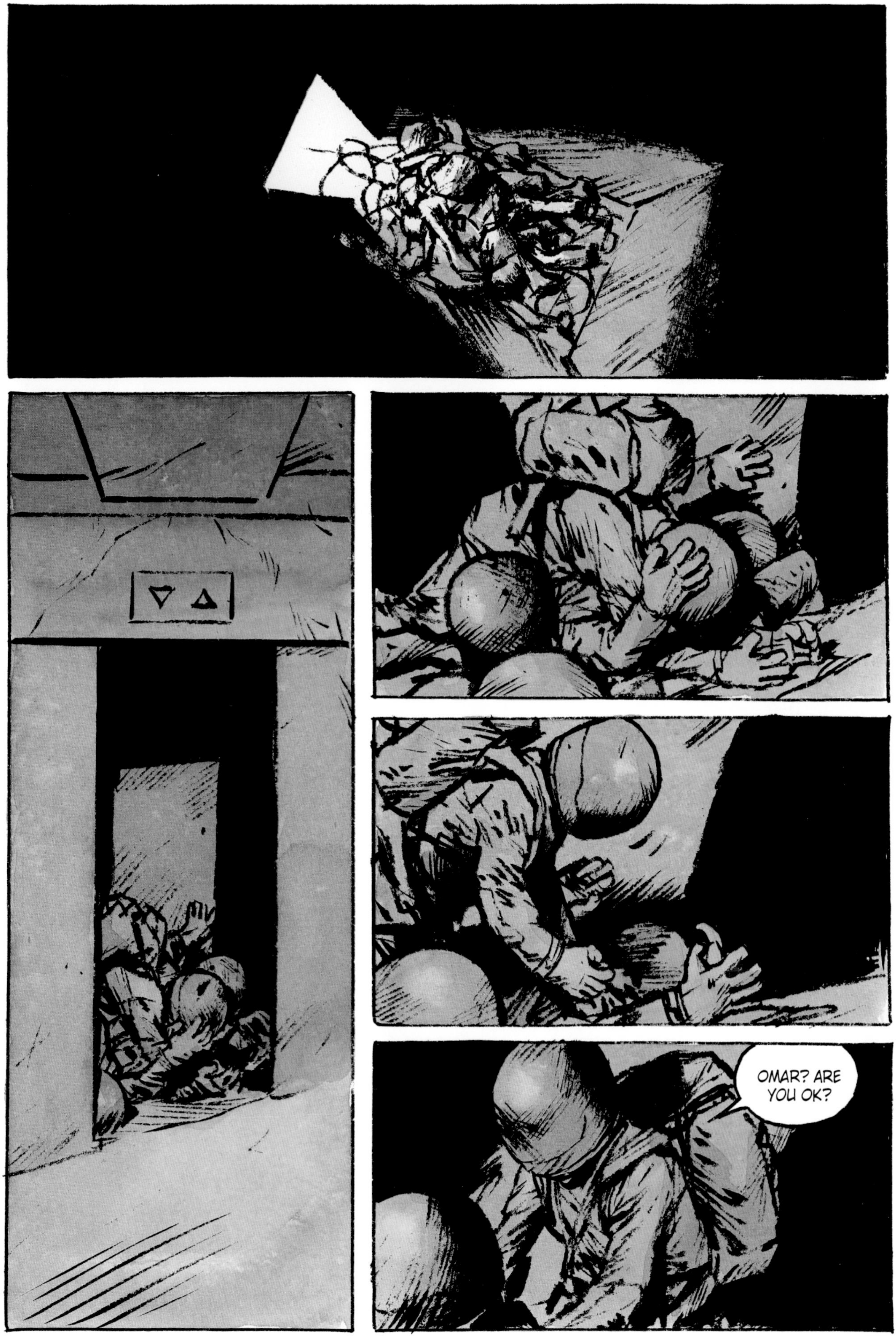
OMAR? ARE YOU OK?

YES. I THINK SO.

OUCH! SHIT, OMAR, YOU'RE SQUASHING ME!

FUCK, MY ARM!

YOU BROKE IT WHEN YOU FELL ON ME.

IT'S OK. I'M ALIVE, WE'RE ALL ALIVE, IT'S ALL THAT MATTERS. THE SNOW ABSORBED THE FALL.

MATT? MATTEO? MATTEO, CAN YOU HEAR ME? OH SHIT, NO...

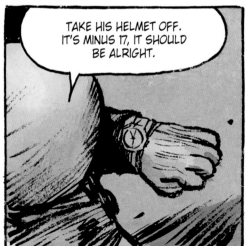

TAKE HIS HELMET OFF. IT'S MINUS 17, IT SHOULD BE ALRIGHT.

HE'S NOT BREATHING...

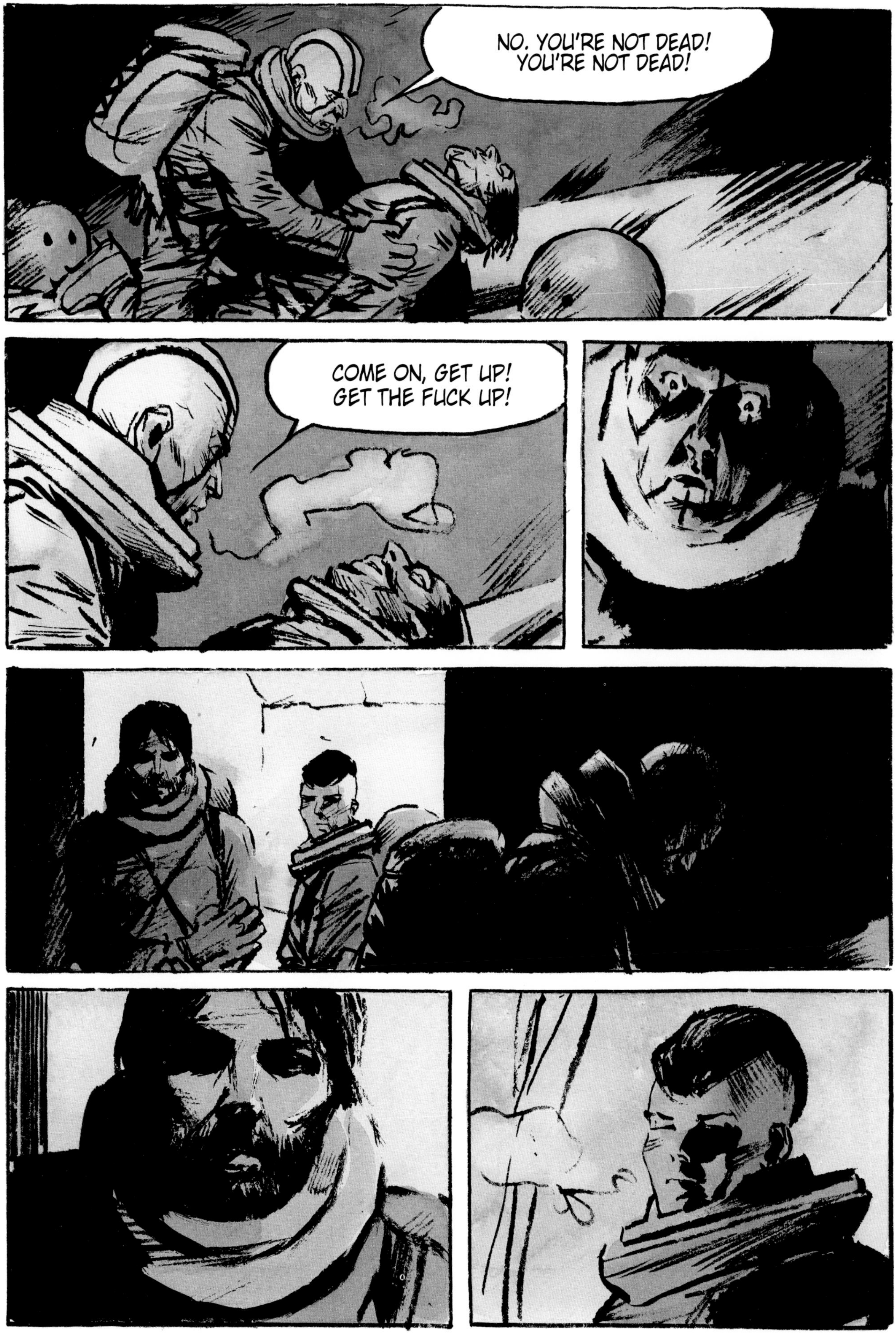
NO. YOU'RE NOT DEAD!
YOU'RE NOT DEAD!
COME ON, GET UP!
GET THE FUCK UP!

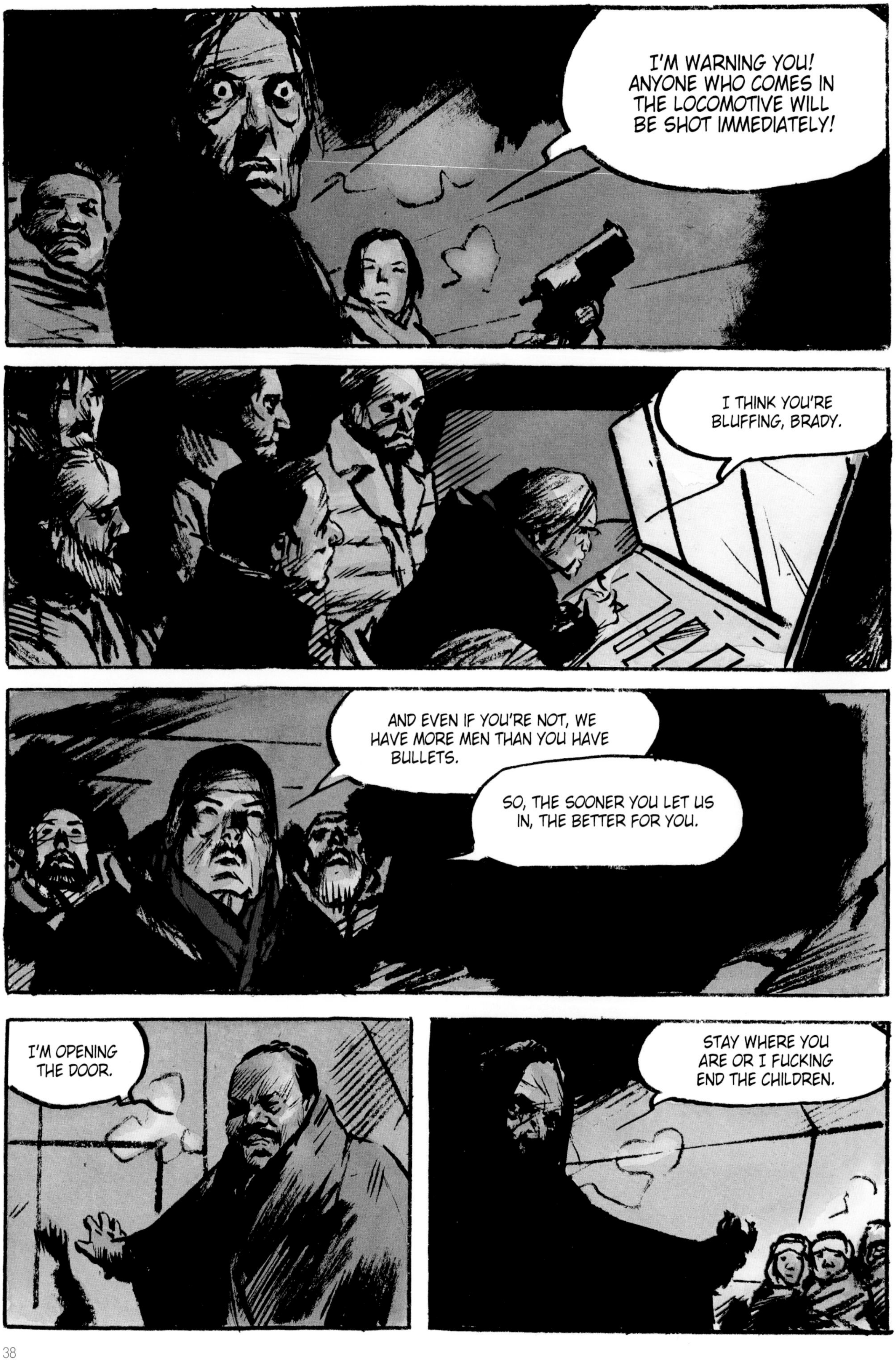
I'M WARNING YOU! ANYONE WHO COMES IN THE LOCOMOTIVE WILL BE SHOT IMMEDIATELY!
I THINK YOU'RE BLUFFING, BRADY.
AND EVEN IF YOU'RE NOT, WE HAVE MORE MEN THAN YOU HAVE BULLETS.
SO, THE SOONER YOU LET US IN, THE BETTER FOR YOU.
I'M OPENING THE DOOR.
STAY WHERE YOU ARE OR I FUCKING END THE CHILDREN.

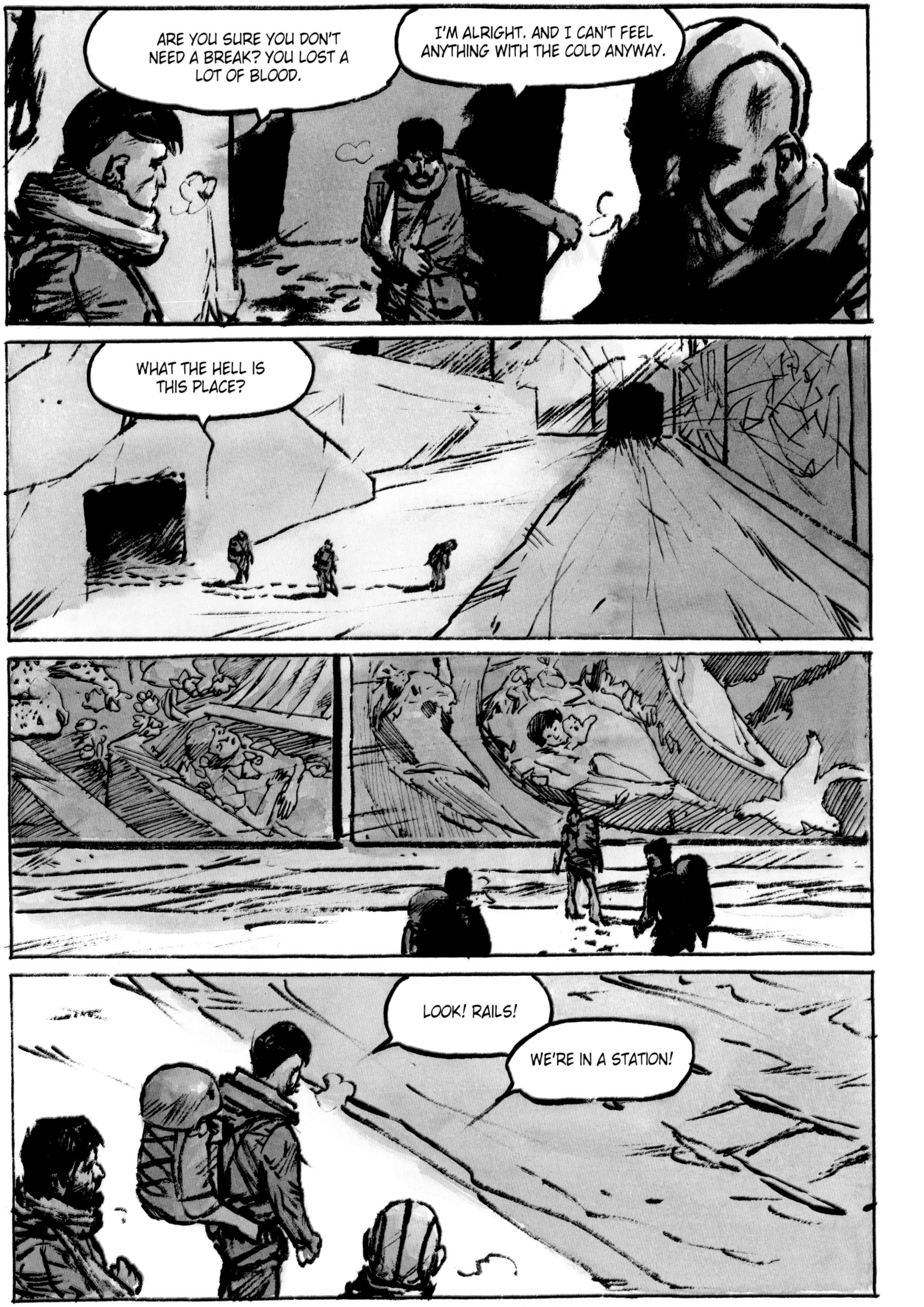
ARE YOU SURE YOU DON'T NEED A BREAK? YOU LOST A LOT OF BLOOD.
I'M ALRIGHT. AND I CAN'T FEEL ANYTHING WITH THE COLD ANYWAY.
WHAT THE HELL IS THIS PLACE?
LOOK! RAILS!
WE'RE IN A STATION!

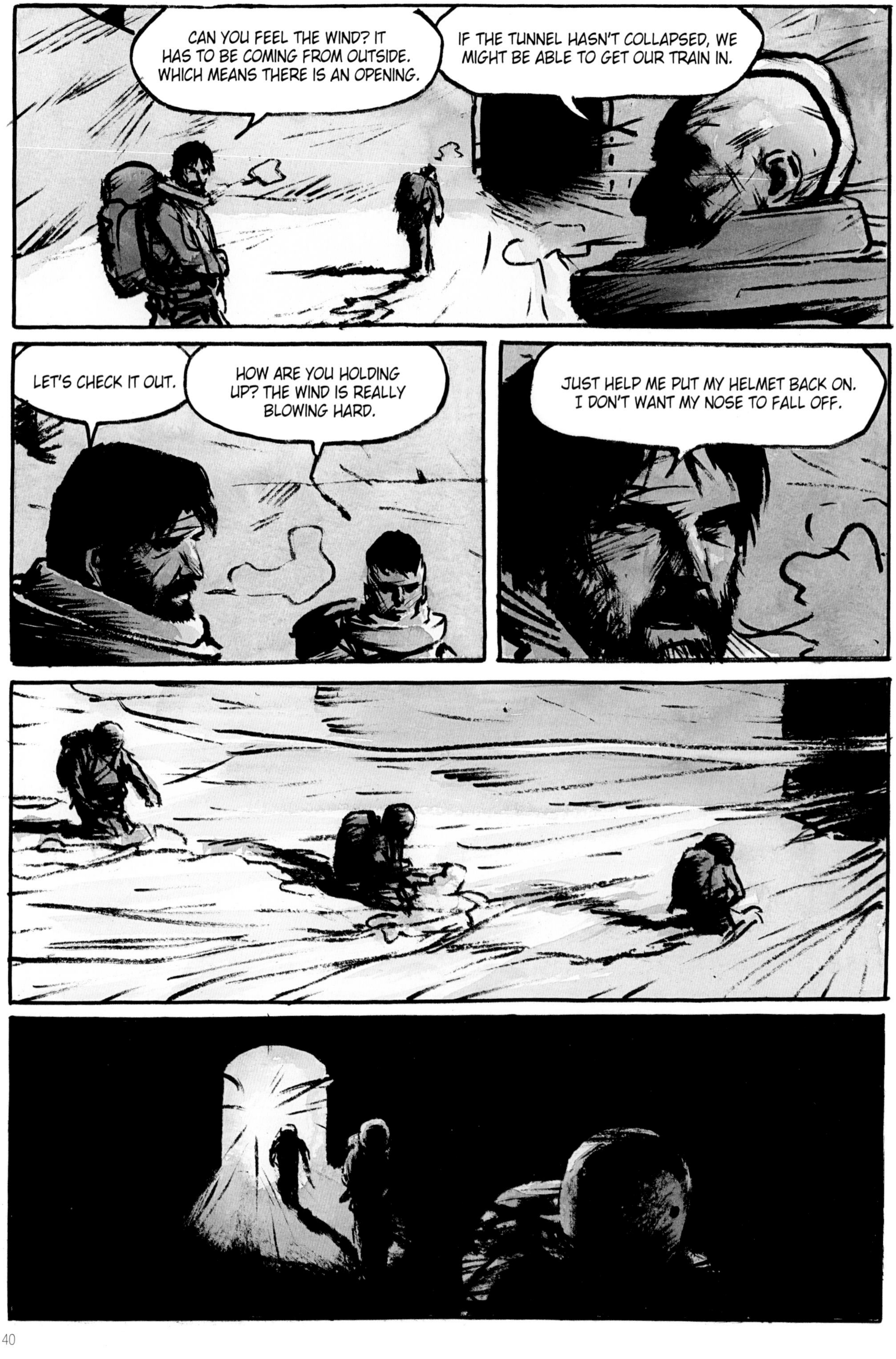
CAN YOU FEEL THE WIND? IT HAS TO BE COMING FROM OUTSIDE. WHICH MEANS THERE IS AN OPENING.
IF THE TUNNEL HASN'T COLLAPSED, WE MIGHT BE ABLE TO GET OUR TRAIN IN.
LET'S CHECK IT OUT.
HOW ARE YOU HOLDING UP? THE WIND IS REALLY BLOWING HARD.
JUST HELP ME PUT MY HELMET BACK ON. I DON'T WANT MY NOSE TO FALL OFF.

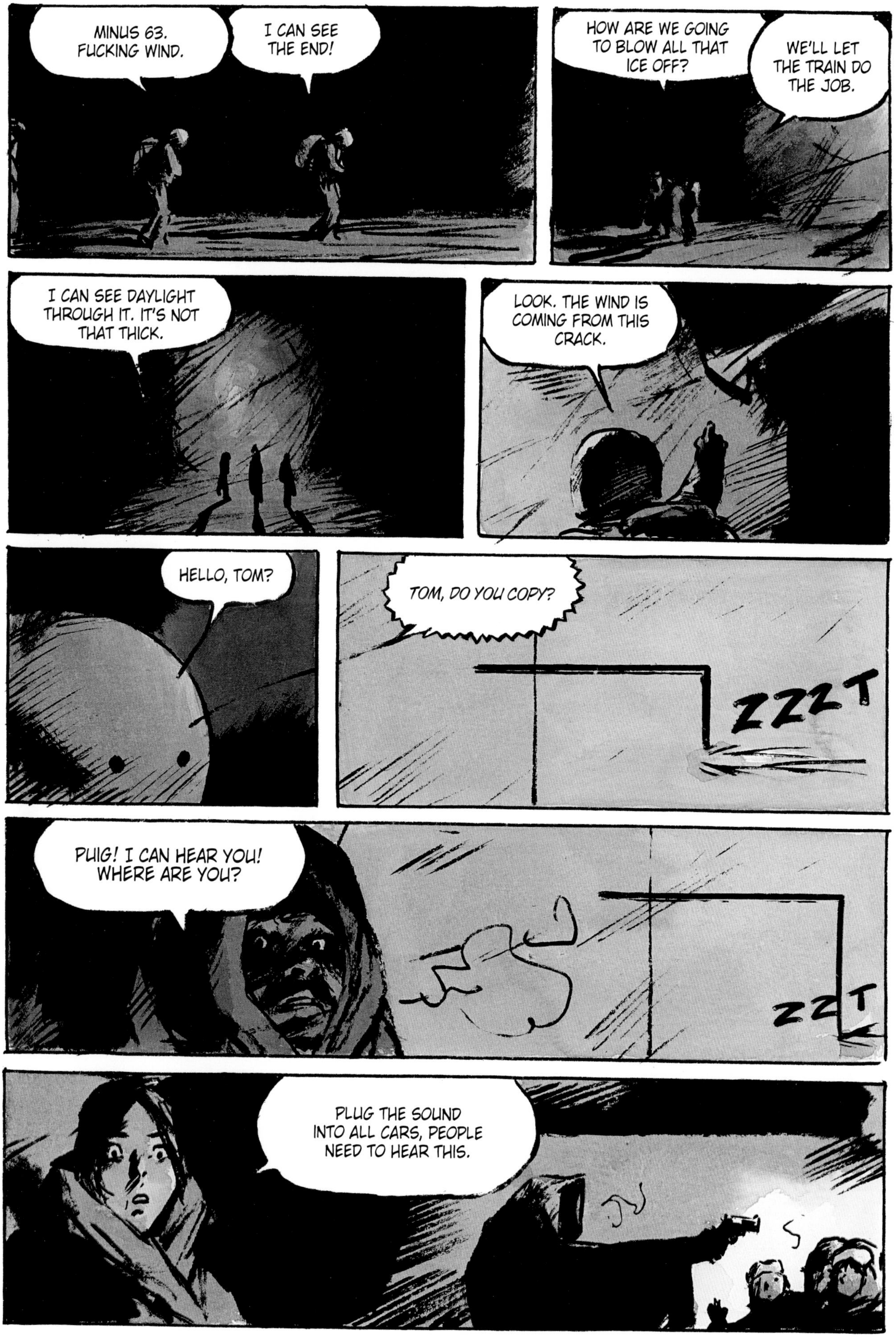
MINUS 63. FUCKING WIND.
I CAN SEE THE END!
HOW ARE WE GOING TO BLOW ALL THAT ICE OFF?
WE'LL LET THE TRAIN DO THE JOB.
I CAN SEE DAYLIGHT THROUGH IT. IT'S NOT THAT THICK.
LOOK. THE WIND IS COMING FROM THIS CRACK.
HELLO, TOM?
TOM, DO YOU COPY?
ZZZT
PUIG! I CAN HEAR YOU! WHERE ARE YOU?
ZZT
PLUG THE SOUND INTO ALL CARS, PEOPLE NEED TO HEAR THIS.

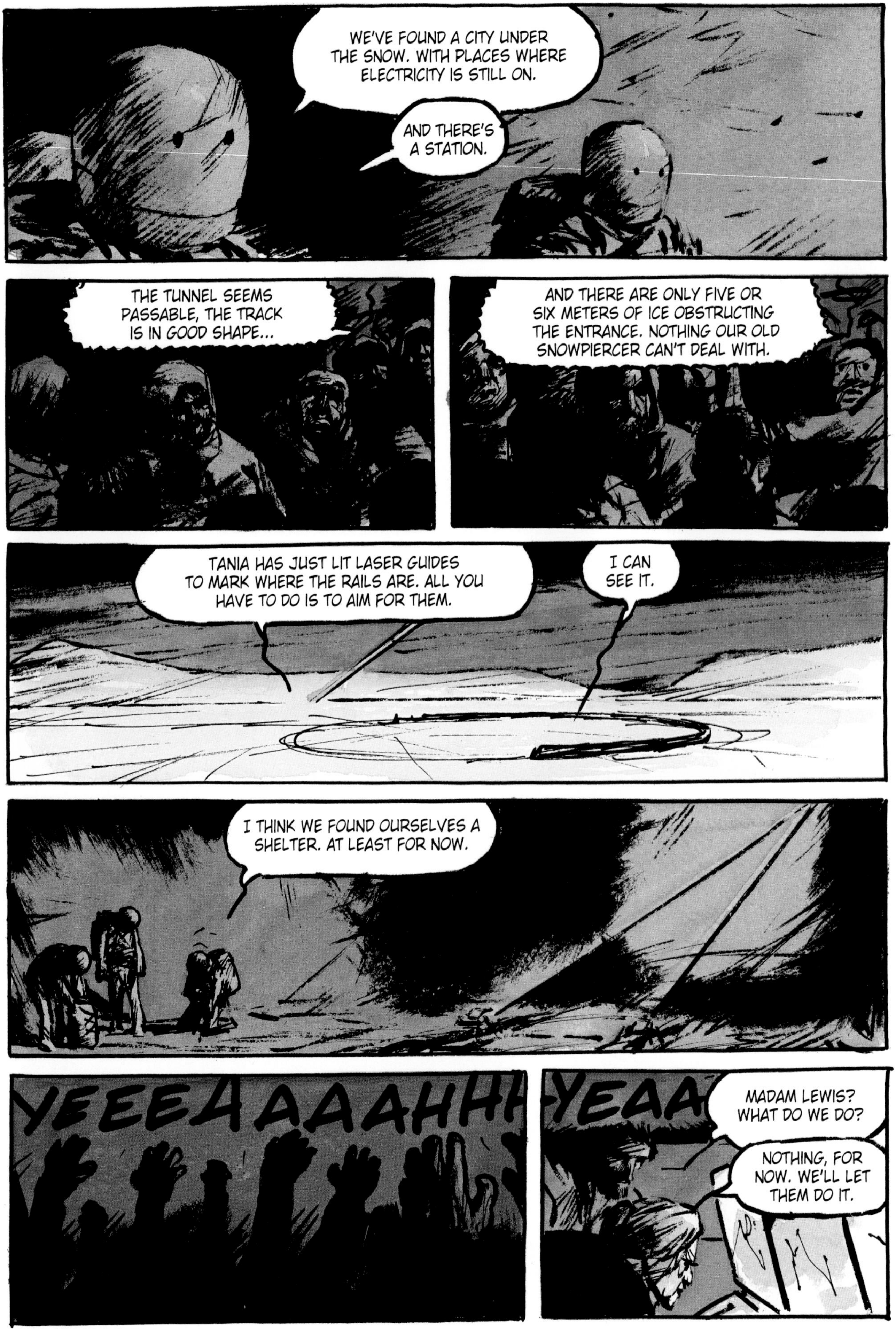
WE'VE FOUND A CITY UNDER THE SNOW. WITH PLACES WHERE ELECTRICITY IS STILL ON.
AND THERE'S A STATION.
THE TUNNEL SEEMS PASSABLE, THE TRACK IS IN GOOD SHAPE...
AND THERE ARE ONLY FIVE OR SIX METERS OF ICE OBSTRUCTING THE ENTRANCE. NOTHING OUR OLD SNOWPIERCER CAN'T DEAL WITH.
TANIA HAS JUST LIT LASER GUIDES TO MARK WHERE THE RAILS ARE. ALL YOU HAVE TO DO IS TO AIM FOR THEM.
I CAN SEE IT.
I THINK WE FOUND OURSELVES A SHELTER. AT LEAST FOR NOW.
YEEEAAAAHH-YEAA
MADAM LEWIS? WHAT DO WE DO?
NOTHING, FOR NOW. WE'LL LET THEM DO IT.

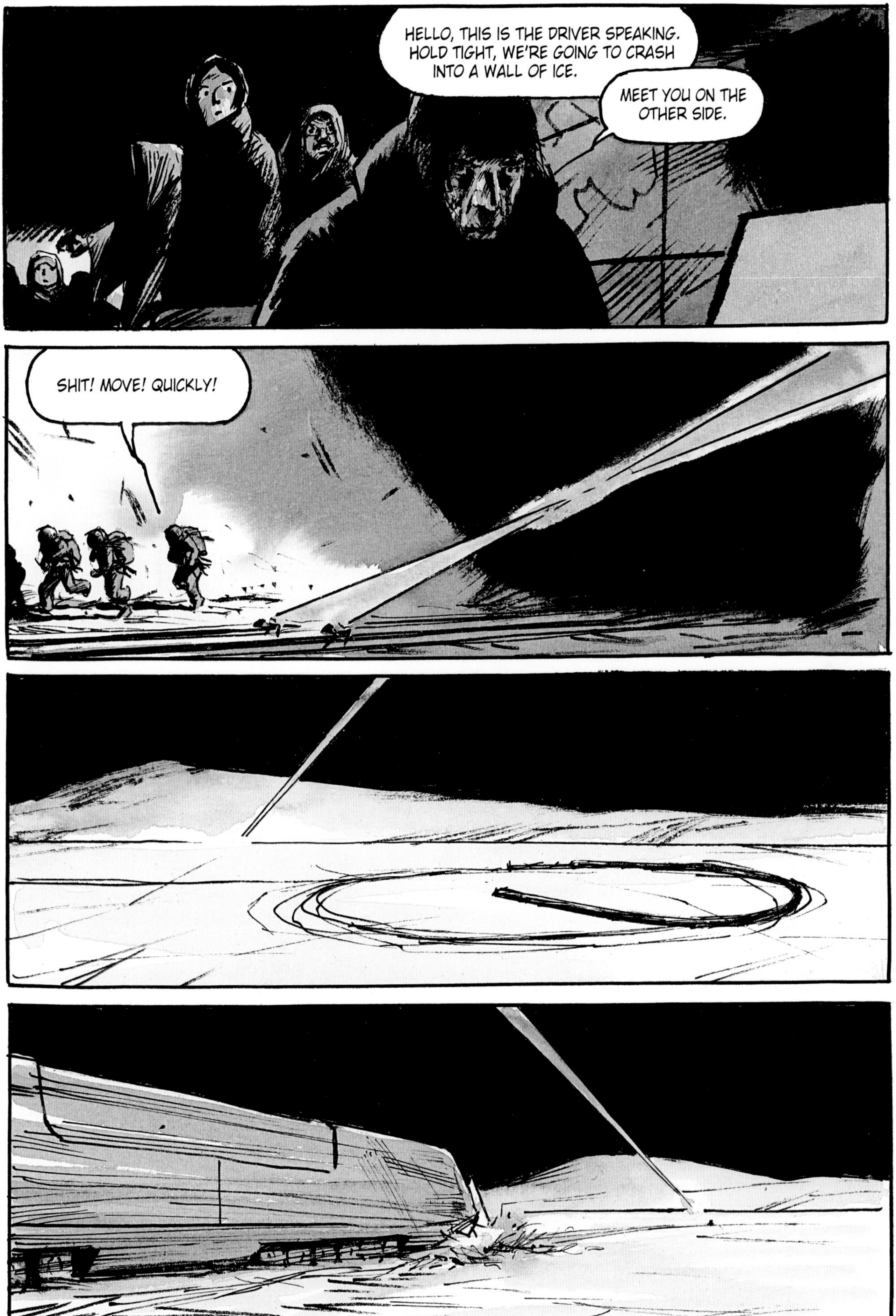
HELLO, THIS IS THE DRIVER SPEAKING. HOLD TIGHT, WE'RE GOING TO CRASH INTO A WALL OF ICE.
MEET YOU ON THE OTHER SIDE.
SHIT! MOVE! QUICKLY!

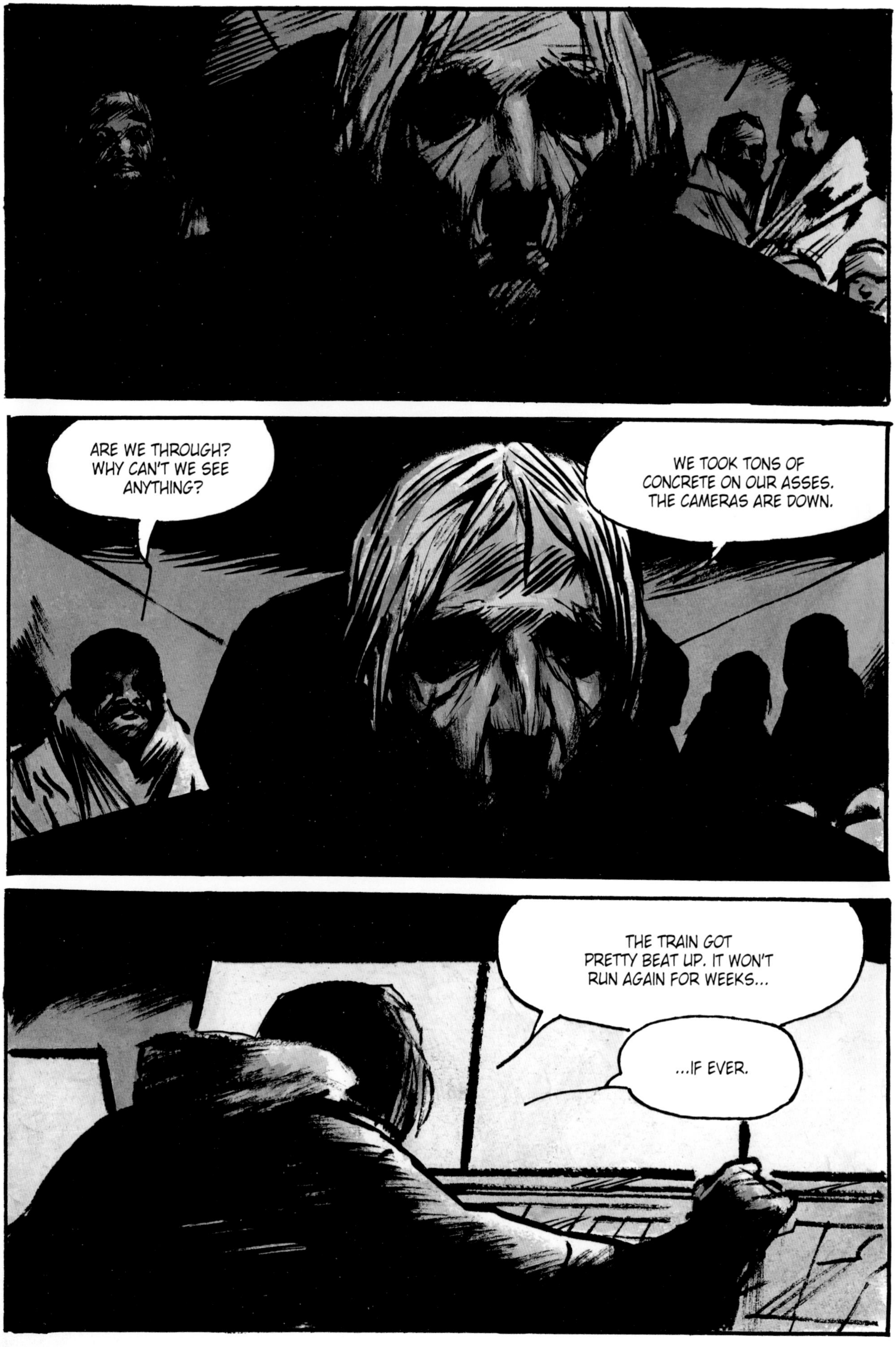
ARE WE THROUGH? WHY CAN'T WE SEE ANYTHING?
WE TOOK TONS OF CONCRETE ON OUR ASSES. THE CAMERAS ARE DOWN.
THE TRAIN GOT PRETTY BEAT UP. IT WON'T RUN AGAIN FOR WEEKS...
...IF EVER.

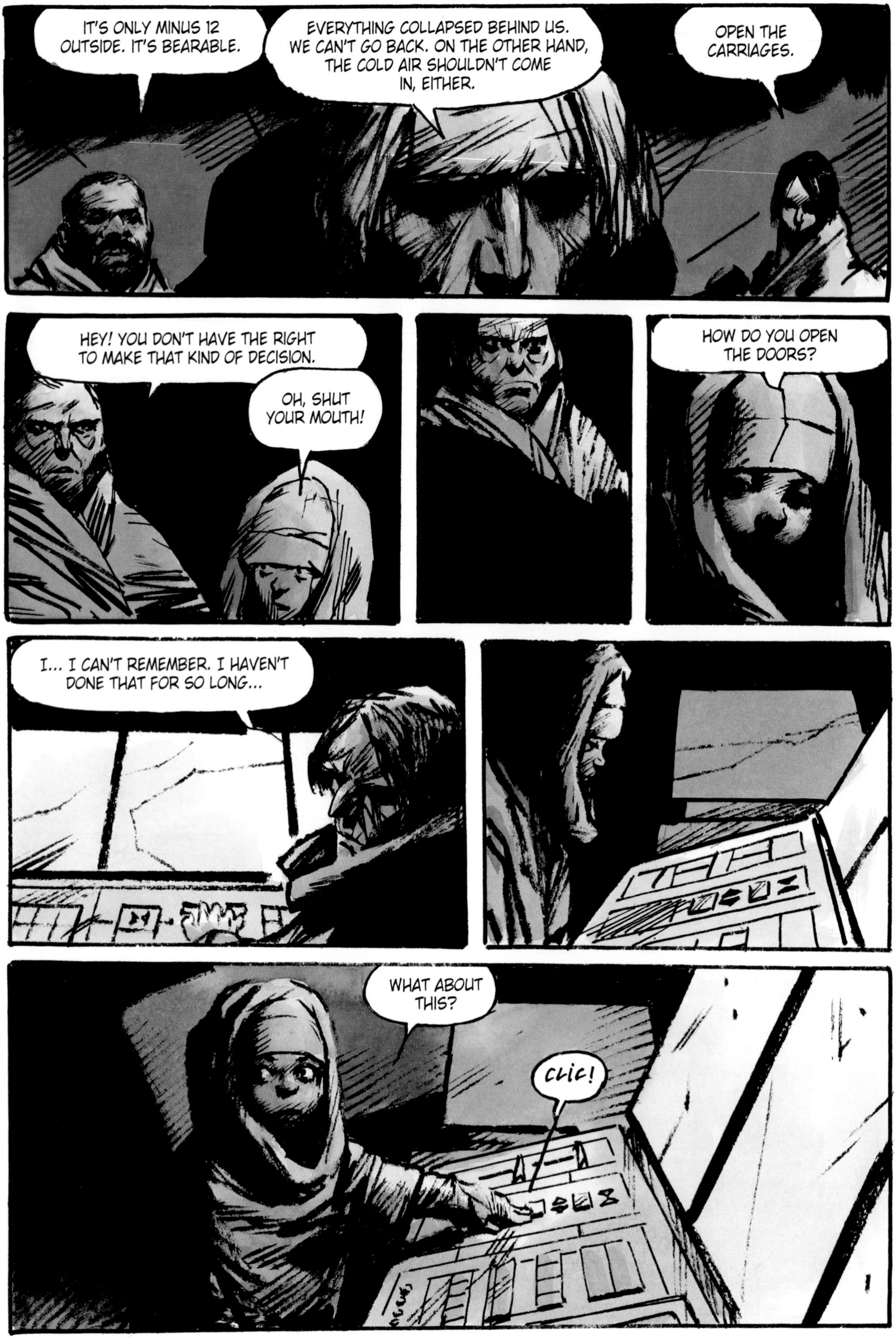
IT'S ONLY MINUS 12 OUTSIDE. IT'S BEARABLE.
EVERYTHING COLLAPSED BEHIND US. WE CAN'T GO BACK. ON THE OTHER HAND, THE COLD AIR SHOULDN'T COME IN, EITHER.
OPEN THE CARRIAGES.
HEY! YOU DON'T HAVE THE RIGHT TO MAKE THAT KIND OF DECISION.
OH, SHUT YOUR MOUTH!
HOW DO YOU OPEN THE DOORS?
I... I CAN'T REMEMBER. I HAVEN'T DONE THAT FOR SO LONG...
WHAT ABOUT THIS?
CLIC!

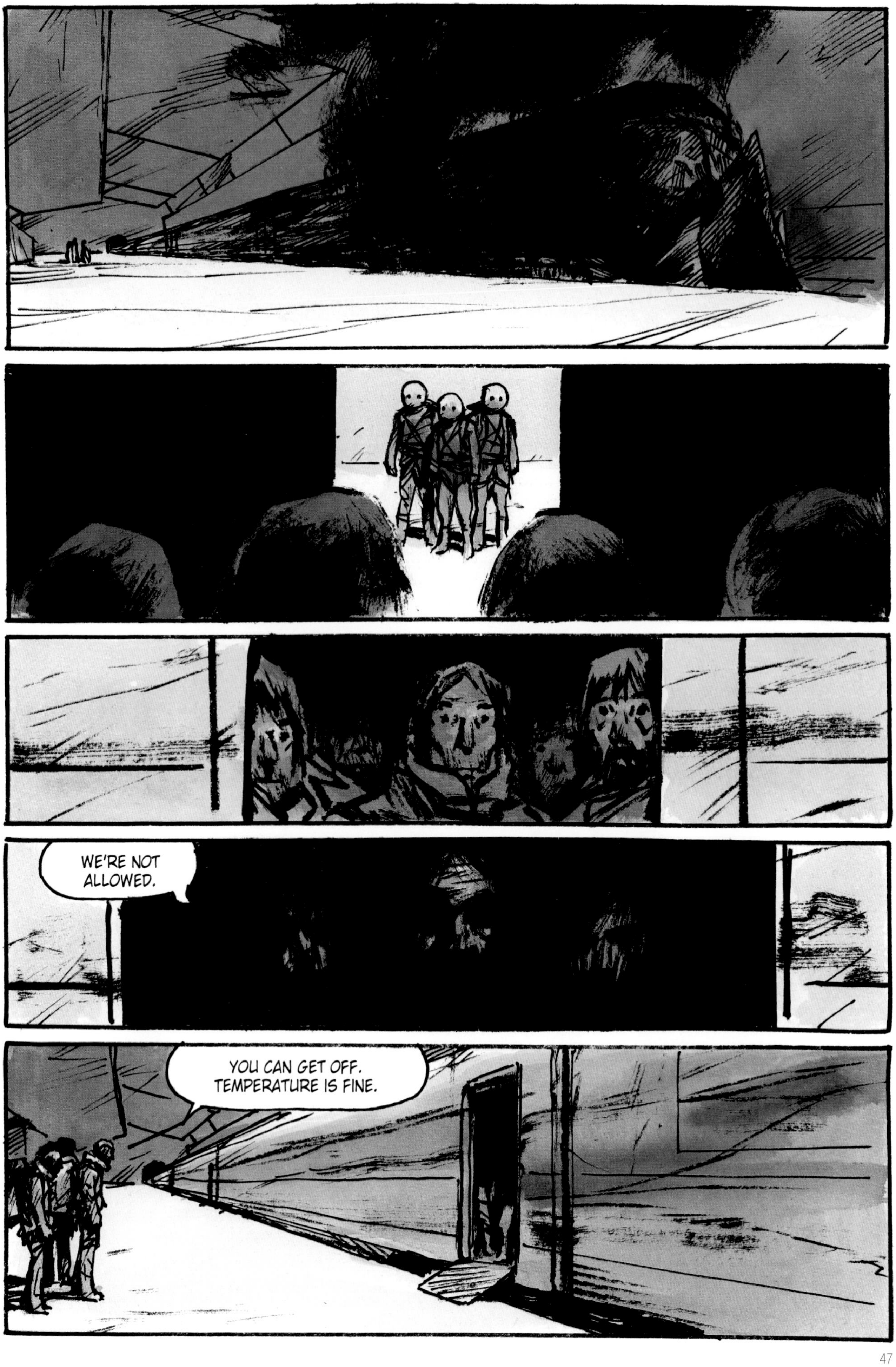
WE'RE NOT ALLOWED.
YOU CAN GET OFF. TEMPERATURE IS FINE.

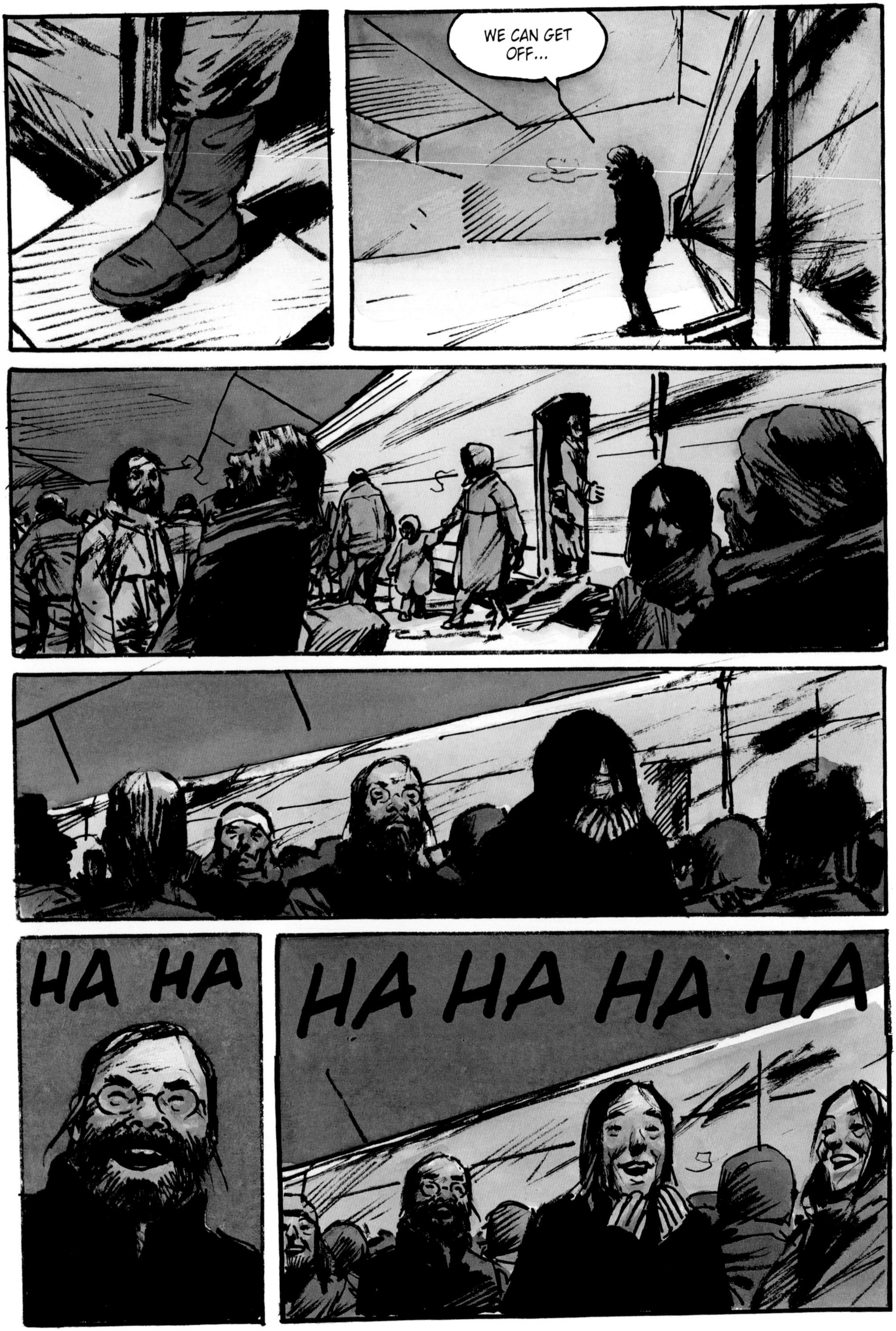
WE CAN GET OFF...
HA HA
HA HA HA HA

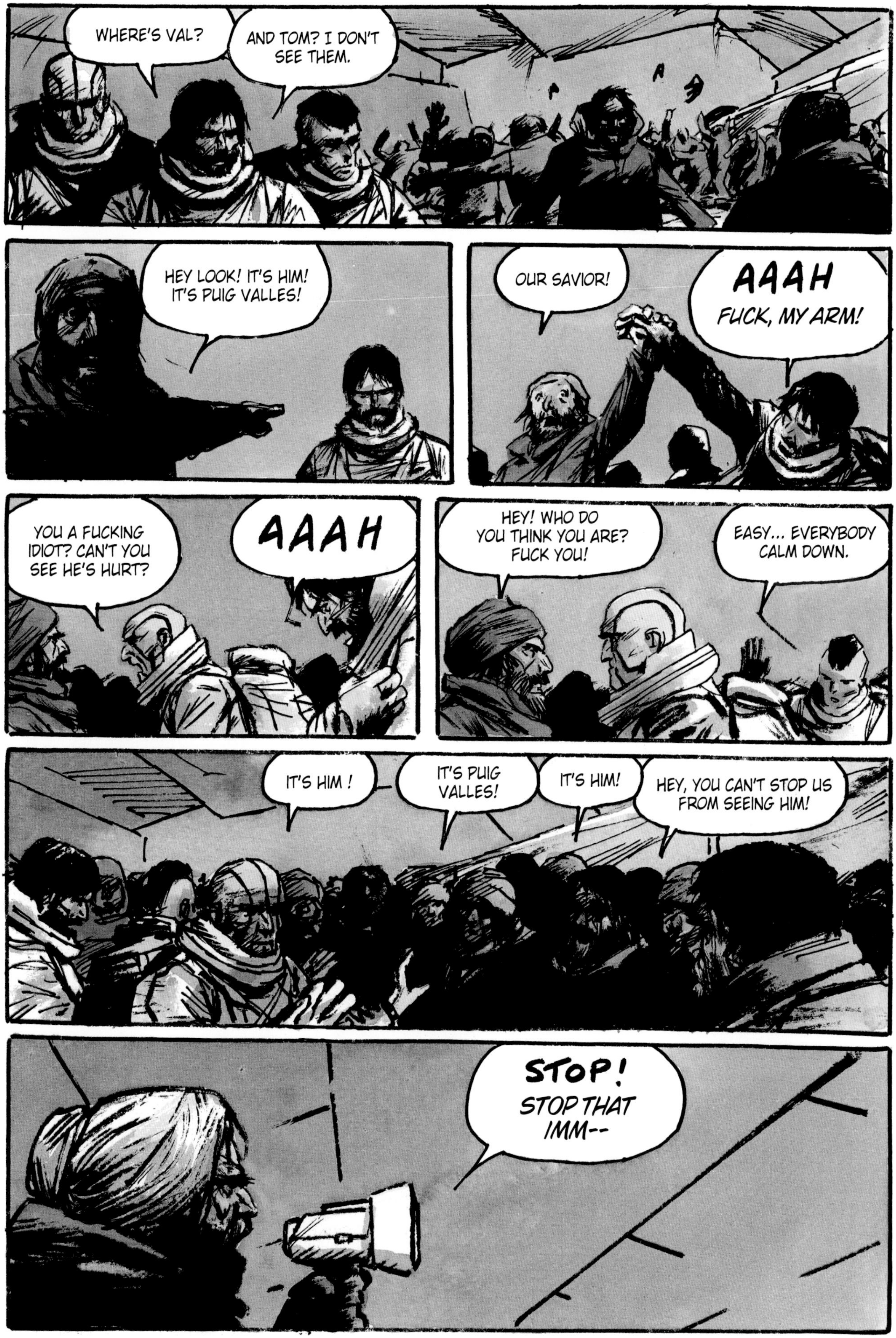
WHERE'S VAL?
AND TOM? I DON'T SEE THEM.
HEY LOOK! IT'S HIM! IT'S PUIG VALLES!
OUR SAVIOR!
AAAH
FUCK, MY ARM!
YOU A FUCKING IDIOT? CAN'T YOU SEE HE'S HURT?
AAAH
HEY! WHO DO YOU THINK YOU ARE? FUCK YOU!
EASY... EVERYBODY CALM DOWN.
IT'S HIM !
IT'S PUIG VALLES!
IT'S HIM!
HEY, YOU CAN'T STOP US FROM SEEING HIM!
STOP!
STOP THAT IMM--

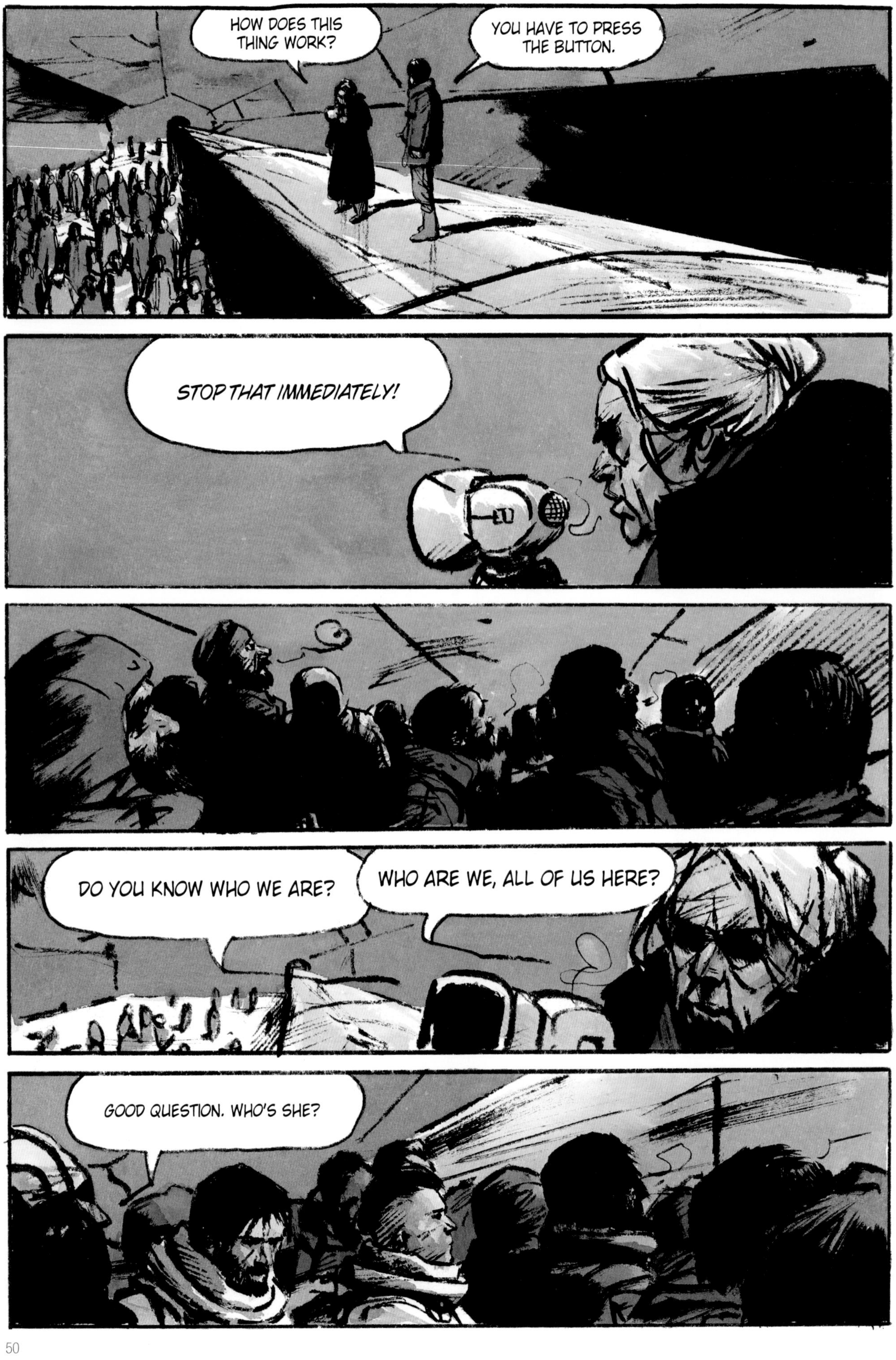
HOW DOES THIS THING WORK?
YOU HAVE TO PRESS THE BUTTON.
STOP THAT IMMEDIATELY!
DO YOU KNOW WHO WE ARE?
WHO ARE WE, ALL OF US HERE?
GOOD QUESTION. WHO'S SHE?

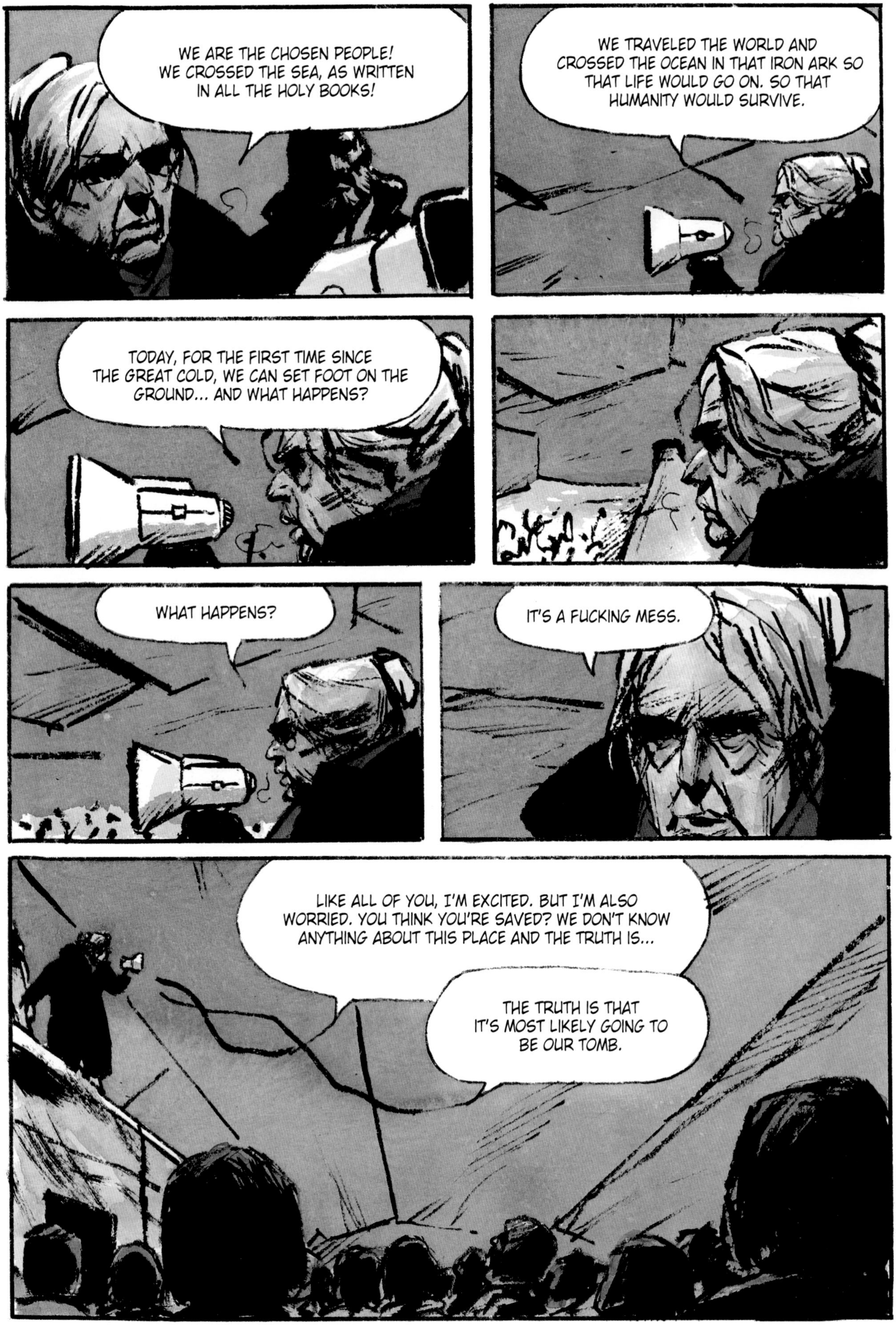
WE ARE THE CHOSEN PEOPLE! WE CROSSED THE SEA, AS WRITTEN IN ALL THE HOLY BOOKS!
WE TRAVELED THE WORLD AND CROSSED THE OCEAN IN THAT IRON ARK SO THAT LIFE WOULD GO ON. SO THAT HUMANITY WOULD SURVIVE.
TODAY, FOR THE FIRST TIME SINCE THE GREAT COLD, WE CAN SET FOOT ON THE GROUND... AND WHAT HAPPENS?
WHAT HAPPENS?
IT'S A FUCKING MESS.
LIKE ALL OF YOU, I'M EXCITED. BUT I'M ALSO WORRIED. YOU THINK YOU'RE SAVED? WE DON'T KNOW ANYTHING ABOUT THIS PLACE AND THE TRUTH IS...
THE TRUTH IS THAT IT'S MOST LIKELY GOING TO BE OUR TOMB.

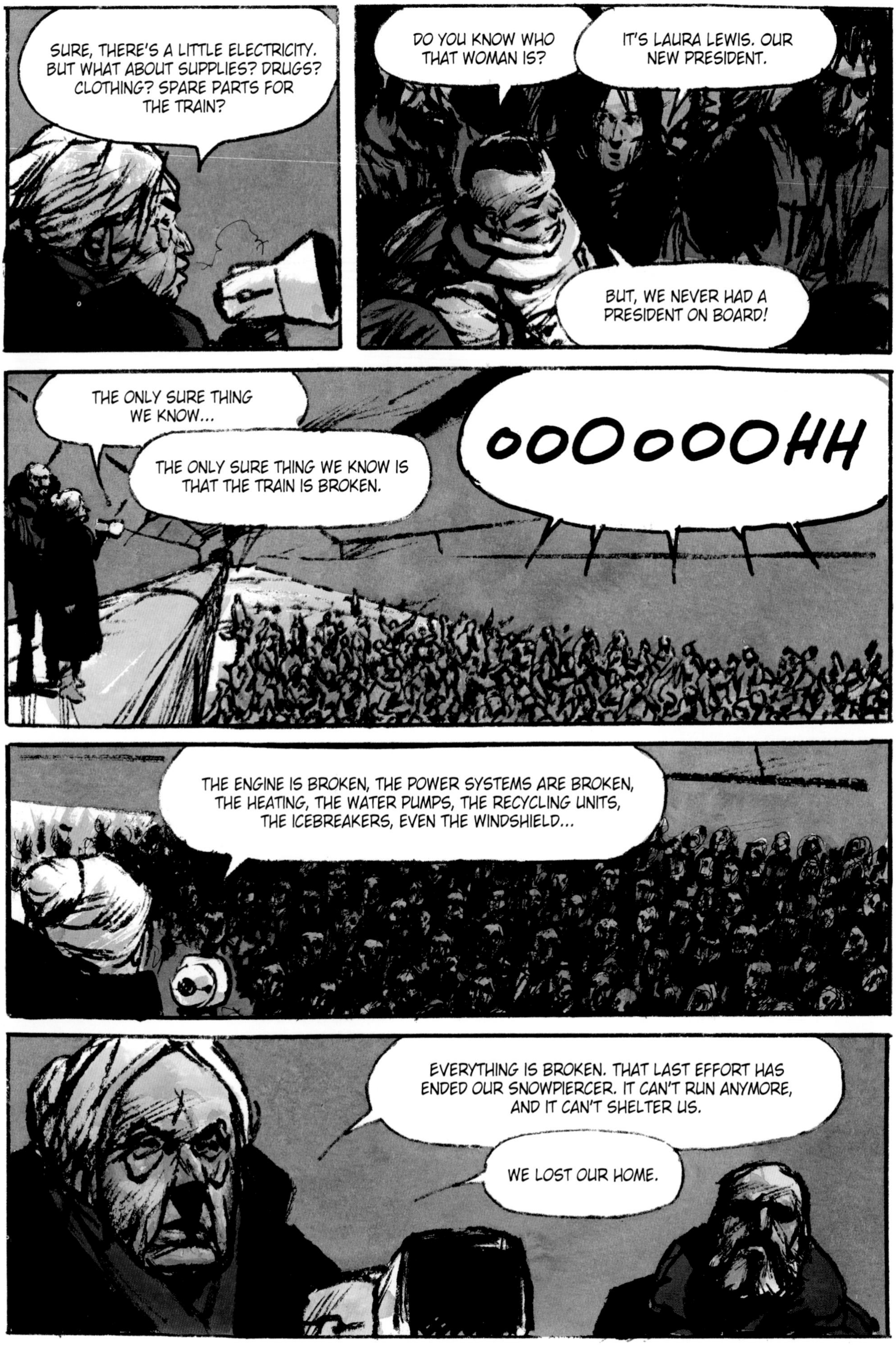
SURE, THERE'S A LITTLE ELECTRICITY. BUT WHAT ABOUT SUPPLIES? DRUGS? CLOTHING? SPARE PARTS FOR THE TRAIN?
DO YOU KNOW WHO THAT WOMAN IS?
IT'S LAURA LEWIS. OUR NEW PRESIDENT.
BUT, WE NEVER HAD A PRESIDENT ON BOARD!
THE ONLY SURE THING WE KNOW...
THE ONLY SURE THING WE KNOW IS THAT THE TRAIN IS BROKEN.
OOOOOOOHH
THE ENGINE IS BROKEN, THE POWER SYSTEMS ARE BROKEN, THE HEATING, THE WATER PUMPS, THE RECYCLING UNITS, THE ICEBREAKERS, EVEN THE WINDSHIELD...
EVERYTHING IS BROKEN. THAT LAST EFFORT HAS ENDED OUR SNOWPIERCER. IT CAN'T RUN ANYMORE, AND IT CAN'T SHELTER US.
WE LOST OUR HOME.

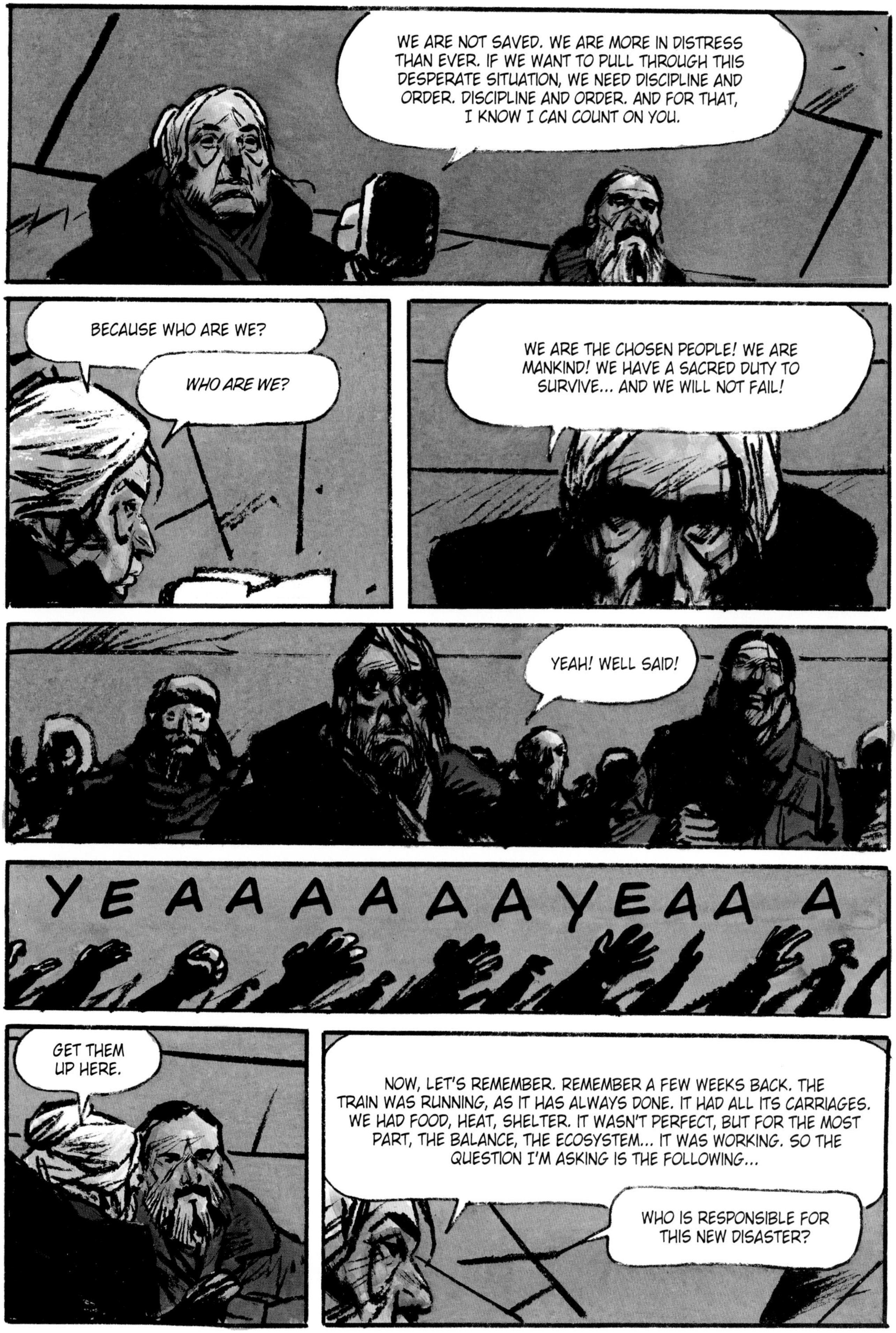
WE ARE NOT SAVED. WE ARE MORE IN DISTRESS THAN EVER. IF WE WANT TO PULL THROUGH THIS DESPERATE SITUATION, WE NEED DISCIPLINE AND ORDER. DISCIPLINE AND ORDER. AND FOR THAT, I KNOW I CAN COUNT ON YOU.
BECAUSE WHO ARE WE?
WHO ARE WE?
WE ARE THE CHOSEN PEOPLE! WE ARE MANKIND! WE HAVE A SACRED DUTY TO SURVIVE... AND WE WILL NOT FAIL!
YEAH! WELL SAID!
YEAAAAAAAYEAA A
GET THEM UP HERE.
NOW, LET'S REMEMBER. REMEMBER A FEW WEEKS BACK. THE TRAIN WAS RUNNING, AS IT HAS ALWAYS DONE. IT HAD ALL ITS CARRIAGES. WE HAD FOOD, HEAT, SHELTER. IT WASN'T PERFECT, BUT FOR THE MOST PART, THE BALANCE, THE ECOSYSTEM... IT WAS WORKING. SO THE QUESTION I'M ASKING IS THE FOLLOWING...
WHO IS RESPONSIBLE FOR THIS NEW DISASTER?

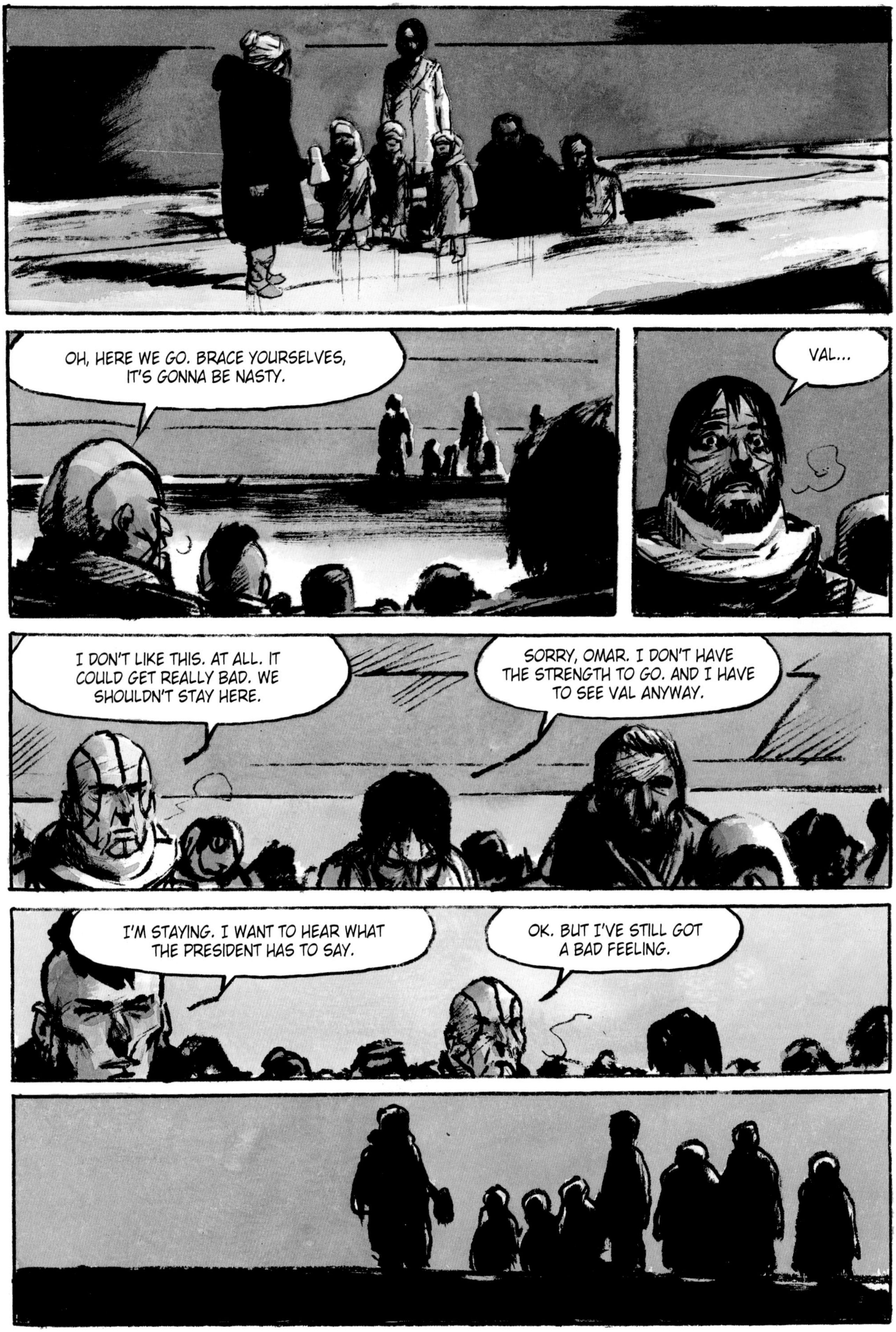
OH, HERE WE GO. BRACE YOURSELVES, IT'S GONNA BE NASTY.
VAL...
I DON'T LIKE THIS. AT ALL. IT COULD GET REALLY BAD. WE SHOULDN'T STAY HERE.
SORRY, OMAR. I DON'T HAVE THE STRENGTH TO GO. AND I HAVE TO SEE VAL ANYWAY.
I'M STAYING. I WANT TO HEAR WHAT THE PRESIDENT HAS TO SAY.
OK. BUT I'VE STILL GOT A BAD FEELING.

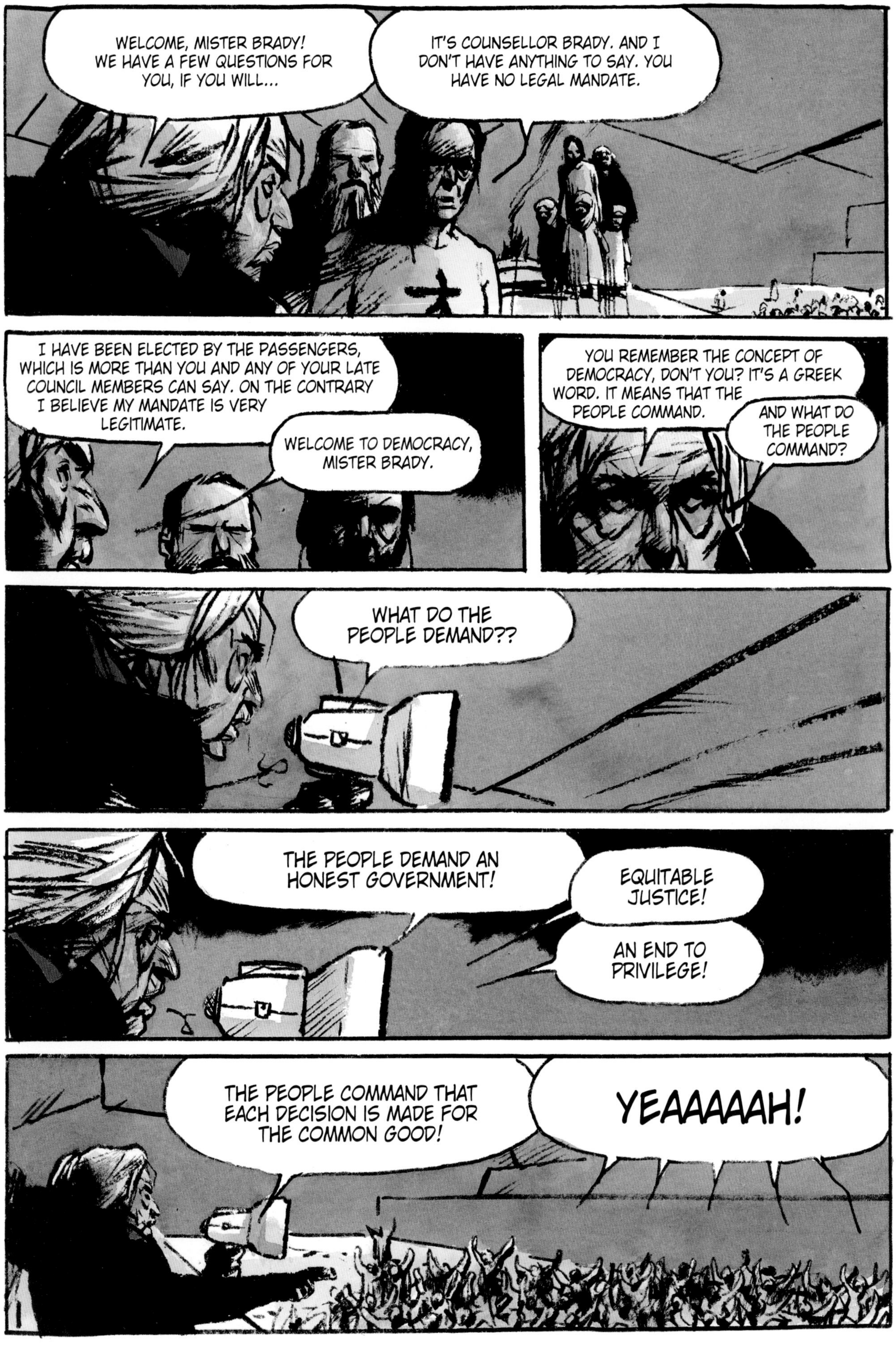
WELCOME, MISTER BRADY! WE HAVE A FEW QUESTIONS FOR YOU, IF YOU WILL...
IT'S COUNSELLOR BRADY. AND I DON'T HAVE ANYTHING TO SAY. YOU HAVE NO LEGAL MANDATE.
I HAVE BEEN ELECTED BY THE PASSENGERS, WHICH IS MORE THAN YOU AND ANY OF YOUR LATE COUNCIL MEMBERS CAN SAY. ON THE CONTRARY I BELIEVE MY MANDATE IS VERY LEGITIMATE.
WELCOME TO DEMOCRACY, MISTER BRADY.
YOU REMEMBER THE CONCEPT OF DEMOCRACY, DON'T YOU? IT'S A GREEK WORD. IT MEANS THAT THE PEOPLE COMMAND.
AND WHAT DO THE PEOPLE COMMAND?
WHAT DO THE PEOPLE DEMAND??
THE PEOPLE DEMAND AN HONEST GOVERNMENT!
EQUITABLE JUSTICE!
AN END TO PRIVILEGE!
THE PEOPLE COMMAND THAT EACH DECISION IS MADE FOR THE COMMON GOOD!
YEAAAAAH!

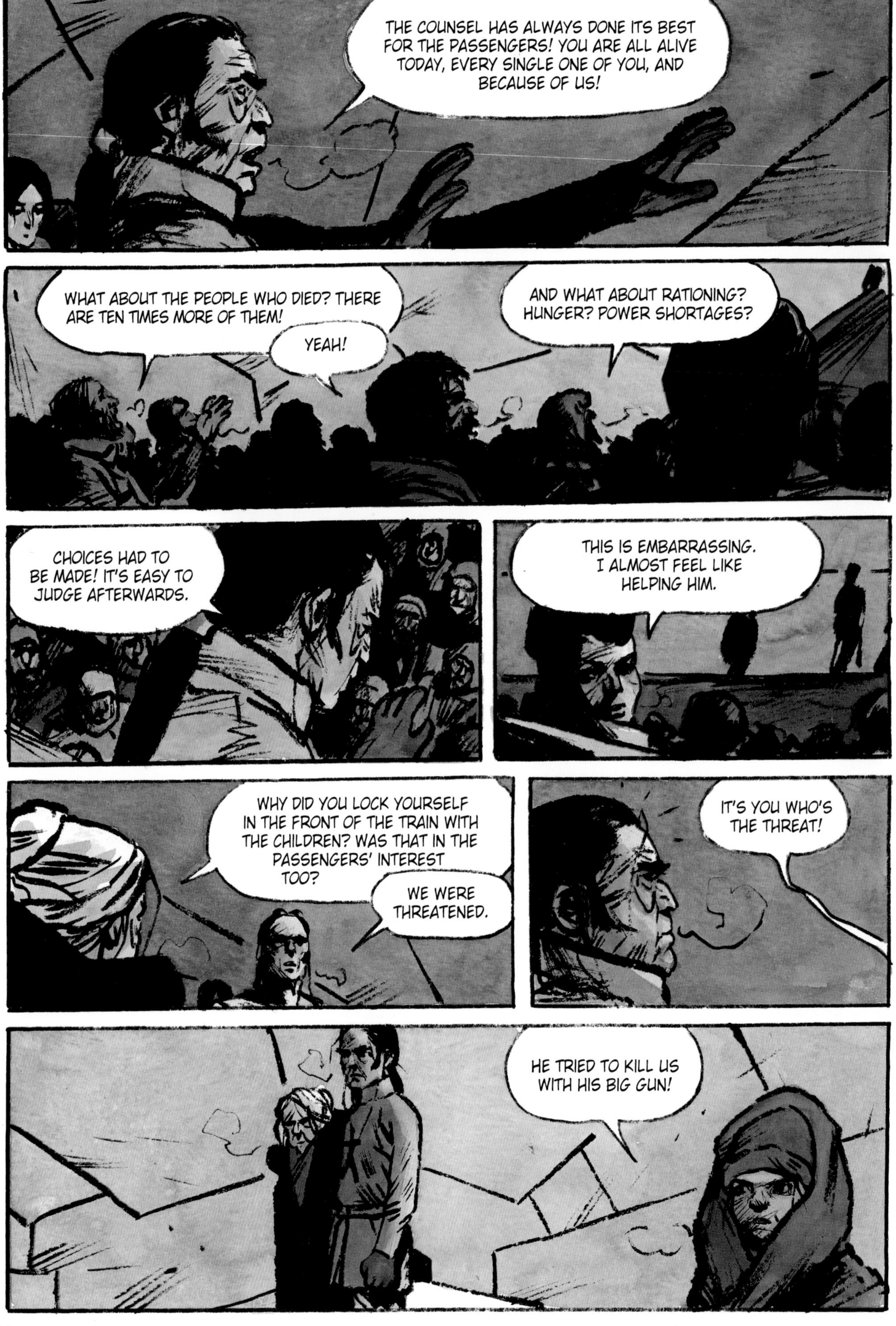
THE COUNSEL HAS ALWAYS DONE ITS BEST FOR THE PASSENGERS! YOU ARE ALL ALIVE TODAY, EVERY SINGLE ONE OF YOU, AND BECAUSE OF US!
WHAT ABOUT THE PEOPLE WHO DIED? THERE ARE TEN TIMES MORE OF THEM!
YEAH!
AND WHAT ABOUT RATIONING? HUNGER? POWER SHORTAGES?
CHOICES HAD TO BE MADE! IT'S EASY TO JUDGE AFTERWARDS.
THIS IS EMBARRASSING. I ALMOST FEEL LIKE HELPING HIM.
WHY DID YOU LOCK YOURSELF IN THE FRONT OF THE TRAIN WITH THE CHILDREN? WAS THAT IN THE PASSENGERS' INTEREST TOO?
WE WERE THREATENED.
IT'S YOU WHO'S THE THREAT!
HE TRIED TO KILL US WITH HIS BIG GUN!

EXCUSE ME, CAN YOU REPEAT THAT?

HE TRIED TO KILL US WITH THAT BIG GUN OF HIS. AND I DON'T KNOW MUCH, BUT I KNOW THERE'S NO BIGGER CRIME ON THE TRAIN THAN TO KILL A CHILD.

YOU'RE NOT GOING TO BELIEVE THAT KID? SHE... SHE STILL HAS HER BABY TEETH !

SHE'S TELLING THE TRUTH. HE TRIED TO SHOOT THE THREE OF US.

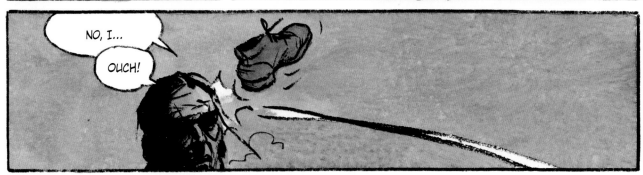

NO, I...

OUCH!

YOU FOOL!

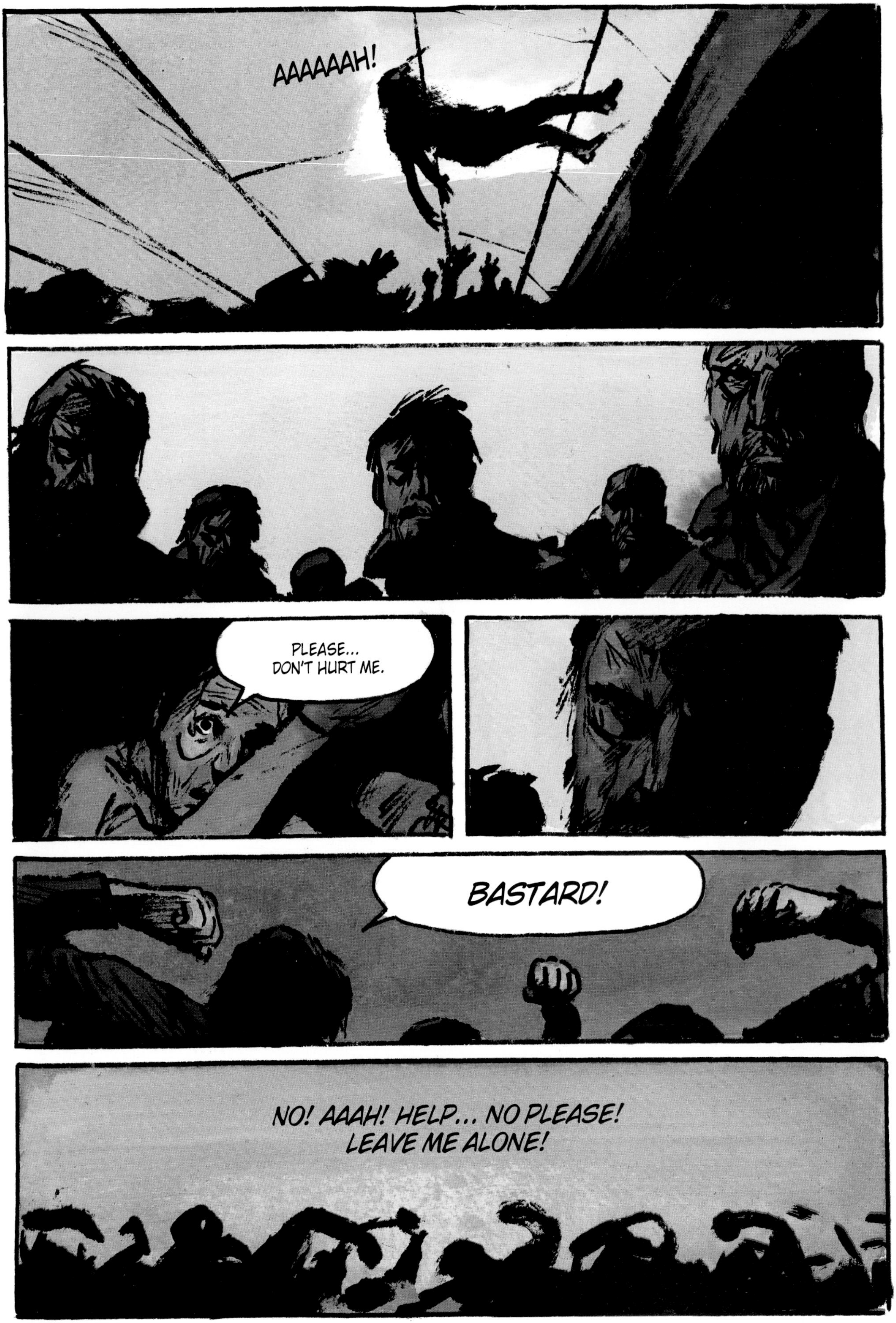
AAAAAAH!
PLEASE... DON'T HURT ME.
BASTARD!
NO! AAAH! HELP... NO PLEASE! LEAVE ME ALONE!

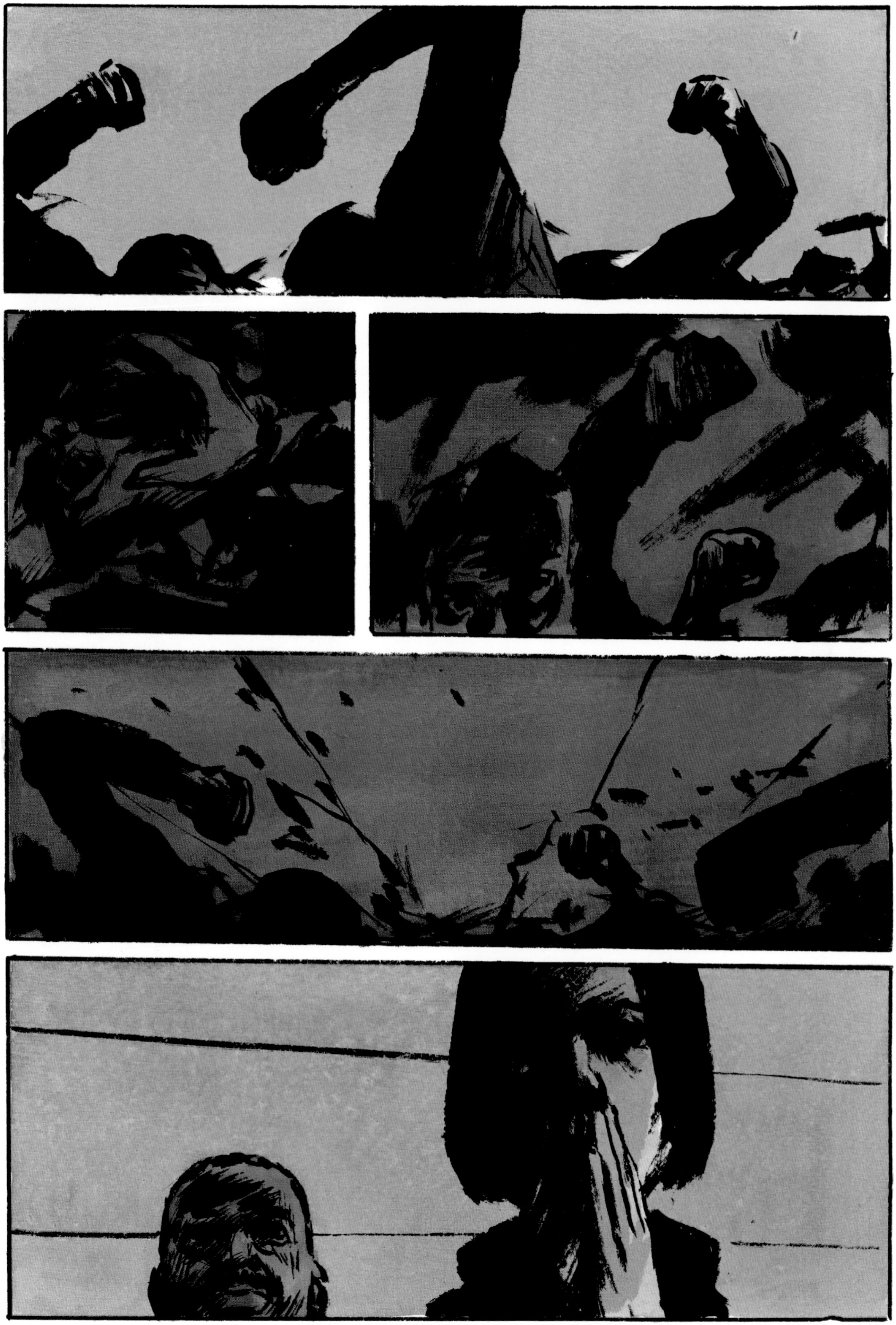

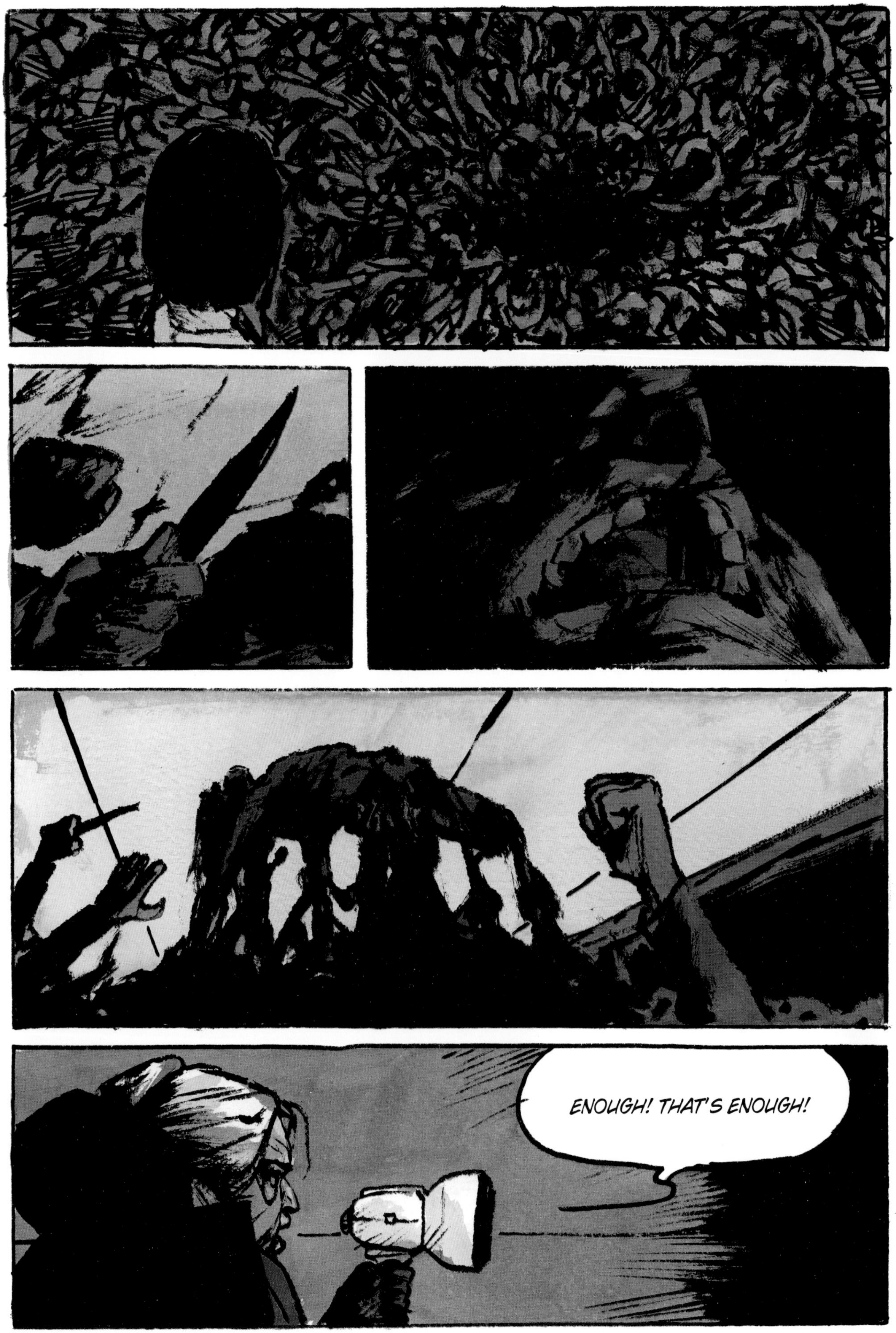
ENOUGH! THAT'S ENOUGH!

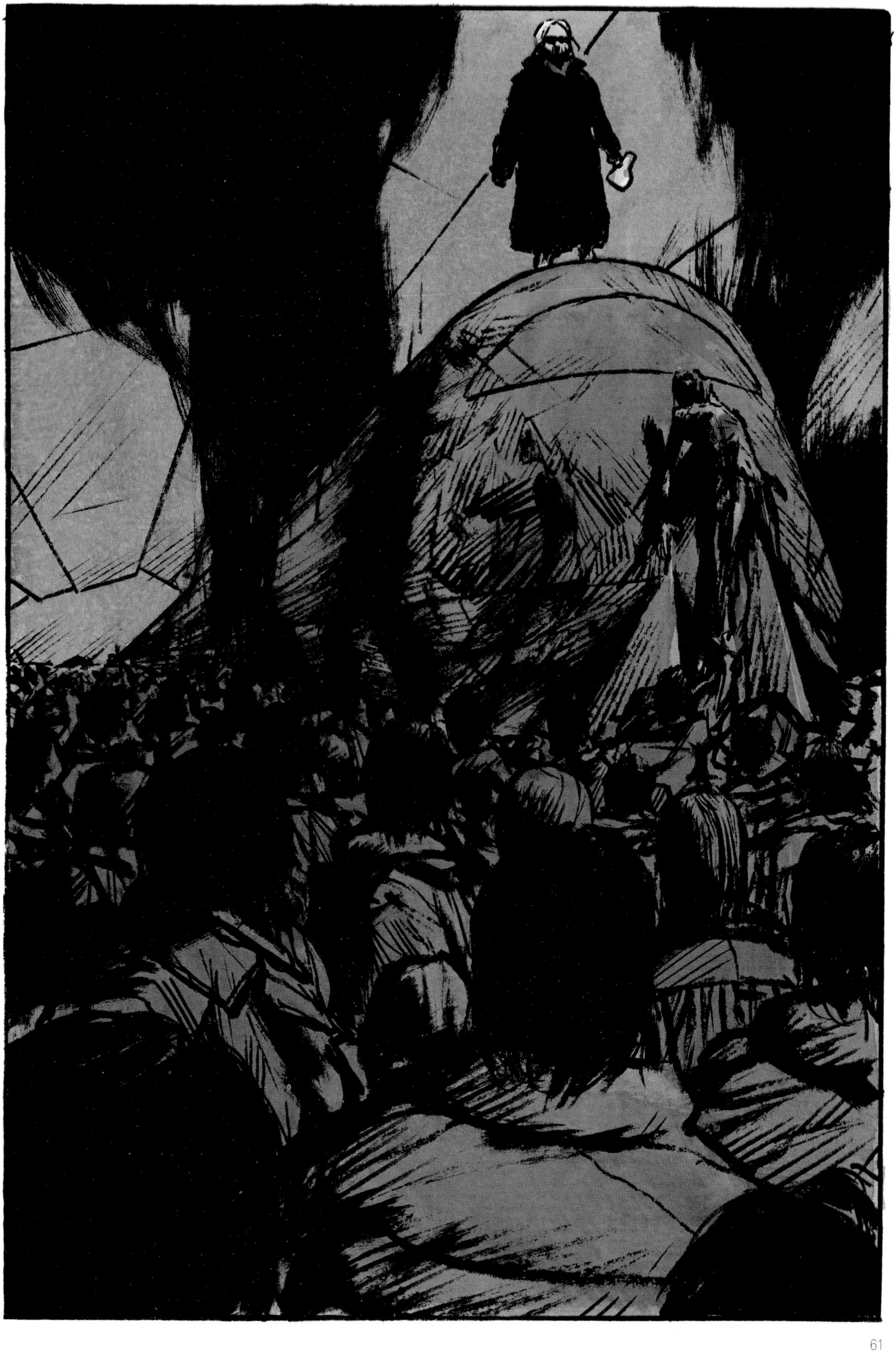

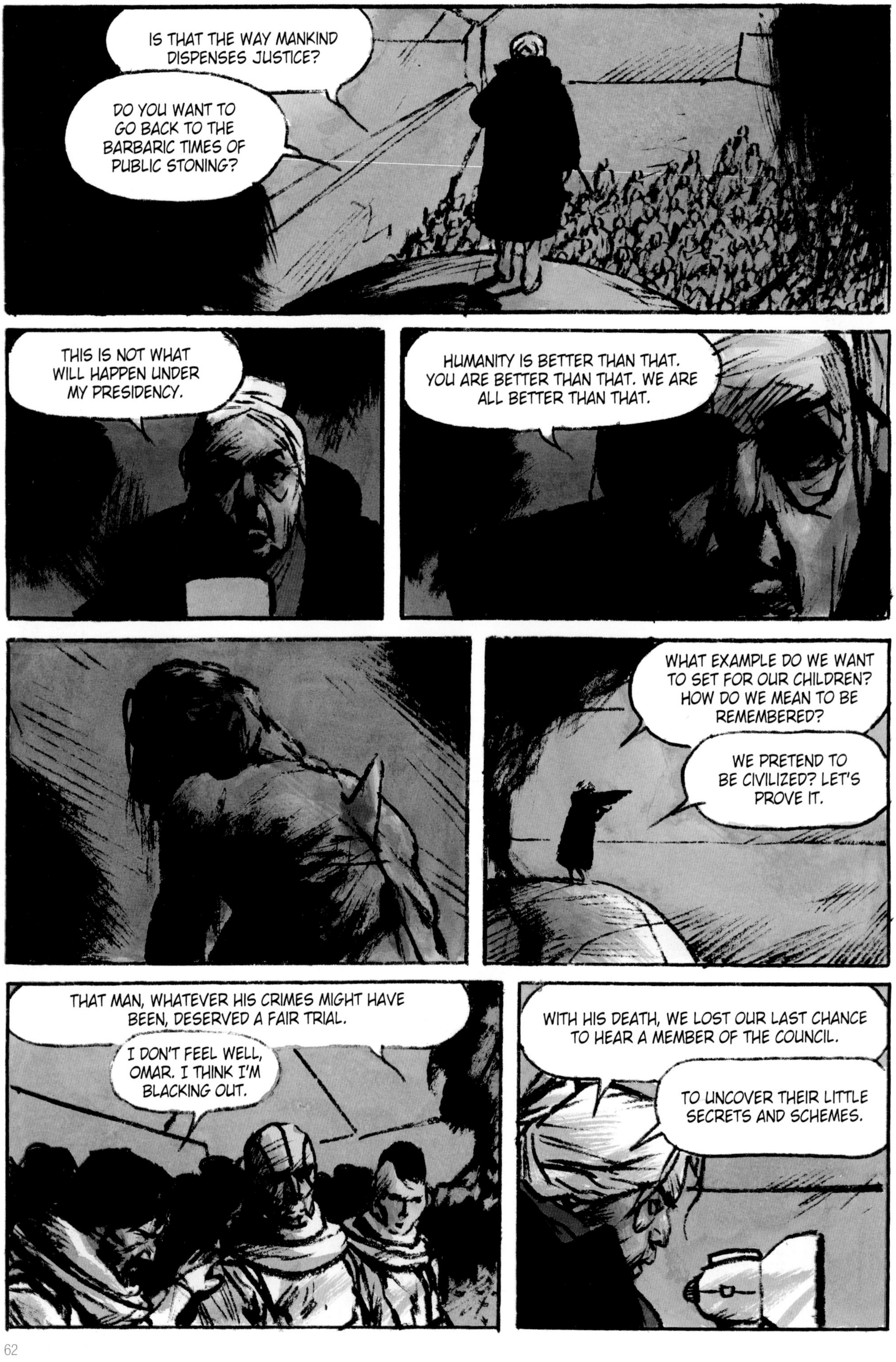
IS THAT THE WAY MANKIND DISPENSES JUSTICE?
DO YOU WANT TO GO BACK TO THE BARBARIC TIMES OF PUBLIC STONING?
THIS IS NOT WHAT WILL HAPPEN UNDER MY PRESIDENCY.
HUMANITY IS BETTER THAN THAT. YOU ARE BETTER THAN THAT. WE ARE ALL BETTER THAN THAT.
WHAT EXAMPLE DO WE WANT TO SET FOR OUR CHILDREN? HOW DO WE MEAN TO BE REMEMBERED?
WE PRETEND TO BE CIVILIZED? LET'S PROVE IT.
THAT MAN, WHATEVER HIS CRIMES MIGHT HAVE BEEN, DESERVED A FAIR TRIAL.
I DON'T FEEL WELL, OMAR. I THINK I'M BLACKING OUT.
WITH HIS DEATH, WE LOST OUR LAST CHANCE TO HEAR A MEMBER OF THE COUNCIL.
TO UNCOVER THEIR LITTLE SECRETS AND SCHEMES.

UNFORTUNATELY, THERE IS NO LIVING COUNSELLOR ANYMORE.

OR IS THERE?

HIM! HE IS A MEMBER OF THE COUNCIL! HE IS COUNSELLOR VALLES!

TRUE. HOW DID I FORGET THAT?

BUT... HE'S OUR SAVIOR!

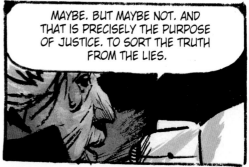

MAYBE. BUT MAYBE NOT. AND THAT IS PRECISELY THE PURPOSE OF JUSTICE. TO SORT THE TRUTH FROM THE LIES.

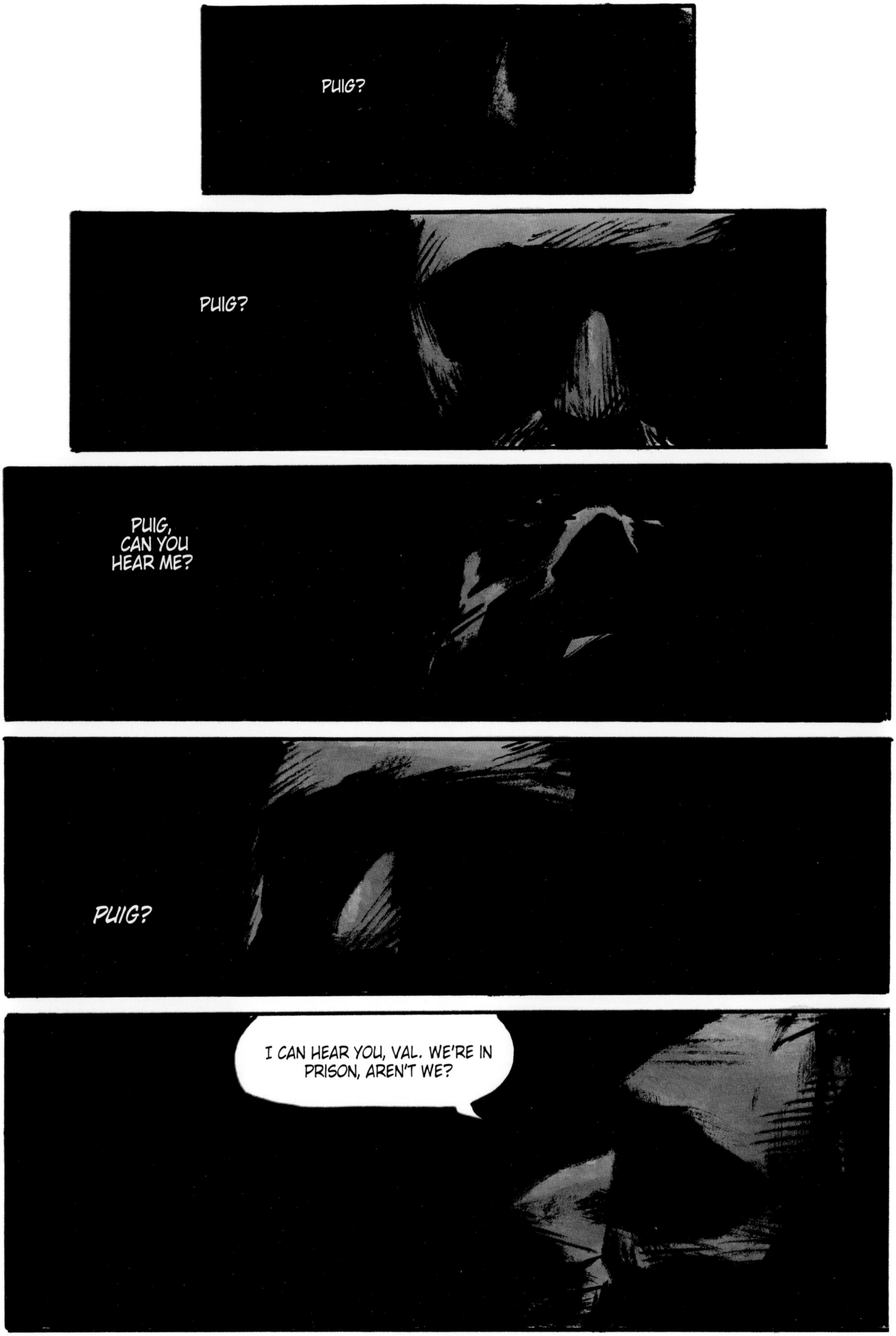
PUIG?
PUIG?
PUIG, CAN YOU HEAR ME?
PUIG?
I CAN HEAR YOU, VAL. WE'RE IN PRISON, AREN'T WE?

YOU ARE. UNTIL YOUR TRIAL. BUT I'M FREE. THEY AUTHORIZED ME TO TALK WITH YOU.

DIDN'T THEY ARREST YOU?

LAURA LEWIS WOULD HAVE LOVED IT, BUT THE CHILDREN DEFENDED TOM AND ME. SAID WE SAVED THEM. I GUESS THAT'S AN EQUIVALENT TO AMNESTY.

THAT'S WHAT THE CROWD THOUGHT, ANYWAY. SO LEWIS DIDN'T INSIST.

A TRIAL... WHAT A CHARADE.

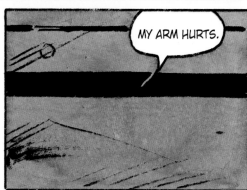

MY ARM HURTS.

THEY SAY THEY'VE FIXED IT.

THEY STRAPPED SOME KIND OF METAL SPLINT TO MY FOREARM. I THINK THEY SCREWED UP THE JOB.

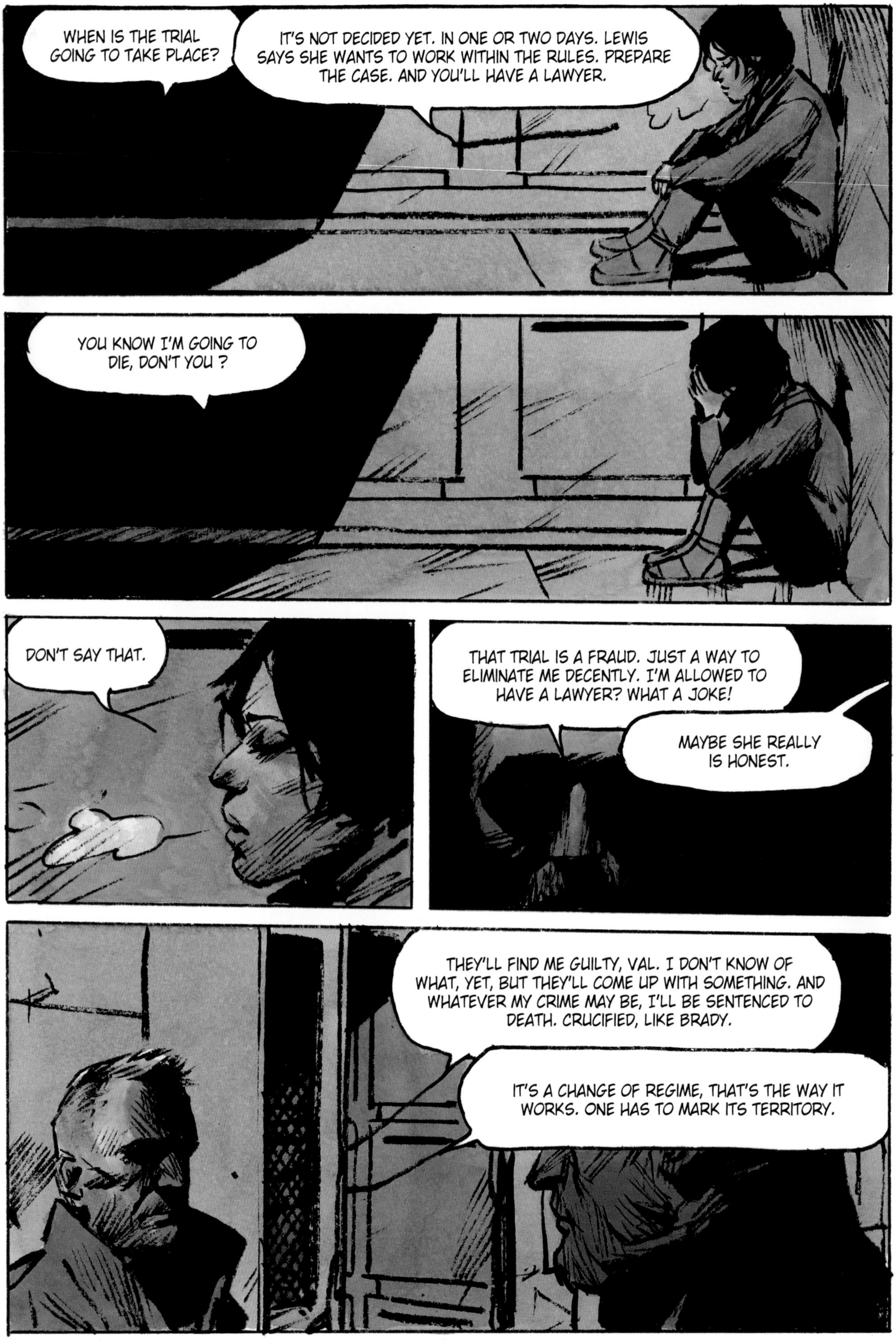
WHEN IS THE TRIAL GOING TO TAKE PLACE?
IT'S NOT DECIDED YET. IN ONE OR TWO DAYS. LEWIS SAYS SHE WANTS TO WORK WITHIN THE RULES. PREPARE THE CASE. AND YOU'LL HAVE A LAWYER.
YOU KNOW I'M GOING TO DIE, DON'T YOU ?
DON'T SAY THAT.
THAT TRIAL IS A FRAUD. JUST A WAY TO ELIMINATE ME DECENTLY. I'M ALLOWED TO HAVE A LAWYER? WHAT A JOKE!
MAYBE SHE REALLY IS HONEST.
THEY'LL FIND ME GUILTY, VAL. I DON'T KNOW OF WHAT, YET, BUT THEY'LL COME UP WITH SOMETHING. AND WHATEVER MY CRIME MAY BE, I'LL BE SENTENCED TO DEATH. CRUCIFIED, LIKE BRADY.
IT'S A CHANGE OF REGIME, THAT'S THE WAY IT WORKS. ONE HAS TO MARK ITS TERRITORY.

I'LL BE YOUR LAWYER. WE'LL START TO PANIC WHEN THE TRIAL BEGINS. IT WILL BE PUBLIC, LAURA WON'T HAVE A FREE HAND.

YOU'LL BE MY LAWYER?

OF COURSE, WHO ELSE?

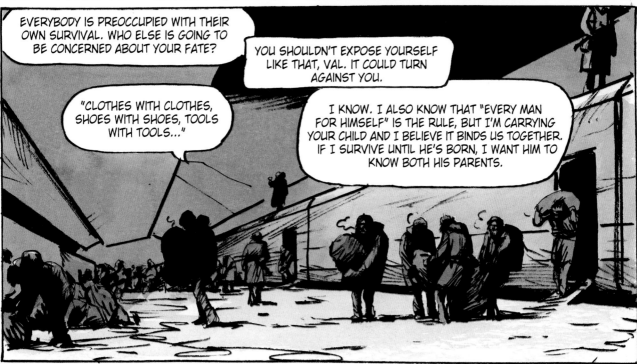

EVERYBODY IS PREOCCUPIED WITH THEIR OWN SURVIVAL. WHO ELSE IS GOING TO BE CONCERNED ABOUT YOUR FATE?

YOU SHOULDN'T EXPOSE YOURSELF LIKE THAT, VAL. IT COULD TURN AGAINST YOU.

"CLOTHES WITH CLOTHES, SHOES WITH SHOES, TOOLS WITH TOOLS..."

I KNOW. I ALSO KNOW THAT "EVERY MAN FOR HIMSELF" IS THE RULE, BUT I'M CARRYING YOUR CHILD AND I BELIEVE IT BINDS US TOGETHER. IF I SURVIVE UNTIL HE'S BORN, I WANT HIM TO KNOW BOTH HIS PARENTS.

I WON'T LET YOU DIE WITHOUT A FIGHT.

DO YOU HEAR ME, PUIG?

I HEAR YOU.

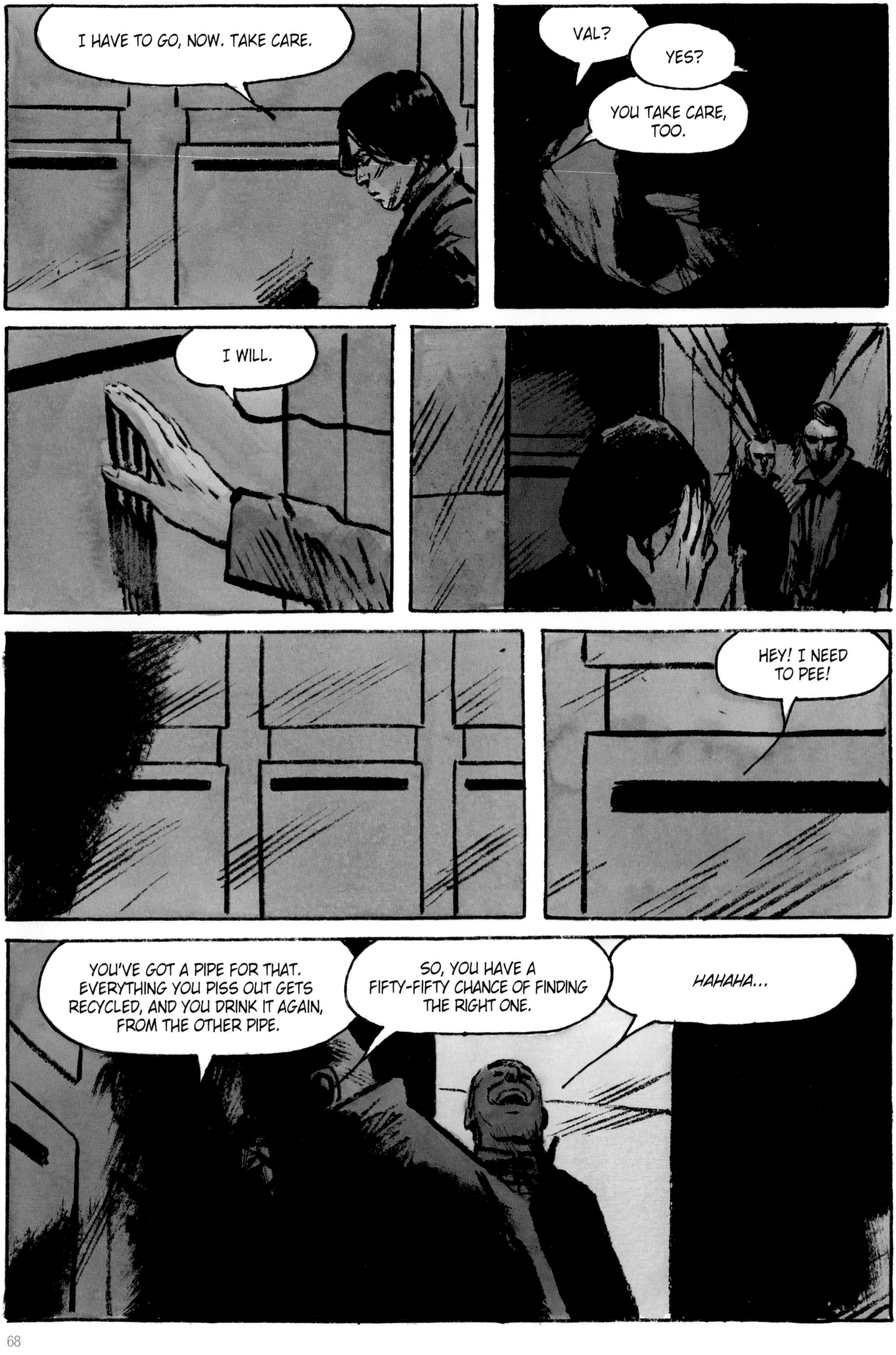
I HAVE TO GO, NOW. TAKE CARE.
VAL?
YES?
YOU TAKE CARE, TOO.
I WILL.
HEY! I NEED TO PEE!
YOU'VE GOT A PIPE FOR THAT. EVERYTHING YOU PISS OUT GETS RECYCLED, AND YOU DRINK IT AGAIN, FROM THE OTHER PIPE.
SO, YOU HAVE A FIFTY-FIFTY CHANCE OF FINDING THE RIGHT ONE.
HAHAHA...

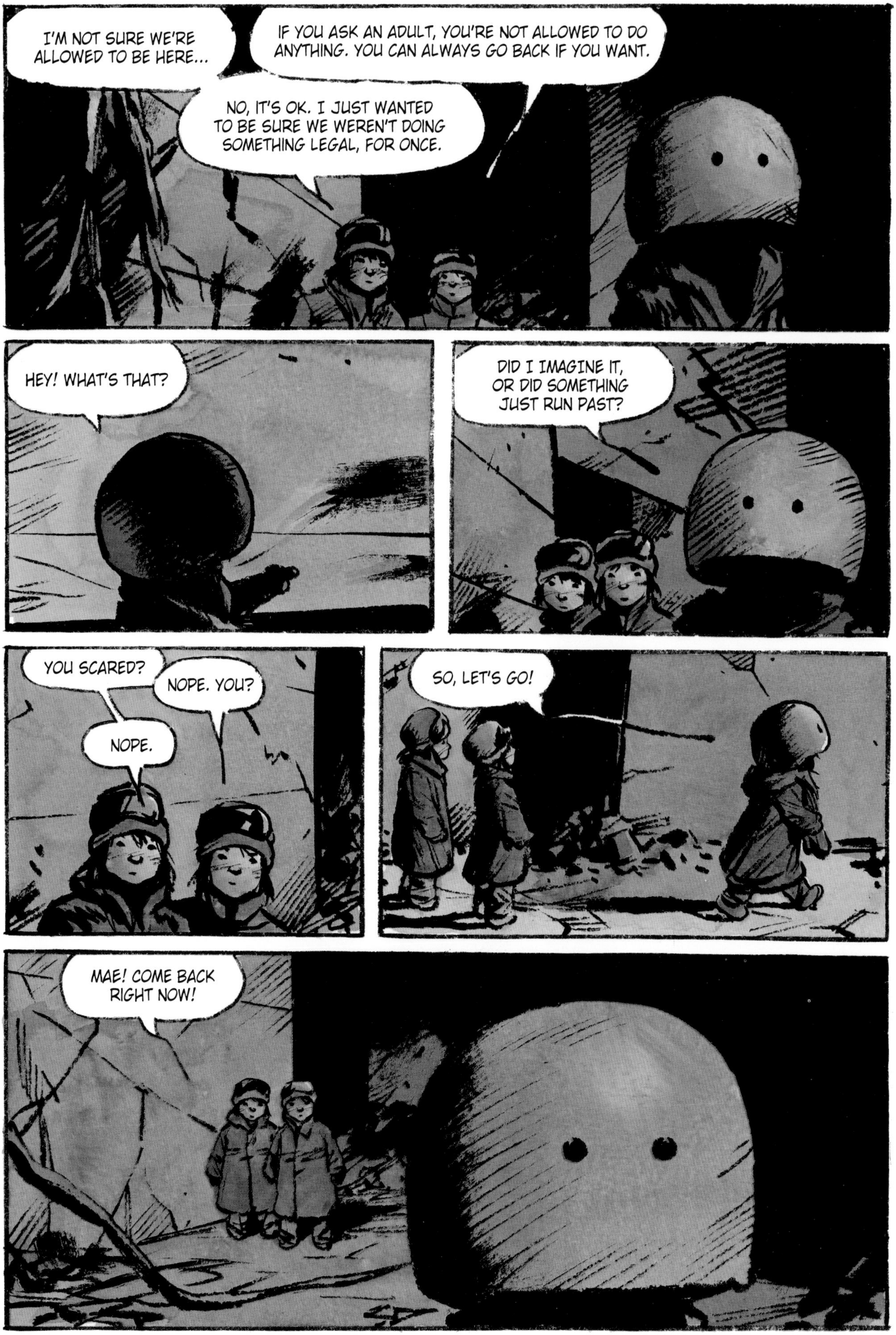

I'M NOT SURE WE'RE ALLOWED TO BE HERE...
IF YOU ASK AN ADULT, YOU'RE NOT ALLOWED TO DO ANYTHING. YOU CAN ALWAYS GO BACK IF YOU WANT.
NO, IT'S OK. I JUST WANTED TO BE SURE WE WEREN'T DOING SOMETHING LEGAL, FOR ONCE.
HEY! WHAT'S THAT?
DID I IMAGINE IT, OR DID SOMETHING JUST RUN PAST?
YOU SCARED?
NOPE. YOU?
NOPE.
SO, LET'S GO!
MAE! COME BACK RIGHT NOW!

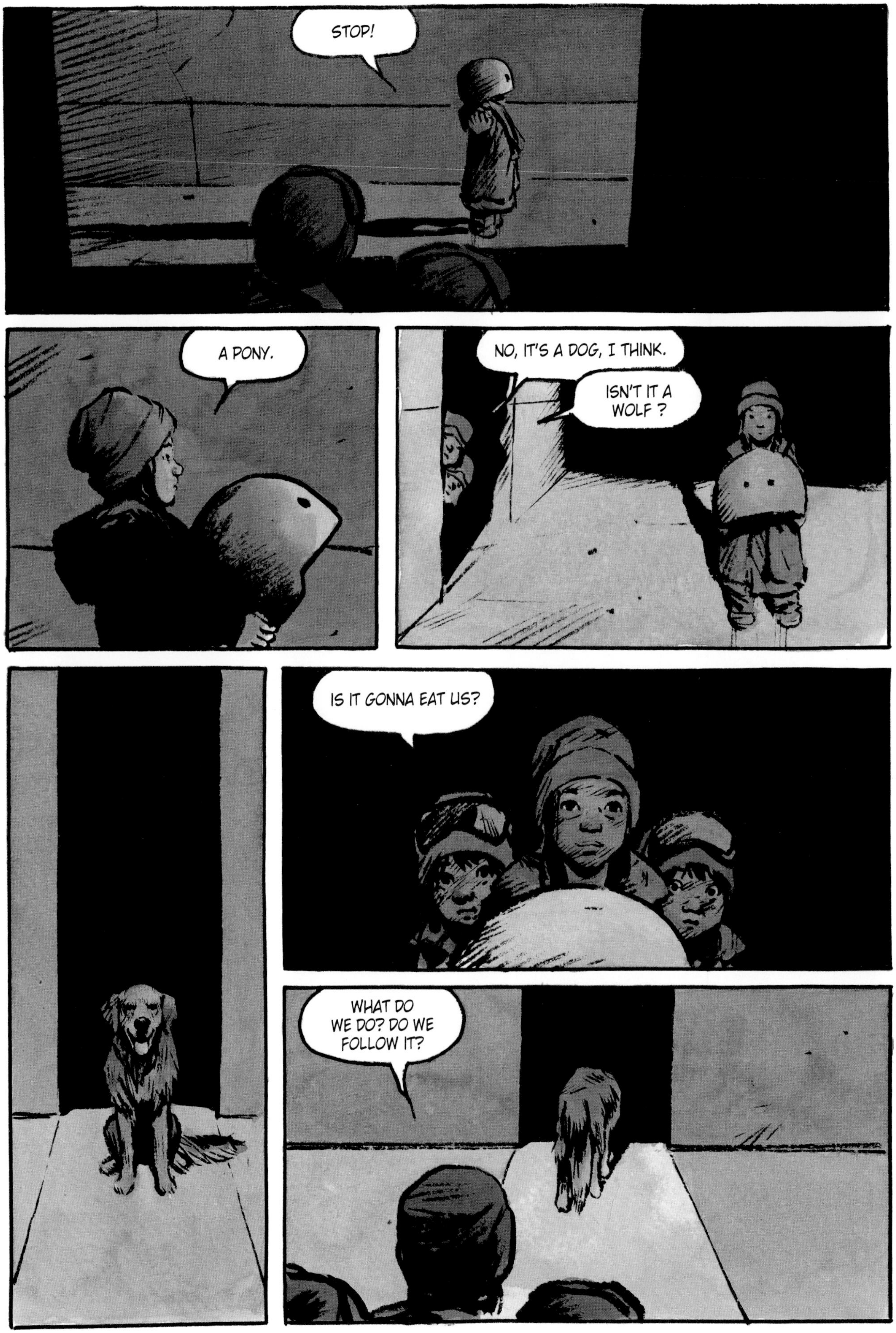
STOP!
A PONY.
NO, IT'S A DOG, I THINK.
ISN'T IT A WOLF ?
IS IT GONNA EAT US?
WHAT DO WE DO? DO WE FOLLOW IT?

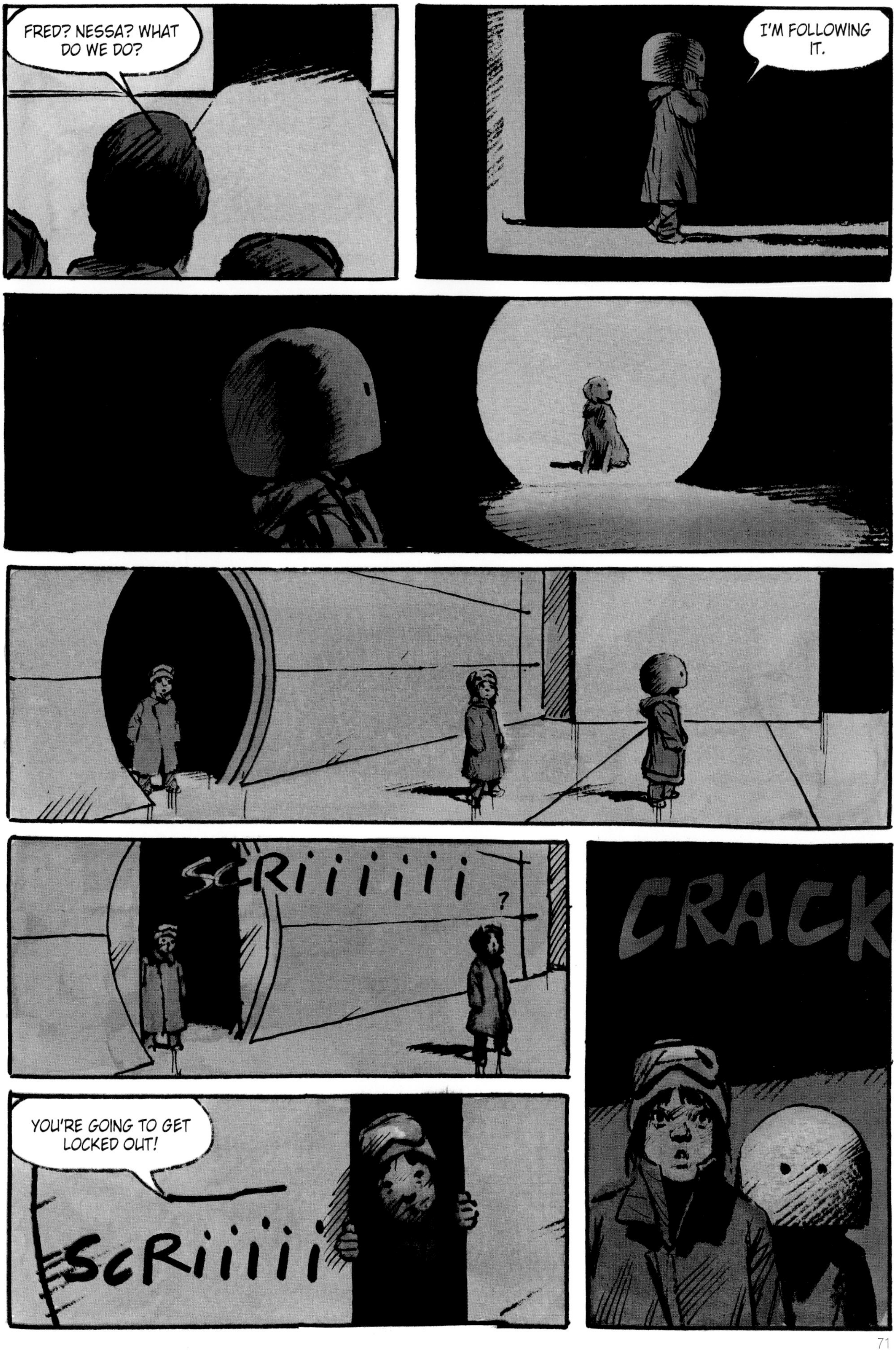
FRED? NESSA? WHAT DO WE DO?
I'M FOLLOWING IT.
SCRIIIIIII
?
CRACK
YOU'RE GOING TO GET LOCKED OUT!
SCRIIIII

I WANT TO BE PUIG VALLES' LAWYER.

IT'S OK, BORIS. LET THE DAUGHTER OF LATE COUNSELLOR KENNEL PASS.

FIVE PEOPLE JUST DIED IN A CAVE-IN. THEY SET THEIR MINDS ON VISITING THIS PLACE WITHOUT BEING PREPARED.

I'M VERY SORRY. BUT...

I NEED SOME VOLUNTEERS TO EXPLORE THE PLACE IN A METHODICAL WAY. I WAS THINKING OF YOU.

PUIG VALLES WOULD DO A GREAT JOB. HE'S TRAINED FOR THAT.

BUT, UNFORTUNATELY, HE IS IN PRISON.

YOU'D LOVE TO SEE ME DIE UNDER A TON OF RUBBLE, WOULDN'T YOU?

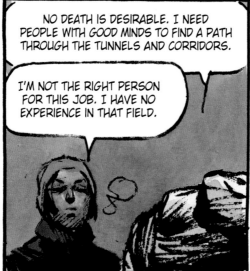
NO DEATH IS DESIRABLE. I NEED PEOPLE WITH GOOD MINDS TO FIND A PATH THROUGH THE TUNNELS AND CORRIDORS.

I'M NOT THE RIGHT PERSON FOR THIS JOB. I HAVE NO EXPERIENCE IN THAT FIELD.

AS YOU WISH, BUT...

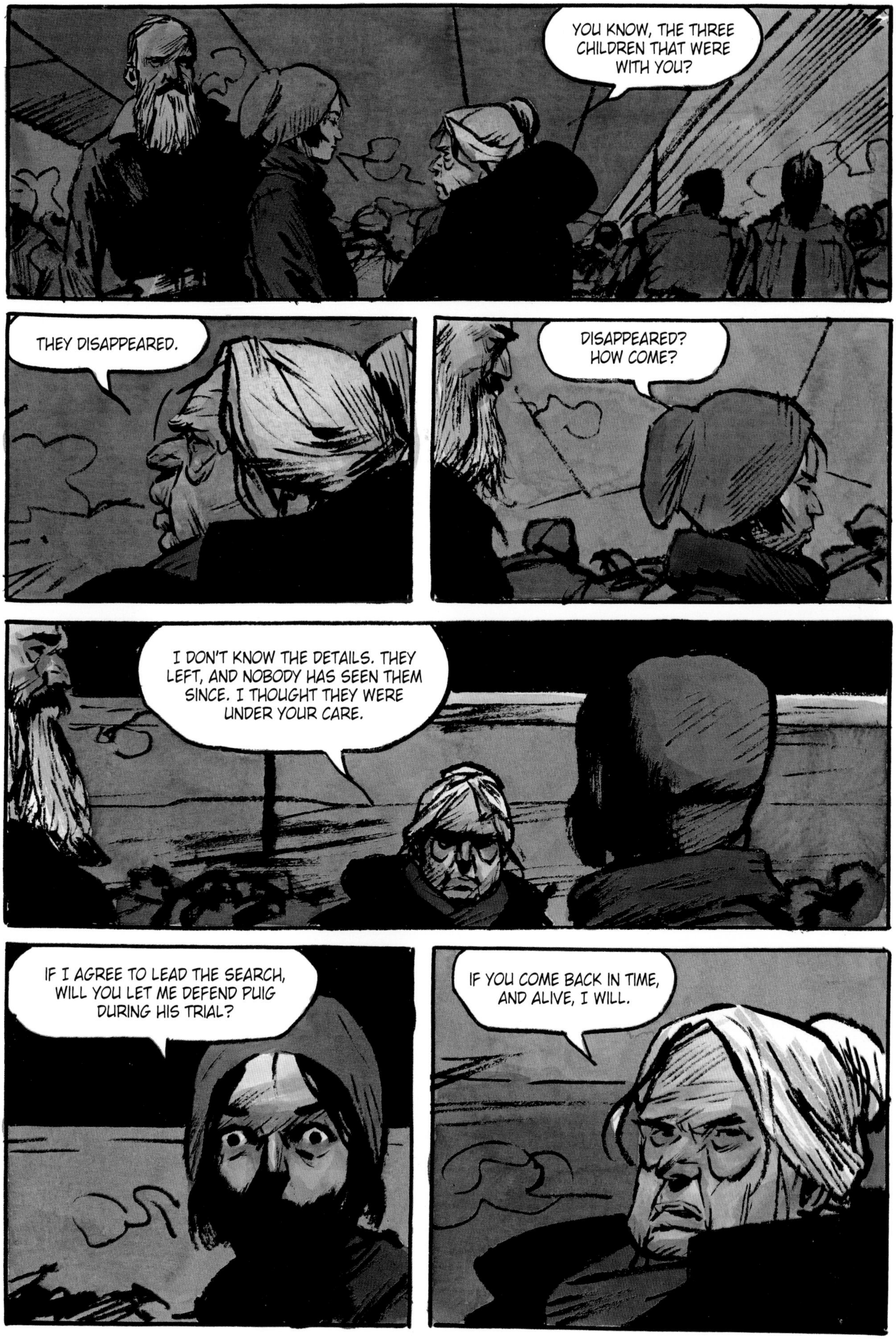
YOU KNOW, THE THREE CHILDREN THAT WERE WITH YOU?
THEY DISAPPEARED.
DISAPPEARED? HOW COME?
I DON'T KNOW THE DETAILS. THEY LEFT, AND NOBODY HAS SEEN THEM SINCE. I THOUGHT THEY WERE UNDER YOUR CARE.
IF I AGREE TO LEAD THE SEARCH, WILL YOU LET ME DEFEND PUIG DURING HIS TRIAL?
IF YOU COME BACK IN TIME, AND ALIVE, I WILL.

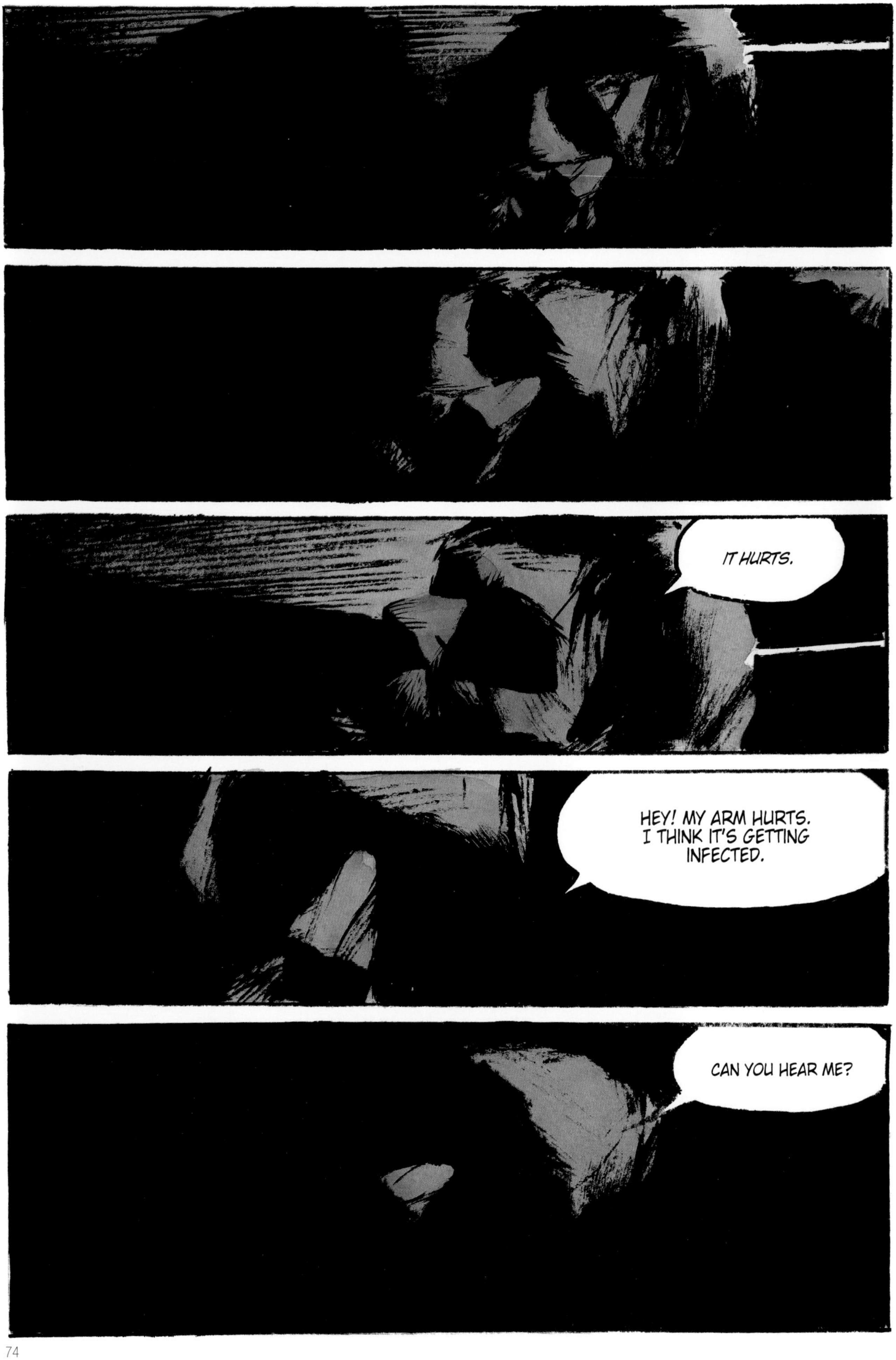
IT HURTS.
HEY! MY ARM HURTS. I THINK IT'S GETTING INFECTED.
CAN YOU HEAR ME?

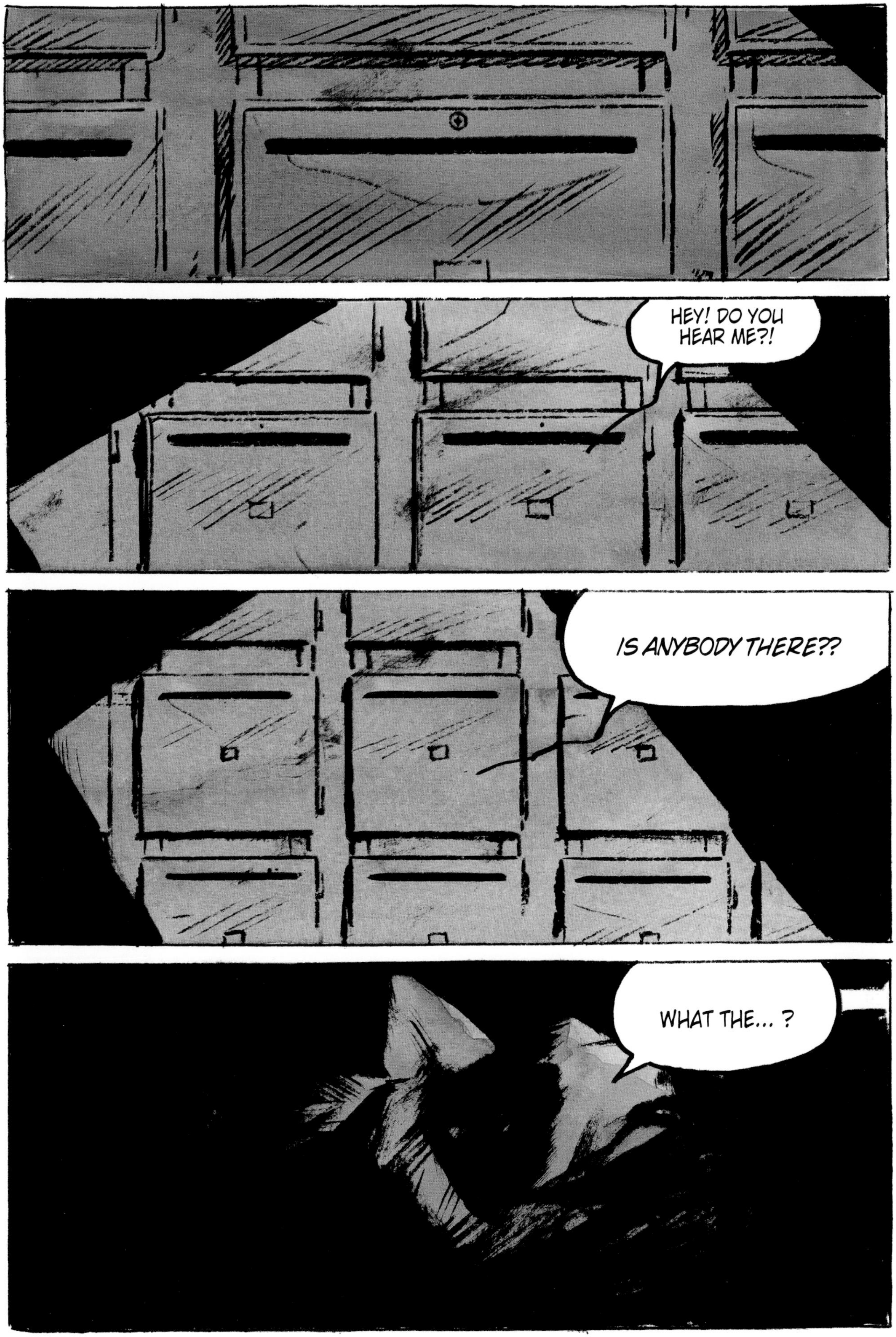
HEY! DO YOU HEAR ME?!
IS ANYBODY THERE??
WHAT THE... ?

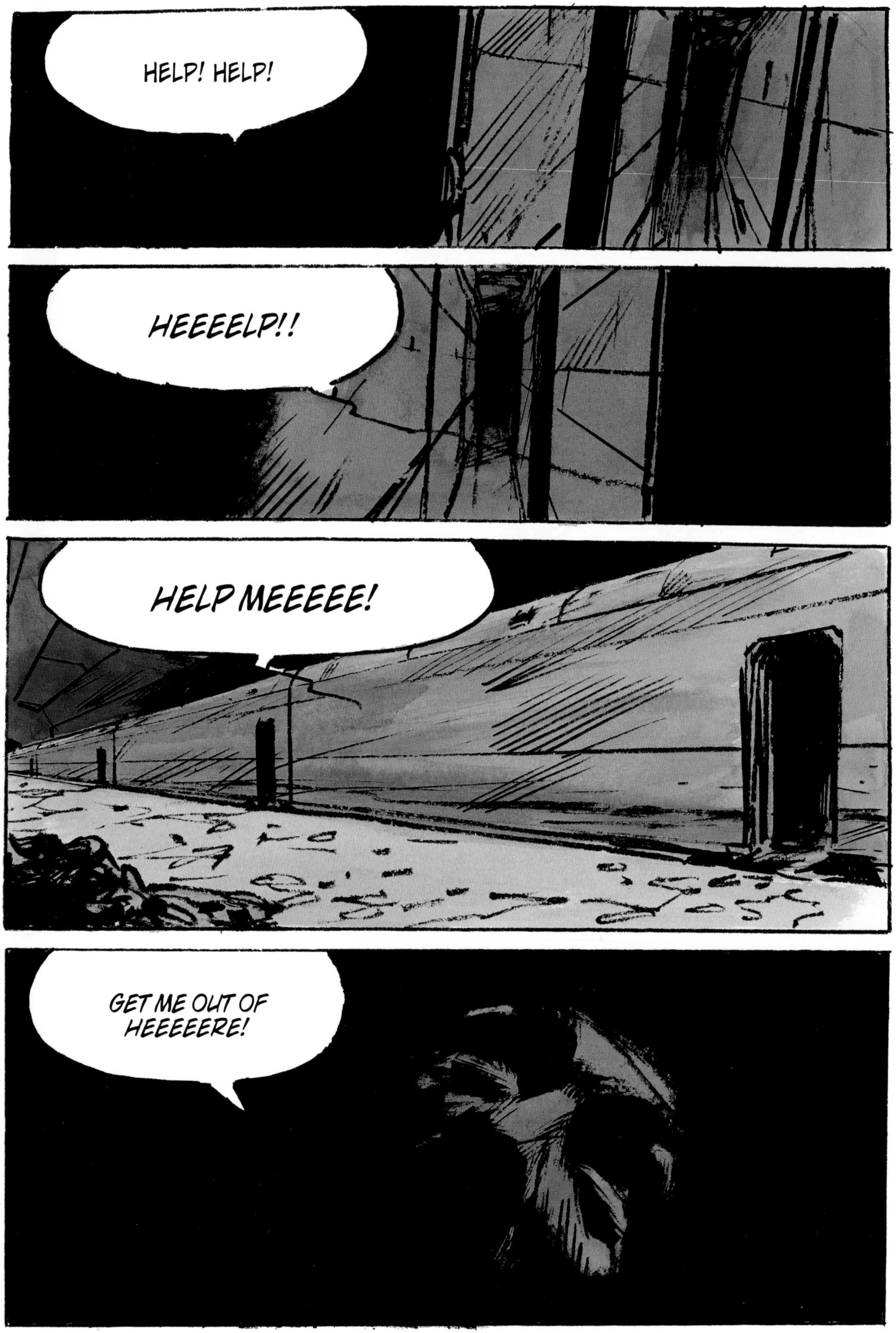
HELP! HELP!
HEEEELP!!
HELP MEEEEE!
GET ME OUT OF HEEEEERE!

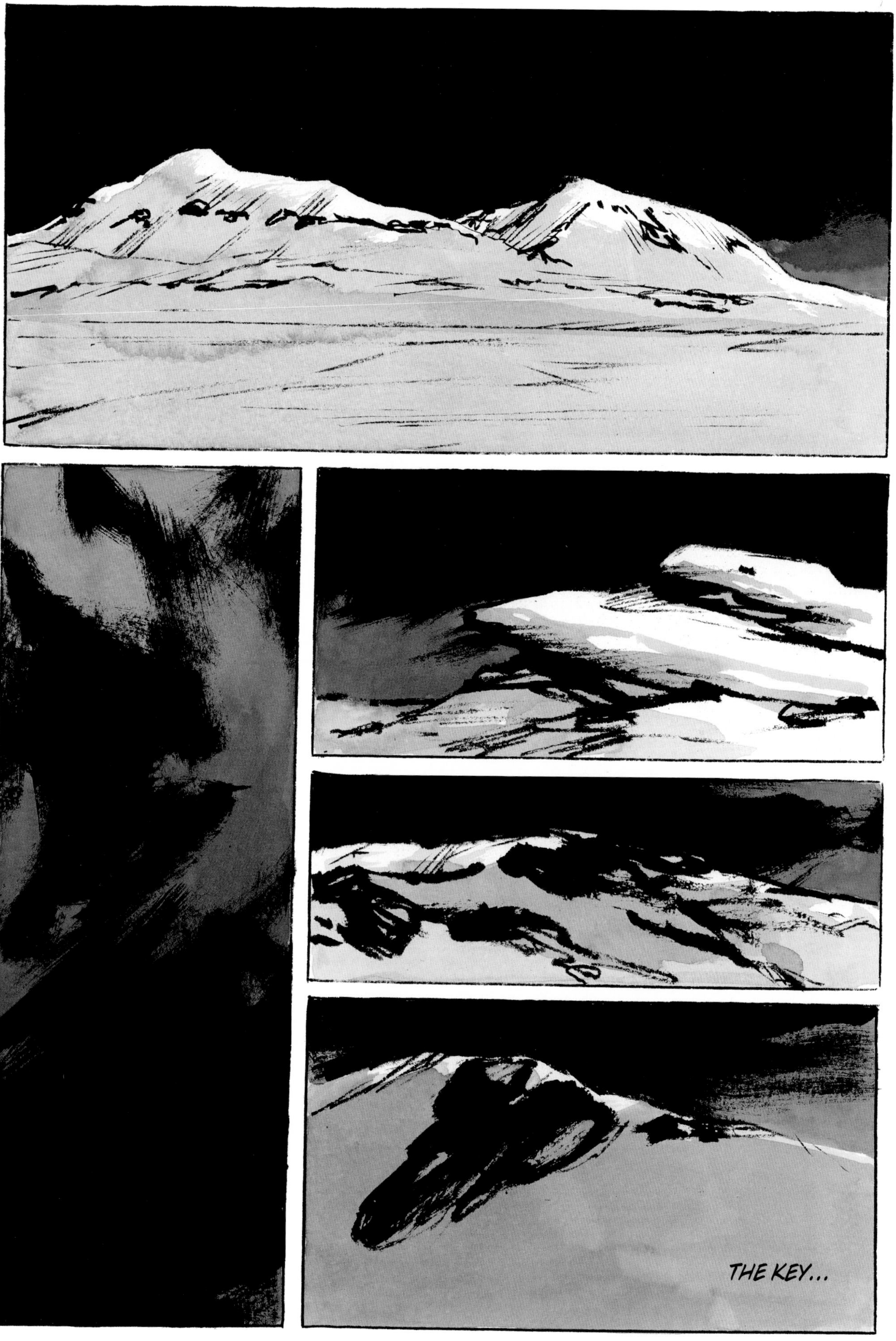
THE KEY...

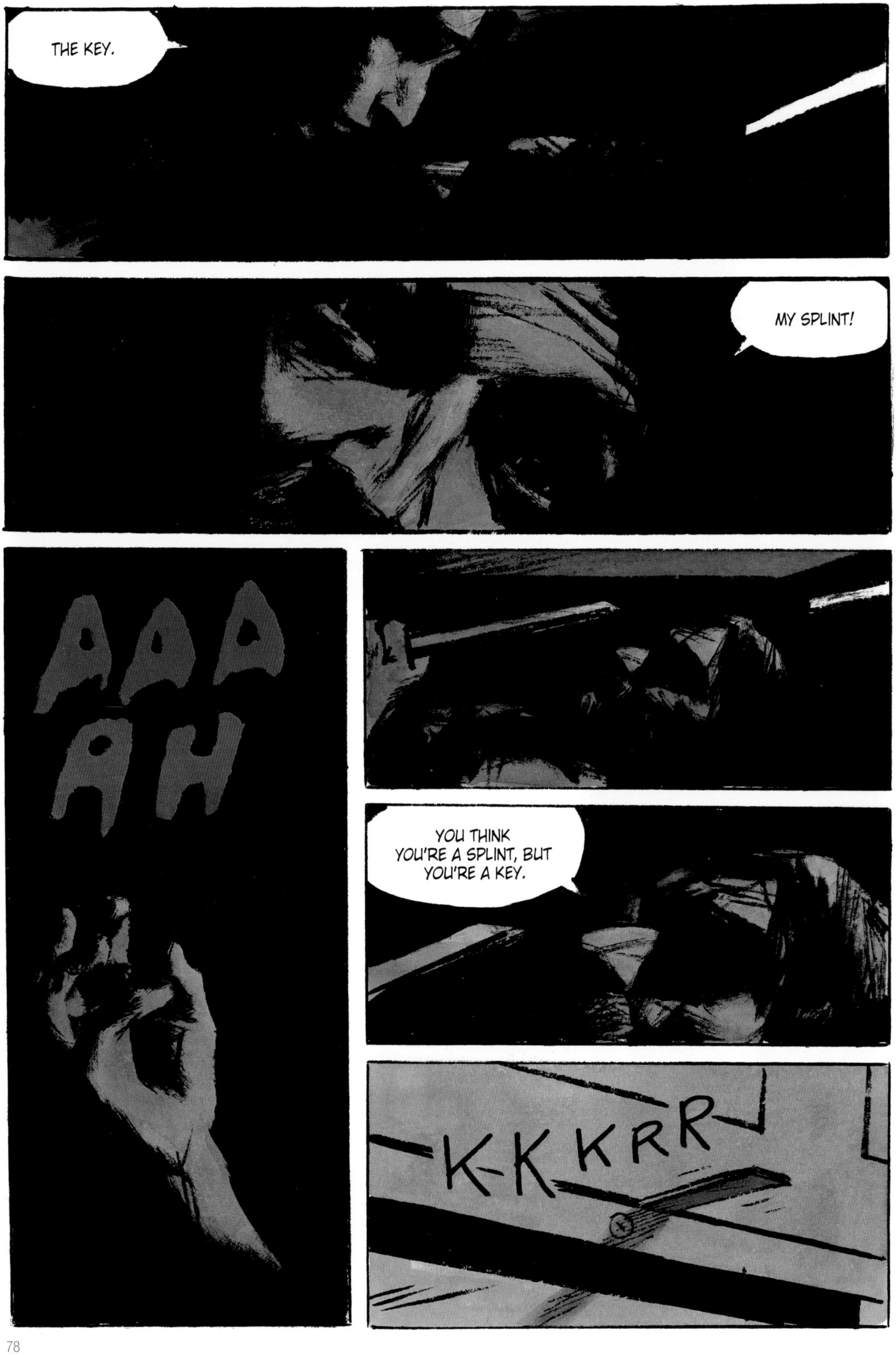
THE KEY.
MY SPLINT!
AAAAAH
YOU THINK YOU'RE A SPLINT, BUT YOU'RE A KEY.
K-KKRR

KRRR
KKRR
KRR
KRR
KRRKRRRR
IT WILL TAKE ME DAYS TO FILE DOWN THAT BOLT.

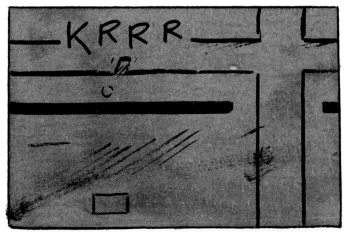

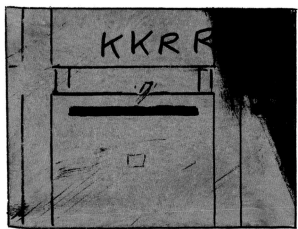

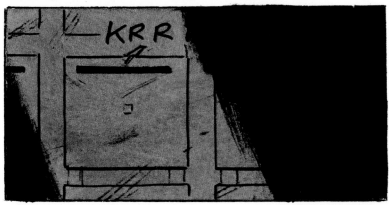

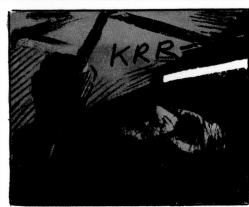

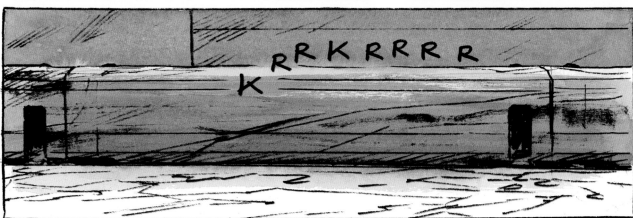

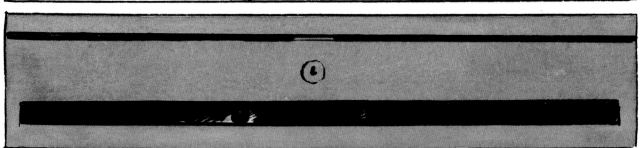

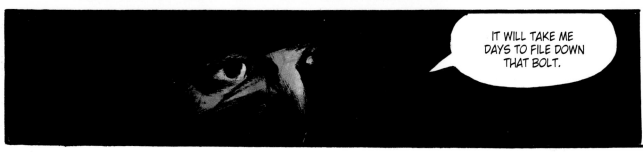

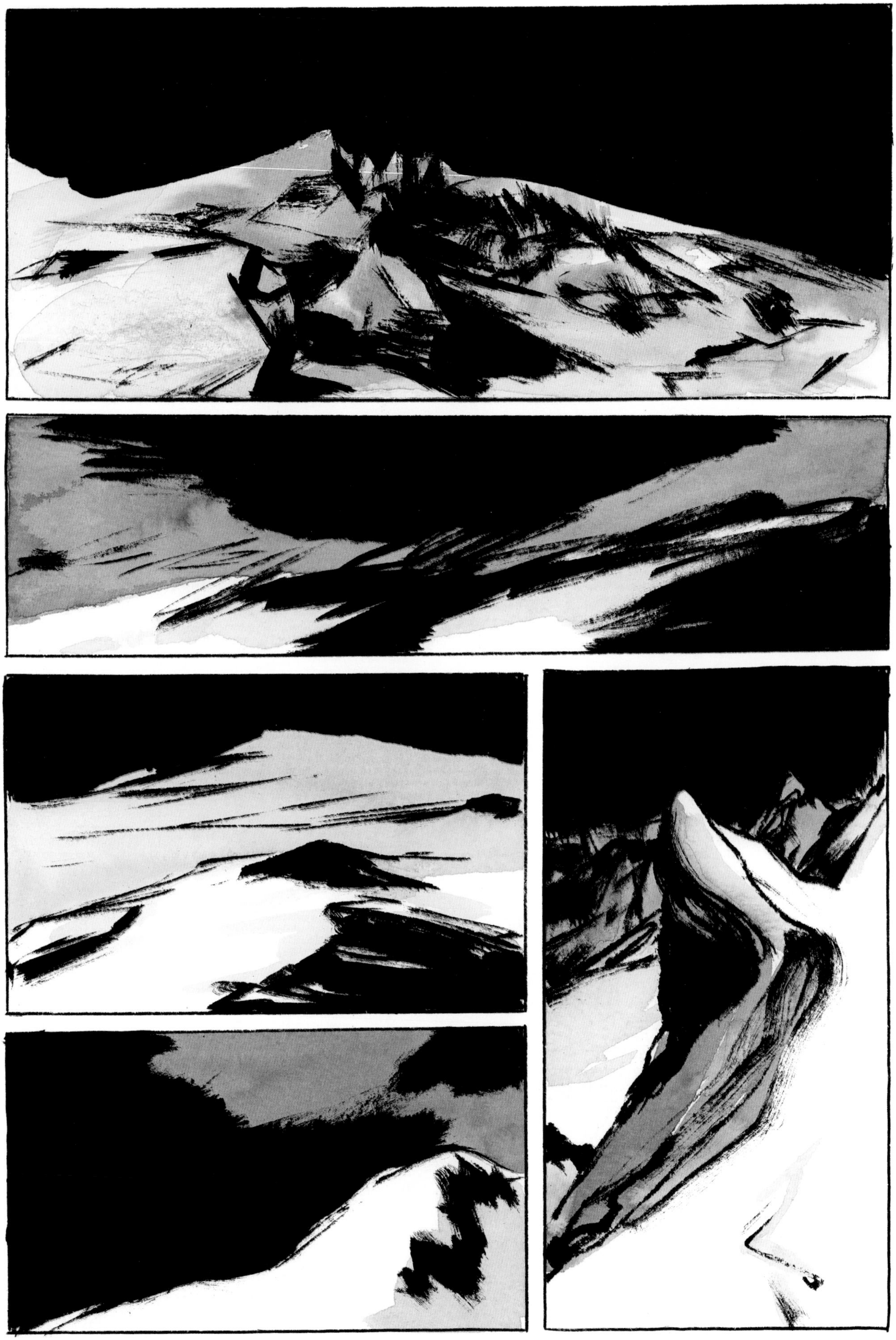

THE KEY.

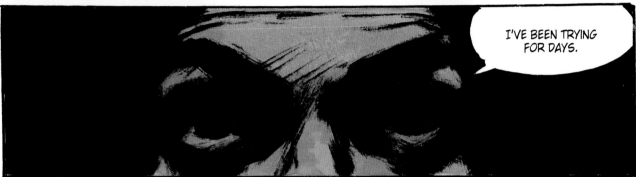

I'VE BEEN TRYING FOR DAYS.

IT'LL NEVER END.

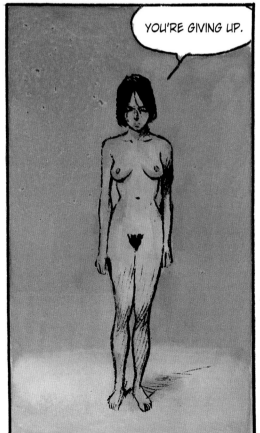

YOU'RE GIVING UP.

COME AND GET ME.

I CAN'T.

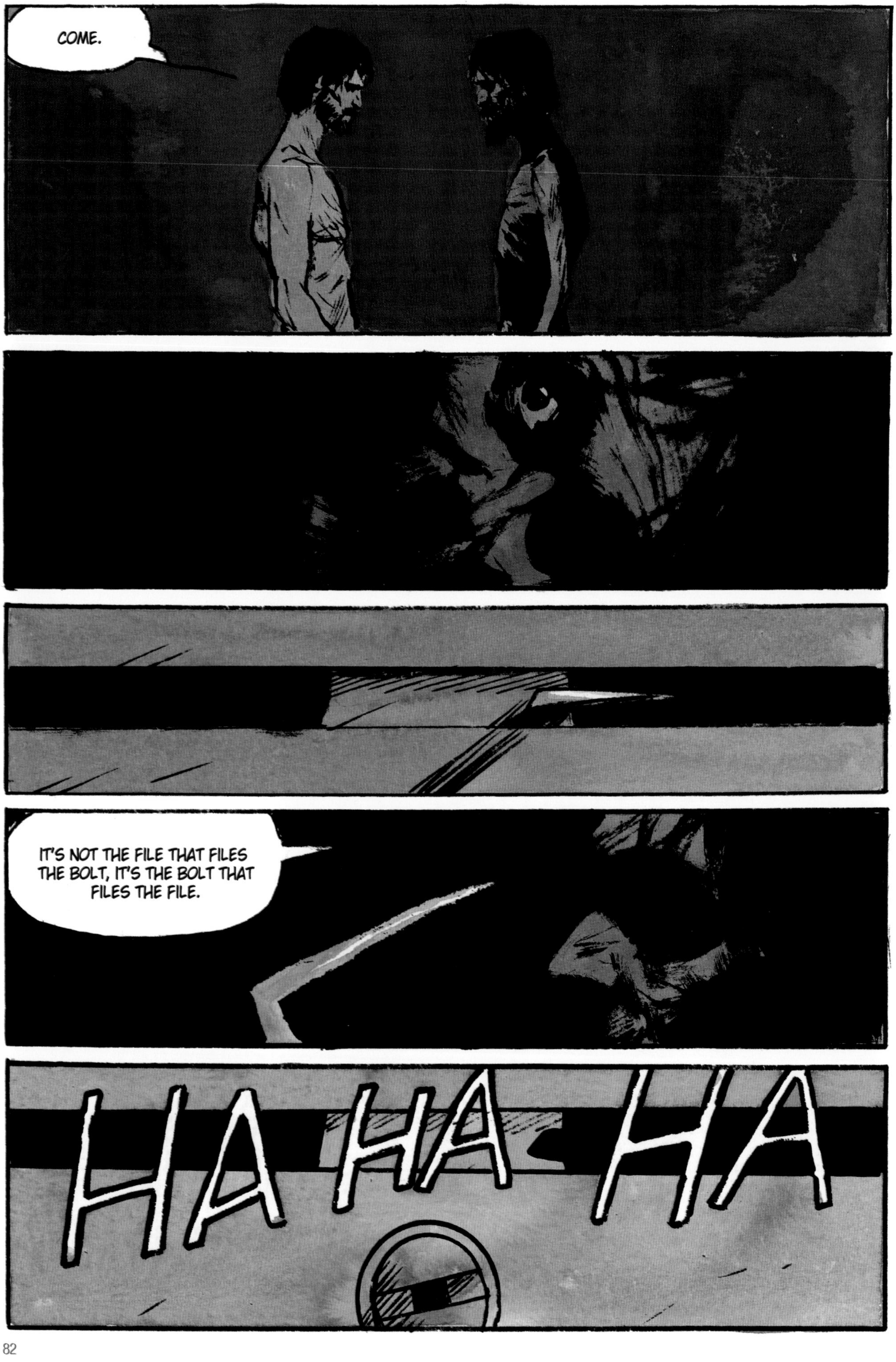
COME.
IT'S NOT THE FILE THAT FILES THE BOLT, IT'S THE BOLT THAT FILES THE FILE.
HA HA HA

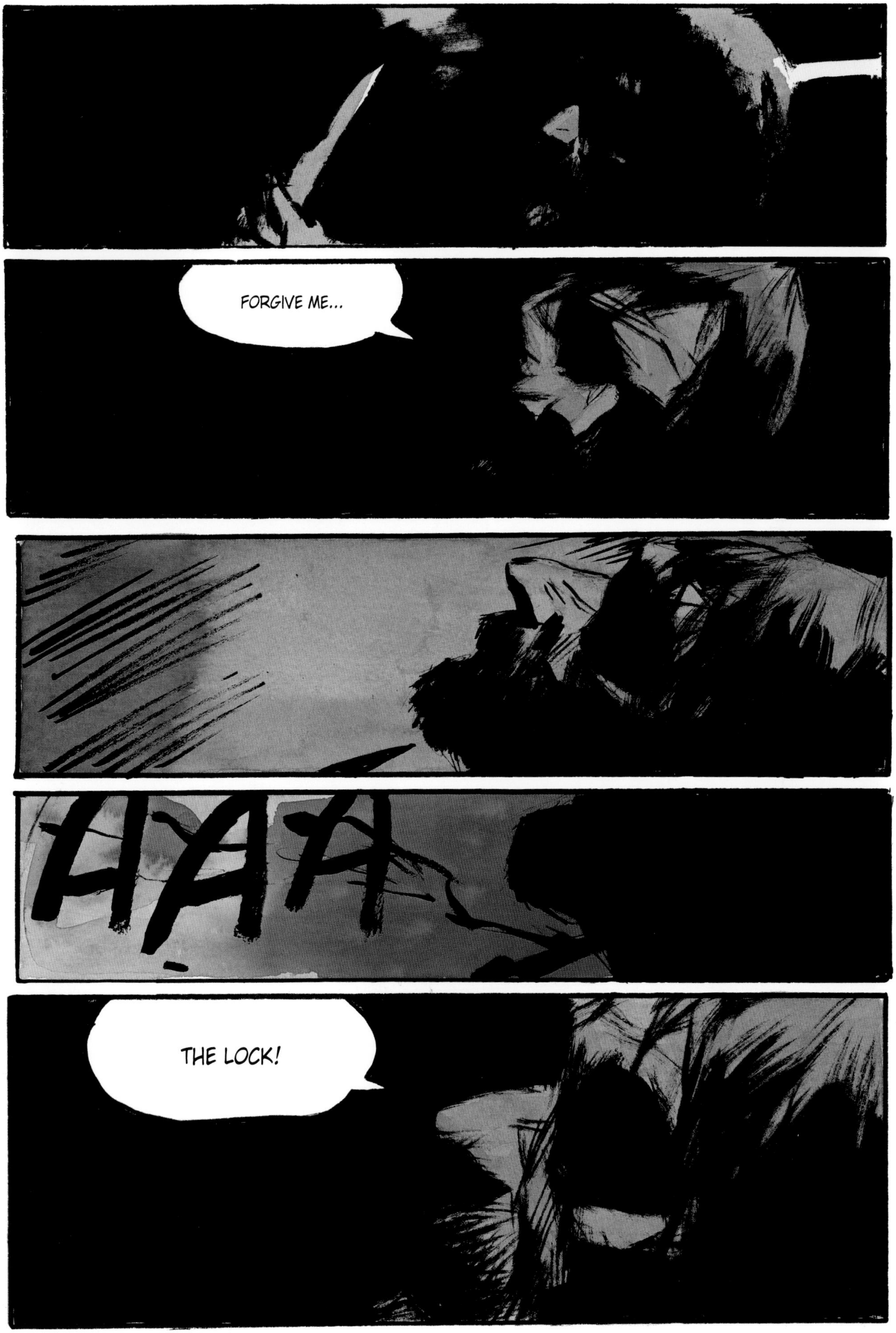
FORGIVE ME...
HAAA
THE LOCK!

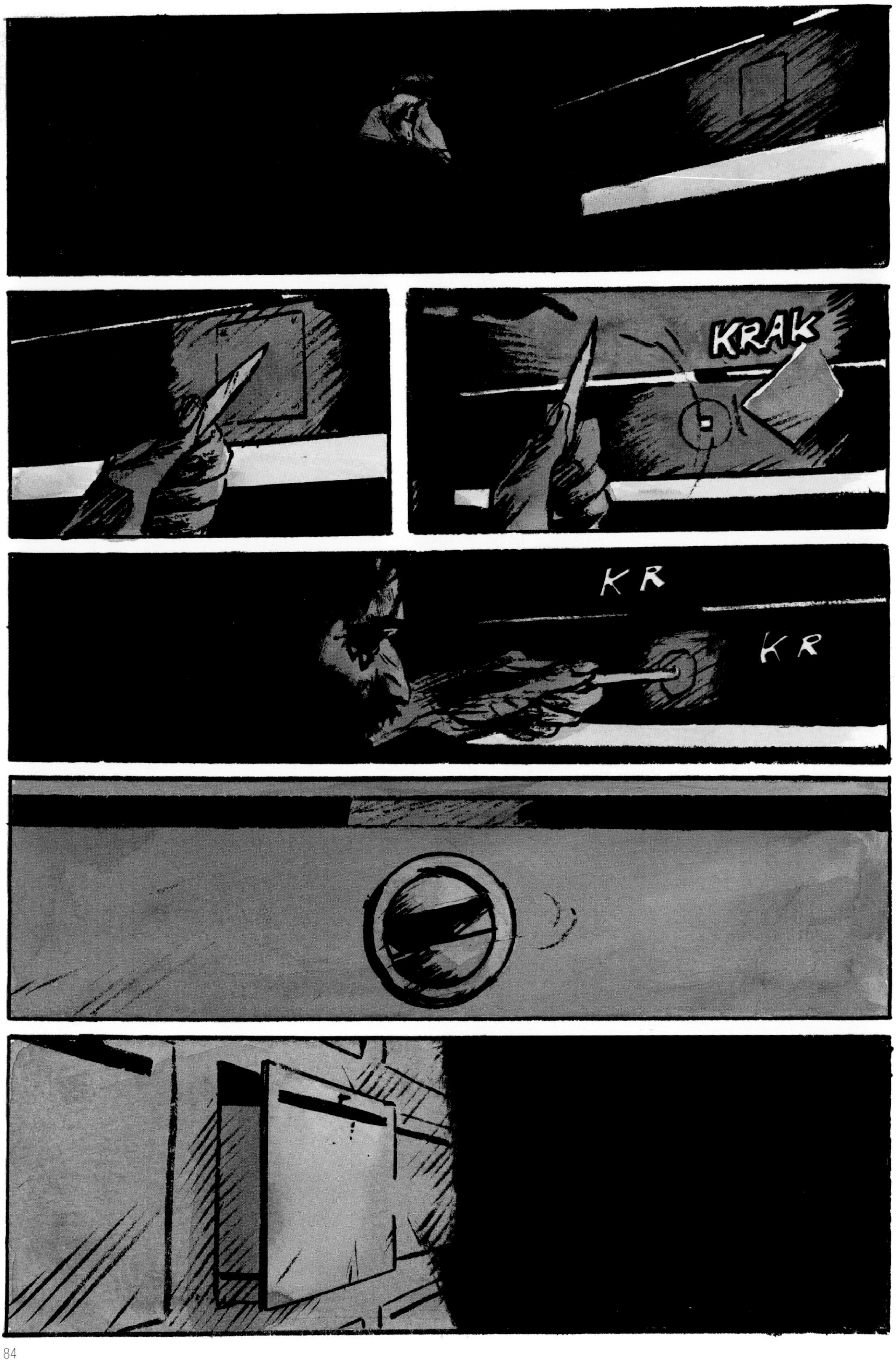
KRAK
KR
KR

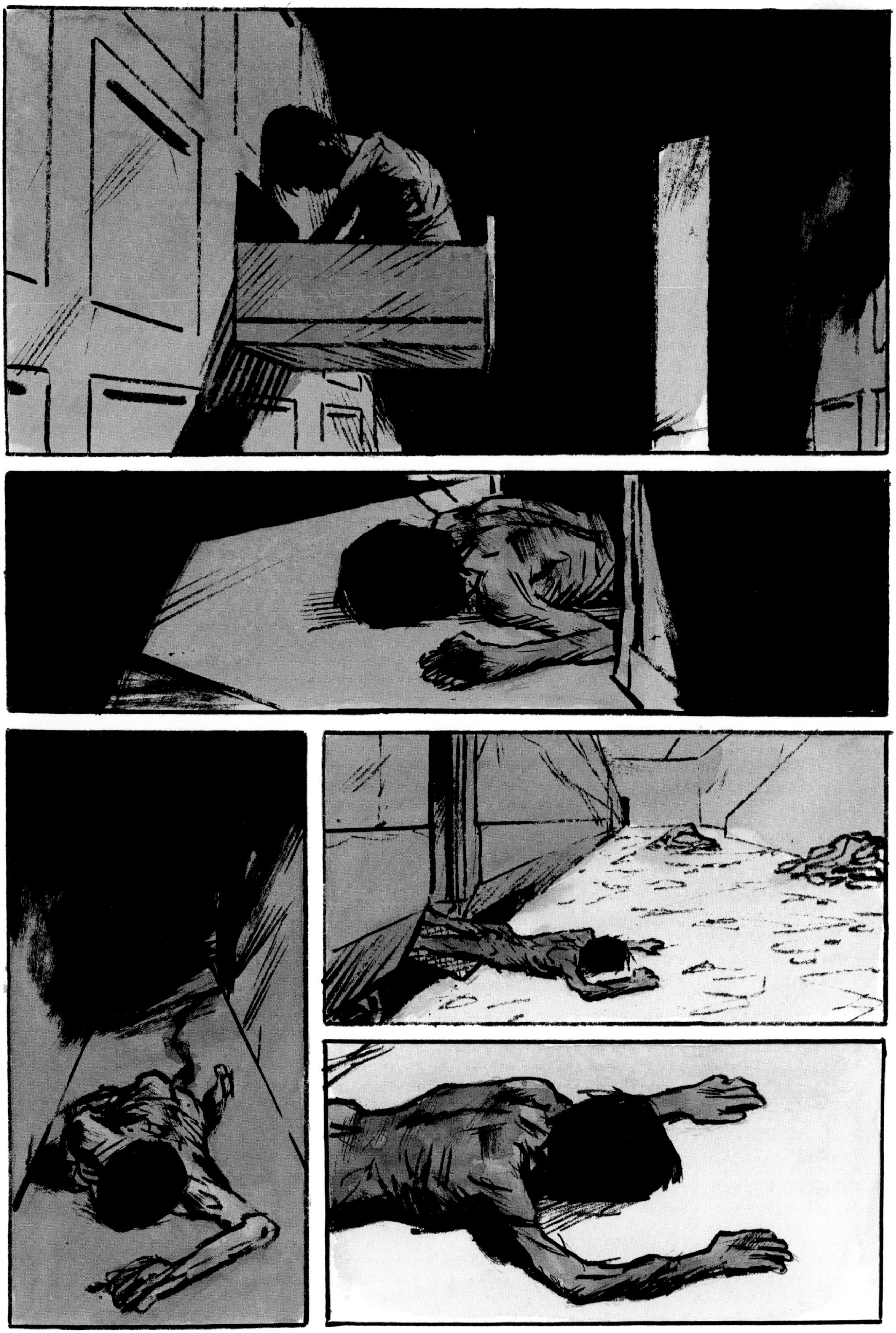

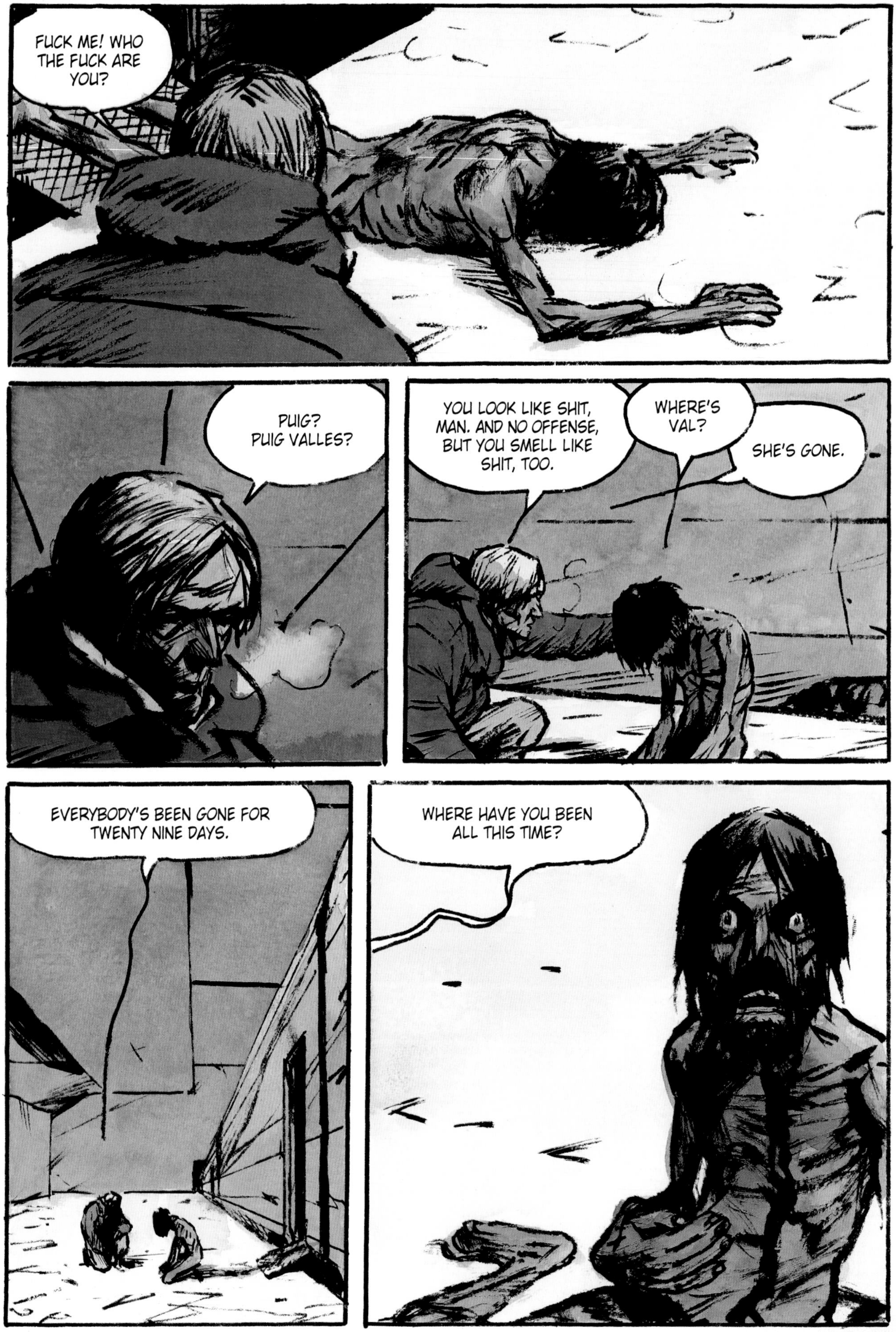
FUCK ME! WHO THE FUCK ARE YOU?
PUIG? PUIG VALLES?
YOU LOOK LIKE SHIT, MAN. AND NO OFFENSE, BUT YOU SMELL LIKE SHIT, TOO.
WHERE'S VAL?
SHE'S GONE.
EVERYBODY'S BEEN GONE FOR TWENTY NINE DAYS.
WHERE HAVE YOU BEEN ALL THIS TIME?

29 DAYS EARLIER...

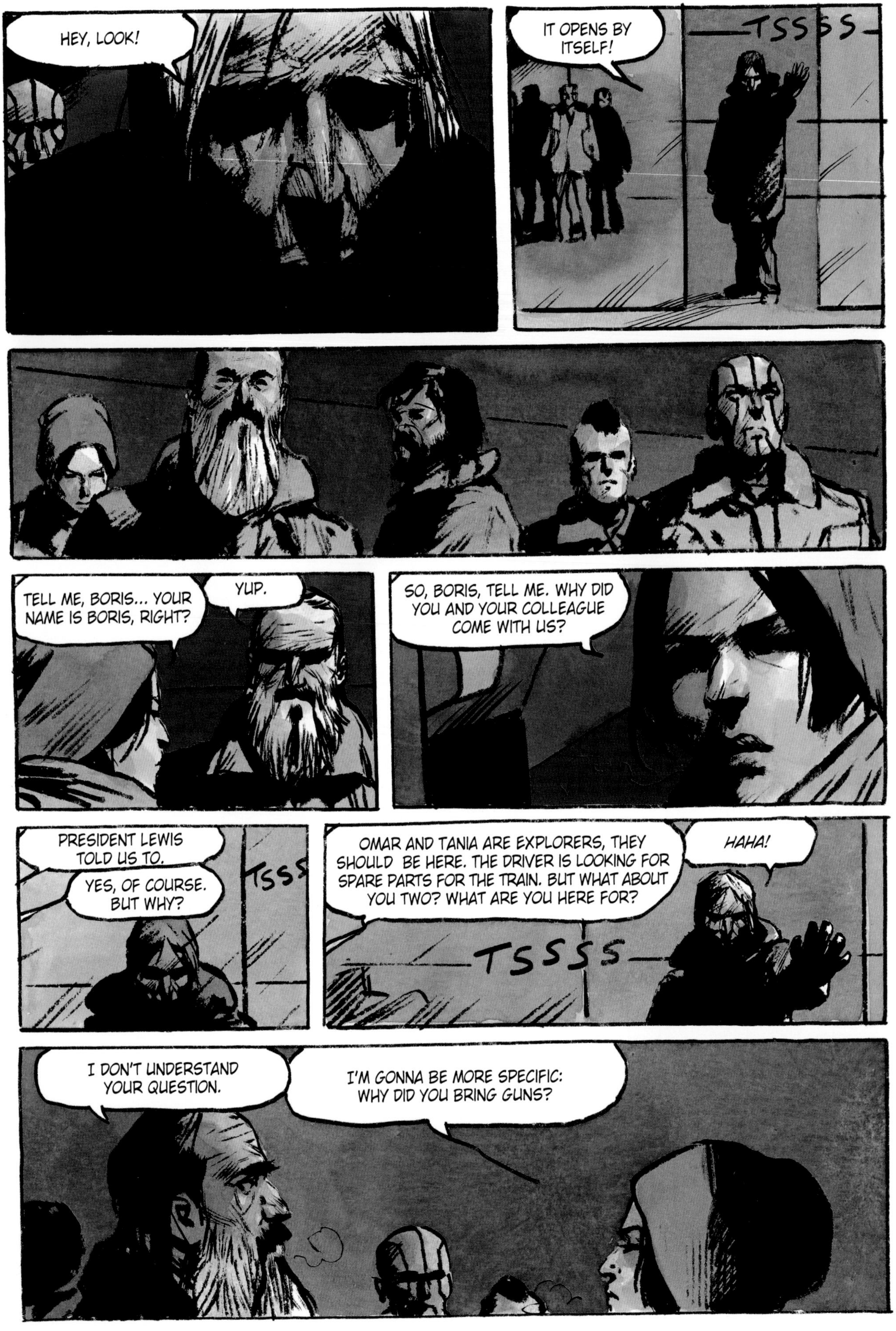
HEY, LOOK!
IT OPENS BY ITSELF!
TSSSS
TELL ME, BORIS... YOUR NAME IS BORIS, RIGHT?
YUP.
SO, BORIS, TELL ME. WHY DID YOU AND YOUR COLLEAGUE COME WITH US?
PRESIDENT LEWIS TOLD US TO.
YES, OF COURSE. BUT WHY?
TSSS
OMAR AND TANIA ARE EXPLORERS, THEY SHOULD BE HERE. THE DRIVER IS LOOKING FOR SPARE PARTS FOR THE TRAIN. BUT WHAT ABOUT YOU TWO? WHAT ARE YOU HERE FOR?
HAHA!
TSSSS
I DON'T UNDERSTAND YOUR QUESTION.
I'M GONNA BE MORE SPECIFIC: WHY DID YOU BRING GUNS?

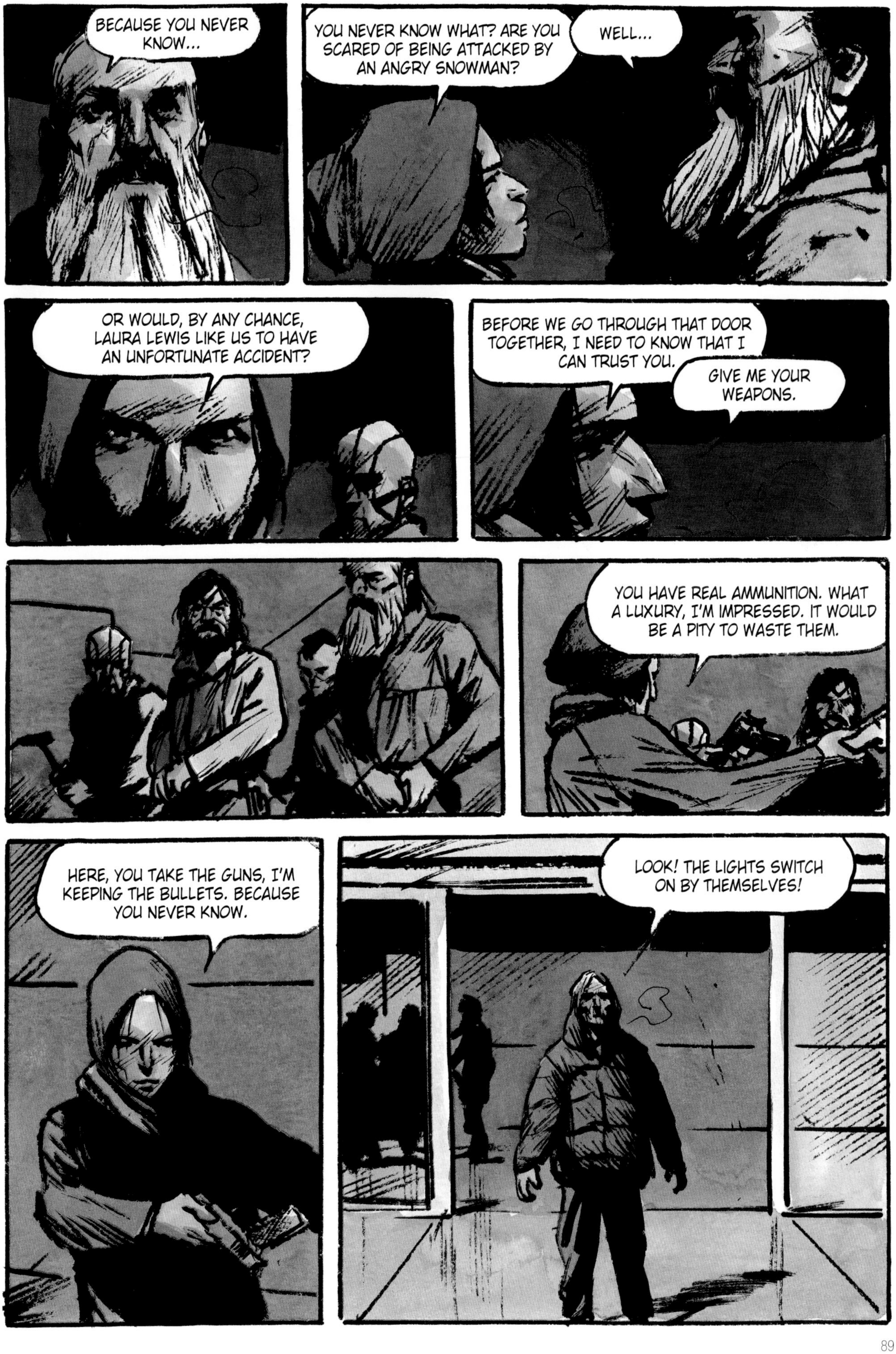
BECAUSE YOU NEVER KNOW...
YOU NEVER KNOW WHAT? ARE YOU SCARED OF BEING ATTACKED BY AN ANGRY SNOWMAN?
WELL...
OR WOULD, BY ANY CHANCE, LAURA LEWIS LIKE US TO HAVE AN UNFORTUNATE ACCIDENT?
BEFORE WE GO THROUGH THAT DOOR TOGETHER, I NEED TO KNOW THAT I CAN TRUST YOU.
GIVE ME YOUR WEAPONS.
YOU HAVE REAL AMMUNITION. WHAT A LUXURY, I'M IMPRESSED. IT WOULD BE A PITY TO WASTE THEM.
HERE, YOU TAKE THE GUNS, I'M KEEPING THE BULLETS. BECAUSE YOU NEVER KNOW.
LOOK! THE LIGHTS SWITCH ON BY THEMSELVES!

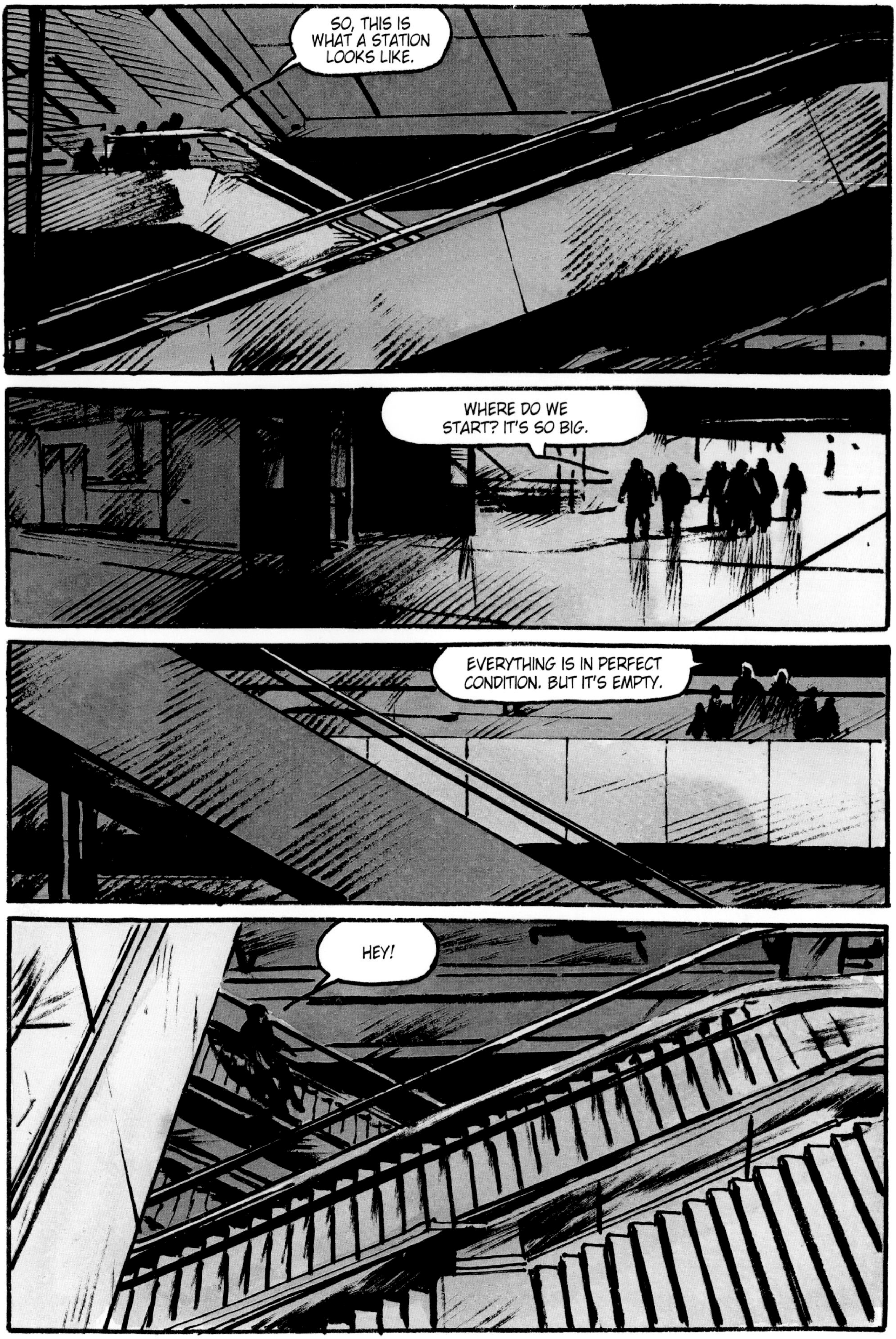
SO, THIS IS WHAT A STATION LOOKS LIKE.
WHERE DO WE START? IT'S SO BIG.
EVERYTHING IS IN PERFECT CONDITION. BUT IT'S EMPTY.
HEY!

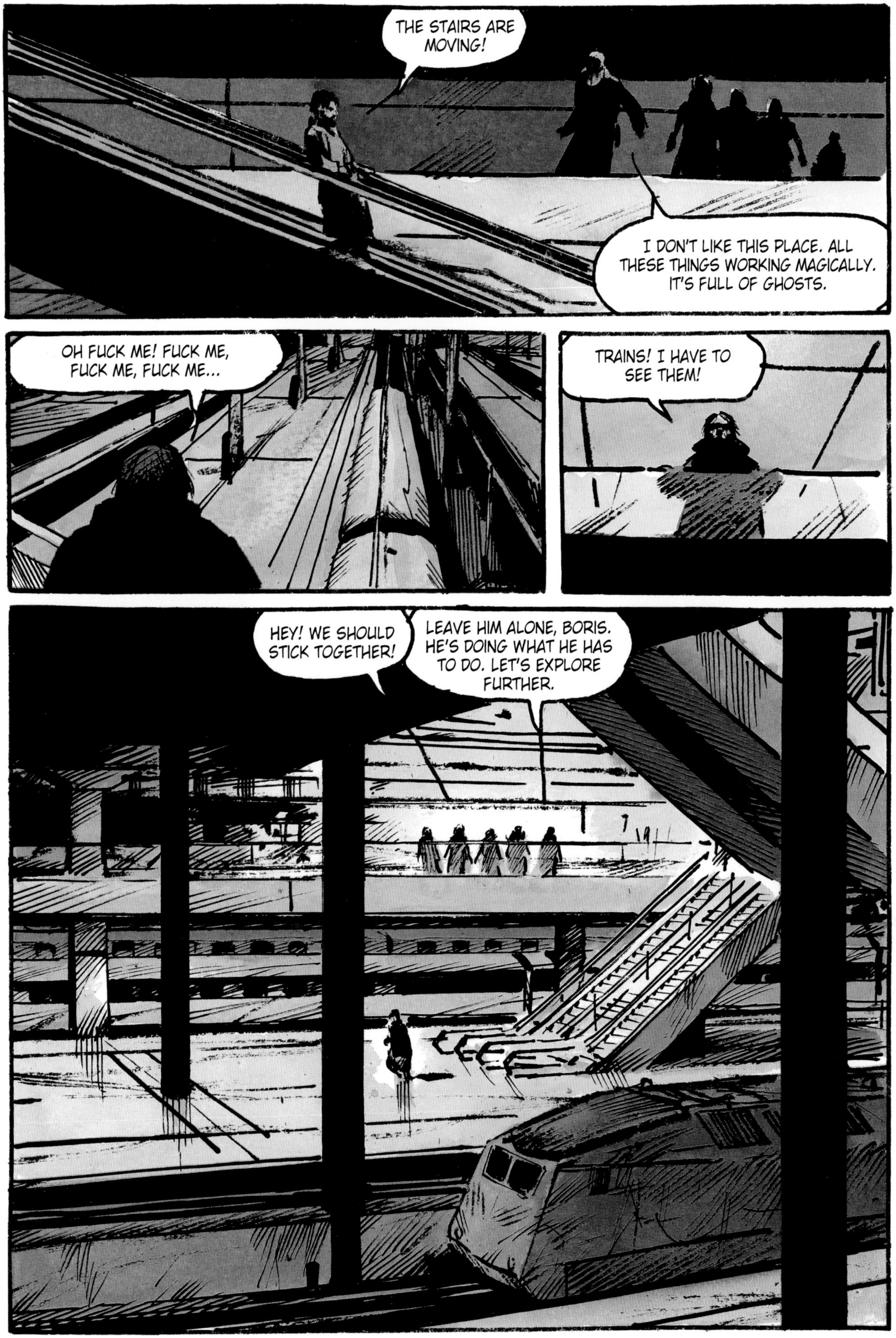
THE STAIRS ARE MOVING!
I DON'T LIKE THIS PLACE. ALL THESE THINGS WORKING MAGICALLY. IT'S FULL OF GHOSTS.
OH FUCK ME! FUCK ME, FUCK ME, FUCK ME...
TRAINS! I HAVE TO SEE THEM!
HEY! WE SHOULD STICK TOGETHER!
LEAVE HIM ALONE, BORIS. HE'S DOING WHAT HE HAS TO DO. LET'S EXPLORE FURTHER.

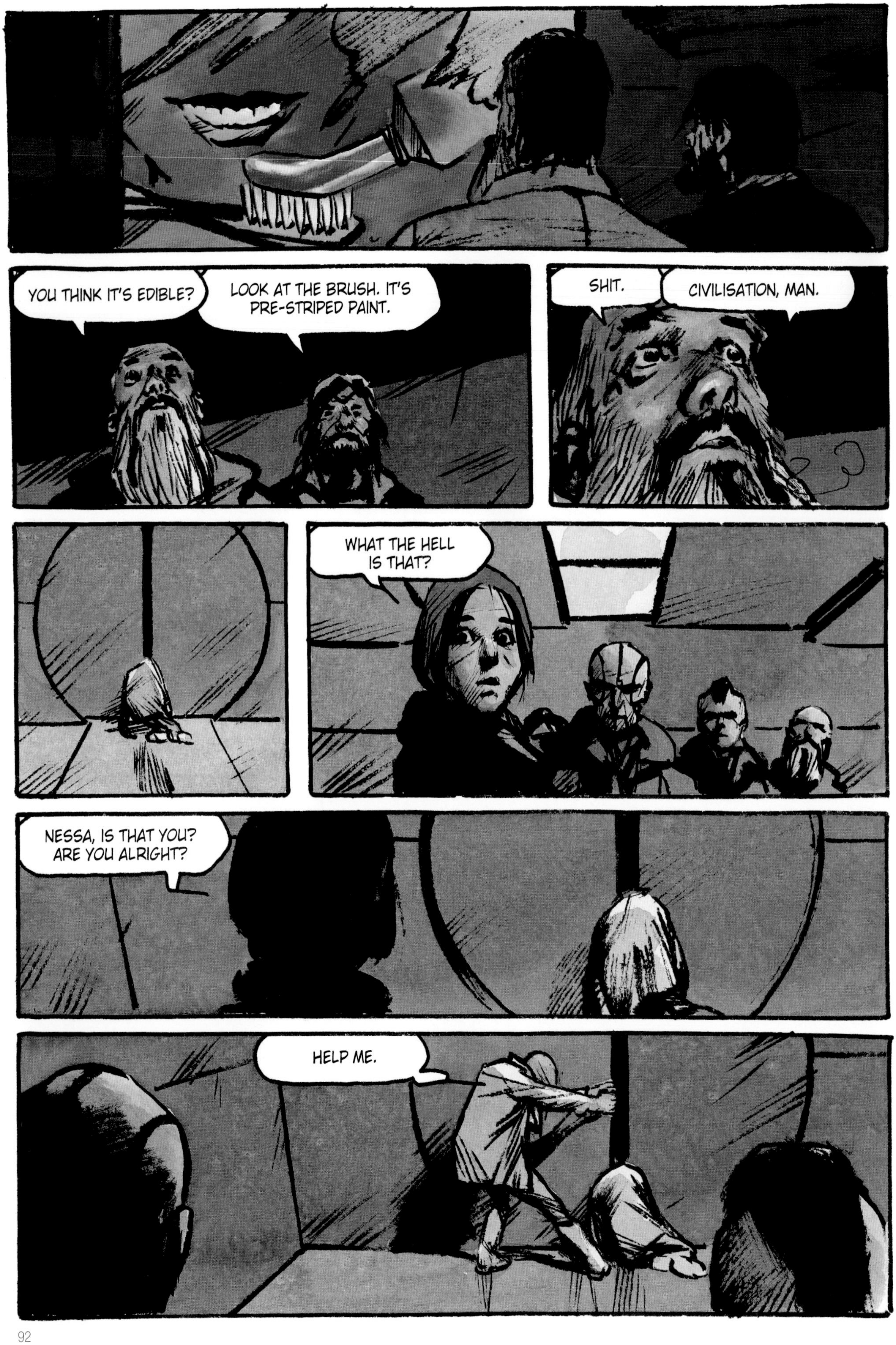
YOU THINK IT'S EDIBLE?
LOOK AT THE BRUSH. IT'S PRE-STRIPED PAINT.
SHIT.
CIVILISATION, MAN.
WHAT THE HELL IS THAT?
NESSA, IS THAT YOU? ARE YOU ALRIGHT?
HELP ME.

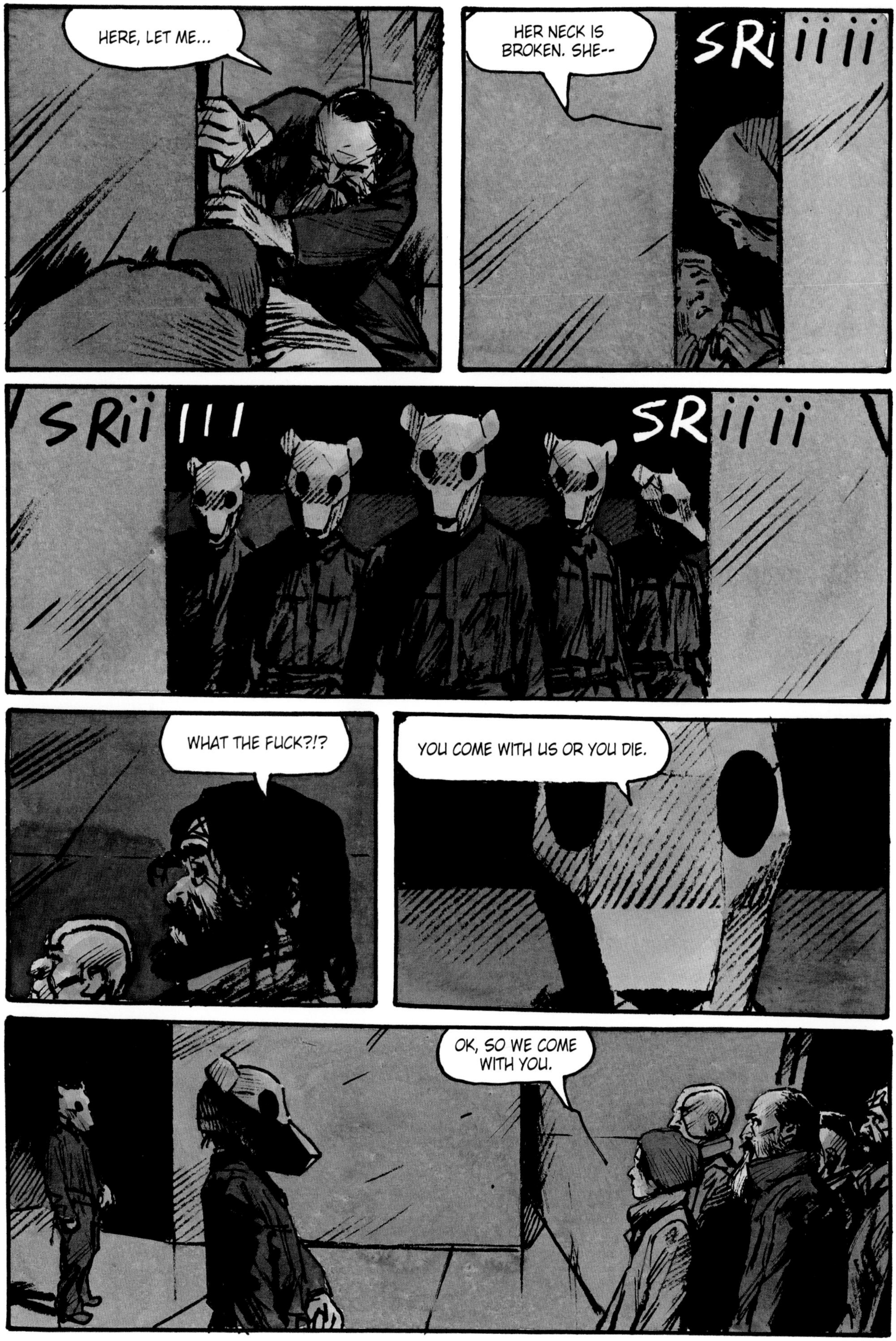
HERE, LET ME...
HER NECK IS BROKEN. SHE--
SRiiiii
SRii III
SRiiii
WHAT THE FUCK?!?
YOU COME WITH US OR YOU DIE.
OK, SO WE COME WITH YOU.

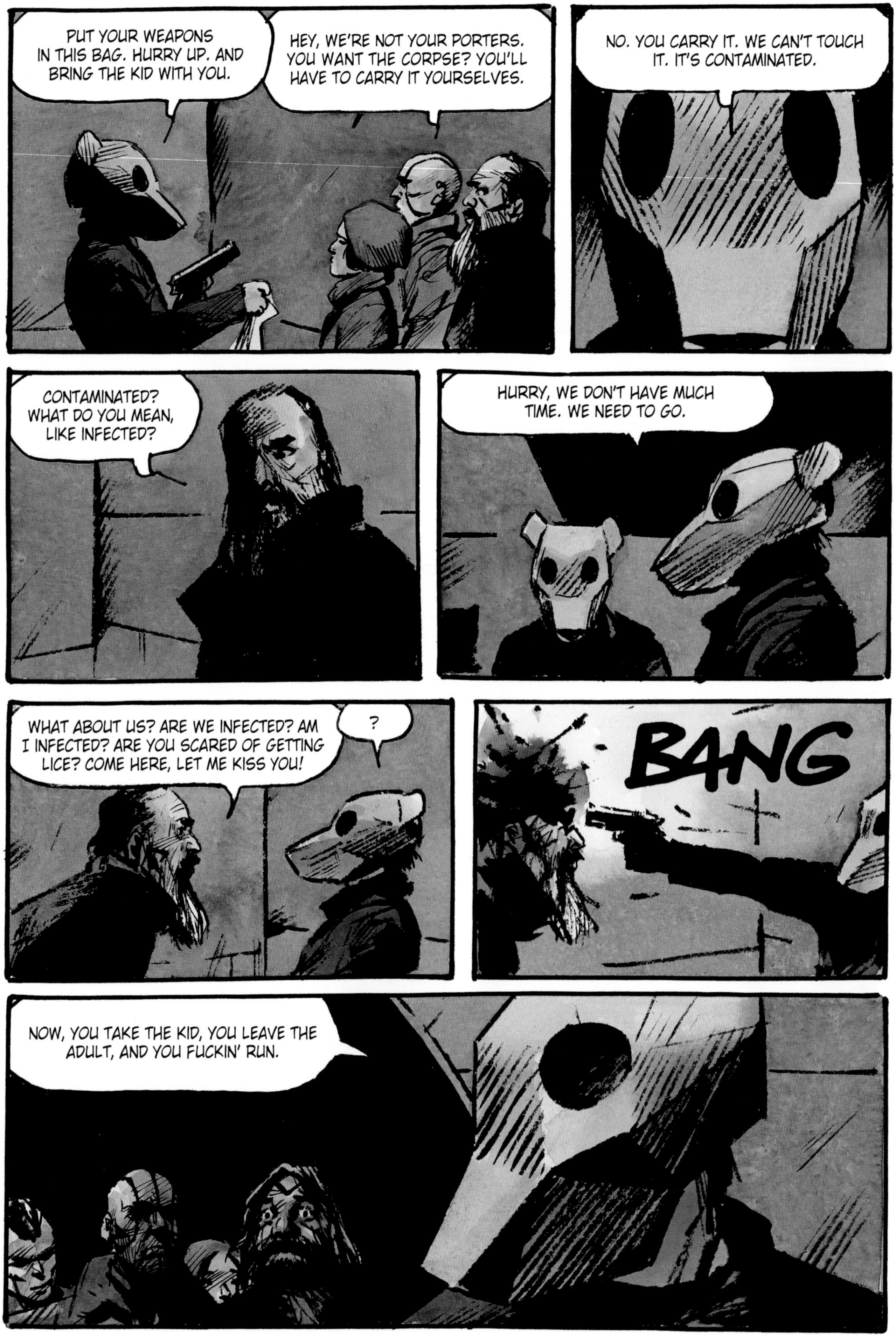
PUT YOUR WEAPONS IN THIS BAG. HURRY UP. AND BRING THE KID WITH YOU.
HEY, WE'RE NOT YOUR PORTERS. YOU WANT THE CORPSE? YOU'LL HAVE TO CARRY IT YOURSELVES.
NO. YOU CARRY IT. WE CAN'T TOUCH IT. IT'S CONTAMINATED.
CONTAMINATED? WHAT DO YOU MEAN, LIKE INFECTED?
HURRY, WE DON'T HAVE MUCH TIME. WE NEED TO GO.
WHAT ABOUT US? ARE WE INFECTED? AM I INFECTED? ARE YOU SCARED OF GETTING LICE? COME HERE, LET ME KISS YOU!
?
BANG
NOW, YOU TAKE THE KID, YOU LEAVE THE ADULT, AND YOU FUCKIN' RUN.

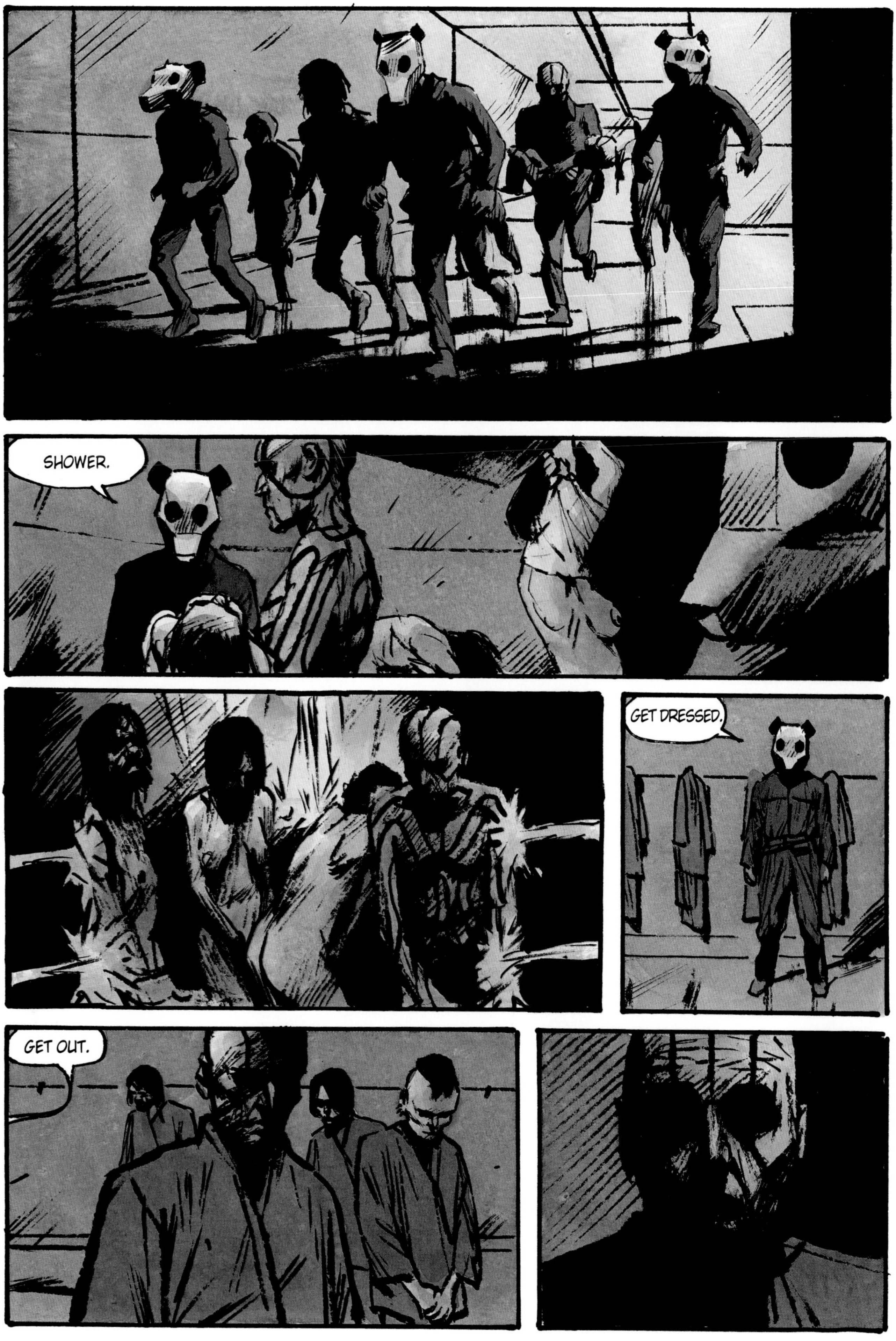
SHOWER.
GET DRESSED.
GET OUT.

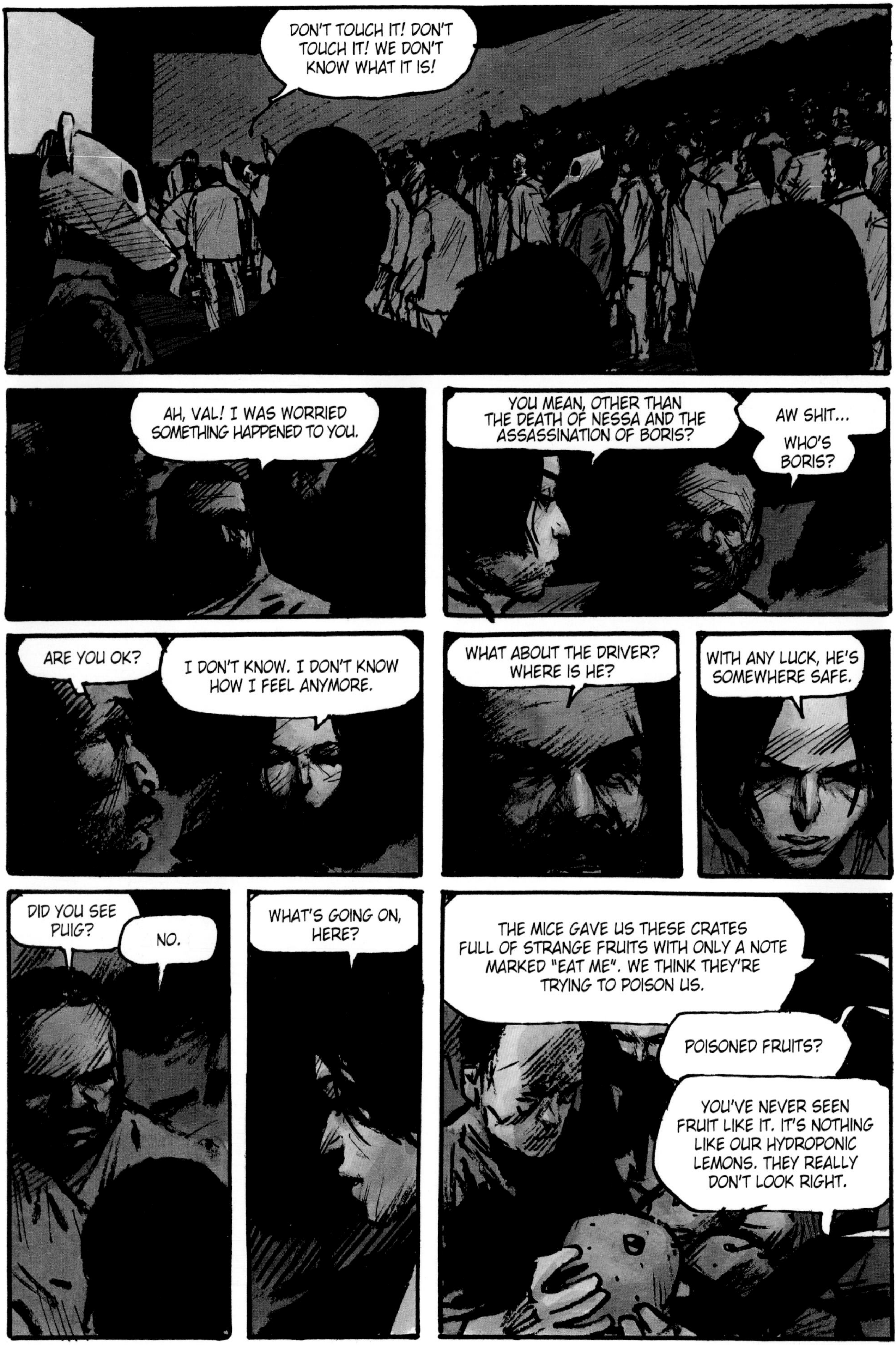
DON'T TOUCH IT! DON'T TOUCH IT! WE DON'T KNOW WHAT IT IS!
AH, VAL! I WAS WORRIED SOMETHING HAPPENED TO YOU.
YOU MEAN, OTHER THAN THE DEATH OF NESSA AND THE ASSASSINATION OF BORIS?
AW SHIT...
WHO'S BORIS?
ARE YOU OK?
I DON'T KNOW. I DON'T KNOW HOW I FEEL ANYMORE.
WHAT ABOUT THE DRIVER? WHERE IS HE?
WITH ANY LUCK, HE'S SOMEWHERE SAFE.
DID YOU SEE PUIG?
NO.
WHAT'S GOING ON, HERE?
THE MICE GAVE US THESE CRATES FULL OF STRANGE FRUITS WITH ONLY A NOTE MARKED "EAT ME". WE THINK THEY'RE TRYING TO POISON US.
POISONED FRUITS?
YOU'VE NEVER SEEN FRUIT LIKE IT. IT'S NOTHING LIKE OUR HYDROPONIC LEMONS. THEY REALLY DON'T LOOK RIGHT.

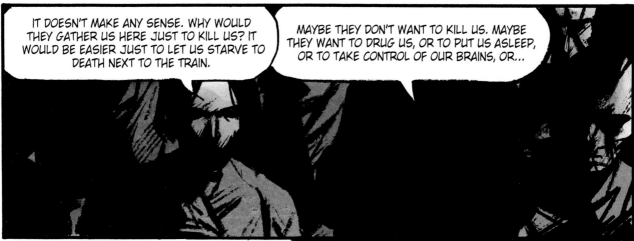

IT DOESN'T MAKE ANY SENSE. WHY WOULD THEY GATHER US HERE JUST TO KILL US? IT WOULD BE EASIER JUST TO LET US STARVE TO DEATH NEXT TO THE TRAIN.

MAYBE THEY DON'T WANT TO KILL US. MAYBE THEY WANT TO DRUG US, OR TO PUT US ASLEEP, OR TO TAKE CONTROL OF OUR BRAINS, OR...

OOOPH...

PROBLEM?

NO, IT'S NOTHING. IT'S... I'M NOT USED TO BEING ON A FLOOR THAT DOESN'T MOVE. AND ALL THIS SPACE... IT MAKES ME DIZZY.

I KNOW WHAT YOU MEAN.

WHERE'S PRESIDENT LEWIS?

THE MICE TOOK HER. WHEN THEY ASKED WHO OUR CHIEF WAS, I HAD THE FEELING THAT THE PRESIDENT WAS SUDDENLY BEING JUST A LITTLE MODEST.

BUT A GOOD SOUL FINALLY PUT HER FRONT AND CENTER.

THAT WAS ME, BY THE WAY.

IT LOOKS LIKE A REAL ONE. IT SMELLS AS GOOD AS IN MY MEMORIES. AS IN MY DREAMS. BUT I DON'T KNOW.

IT'S POISON! HUNDRED PER CENT SURE!

LOOKING AT THEM WON'T GIVE US ANSWERS. THERE'S ONLY ONE WAY TO KNOW.

I'VE NEVER SEEN SUCH A BIG PEAR, BUT IT'S THE TASTIEST THING I'VE EATEN IN MY ENTIRE LIFE.

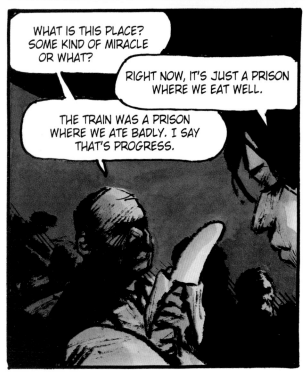

WHAT IS THIS PLACE? SOME KIND OF MIRACLE OR WHAT?

RIGHT NOW, IT'S JUST A PRISON WHERE WE EAT WELL.

THE TRAIN WAS A PRISON WHERE WE ATE BADLY. I SAY THAT'S PROGRESS.

NOW, COME WITH ME, I HAVE SOMETHING TO SHOW YOU.

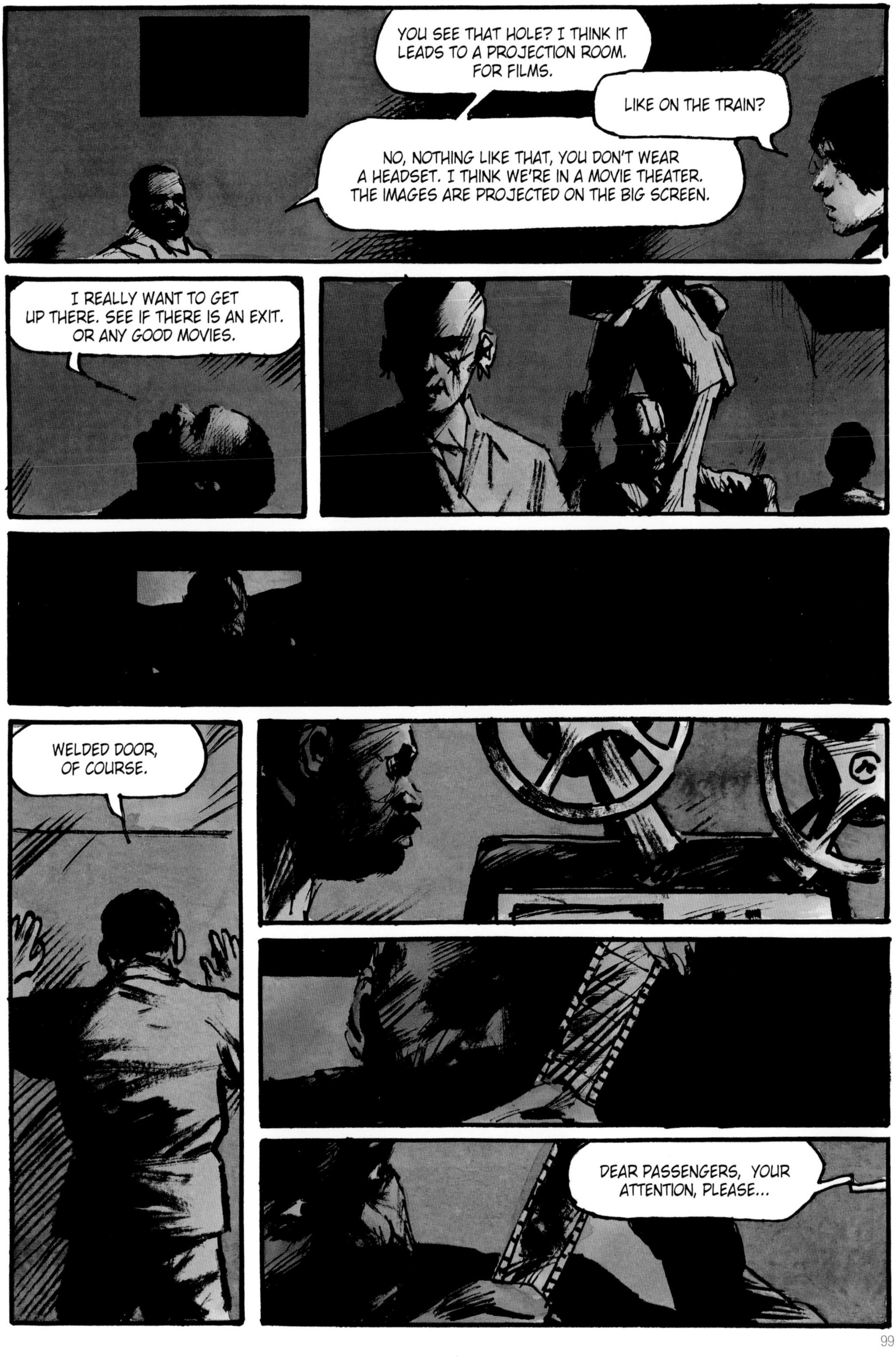
YOU SEE THAT HOLE? I THINK IT LEADS TO A PROJECTION ROOM. FOR FILMS.
LIKE ON THE TRAIN?
NO, NOTHING LIKE THAT, YOU DON'T WEAR A HEADSET. I THINK WE'RE IN A MOVIE THEATER. THE IMAGES ARE PROJECTED ON THE BIG SCREEN.
I REALLY WANT TO GET UP THERE. SEE IF THERE IS AN EXIT. OR ANY GOOD MOVIES.
WELDED DOOR, OF COURSE.
DEAR PASSENGERS, YOUR ATTENTION, PLEASE...

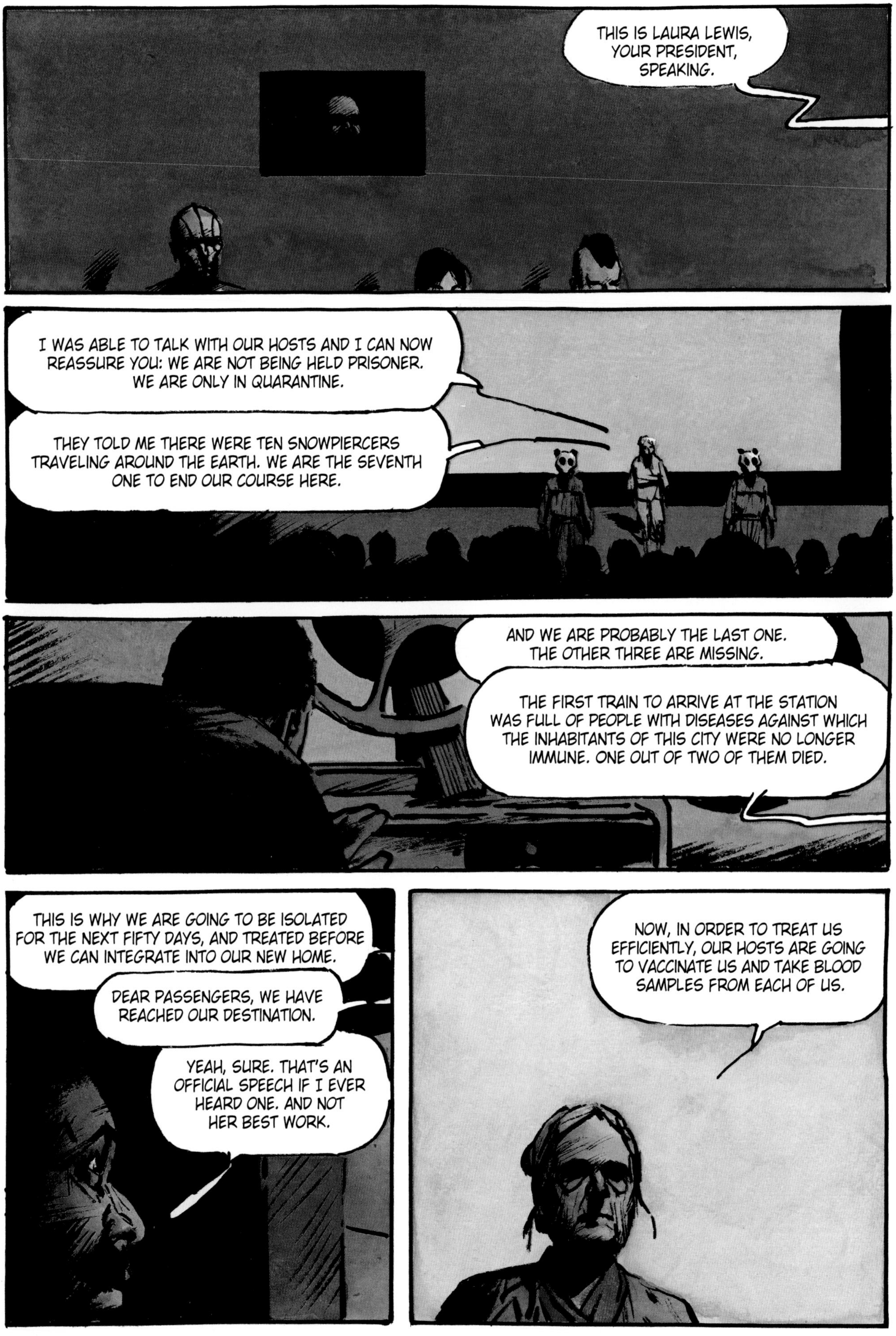
THIS IS LAURA LEWIS, YOUR PRESIDENT, SPEAKING.
I WAS ABLE TO TALK WITH OUR HOSTS AND I CAN NOW REASSURE YOU: WE ARE NOT BEING HELD PRISONER. WE ARE ONLY IN QUARANTINE.
THEY TOLD ME THERE WERE TEN SNOWPIERCERS TRAVELING AROUND THE EARTH. WE ARE THE SEVENTH ONE TO END OUR COURSE HERE.
AND WE ARE PROBABLY THE LAST ONE. THE OTHER THREE ARE MISSING.
THE FIRST TRAIN TO ARRIVE AT THE STATION WAS FULL OF PEOPLE WITH DISEASES AGAINST WHICH THE INHABITANTS OF THIS CITY WERE NO LONGER IMMUNE. ONE OUT OF TWO OF THEM DIED.
THIS IS WHY WE ARE GOING TO BE ISOLATED FOR THE NEXT FIFTY DAYS, AND TREATED BEFORE WE CAN INTEGRATE INTO OUR NEW HOME.
DEAR PASSENGERS, WE HAVE REACHED OUR DESTINATION.
YEAH, SURE. THAT'S AN OFFICIAL SPEECH IF I EVER HEARD ONE. AND NOT HER BEST WORK.
NOW, IN ORDER TO TREAT US EFFICIENTLY, OUR HOSTS ARE GOING TO VACCINATE US AND TAKE BLOOD SAMPLES FROM EACH OF US.

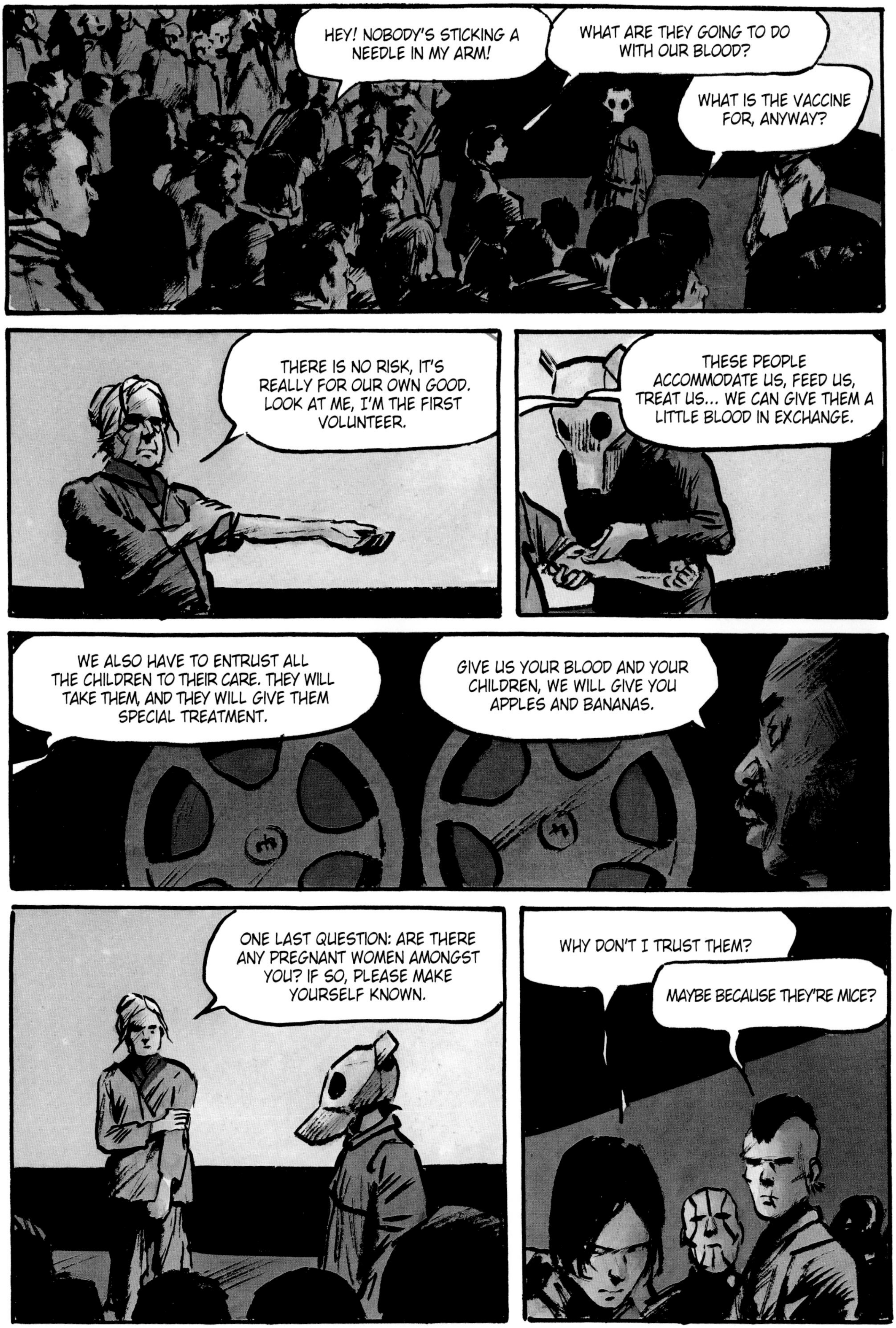
HEY! NOBODY'S STICKING A NEEDLE IN MY ARM!
WHAT ARE THEY GOING TO DO WITH OUR BLOOD?
WHAT IS THE VACCINE FOR, ANYWAY?
THERE IS NO RISK, IT'S REALLY FOR OUR OWN GOOD. LOOK AT ME, I'M THE FIRST VOLUNTEER.
THESE PEOPLE ACCOMMODATE US, FEED US, TREAT US... WE CAN GIVE THEM A LITTLE BLOOD IN EXCHANGE.
WE ALSO HAVE TO ENTRUST ALL THE CHILDREN TO THEIR CARE. THEY WILL TAKE THEM, AND THEY WILL GIVE THEM SPECIAL TREATMENT.
GIVE US YOUR BLOOD AND YOUR CHILDREN, WE WILL GIVE YOU APPLES AND BANANAS.
ONE LAST QUESTION: ARE THERE ANY PREGNANT WOMEN AMONGST YOU? IF SO, PLEASE MAKE YOURSELF KNOWN.
WHY DON'T I TRUST THEM?
MAYBE BECAUSE THEY'RE MICE?

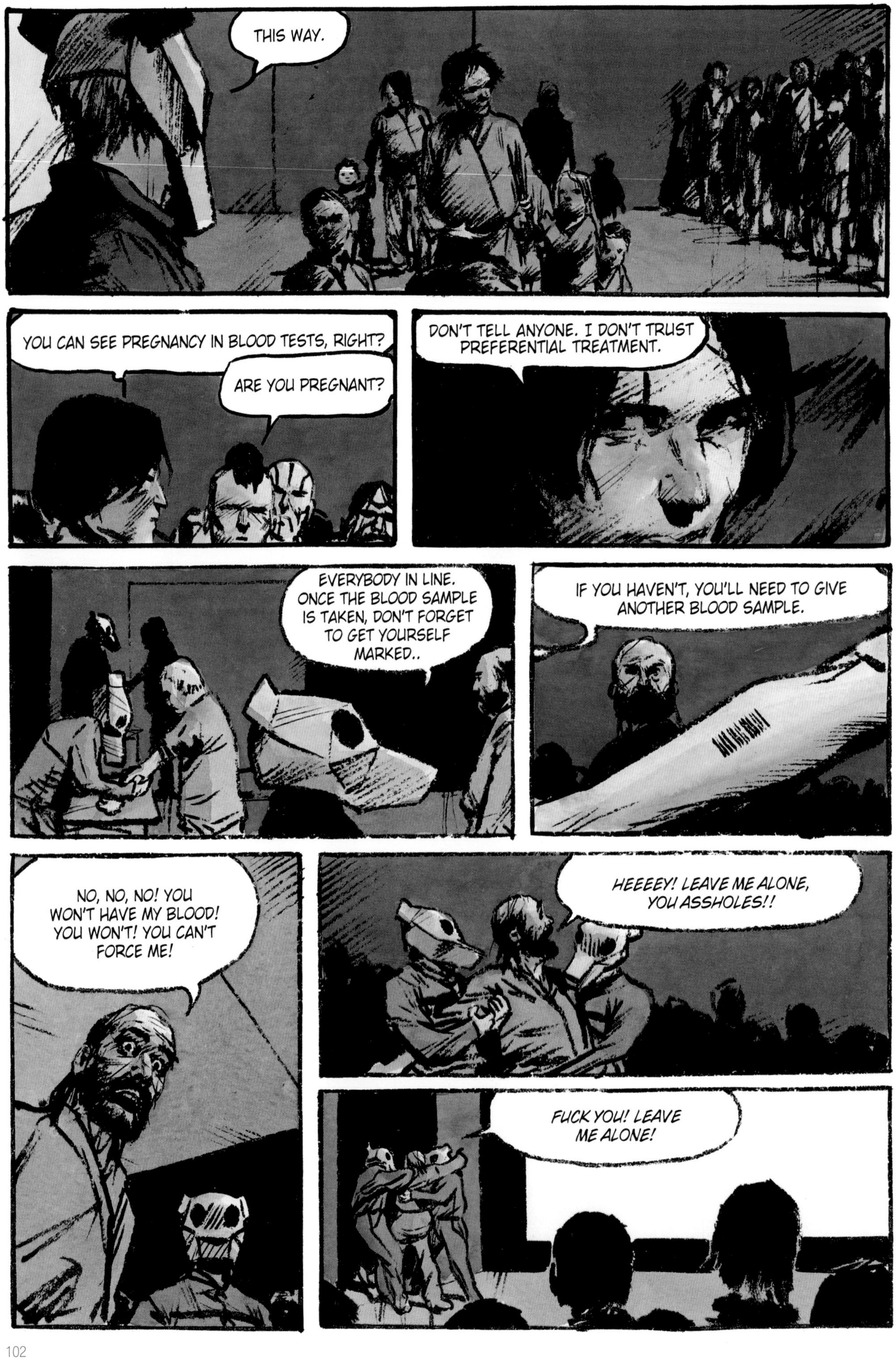
THIS WAY.
YOU CAN SEE PREGNANCY IN BLOOD TESTS, RIGHT?
ARE YOU PREGNANT?
DON'T TELL ANYONE. I DON'T TRUST PREFERENTIAL TREATMENT.
EVERYBODY IN LINE. ONCE THE BLOOD SAMPLE IS TAKEN, DON'T FORGET TO GET YOURSELF MARKED..
IF YOU HAVEN'T, YOU'LL NEED TO GIVE ANOTHER BLOOD SAMPLE.
NO, NO, NO! YOU WON'T HAVE MY BLOOD! YOU WON'T! YOU CAN'T FORCE ME!
HEEEEY! LEAVE ME ALONE, YOU ASSHOLES!!
FUCK YOU! LEAVE ME ALONE!

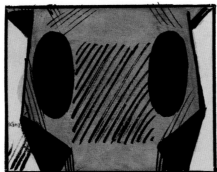

ALL RIGHT, ALL RIGHT, GO ON! STAY FOCUSED, GO ON!

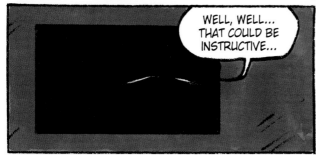

I'M AFRAID YOU CAN'T AVOID THAT BLOOD SAMPLE THING.

WELL, WELL... THAT COULD BE INSTRUCTIVE...

PRESENTATION

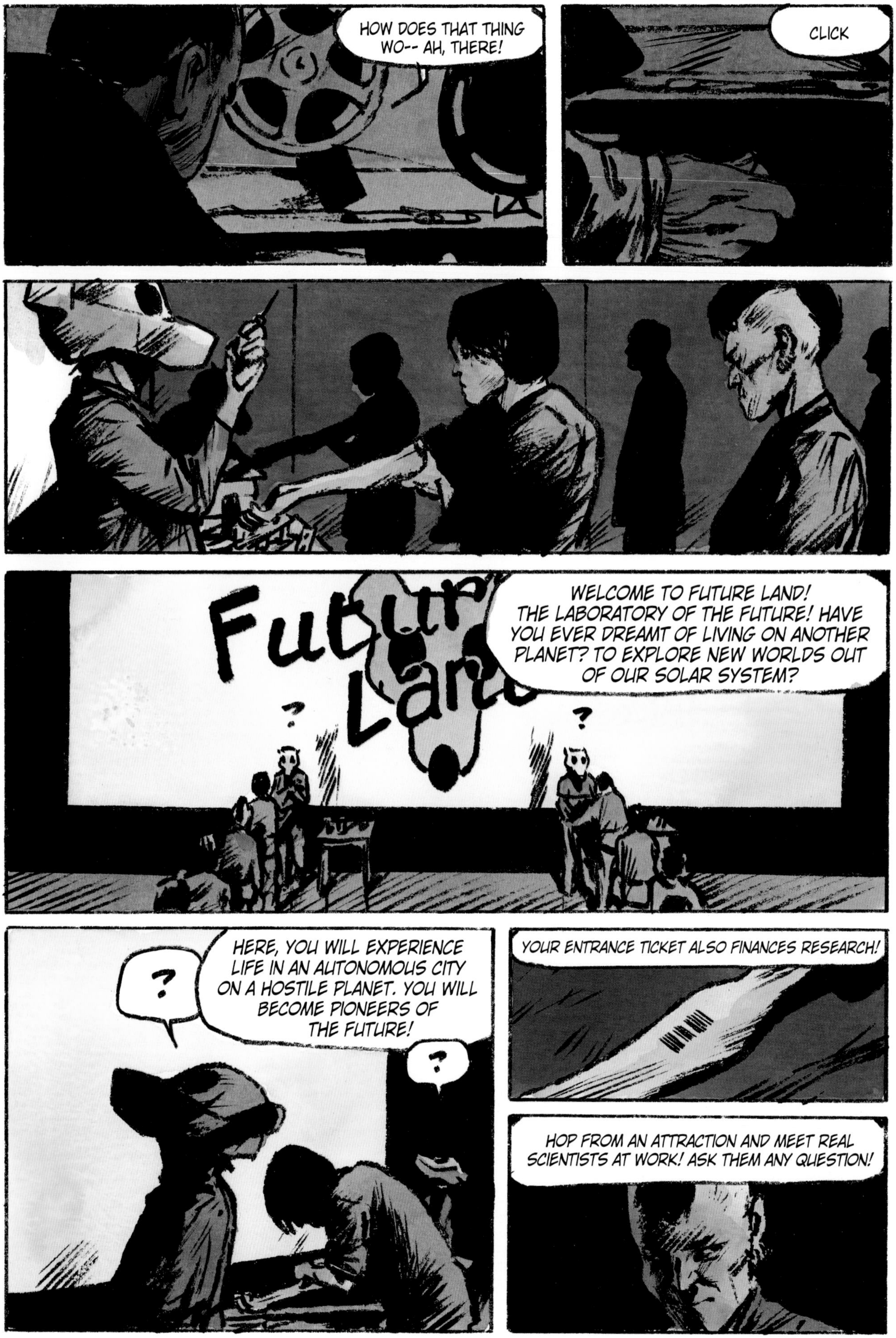
HOW DOES THAT THING WO-- AH, THERE!
CLICK
Futur Land
WELCOME TO FUTURE LAND! THE LABORATORY OF THE FUTURE! HAVE YOU EVER DREAMT OF LIVING ON ANOTHER PLANET? TO EXPLORE NEW WORLDS OUT OF OUR SOLAR SYSTEM?
?
?
?
HERE, YOU WILL EXPERIENCE LIFE IN AN AUTONOMOUS CITY ON A HOSTILE PLANET. YOU WILL BECOME PIONEERS OF THE FUTURE!
?
YOUR ENTRANCE TICKET ALSO FINANCES RESEARCH!
HOP FROM AN ATTRACTION AND MEET REAL SCIENTISTS AT WORK! ASK THEM ANY QUESTION!

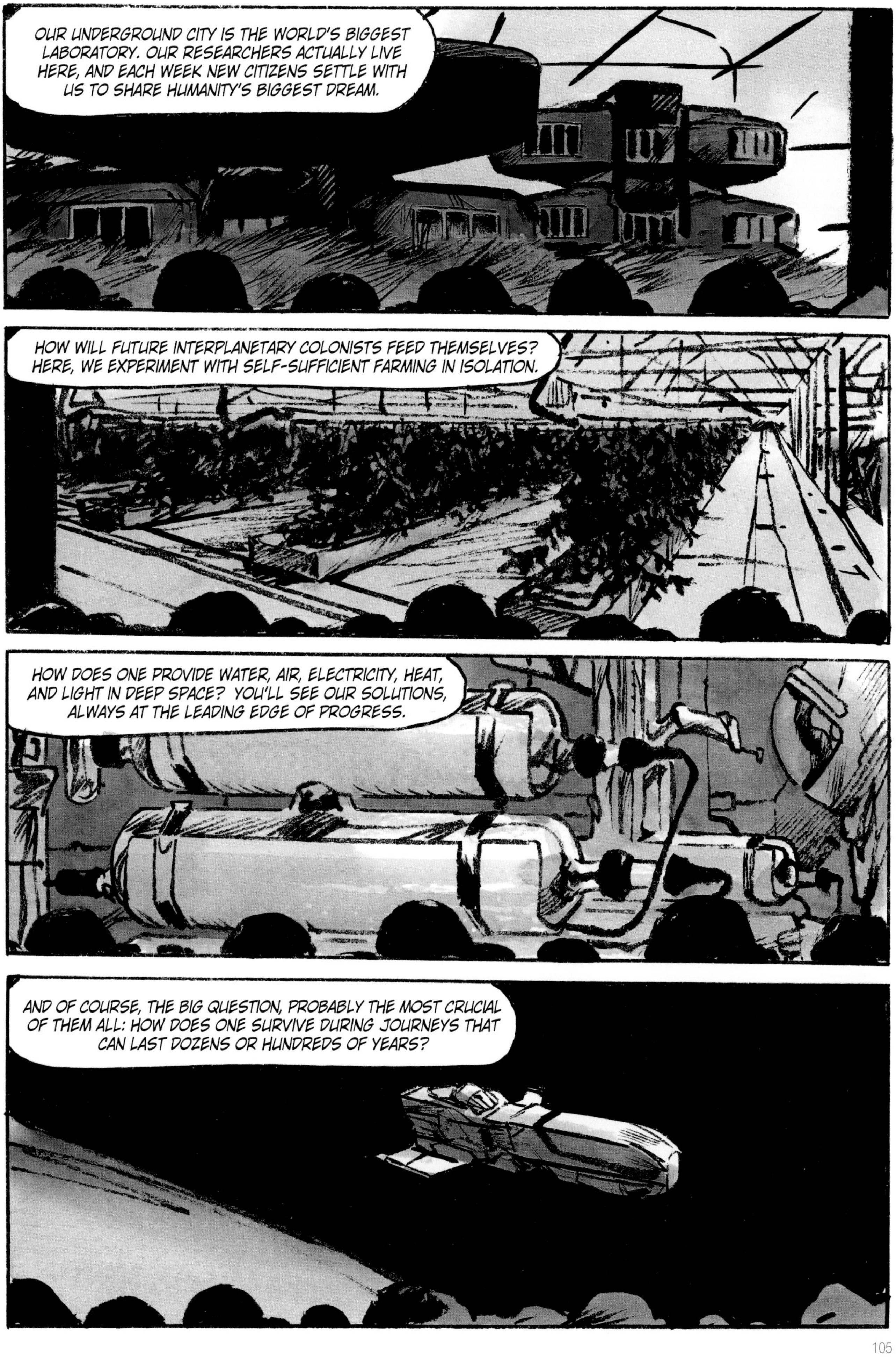
OUR UNDERGROUND CITY IS THE WORLD'S BIGGEST LABORATORY. OUR RESEARCHERS ACTUALLY LIVE HERE, AND EACH WEEK NEW CITIZENS SETTLE WITH US TO SHARE HUMANITY'S BIGGEST DREAM.
HOW WILL FUTURE INTERPLANETARY COLONISTS FEED THEMSELVES? HERE, WE EXPERIMENT WITH SELF-SUFFICIENT FARMING IN ISOLATION.
HOW DOES ONE PROVIDE WATER, AIR, ELECTRICITY, HEAT, AND LIGHT IN DEEP SPACE? YOU'LL SEE OUR SOLUTIONS, ALWAYS AT THE LEADING EDGE OF PROGRESS.
AND OF COURSE, THE BIG QUESTION, PROBABLY THE MOST CRUCIAL OF THEM ALL: HOW DOES ONE SURVIVE DURING JOURNEYS THAT CAN LAST DOZENS OR HUNDREDS OF YEARS?

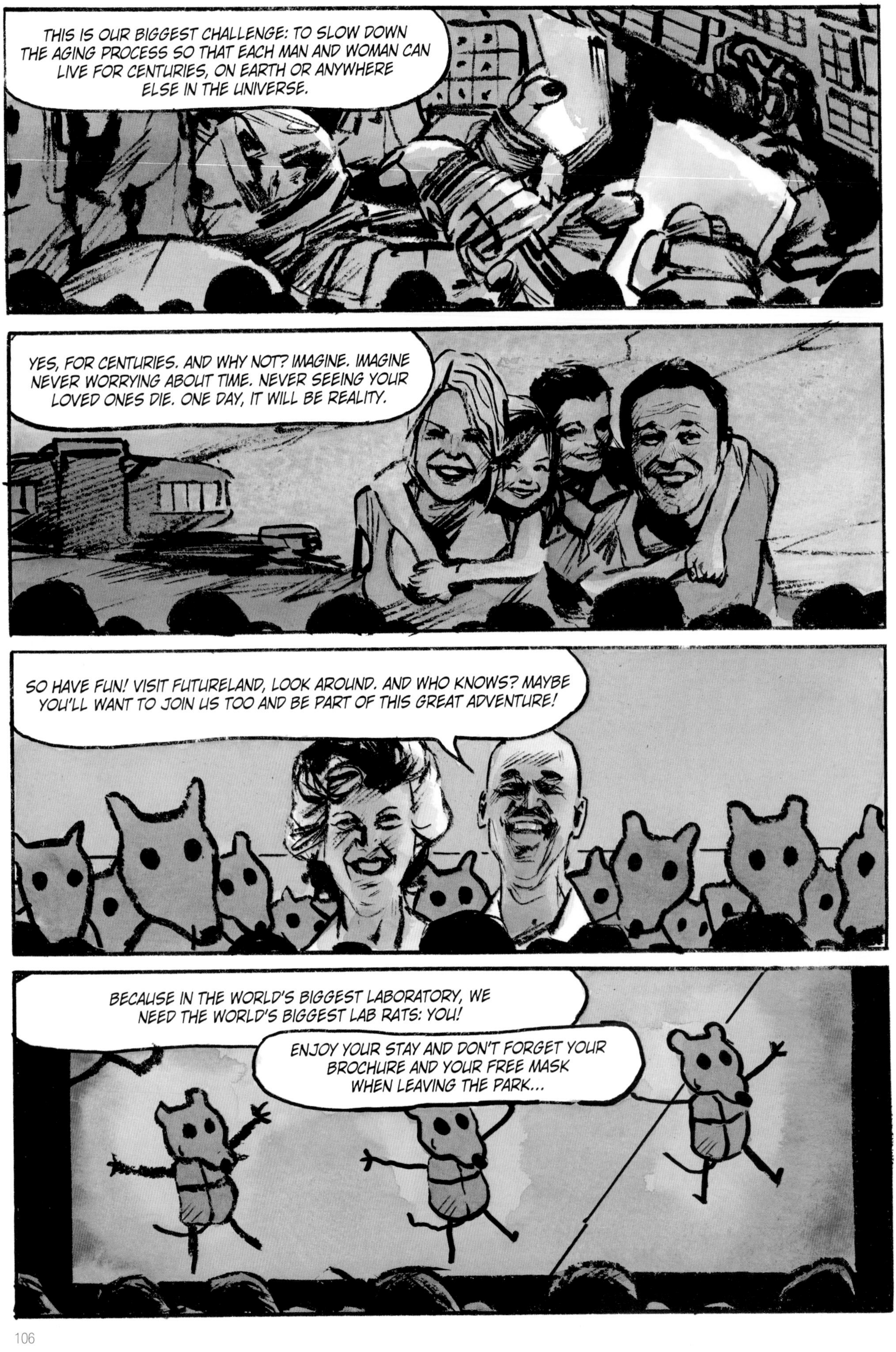
THIS IS OUR BIGGEST CHALLENGE: TO SLOW DOWN THE AGING PROCESS SO THAT EACH MAN AND WOMAN CAN LIVE FOR CENTURIES, ON EARTH OR ANYWHERE ELSE IN THE UNIVERSE.
YES, FOR CENTURIES. AND WHY NOT? IMAGINE. IMAGINE NEVER WORRYING ABOUT TIME. NEVER SEEING YOUR LOVED ONES DIE. ONE DAY, IT WILL BE REALITY.
SO HAVE FUN! VISIT FUTURELAND, LOOK AROUND. AND WHO KNOWS? MAYBE YOU'LL WANT TO JOIN US TOO AND BE PART OF THIS GREAT ADVENTURE!
BECAUSE IN THE WORLD'S BIGGEST LABORATORY, WE NEED THE WORLD'S BIGGEST LAB RATS: YOU!
ENJOY YOUR STAY AND DON'T FORGET YOUR BROCHURE AND YOUR FREE MASK WHEN LEAVING THE PARK...

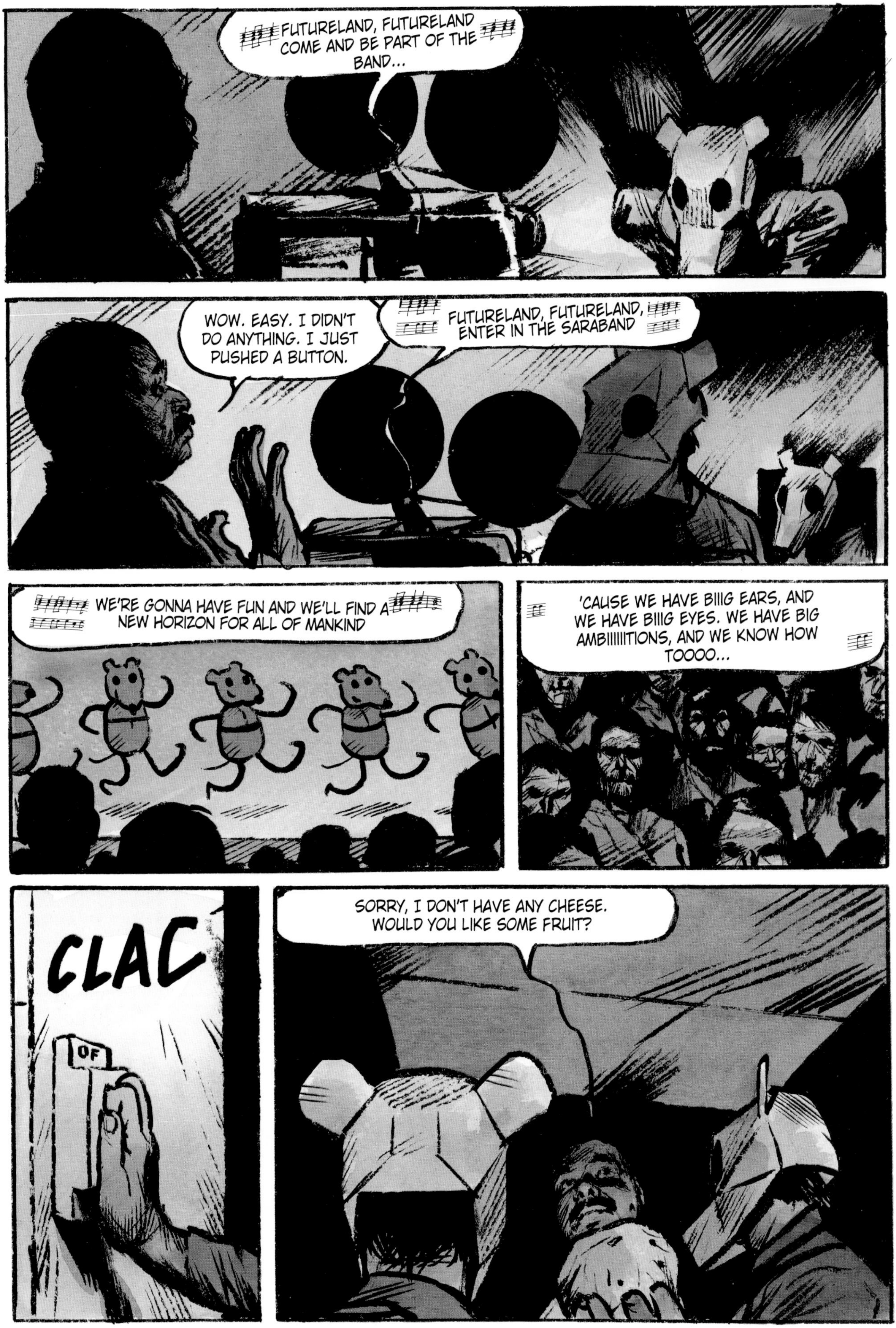
FUTURELAND, FUTURELAND COME AND BE PART OF THE BAND...
WOW. EASY. I DIDN'T DO ANYTHING. I JUST PUSHED A BUTTON.
FUTURELAND, FUTURELAND, ENTER IN THE SARABAND
WE'RE GONNA HAVE FUN AND WE'LL FIND A NEW HORIZON FOR ALL OF MANKIND
'CAUSE WE HAVE BIIIG EARS, AND WE HAVE BIIIG EYES. WE HAVE BIG AMBIIIIITIONS, AND WE KNOW HOW TOOOO...
CLAC
OF
SORRY, I DON'T HAVE ANY CHEESE. WOULD YOU LIKE SOME FRUIT?

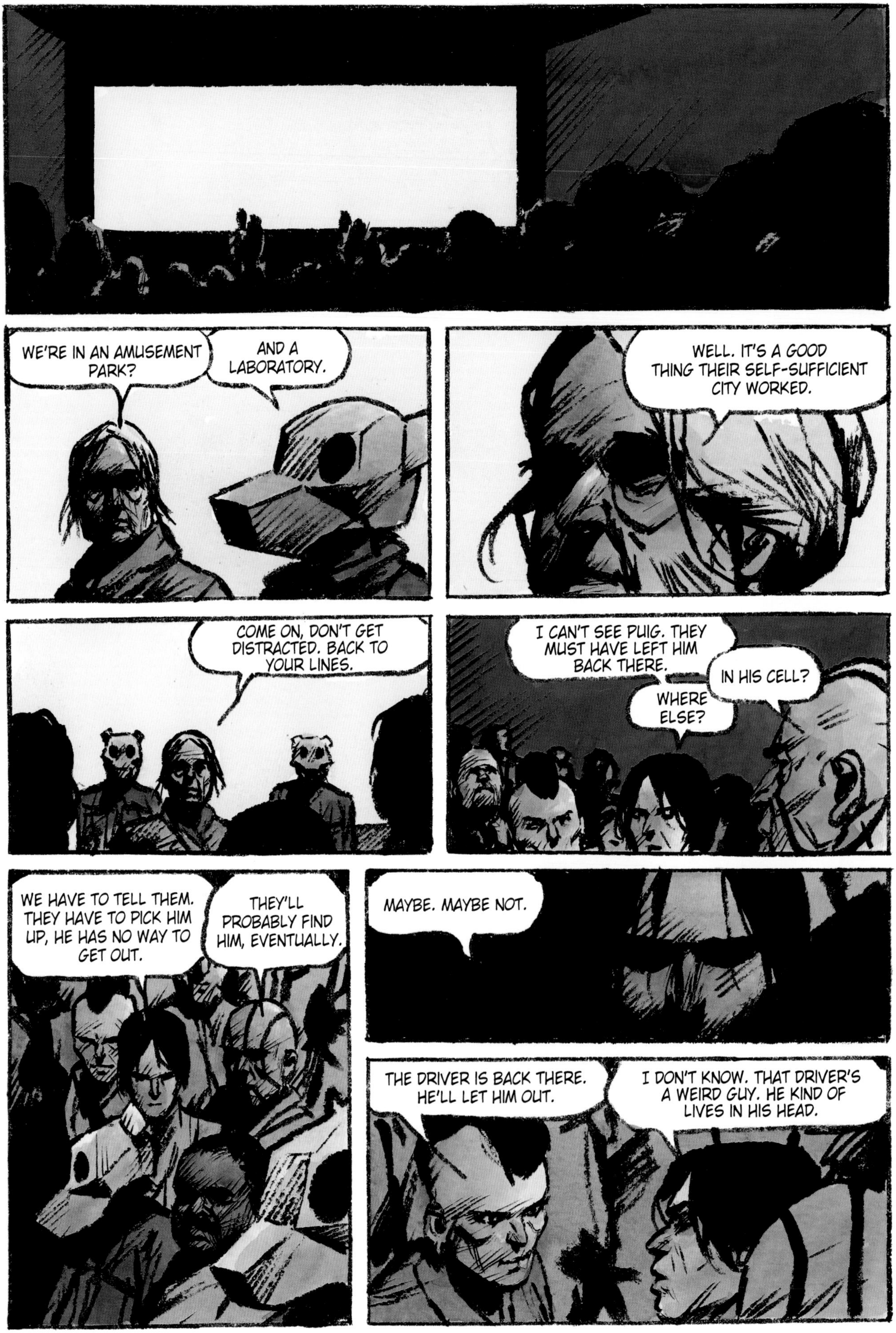
WE'RE IN AN AMUSEMENT PARK?
AND A LABORATORY.
WELL. IT'S A GOOD THING THEIR SELF-SUFFICIENT CITY WORKED.
COME ON, DON'T GET DISTRACTED. BACK TO YOUR LINES.
I CAN'T SEE PUIG. THEY MUST HAVE LEFT HIM BACK THERE.
IN HIS CELL?
WHERE ELSE?
WE HAVE TO TELL THEM. THEY HAVE TO PICK HIM UP, HE HAS NO WAY TO GET OUT.
THEY'LL PROBABLY FIND HIM, EVENTUALLY.
MAYBE. MAYBE NOT.
THE DRIVER IS BACK THERE. HE'LL LET HIM OUT.
I DON'T KNOW. THAT DRIVER'S A WEIRD GUY. HE KIND OF LIVES IN HIS HEAD.

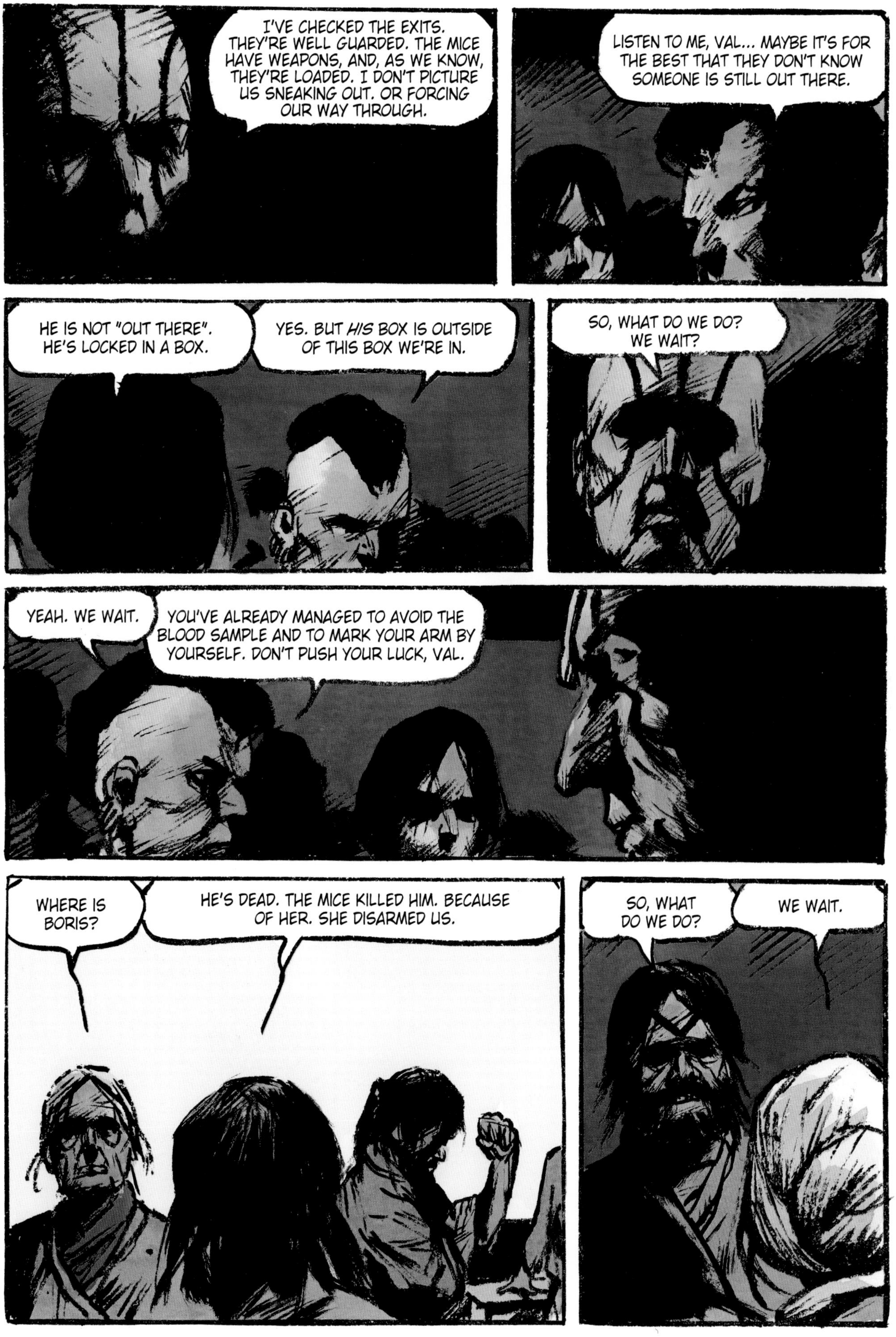
I'VE CHECKED THE EXITS. THEY'RE WELL GUARDED. THE MICE HAVE WEAPONS, AND, AS WE KNOW, THEY'RE LOADED. I DON'T PICTURE US SNEAKING OUT. OR FORCING OUR WAY THROUGH.
LISTEN TO ME, VAL... MAYBE IT'S FOR THE BEST THAT THEY DON'T KNOW SOMEONE IS STILL OUT THERE.
HE IS NOT "OUT THERE". HE'S LOCKED IN A BOX.
YES. BUT *HIS* BOX IS OUTSIDE OF THIS BOX WE'RE IN.
SO, WHAT DO WE DO? WE WAIT?
YEAH. WE WAIT.
YOU'VE ALREADY MANAGED TO AVOID THE BLOOD SAMPLE AND TO MARK YOUR ARM BY YOURSELF. DON'T PUSH YOUR LUCK, VAL.
WHERE IS BORIS?
HE'S DEAD. THE MICE KILLED HIM. BECAUSE OF HER. SHE DISARMED US.
SO, WHAT DO WE DO?
WE WAIT.

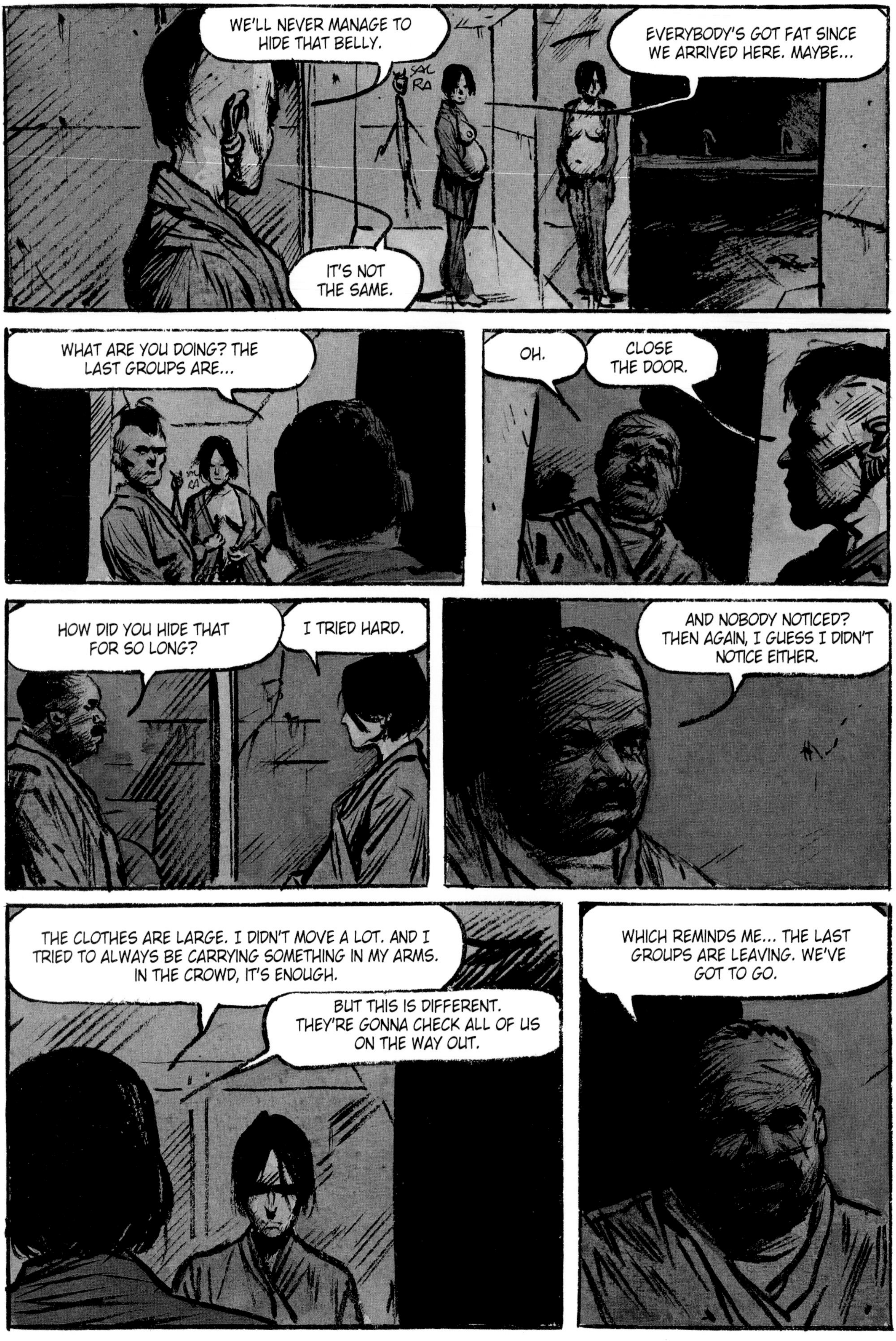
WE'LL NEVER MANAGE TO HIDE THAT BELLY.
EVERYBODY'S GOT FAT SINCE WE ARRIVED HERE. MAYBE...
IT'S NOT THE SAME.
WHAT ARE YOU DOING? THE LAST GROUPS ARE...
OH.
CLOSE THE DOOR.
HOW DID YOU HIDE THAT FOR SO LONG?
I TRIED HARD.
AND NOBODY NOTICED? THEN AGAIN, I GUESS I DIDN'T NOTICE EITHER.
THE CLOTHES ARE LARGE. I DIDN'T MOVE A LOT. AND I TRIED TO ALWAYS BE CARRYING SOMETHING IN MY ARMS. IN THE CROWD, IT'S ENOUGH.
BUT THIS IS DIFFERENT. THEY'RE GONNA CHECK ALL OF US ON THE WAY OUT.
WHICH REMINDS ME... THE LAST GROUPS ARE LEAVING. WE'VE GOT TO GO.

WALK IN FRONT OF ME.

YOUR CONDITION IS NOT GONNA IMPROVE, THEY WILL NOTICE, EVENTUALLY. YOU MIGHT AS WELL TELL THEM NOW.

NO.

YOU DON'T THINK YOU'LL MANAGE TO HIDE THE BIRTH, DO YOU?

WE'LL SEE WHEN WE GET THERE. ALL I KNOW IS THAT WE NEVER SEE A CHILD OR A PREGNANT WOMAN ANYMORE.

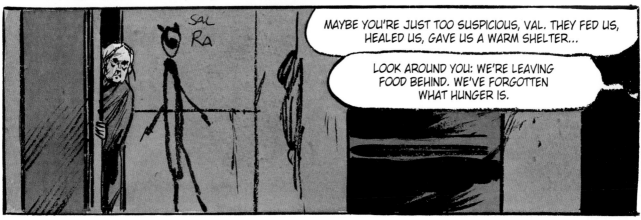

MAYBE YOU'RE JUST TOO SUSPICIOUS, VAL. THEY FED US, HEALED US, GAVE US A WARM SHELTER...

LOOK AROUND YOU: WE'RE LEAVING FOOD BEHIND. WE'VE FORGOTTEN WHAT HUNGER IS.

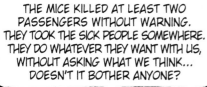

THE MICE KILLED AT LEAST TWO PASSENGERS WITHOUT WARNING. THEY TOOK THE SICK PEOPLE SOMEWHERE. THEY DO WHATEVER THEY WANT WITH US, WITHOUT ASKING WHAT WE THINK... DOESN'T IT BOTHER ANYONE?

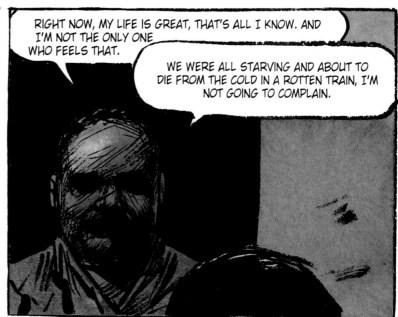

RIGHT NOW, MY LIFE IS GREAT, THAT'S ALL I KNOW. AND I'M NOT THE ONLY ONE WHO FEELS THAT.

WE WERE ALL STARVING AND ABOUT TO DIE FROM THE COLD IN A ROTTEN TRAIN, I'M NOT GOING TO COMPLAIN.

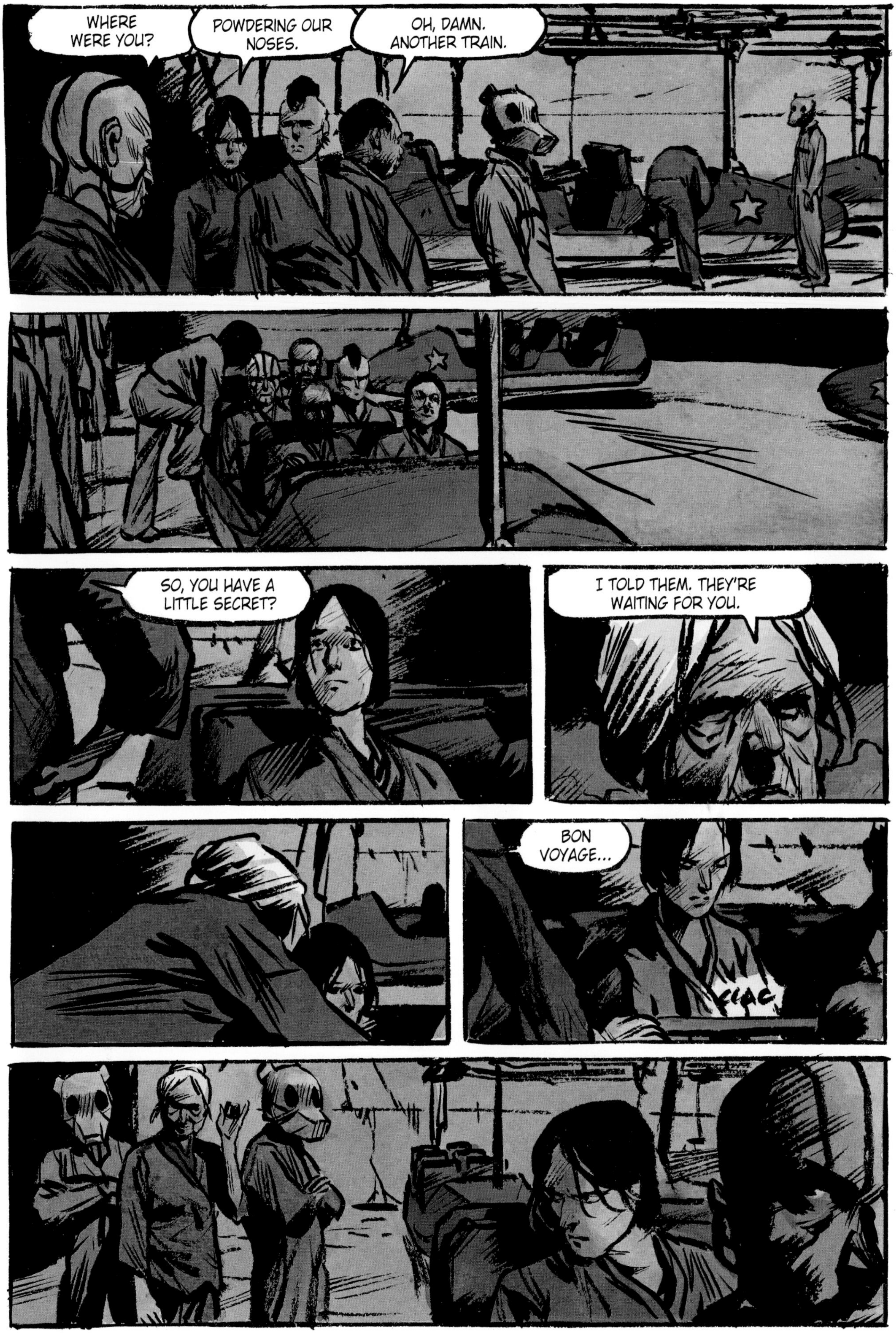
WHERE WERE YOU?
POWDERING OUR NOSES.
OH, DAMN. ANOTHER TRAIN.
SO, YOU HAVE A LITTLE SECRET?
I TOLD THEM. THEY'RE WAITING FOR YOU.
BON VOYAGE...
CLAC

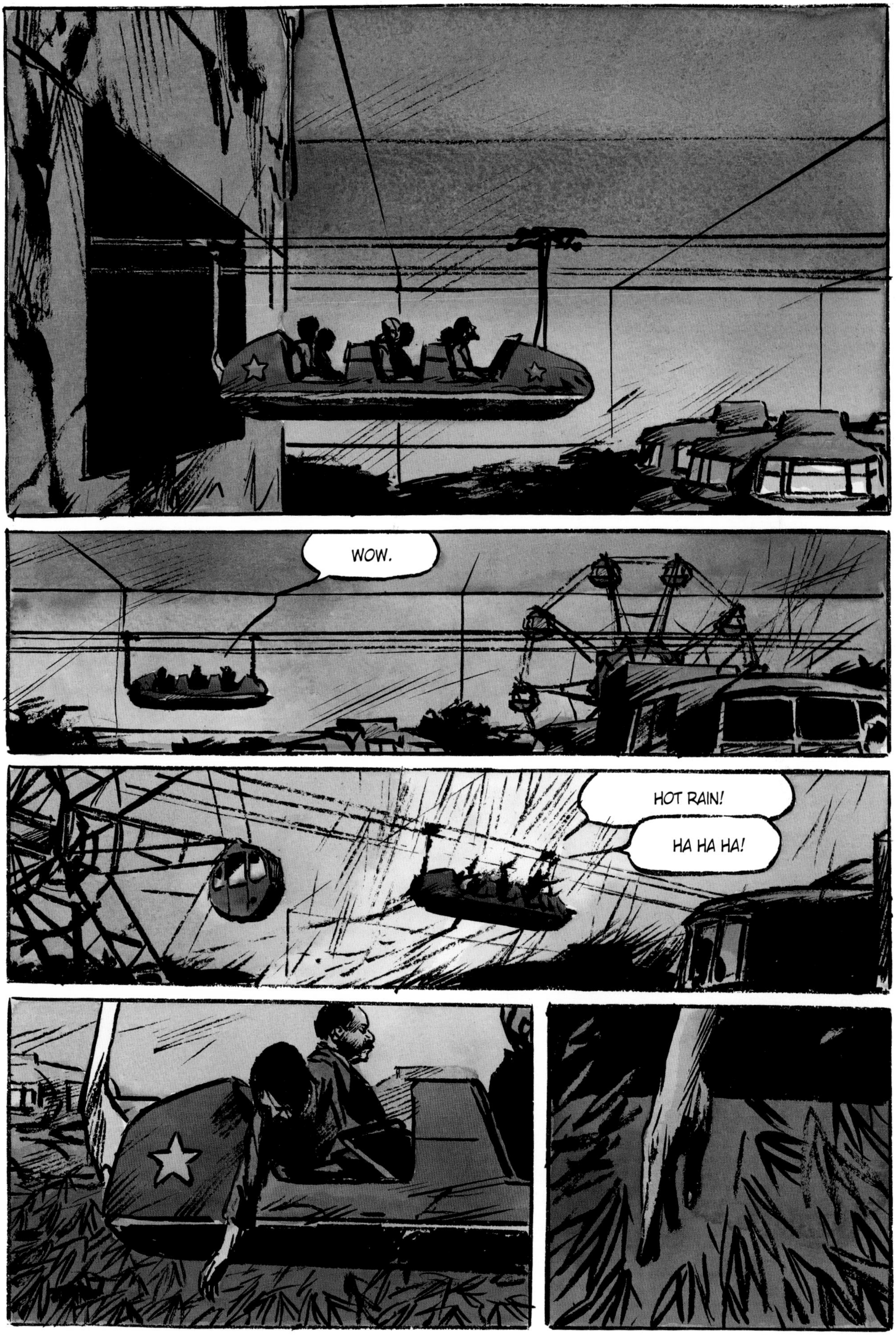
WOW.
HOT RAIN!
HA HA HA!

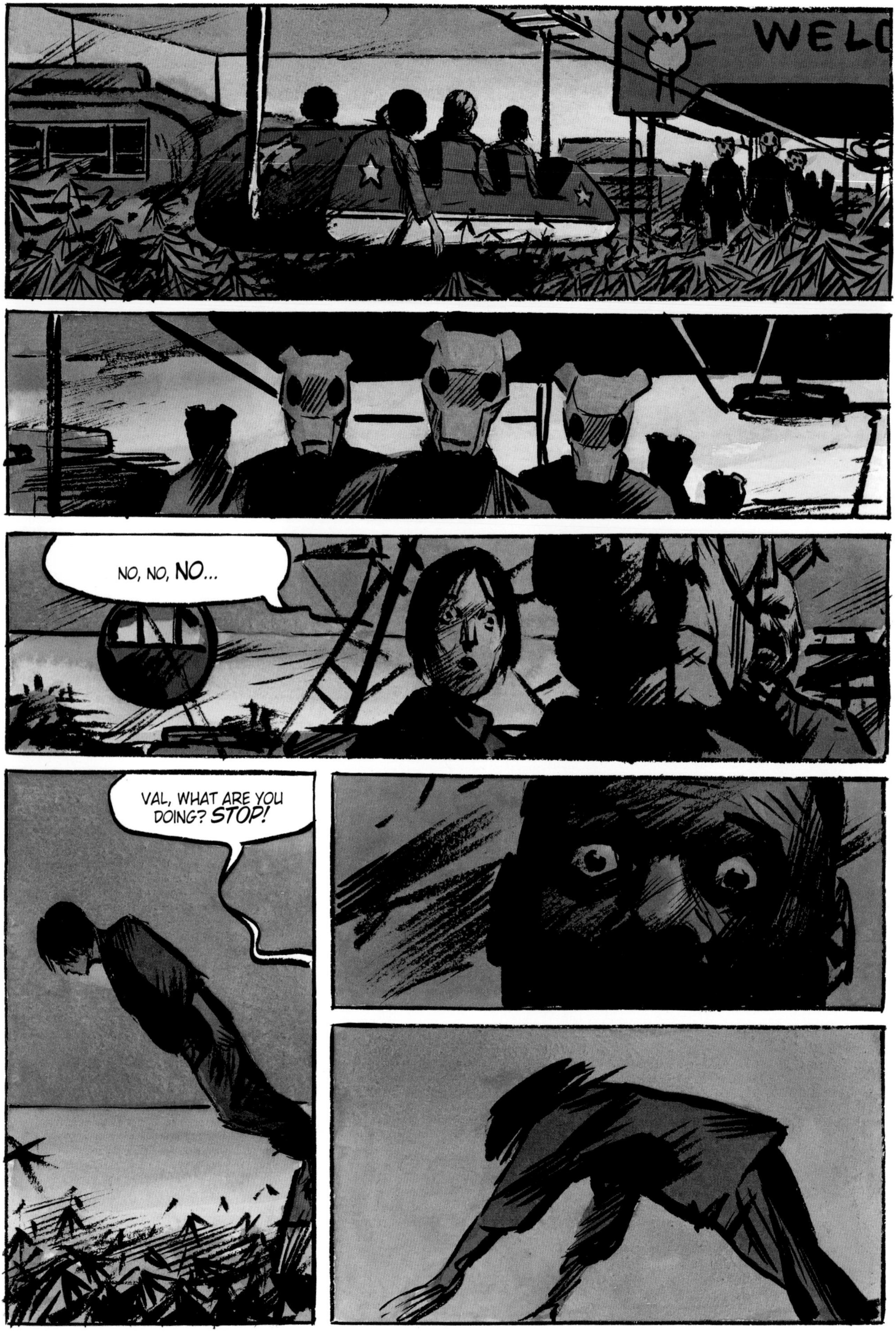
WELC
NO, NO, NO...
VAL, WHAT ARE YOU DOING? STOP!

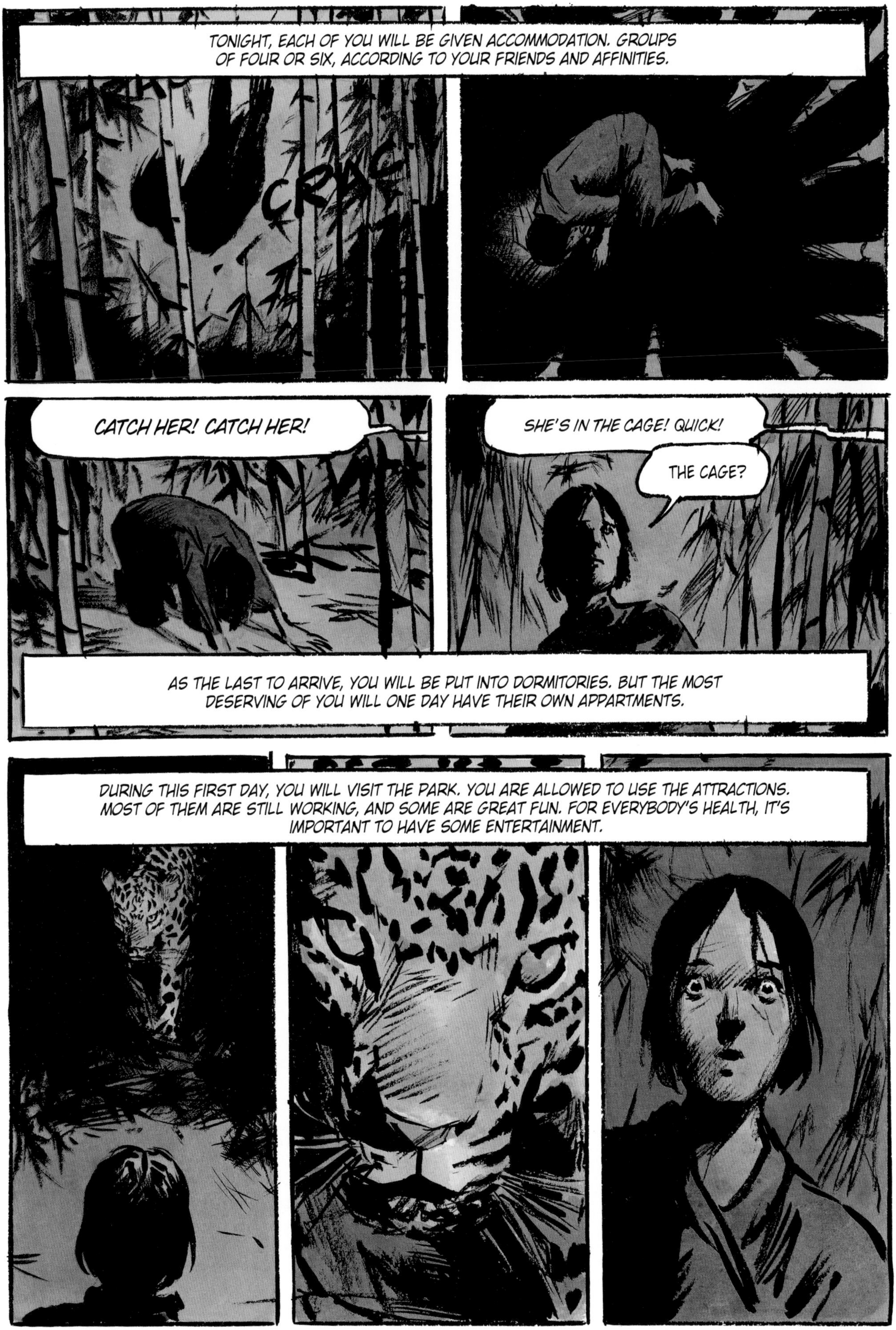

TONIGHT, EACH OF YOU WILL BE GIVEN ACCOMMODATION. GROUPS OF FOUR OR SIX, ACCORDING TO YOUR FRIENDS AND AFFINITIES.
CATCH HER! CATCH HER!
SHE'S IN THE CAGE! QUICK!
THE CAGE?
AS THE LAST TO ARRIVE, YOU WILL BE PUT INTO DORMITORIES. BUT THE MOST DESERVING OF YOU WILL ONE DAY HAVE THEIR OWN APPARTMENTS.
DURING THIS FIRST DAY, YOU WILL VISIT THE PARK. YOU ARE ALLOWED TO USE THE ATTRACTIONS. MOST OF THEM ARE STILL WORKING, AND SOME ARE GREAT FUN. FOR EVERYBODY'S HEALTH, IT'S IMPORTANT TO HAVE SOME ENTERTAINMENT.

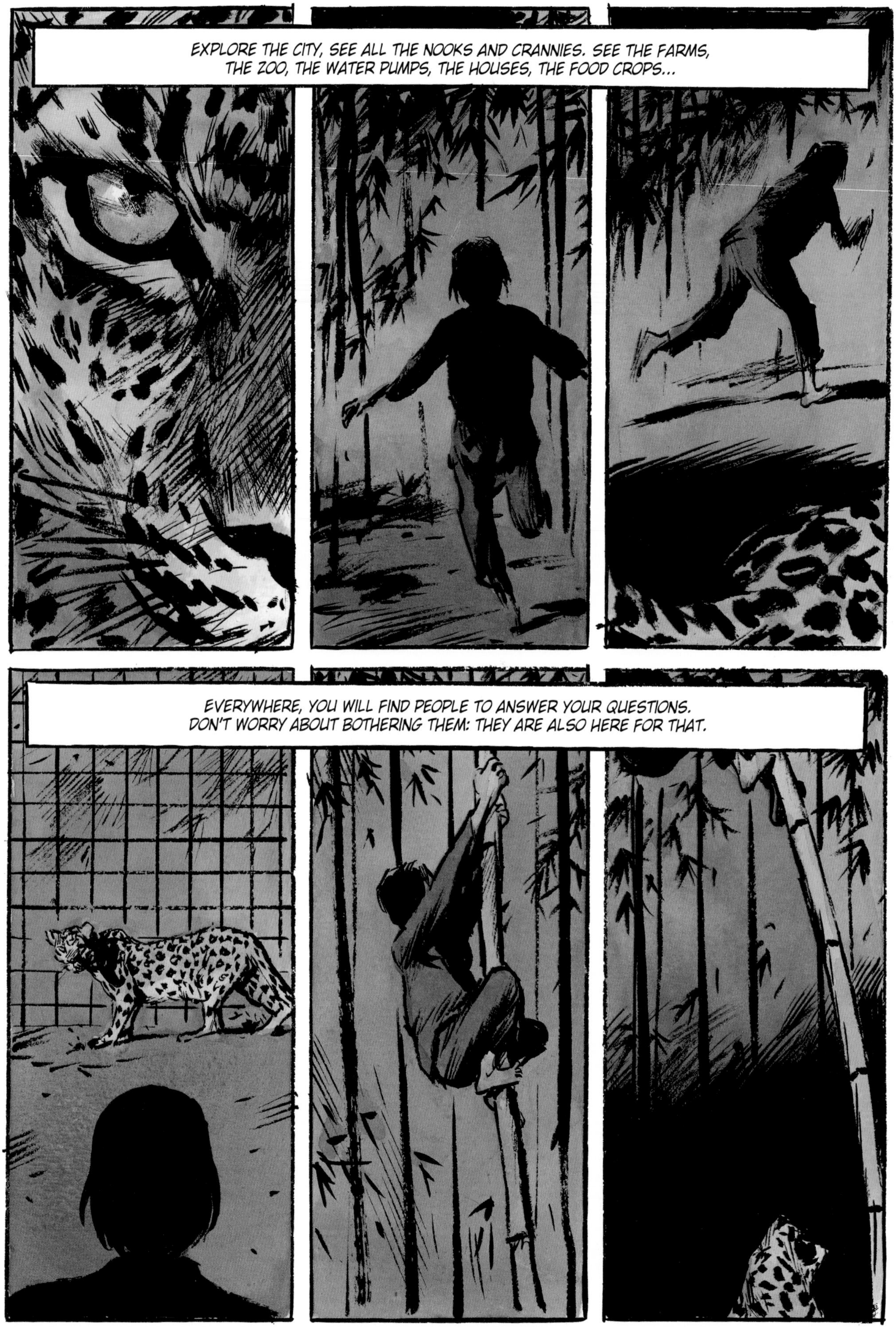
EXPLORE THE CITY, SEE ALL THE NOOKS AND CRANNIES. SEE THE FARMS, THE ZOO, THE WATER PUMPS, THE HOUSES, THE FOOD CROPS...
EVERYWHERE, YOU WILL FIND PEOPLE TO ANSWER YOUR QUESTIONS. DON'T WORRY ABOUT BOTHERING THEM: THEY ARE ALSO HERE FOR THAT.

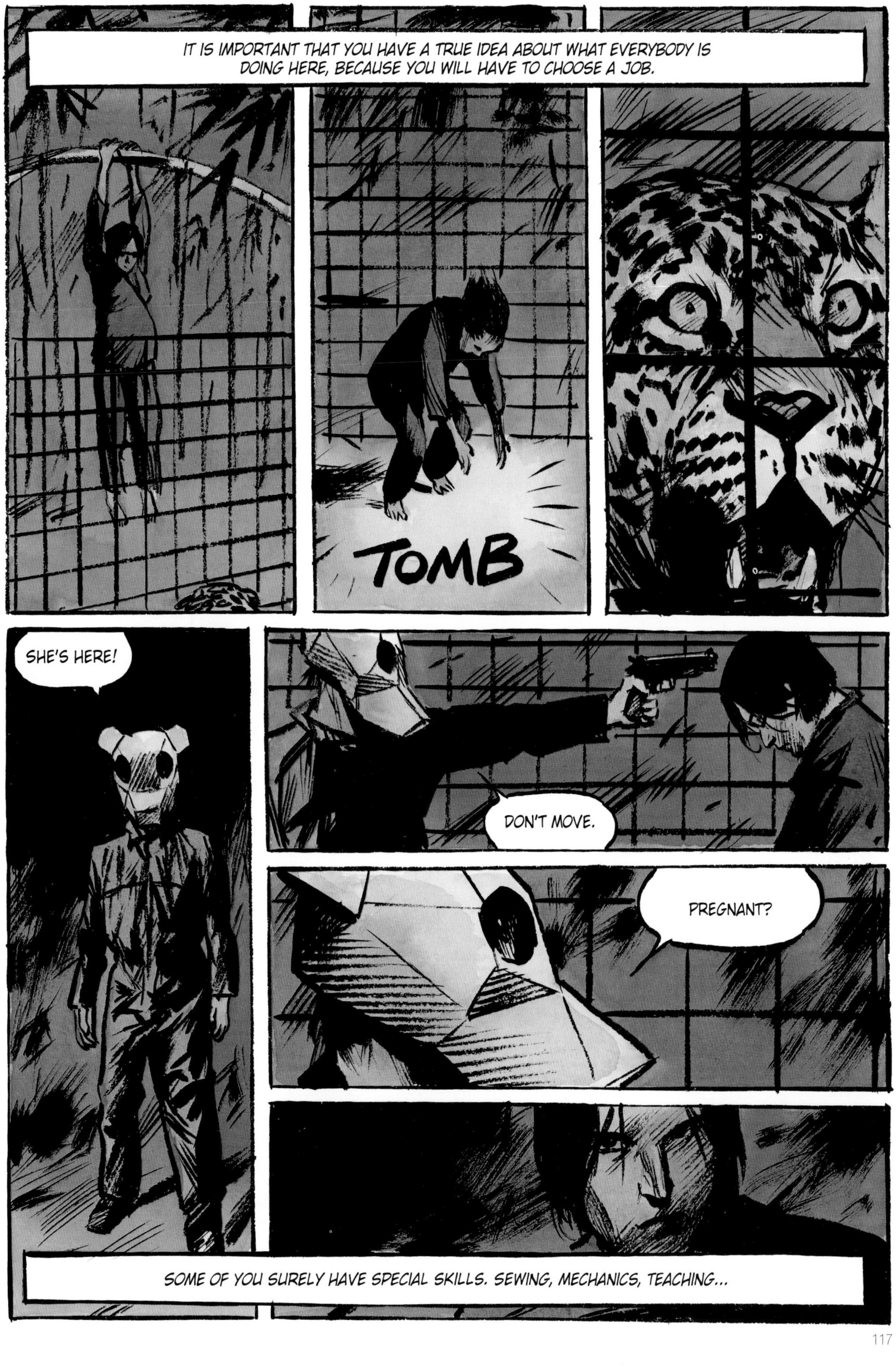
IT IS IMPORTANT THAT YOU HAVE A TRUE IDEA ABOUT WHAT EVERYBODY IS DOING HERE, BECAUSE YOU WILL HAVE TO CHOOSE A JOB.
TOMB
SHE'S HERE!
DON'T MOVE.
PREGNANT?
SOME OF YOU SURELY HAVE SPECIAL SKILLS. SEWING, MECHANICS, TEACHING...

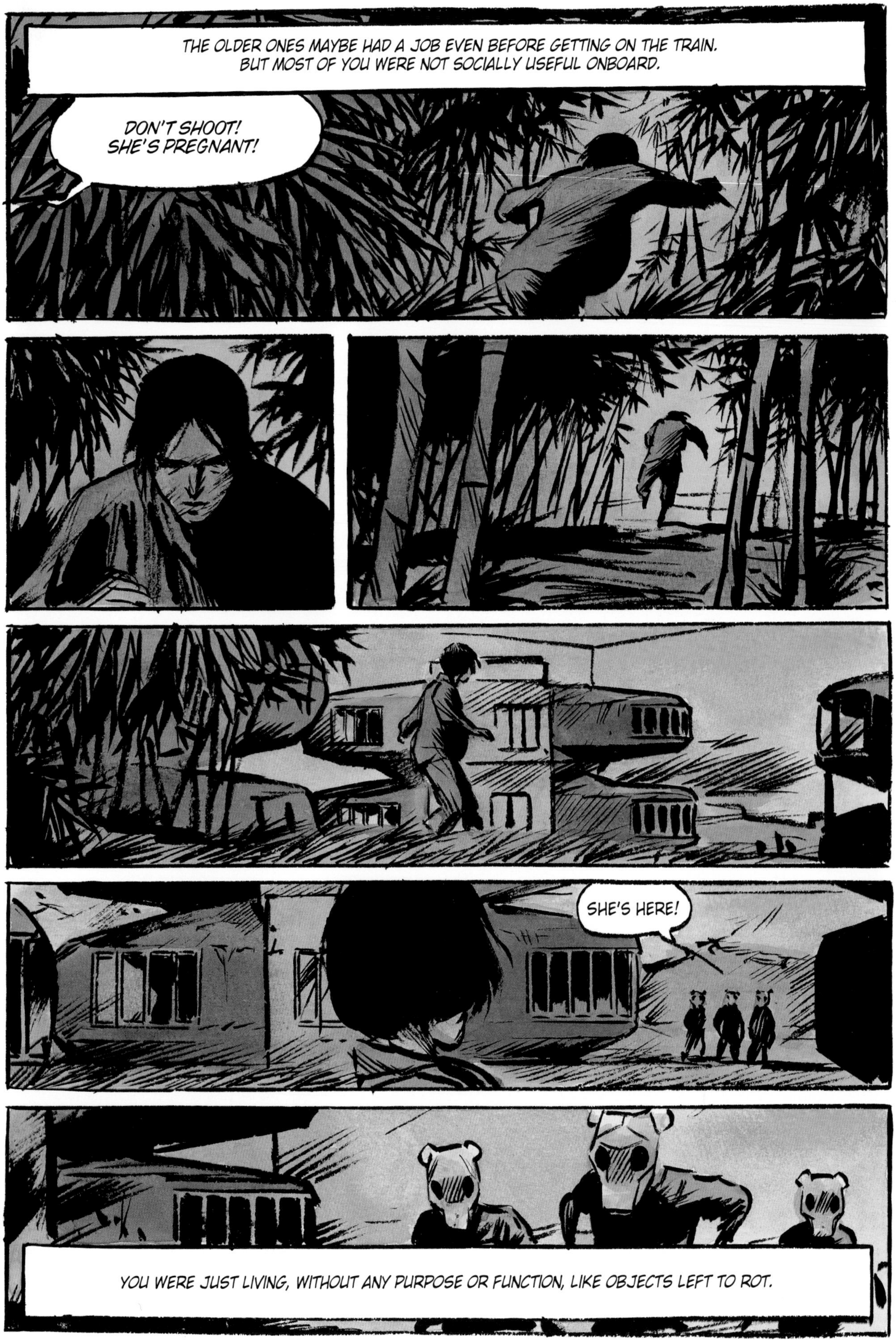
THE OLDER ONES MAYBE HAD A JOB EVEN BEFORE GETTING ON THE TRAIN. BUT MOST OF YOU WERE NOT SOCIALLY USEFUL ONBOARD.
DON'T SHOOT! SHE'S PREGNANT!
SHE'S HERE!
YOU WERE JUST LIVING, WITHOUT ANY PURPOSE OR FUNCTION, LIKE OBJECTS LEFT TO ROT.

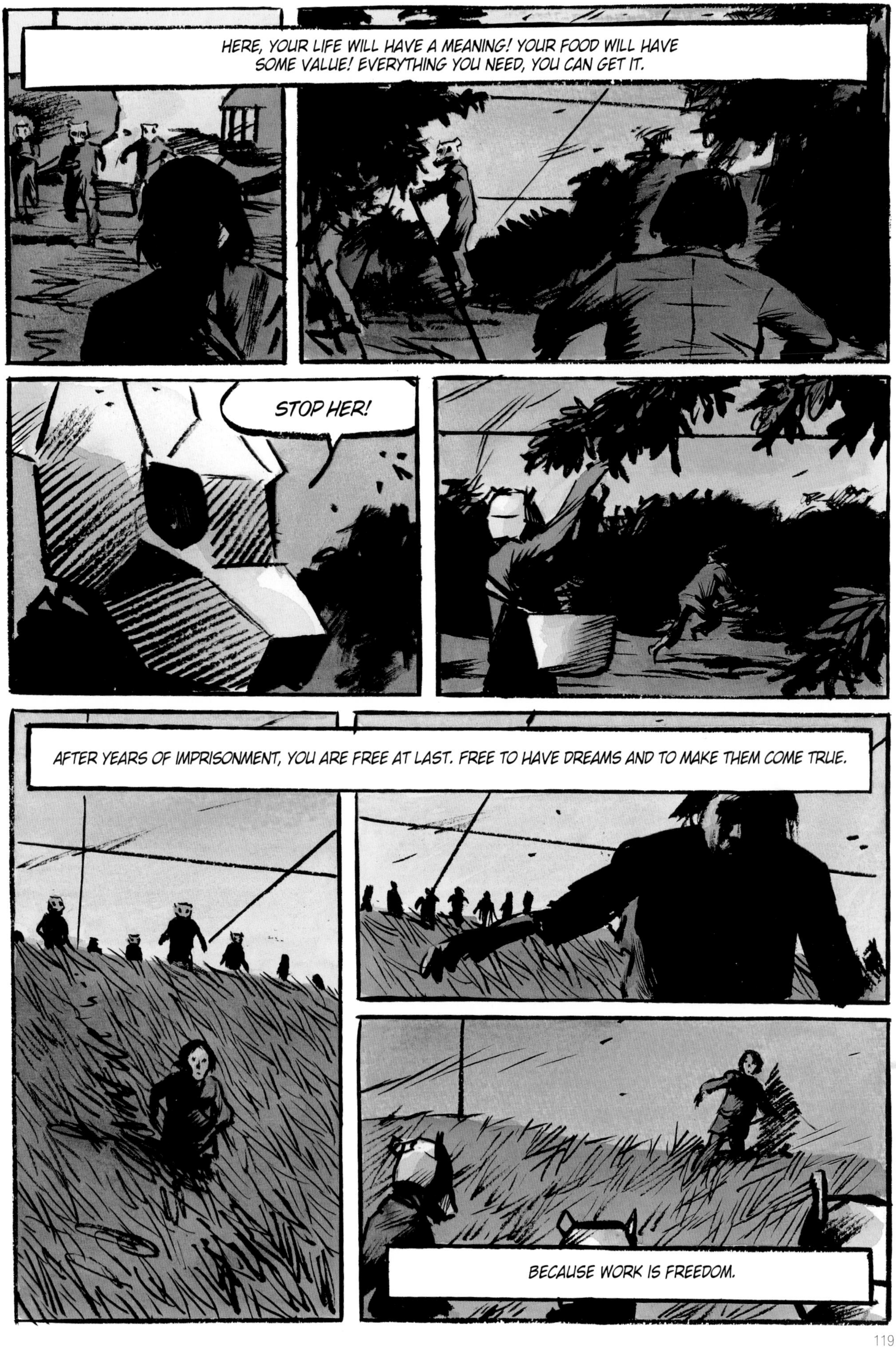
HERE, YOUR LIFE WILL HAVE A MEANING! YOUR FOOD WILL HAVE SOME VALUE! EVERYTHING YOU NEED, YOU CAN GET IT.
STOP HER!
AFTER YEARS OF IMPRISONMENT, YOU ARE FREE AT LAST. FREE TO HAVE DREAMS AND TO MAKE THEM COME TRUE.
BECAUSE WORK IS FREEDOM.

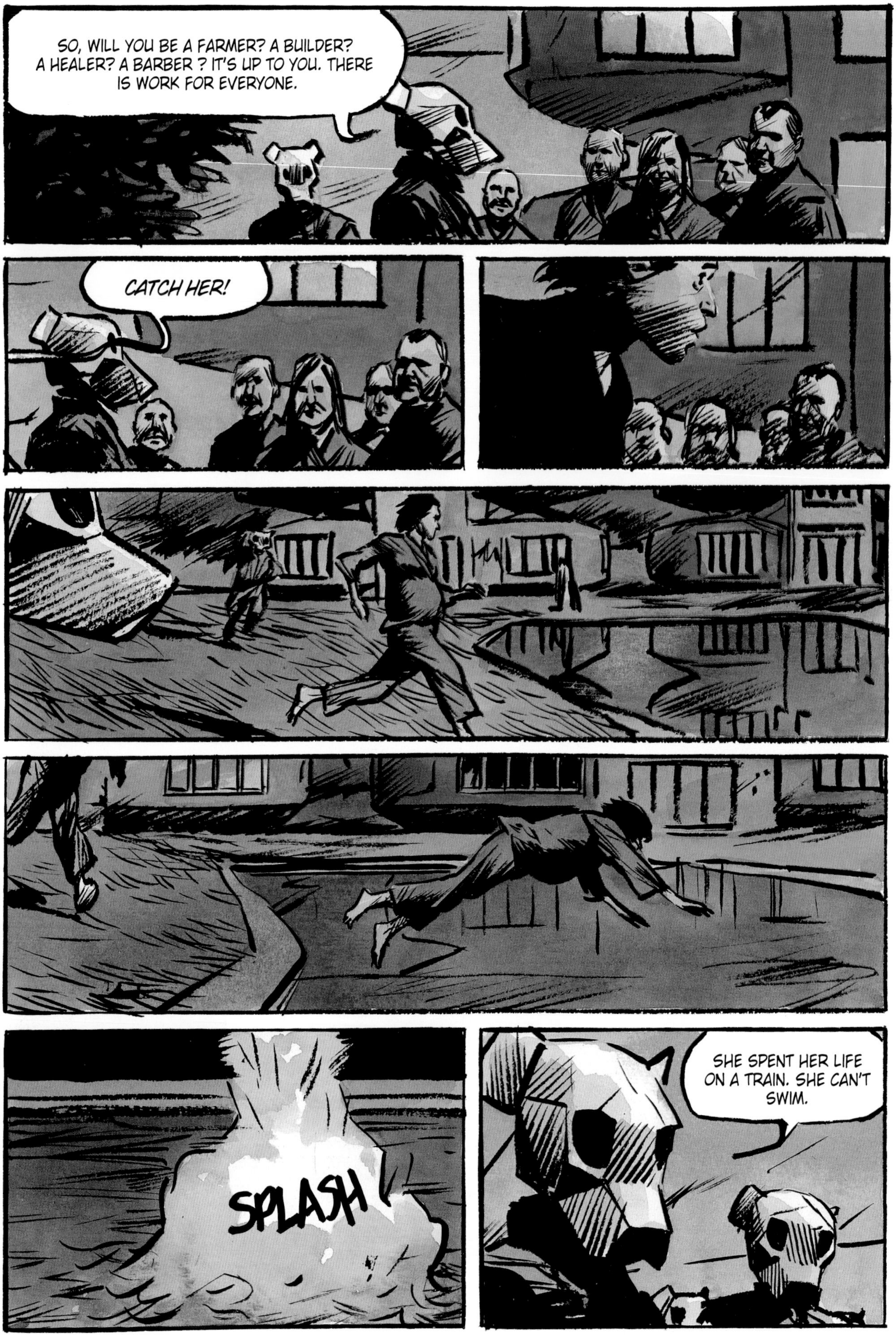
SO, WILL YOU BE A FARMER? A BUILDER? A HEALER? A BARBER ? IT'S UP TO YOU. THERE IS WORK FOR EVERYONE.
CATCH HER!
SPLASH
SHE SPENT HER LIFE ON A TRAIN. SHE CAN'T SWIM.

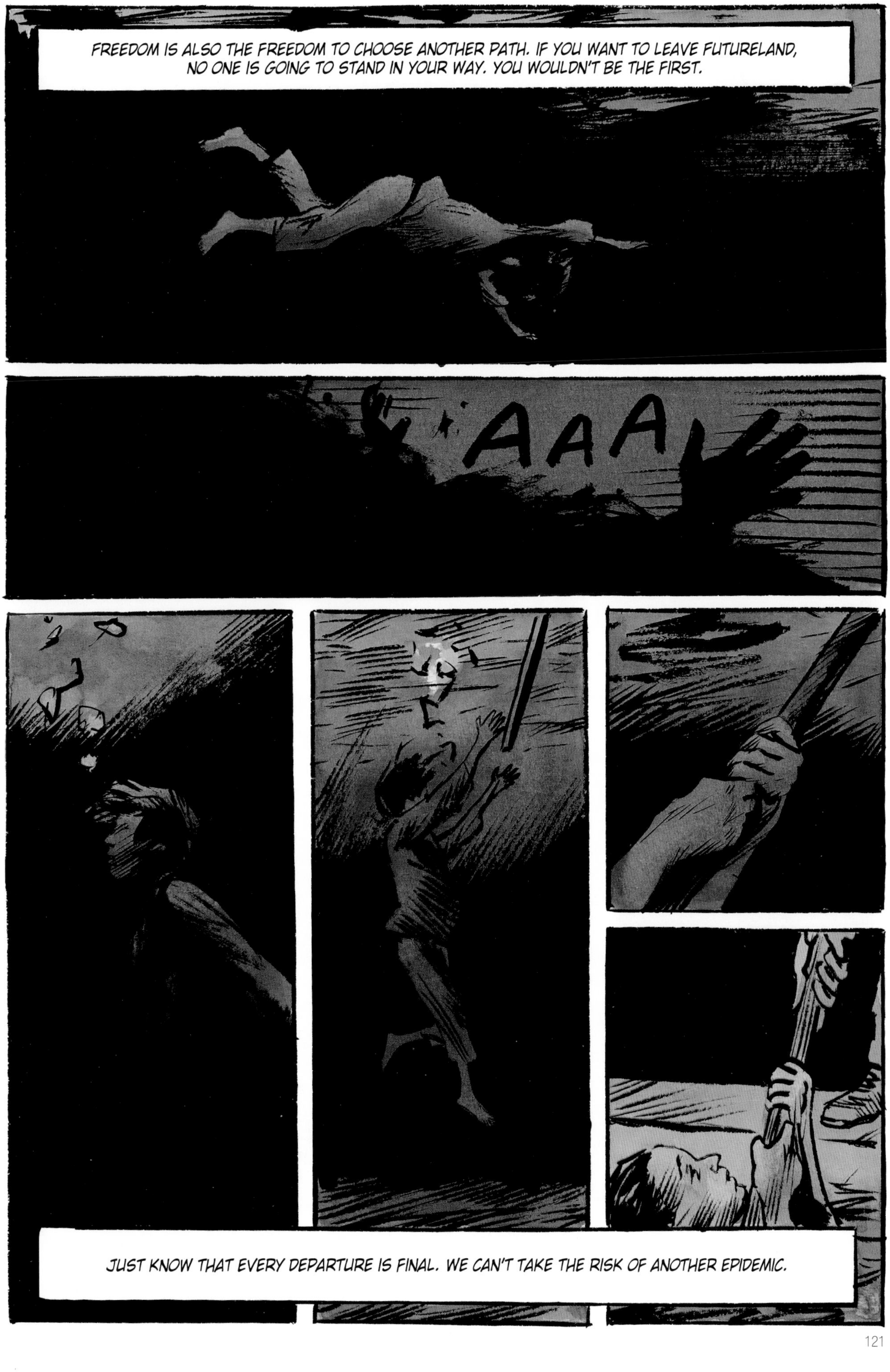
FREEDOM IS ALSO THE FREEDOM TO CHOOSE ANOTHER PATH. IF YOU WANT TO LEAVE FUTURELAND, NO ONE IS GOING TO STAND IN YOUR WAY. YOU WOULDN'T BE THE FIRST.
AAA
JUST KNOW THAT EVERY DEPARTURE IS FINAL. WE CAN'T TAKE THE RISK OF ANOTHER EPIDEMIC.

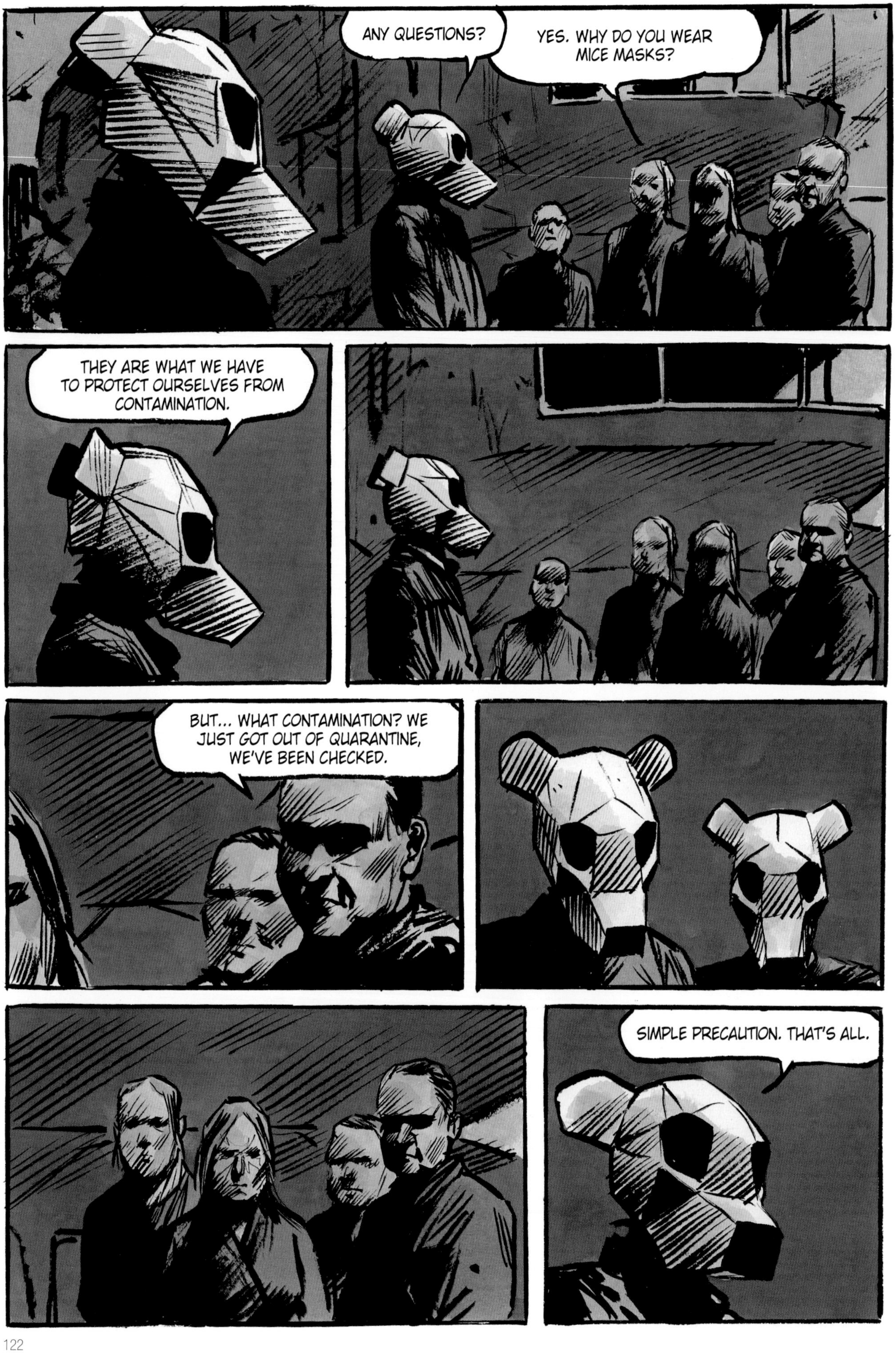
ANY QUESTIONS?
YES. WHY DO YOU WEAR MICE MASKS?
THEY ARE WHAT WE HAVE TO PROTECT OURSELVES FROM CONTAMINATION.
BUT... WHAT CONTAMINATION? WE JUST GOT OUT OF QUARANTINE, WE'VE BEEN CHECKED.
SIMPLE PRECAUTION. THAT'S ALL.

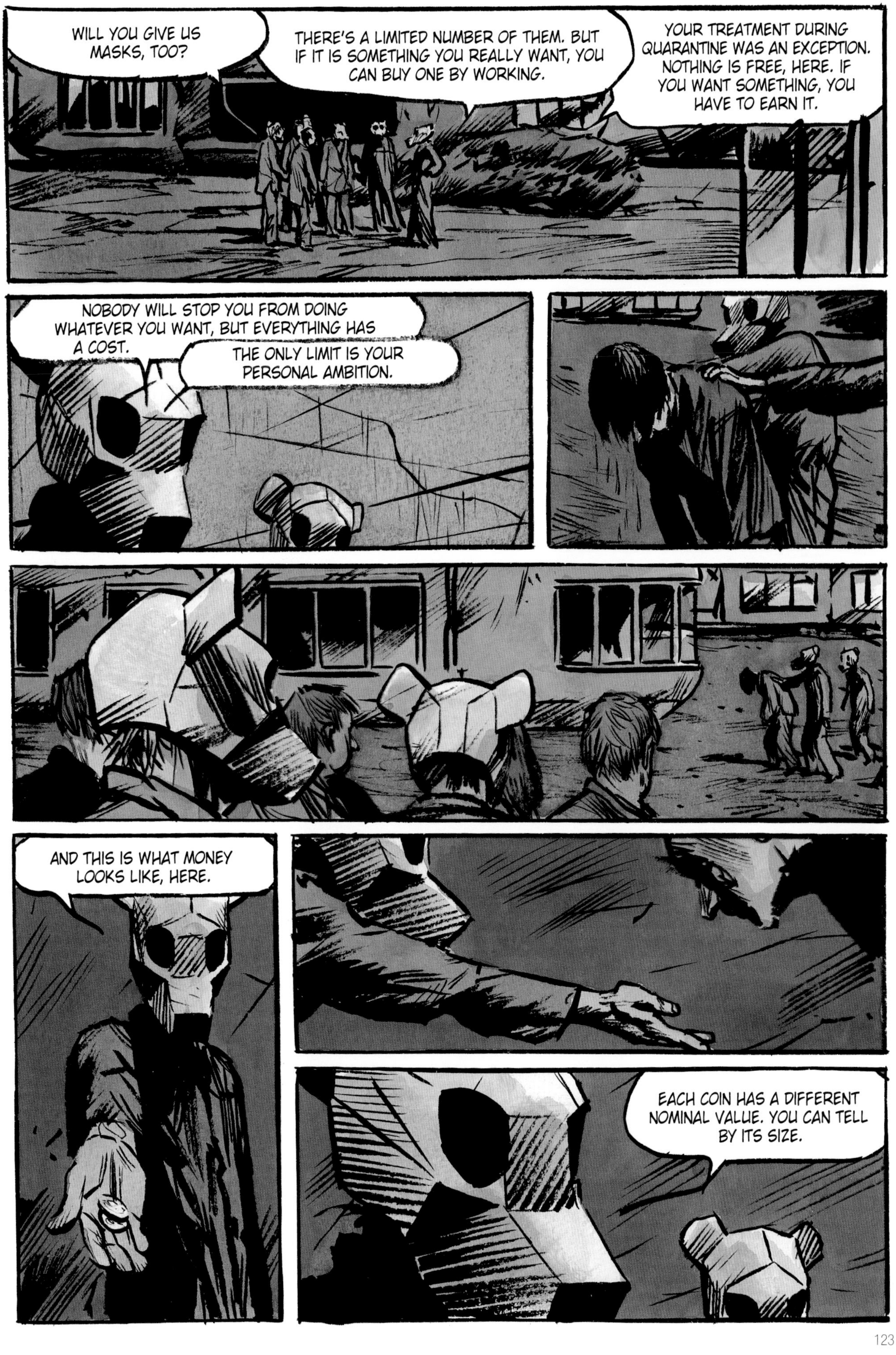
WILL YOU GIVE US MASKS, TOO?
THERE'S A LIMITED NUMBER OF THEM. BUT IF IT IS SOMETHING YOU REALLY WANT, YOU CAN BUY ONE BY WORKING.
YOUR TREATMENT DURING QUARANTINE WAS AN EXCEPTION. NOTHING IS FREE, HERE. IF YOU WANT SOMETHING, YOU HAVE TO EARN IT.
NOBODY WILL STOP YOU FROM DOING WHATEVER YOU WANT, BUT EVERYTHING HAS A COST.
THE ONLY LIMIT IS YOUR PERSONAL AMBITION.
AND THIS IS WHAT MONEY LOOKS LIKE, HERE.
EACH COIN HAS A DIFFERENT NOMINAL VALUE. YOU CAN TELL BY ITS SIZE.

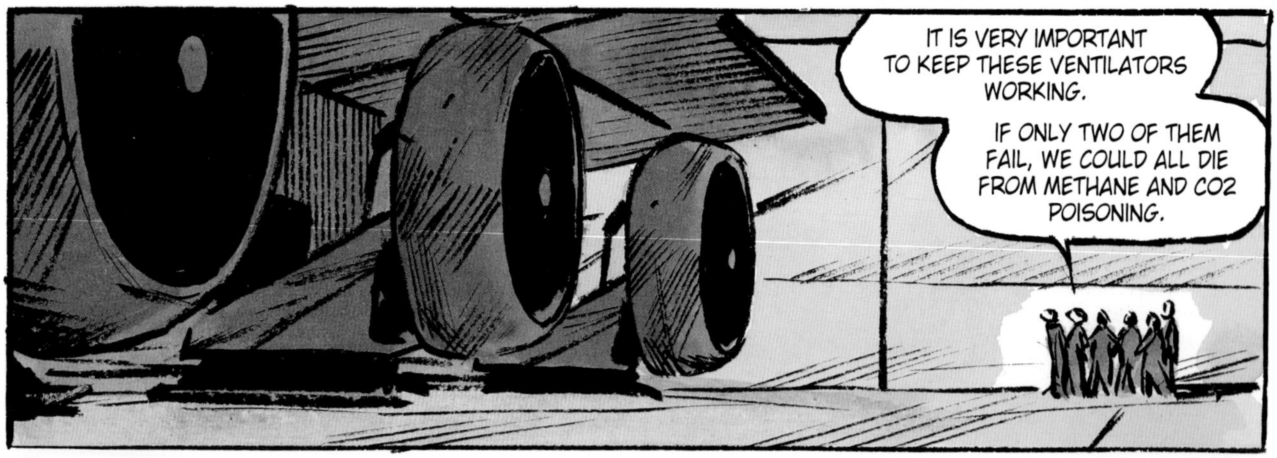

IT IS VERY IMPORTANT TO KEEP THESE VENTILATORS WORKING.
IF ONLY TWO OF THEM FAIL, WE COULD ALL DIE FROM METHANE AND CO2 POISONING.

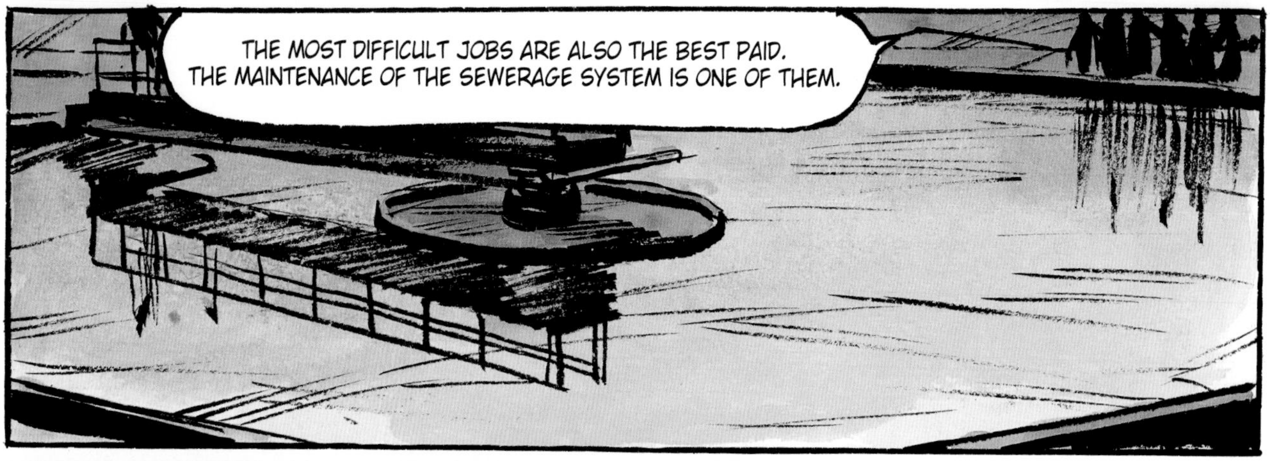

THE MOST DIFFICULT JOBS ARE ALSO THE BEST PAID. THE MAINTENANCE OF THE SEWERAGE SYSTEM IS ONE OF THEM.

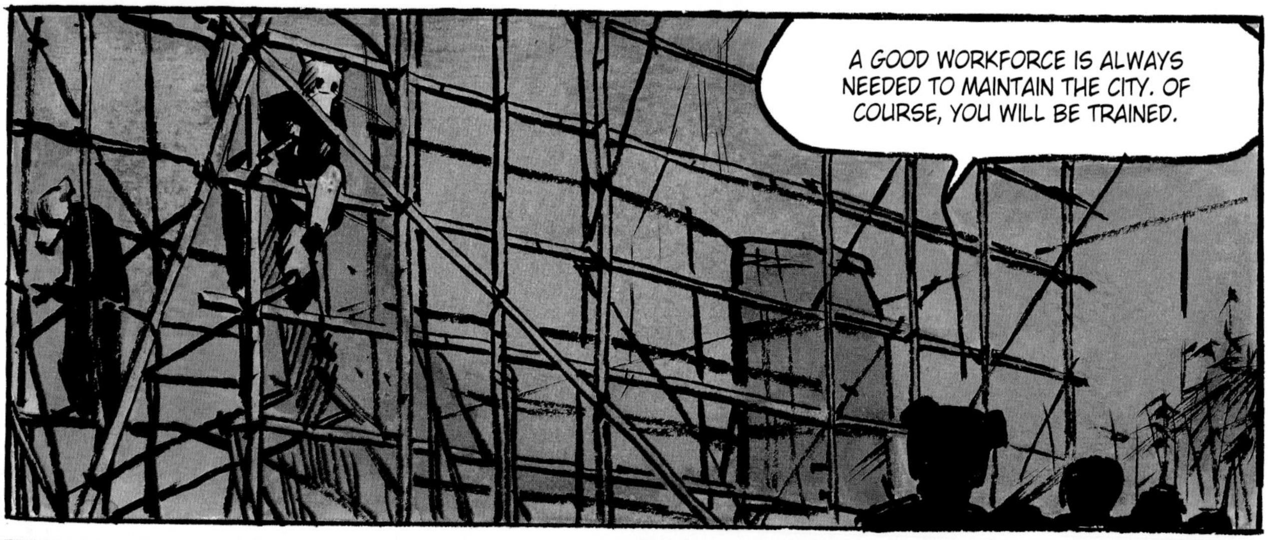

A GOOD WORKFORCE IS ALWAYS NEEDED TO MAINTAIN THE CITY. OF COURSE, YOU WILL BE TRAINED.

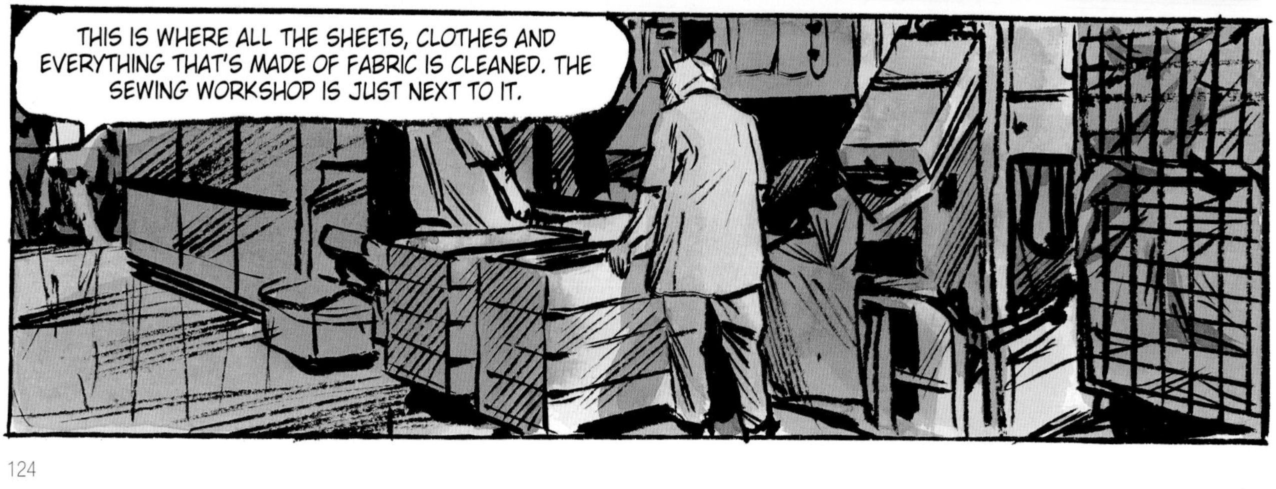

THIS IS WHERE ALL THE SHEETS, CLOTHES AND EVERYTHING THAT'S MADE OF FABRIC IS CLEANED. THE SEWING WORKSHOP IS JUST NEXT TO IT.

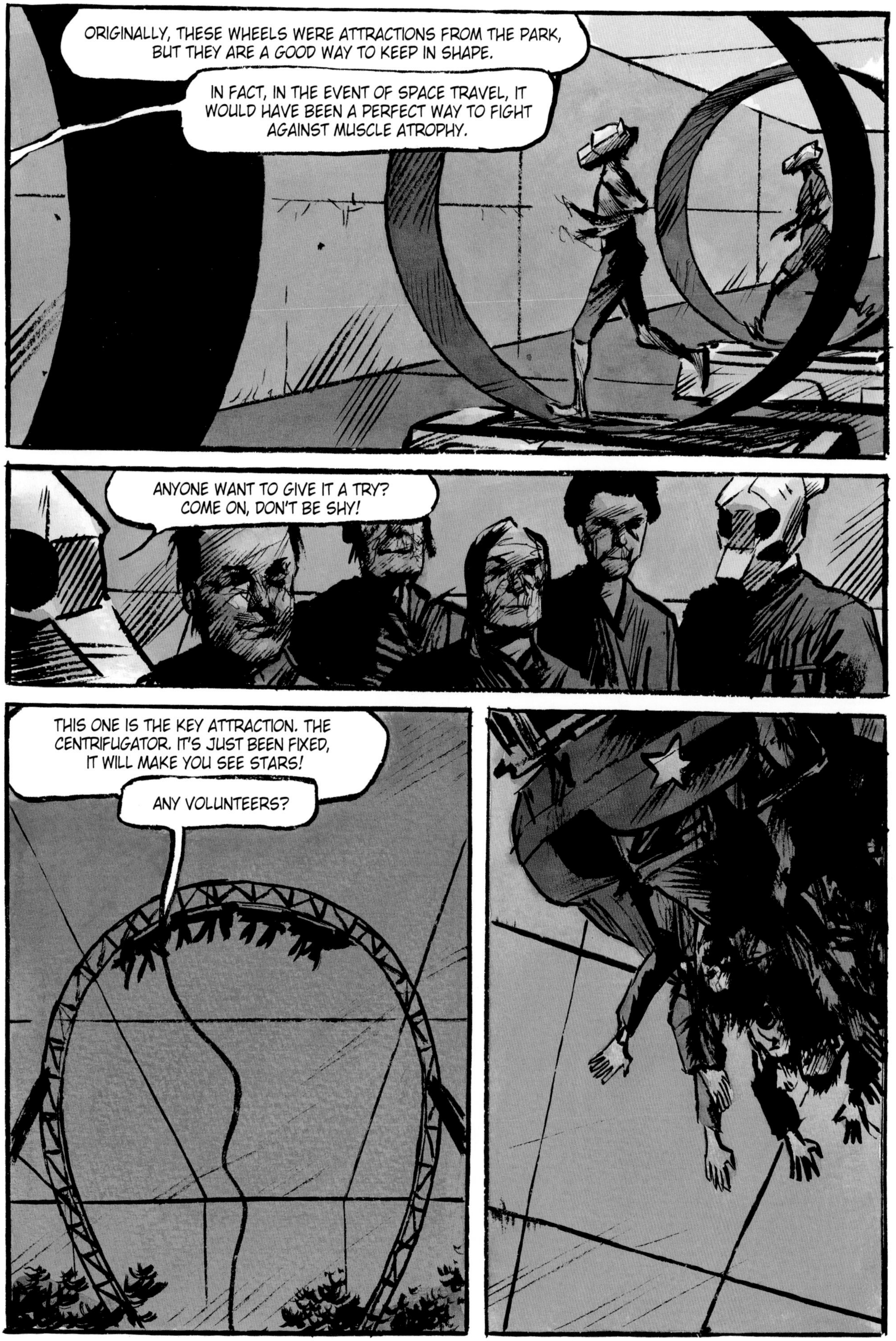
ORIGINALLY, THESE WHEELS WERE ATTRACTIONS FROM THE PARK, BUT THEY ARE A GOOD WAY TO KEEP IN SHAPE.
IN FACT, IN THE EVENT OF SPACE TRAVEL, IT WOULD HAVE BEEN A PERFECT WAY TO FIGHT AGAINST MUSCLE ATROPHY.
ANYONE WANT TO GIVE IT A TRY? COME ON, DON'T BE SHY!
THIS ONE IS THE KEY ATTRACTION. THE CENTRIFUGATOR. IT'S JUST BEEN FIXED, IT WILL MAKE YOU SEE STARS!
ANY VOLUNTEERS?

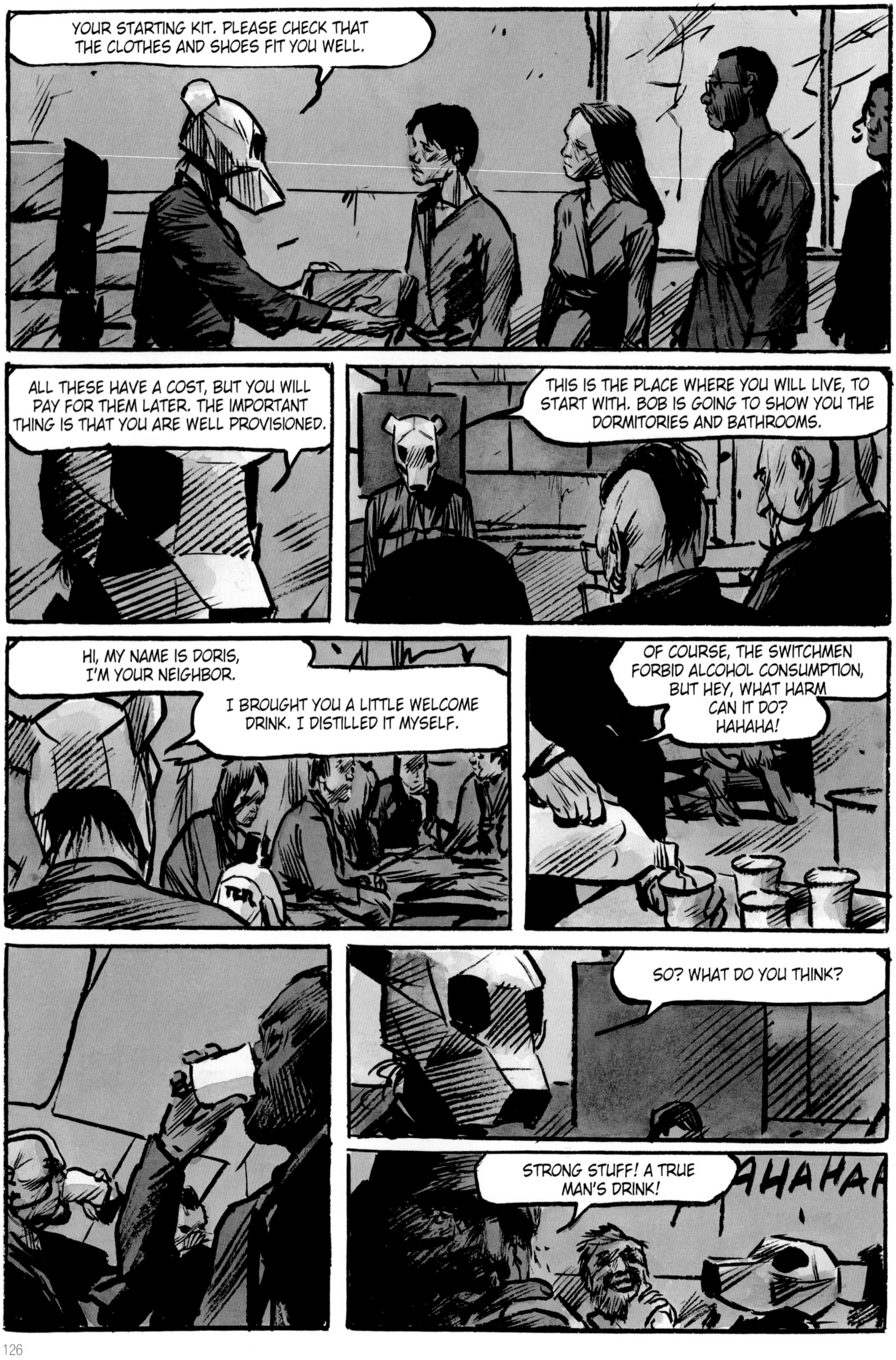
YOUR STARTING KIT. PLEASE CHECK THAT THE CLOTHES AND SHOES FIT YOU WELL.
ALL THESE HAVE A COST, BUT YOU WILL PAY FOR THEM LATER. THE IMPORTANT THING IS THAT YOU ARE WELL PROVISIONED.
THIS IS THE PLACE WHERE YOU WILL LIVE, TO START WITH. BOB IS GOING TO SHOW YOU THE DORMITORIES AND BATHROOMS.
HI, MY NAME IS DORIS, I'M YOUR NEIGHBOR.
I BROUGHT YOU A LITTLE WELCOME DRINK. I DISTILLED IT MYSELF.
OF COURSE, THE SWITCHMEN FORBID ALCOHOL CONSUMPTION, BUT HEY, WHAT HARM CAN IT DO? HAHAHA!
SO? WHAT DO YOU THINK?
STRONG STUFF! A TRUE MAN'S DRINK!
AHAHA

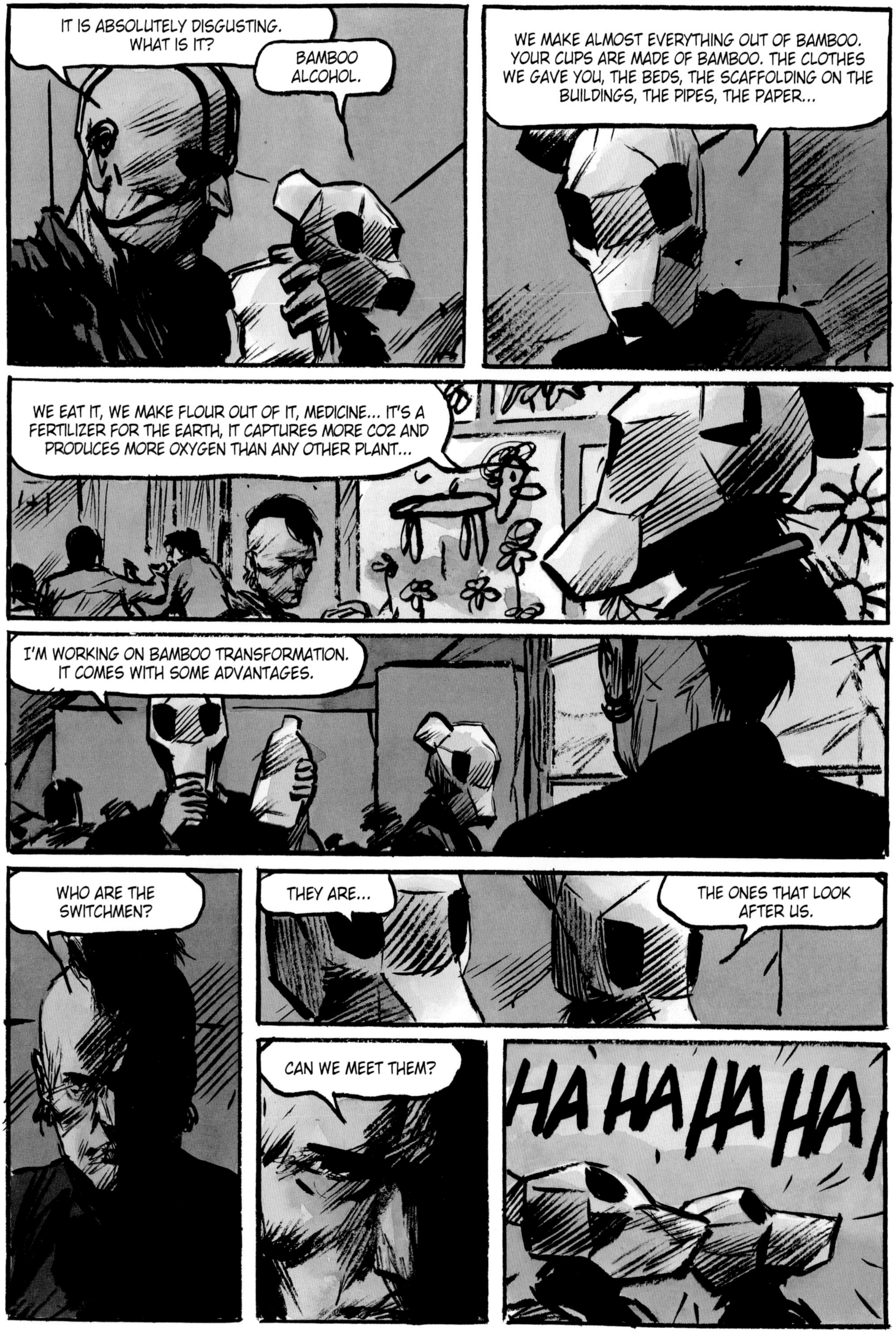
IT IS ABSOLUTELY DISGUSTING. WHAT IS IT?
BAMBOO ALCOHOL.
WE MAKE ALMOST EVERYTHING OUT OF BAMBOO. YOUR CUPS ARE MADE OF BAMBOO. THE CLOTHES WE GAVE YOU, THE BEDS, THE SCAFFOLDING ON THE BUILDINGS, THE PIPES, THE PAPER...
WE EAT IT, WE MAKE FLOUR OUT OF IT, MEDICINE... IT'S A FERTILIZER FOR THE EARTH, IT CAPTURES MORE CO2 AND PRODUCES MORE OXYGEN THAN ANY OTHER PLANT...
I'M WORKING ON BAMBOO TRANSFORMATION. IT COMES WITH SOME ADVANTAGES.
WHO ARE THE SWITCHMEN?
THEY ARE...
THE ONES THAT LOOK AFTER US.
CAN WE MEET THEM?
HA HA HA HA

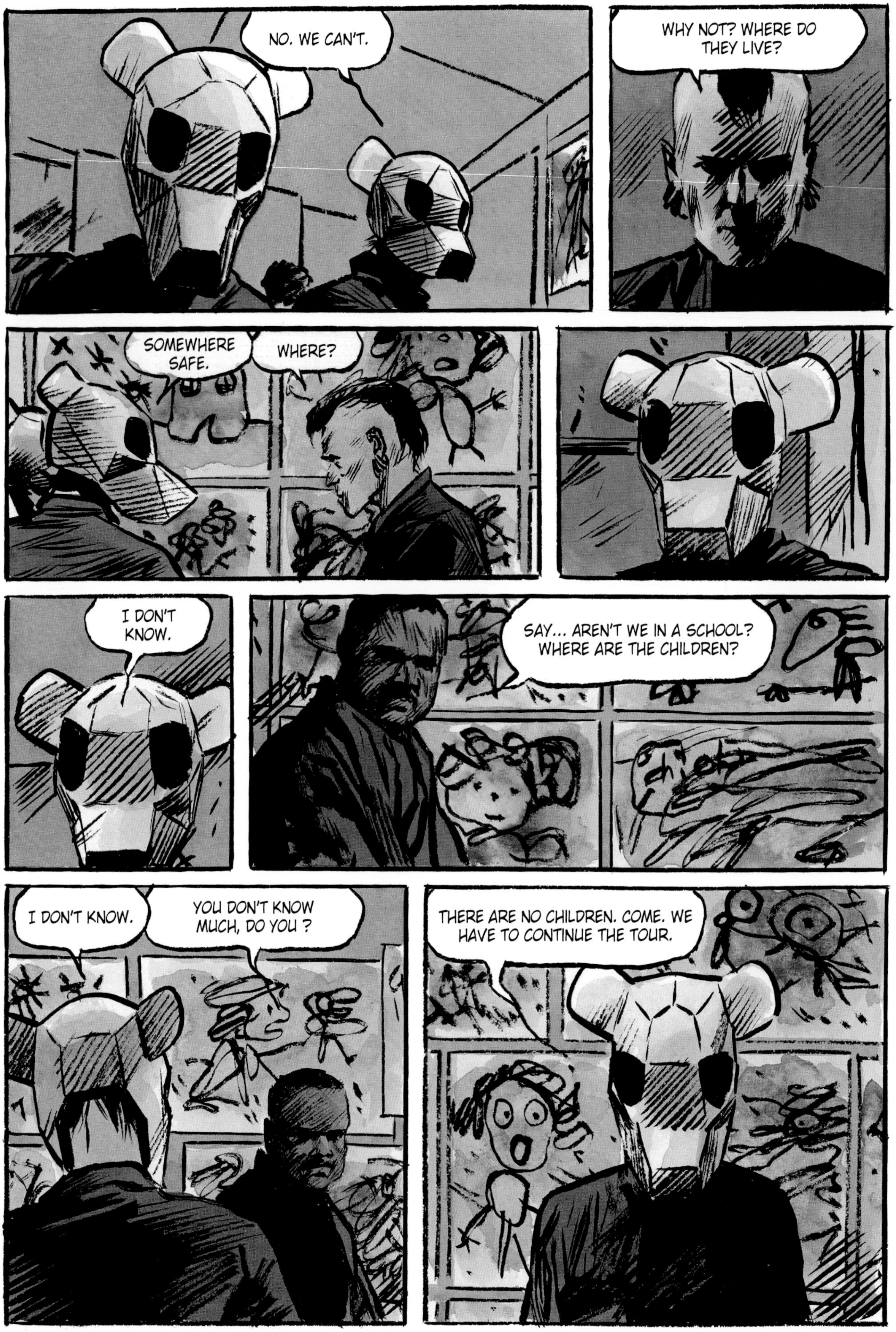
NO. WE CAN'T.
WHY NOT? WHERE DO THEY LIVE?
SOMEWHERE SAFE.
WHERE?
I DON'T KNOW.
SAY... AREN'T WE IN A SCHOOL? WHERE ARE THE CHILDREN?
I DON'T KNOW.
YOU DON'T KNOW MUCH, DO YOU ?
THERE ARE NO CHILDREN. COME. WE HAVE TO CONTINUE THE TOUR.

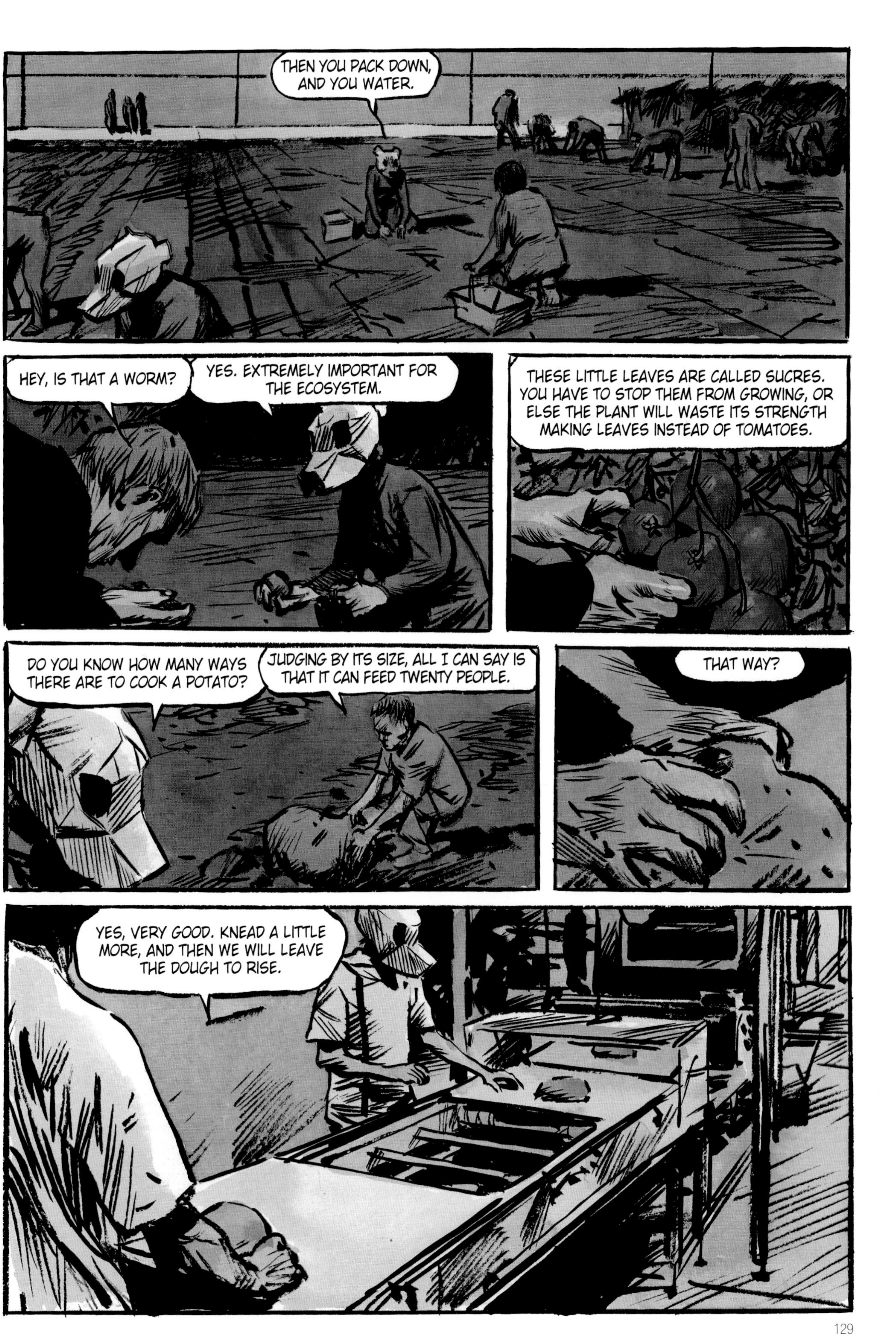
THEN YOU PACK DOWN, AND YOU WATER.
HEY, IS THAT A WORM?
YES. EXTREMELY IMPORTANT FOR THE ECOSYSTEM.
THESE LITTLE LEAVES ARE CALLED SUCRES. YOU HAVE TO STOP THEM FROM GROWING, OR ELSE THE PLANT WILL WASTE ITS STRENGTH MAKING LEAVES INSTEAD OF TOMATOES.
DO YOU KNOW HOW MANY WAYS THERE ARE TO COOK A POTATO?
JUDGING BY ITS SIZE, ALL I CAN SAY IS THAT IT CAN FEED TWENTY PEOPLE.
THAT WAY?
YES, VERY GOOD. KNEAD A LITTLE MORE, AND THEN WE WILL LEAVE THE DOUGH TO RISE.

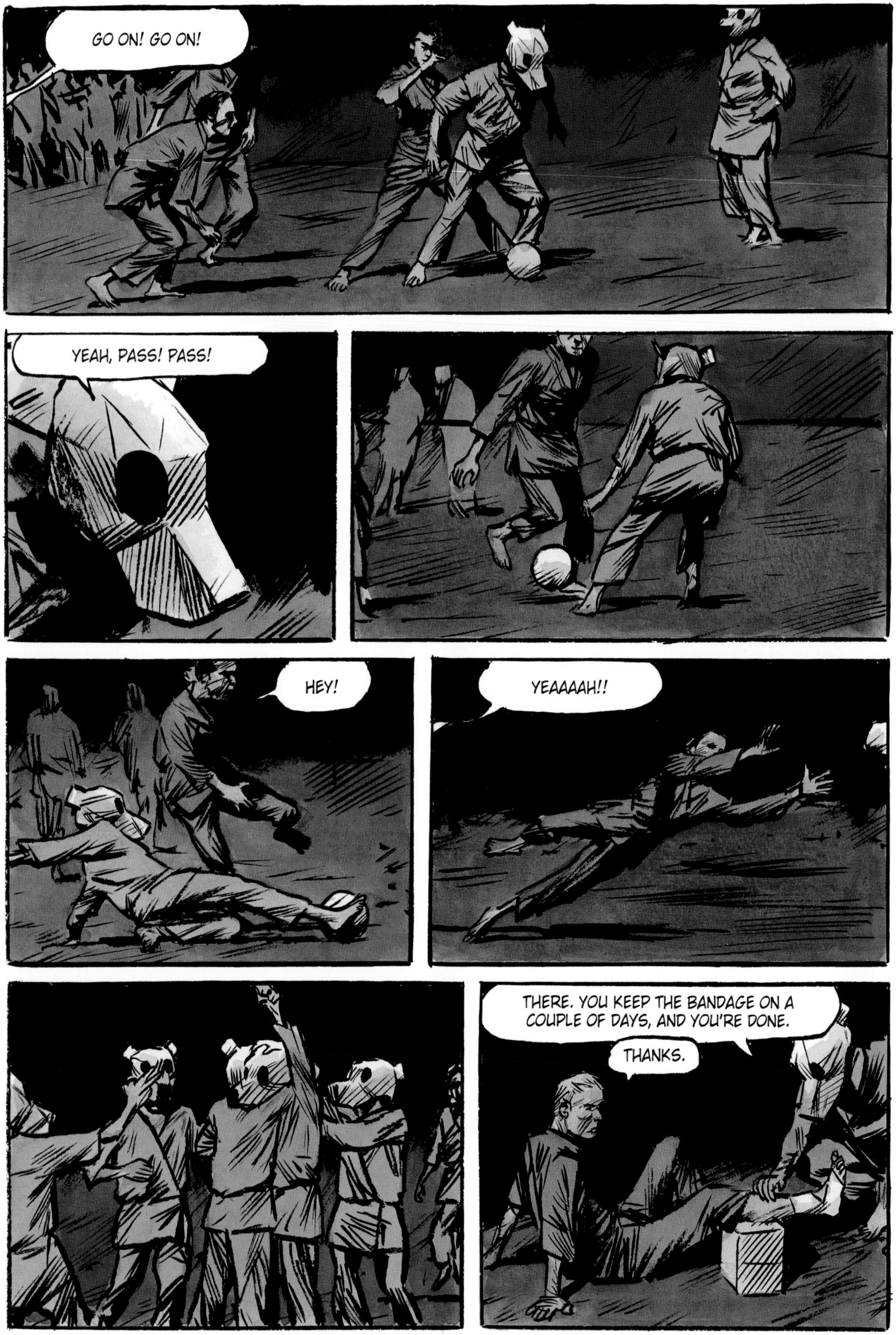
GO ON! GO ON!
YEAH, PASS! PASS!
HEY!
YEAAAAH!!
THERE. YOU KEEP THE BANDAGE ON A COUPLE OF DAYS, AND YOU'RE DONE.
THANKS.

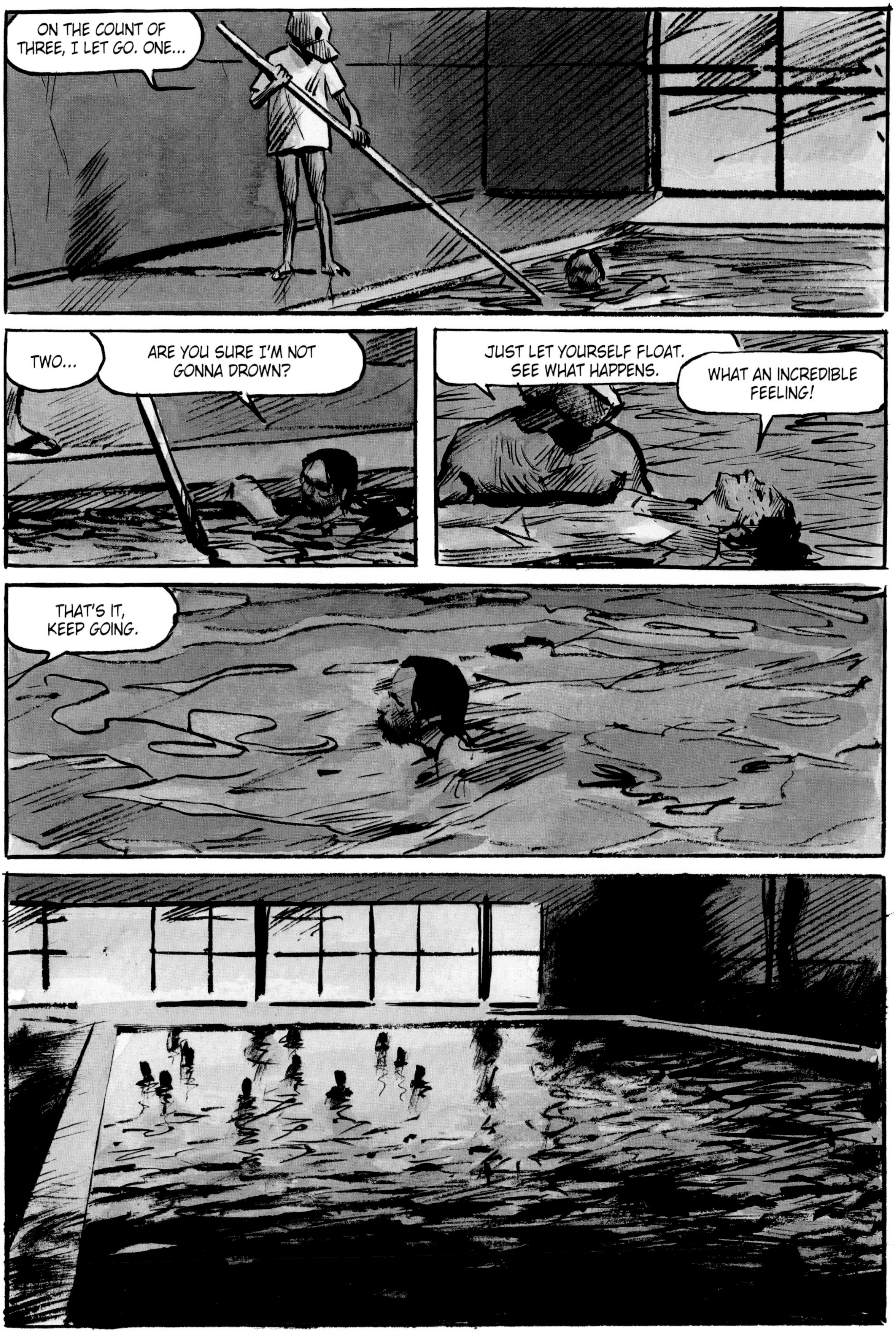
ON THE COUNT OF THREE, I LET GO. ONE...
TWO...
ARE YOU SURE I'M NOT GONNA DROWN?
JUST LET YOURSELF FLOAT. SEE WHAT HAPPENS.
WHAT AN INCREDIBLE FEELING!
THAT'S IT, KEEP GOING.

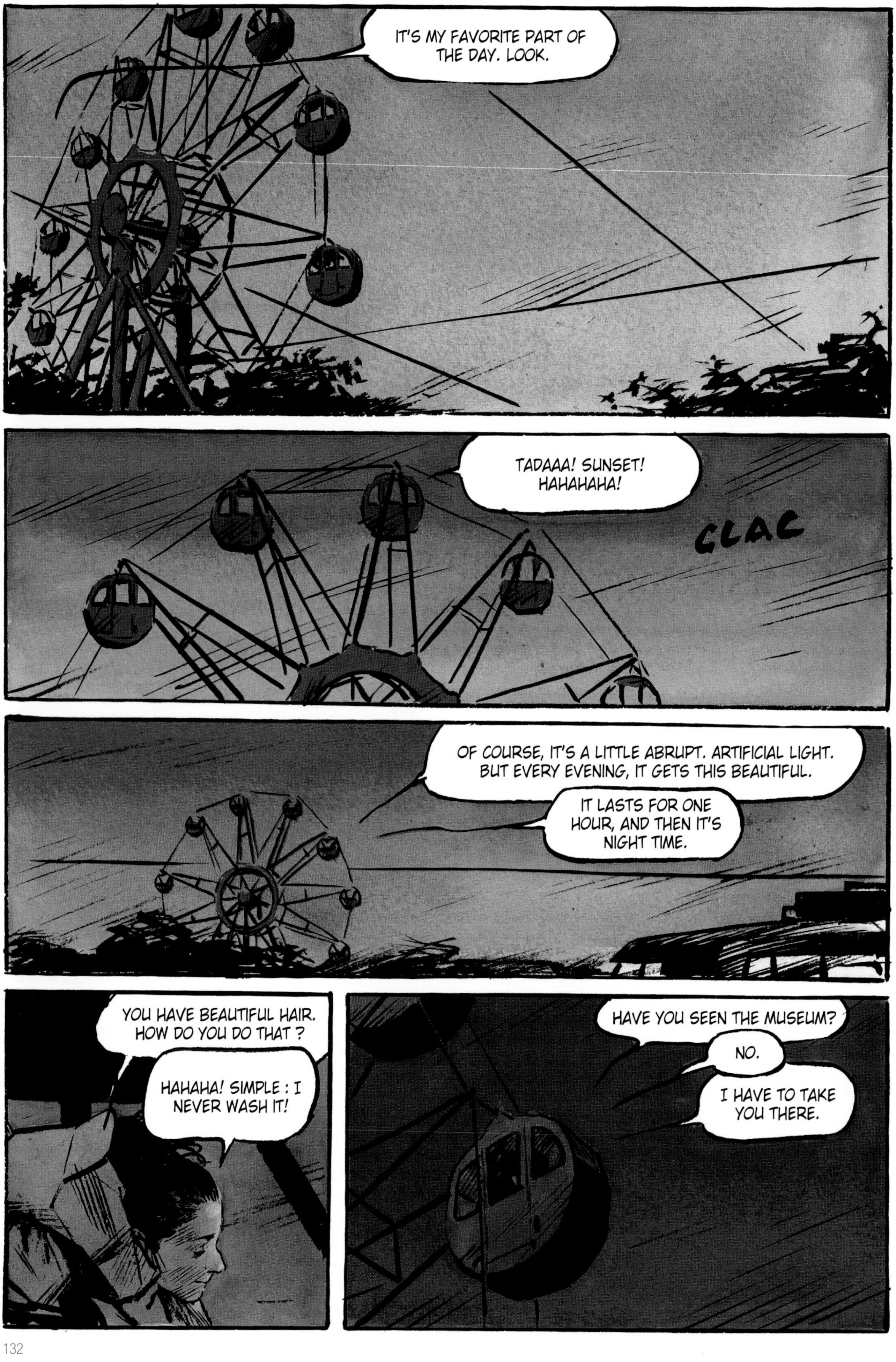
IT'S MY FAVORITE PART OF THE DAY. LOOK.
TADAAA! SUNSET! HAHAHAHA!
CLAC
OF COURSE, IT'S A LITTLE ABRUPT. ARTIFICIAL LIGHT. BUT EVERY EVENING, IT GETS THIS BEAUTIFUL.
IT LASTS FOR ONE HOUR, AND THEN IT'S NIGHT TIME.
YOU HAVE BEAUTIFUL HAIR. HOW DO YOU DO THAT ?
HAHAHA! SIMPLE : I NEVER WASH IT!
HAVE YOU SEEN THE MUSEUM?
NO.
I HAVE TO TAKE YOU THERE.

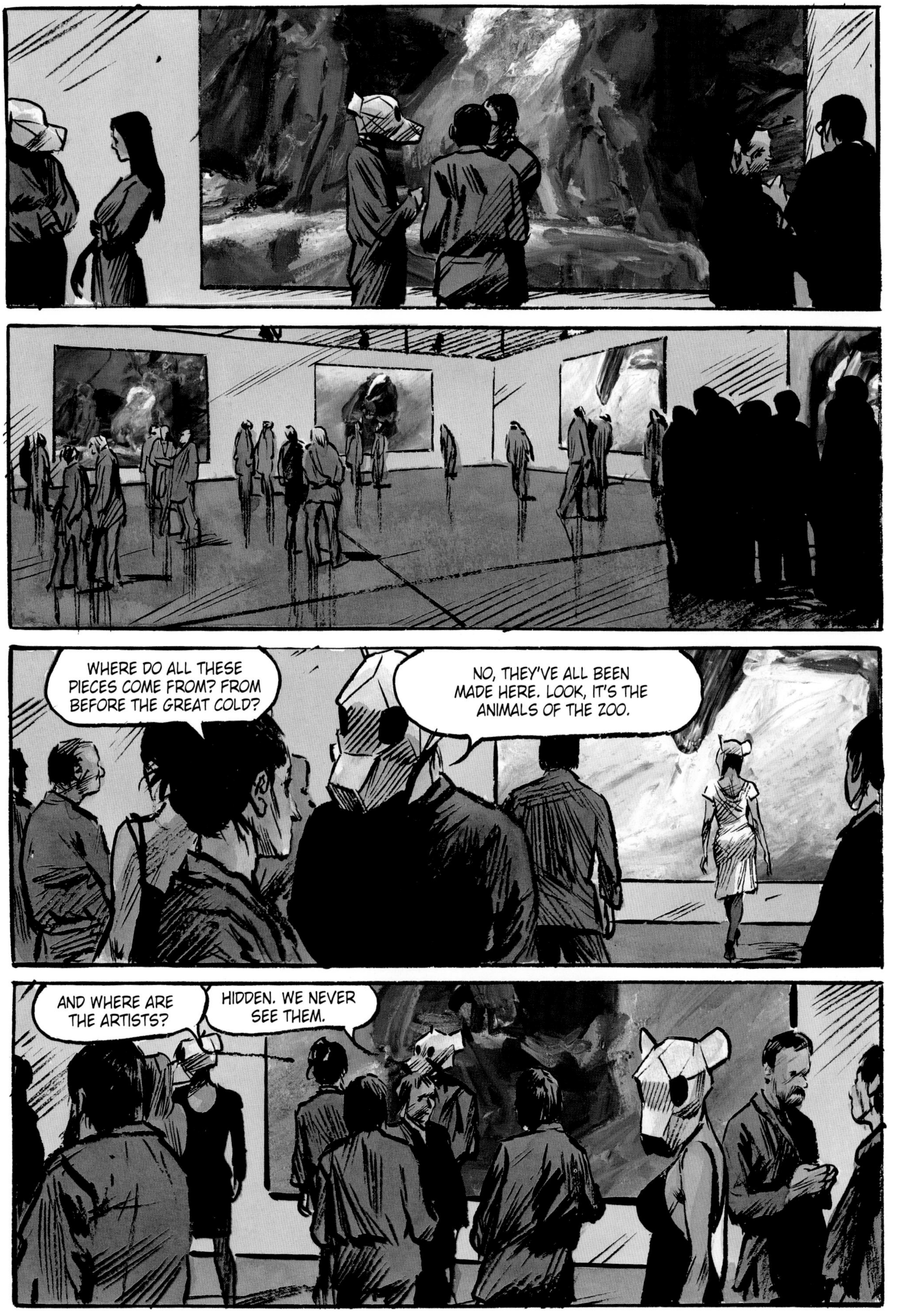
WHERE DO ALL THESE PIECES COME FROM? FROM BEFORE THE GREAT COLD?
NO, THEY'VE ALL BEEN MADE HERE. LOOK, IT'S THE ANIMALS OF THE ZOO.
AND WHERE ARE THE ARTISTS?
HIDDEN. WE NEVER SEE THEM.

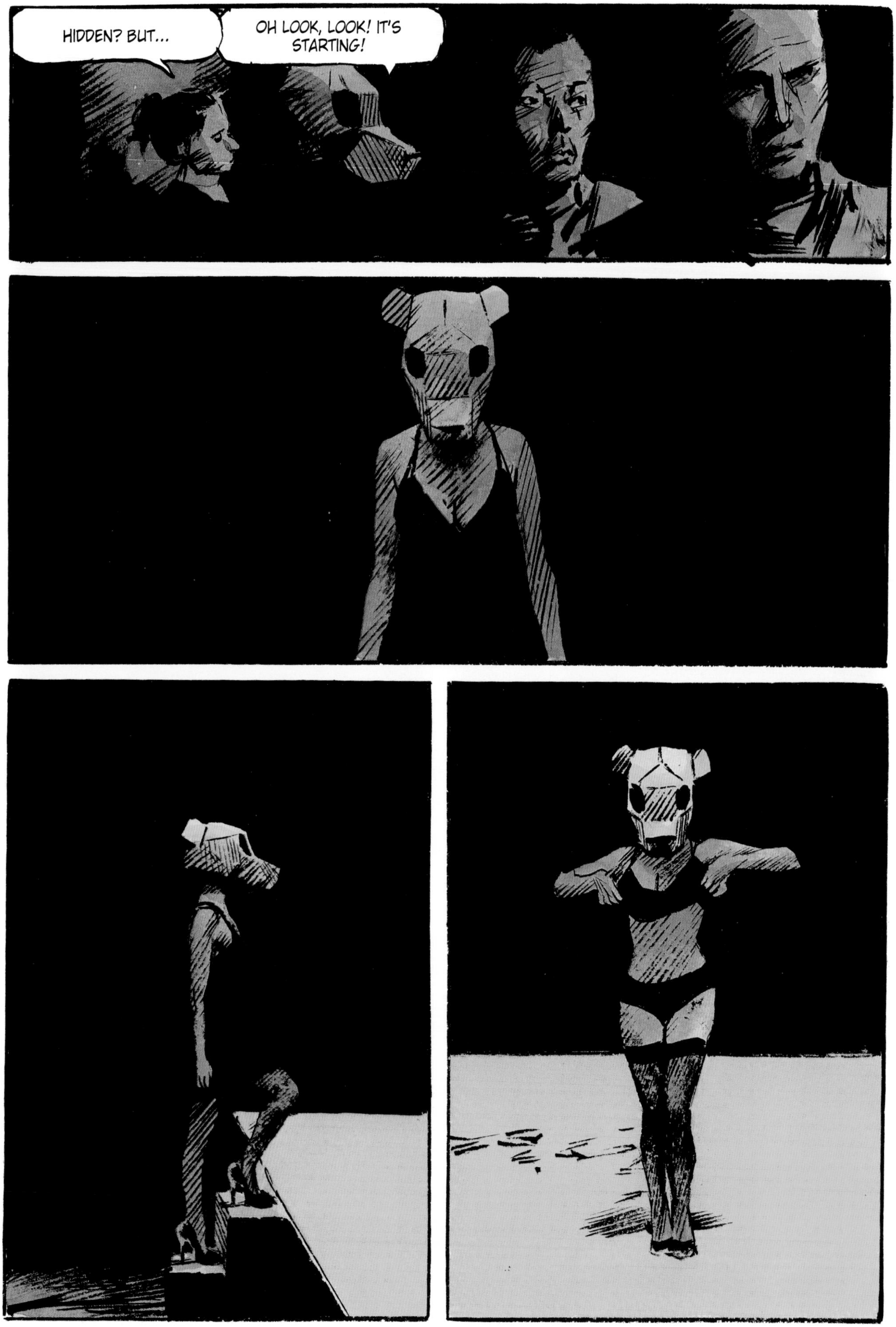
HIDDEN? BUT...
OH LOOK, LOOK! IT'S STARTING!

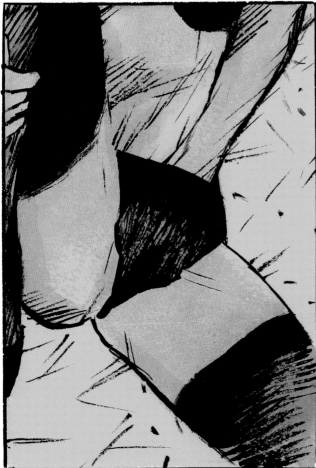

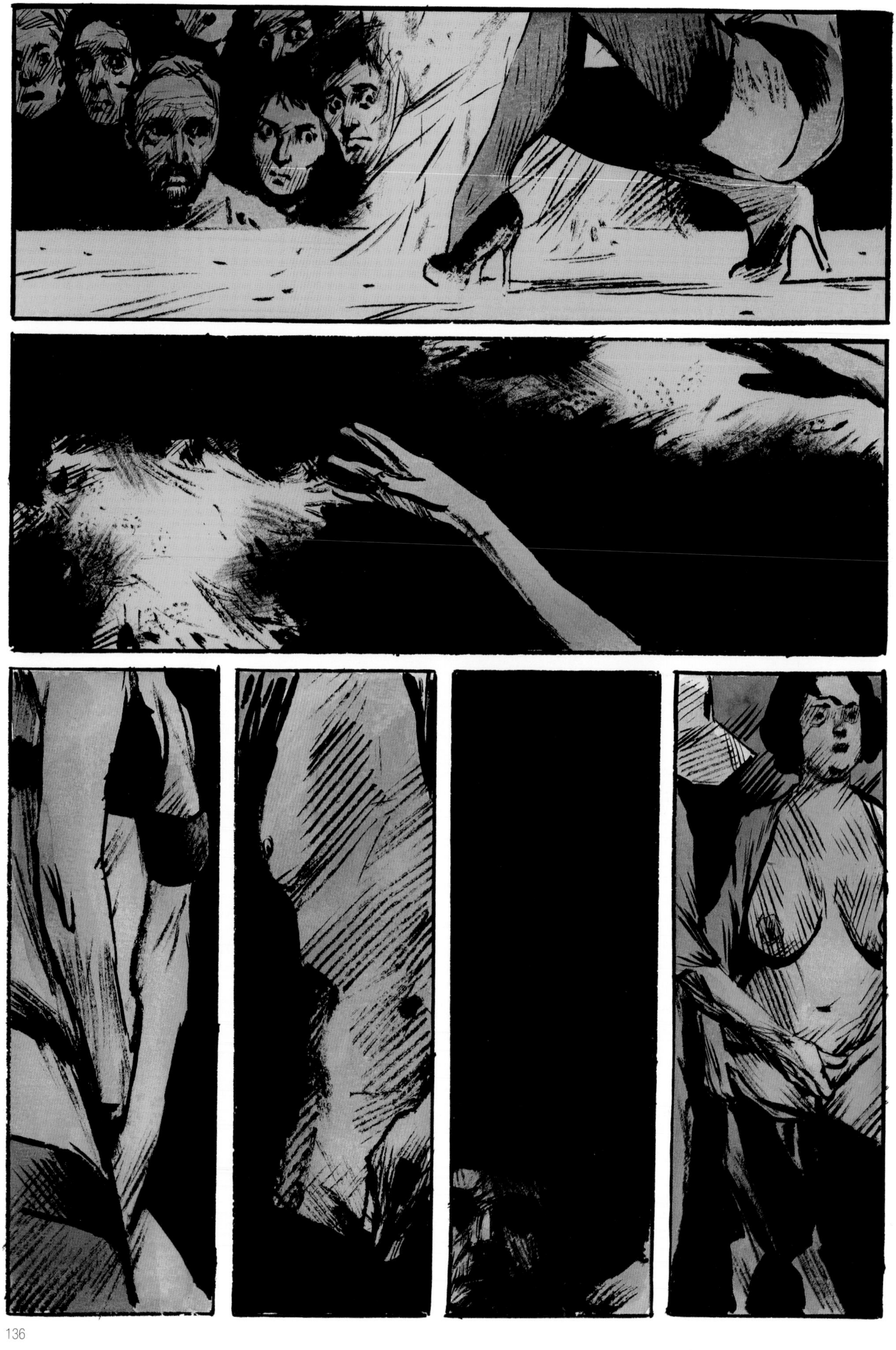

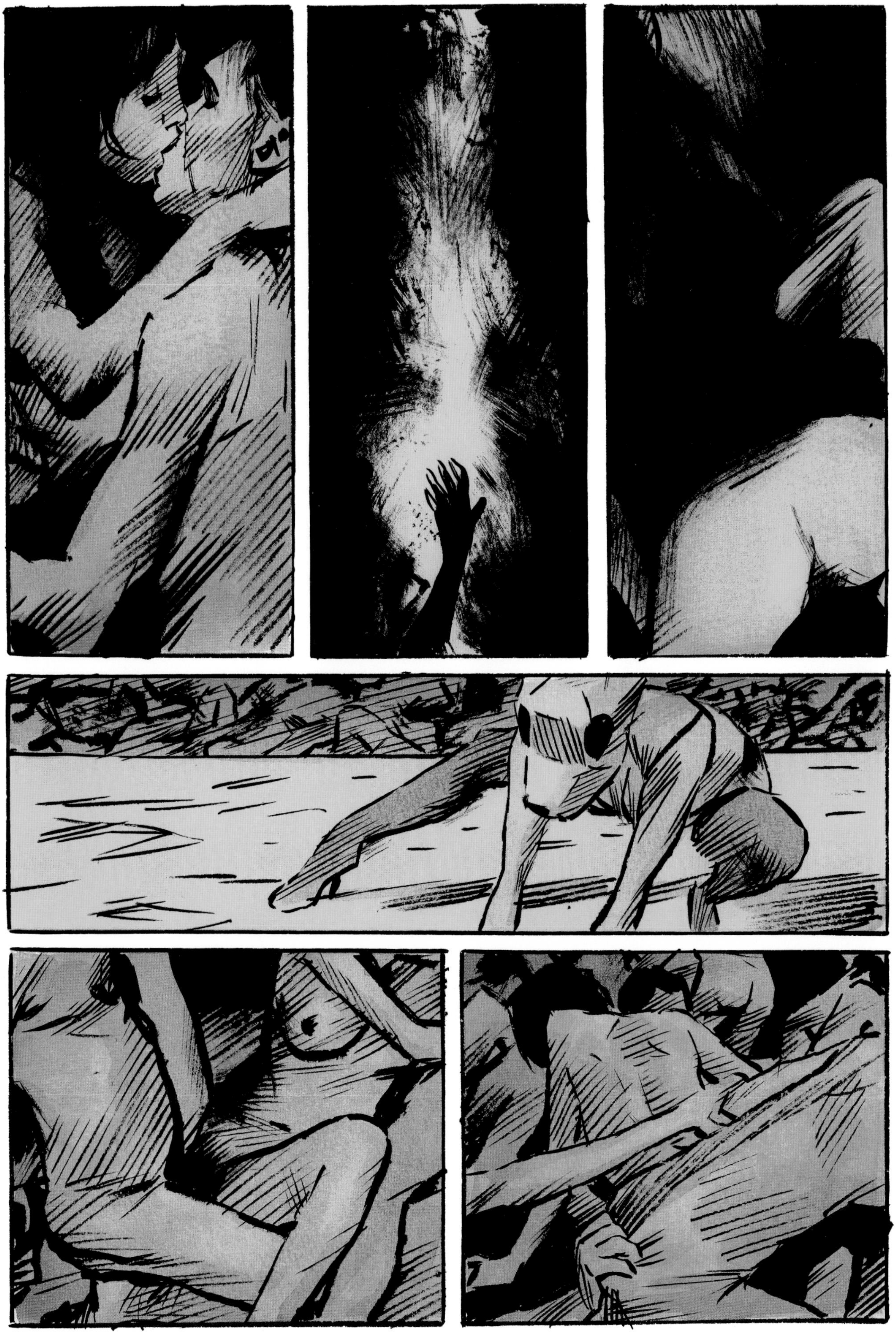

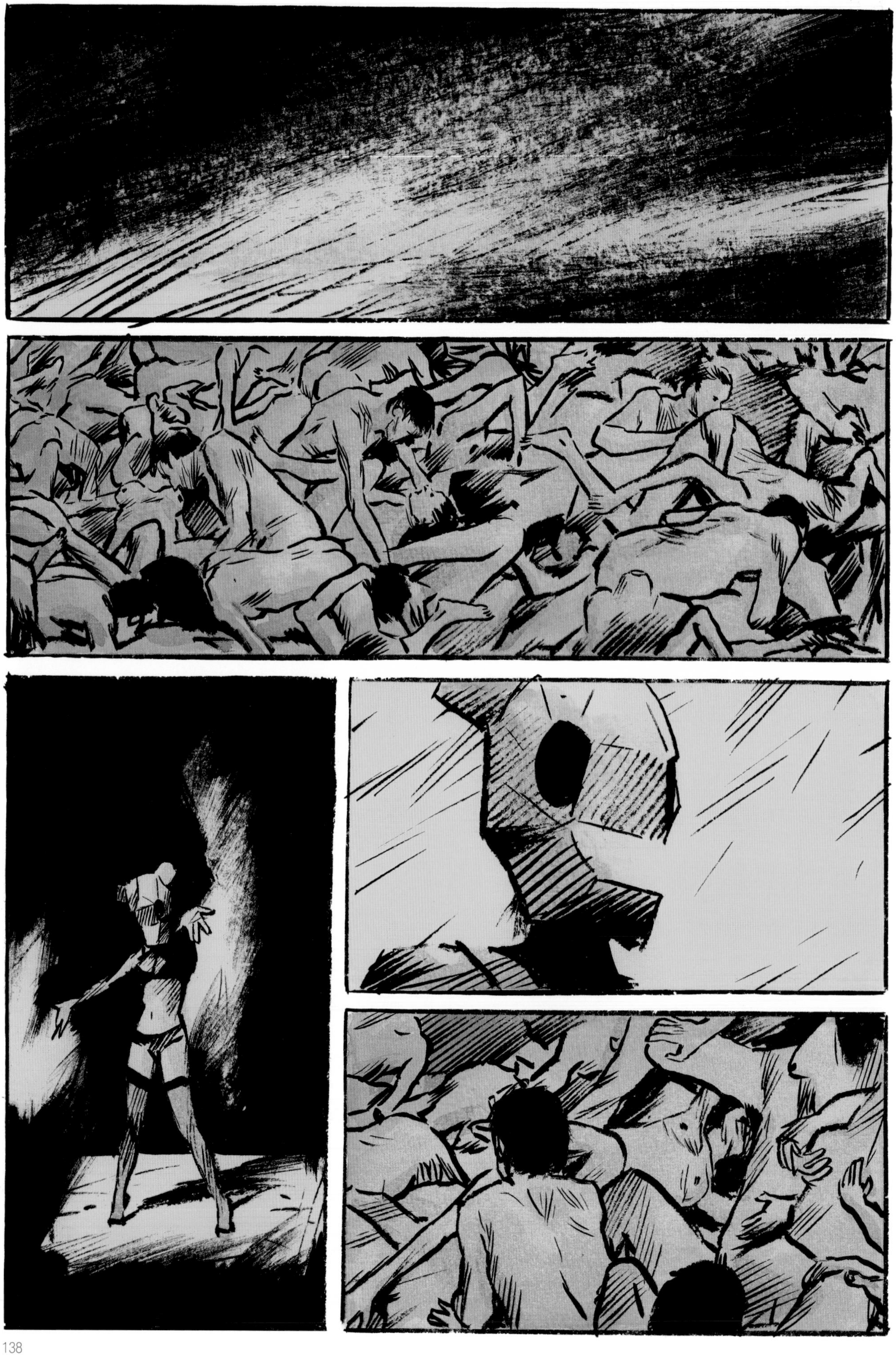

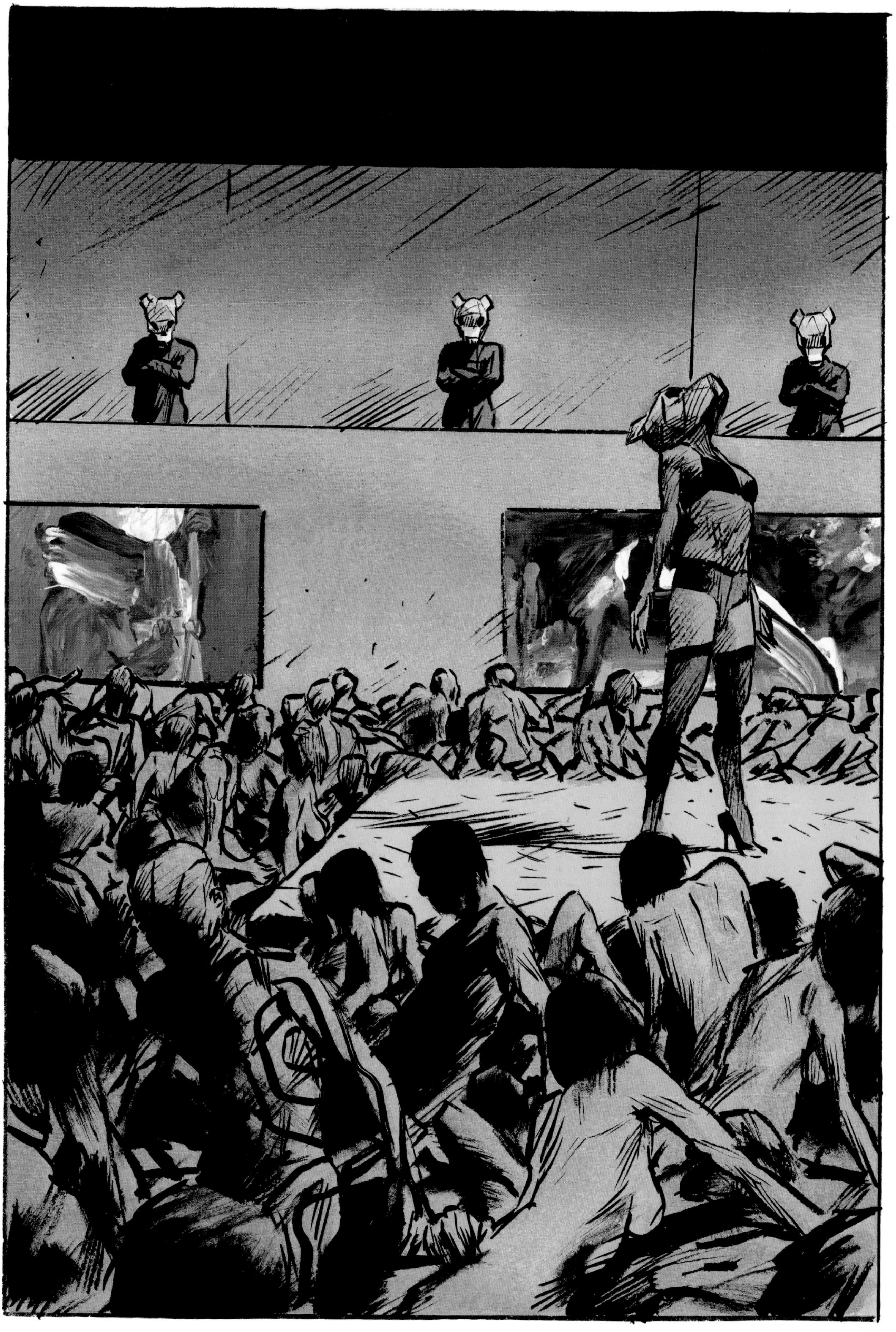

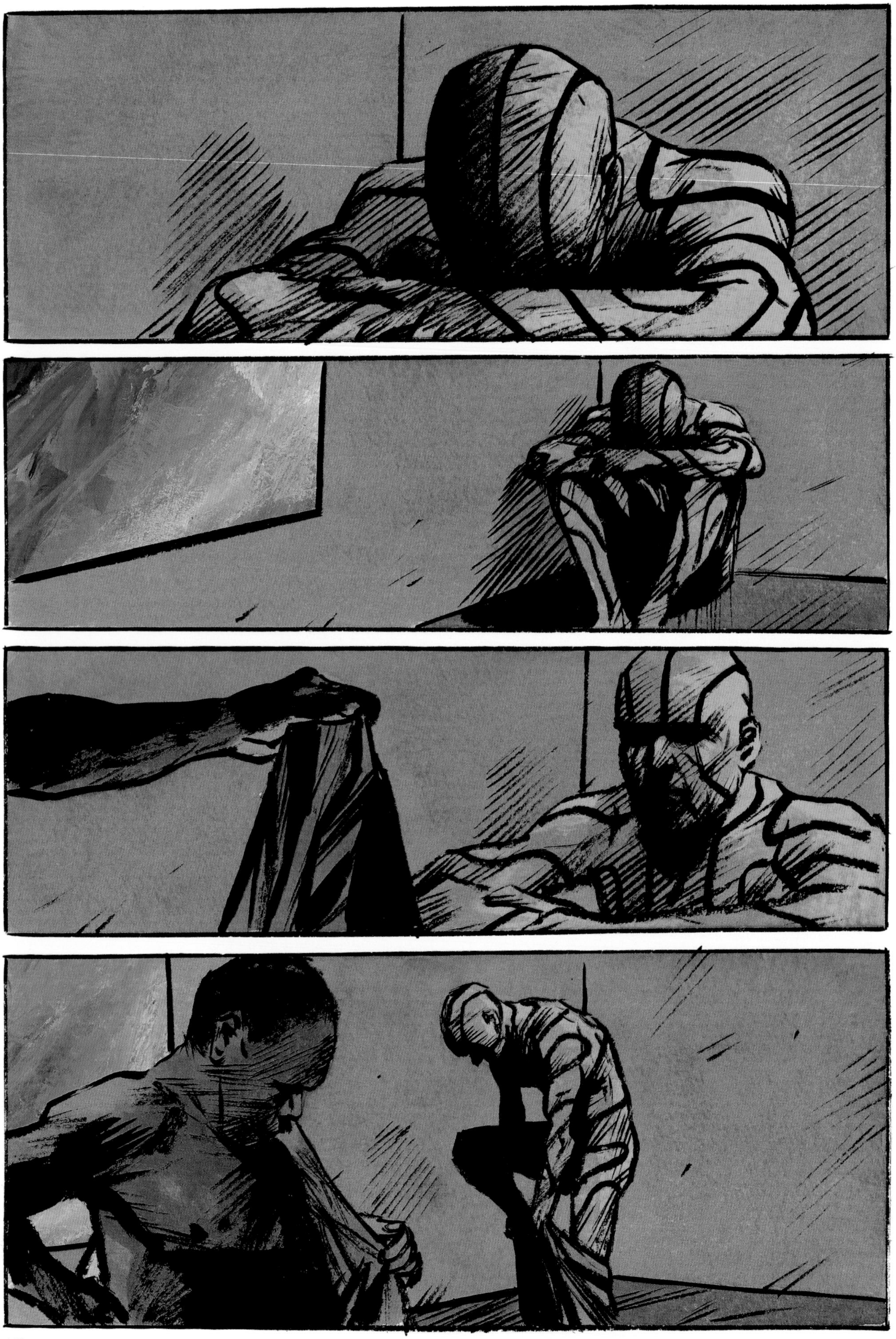

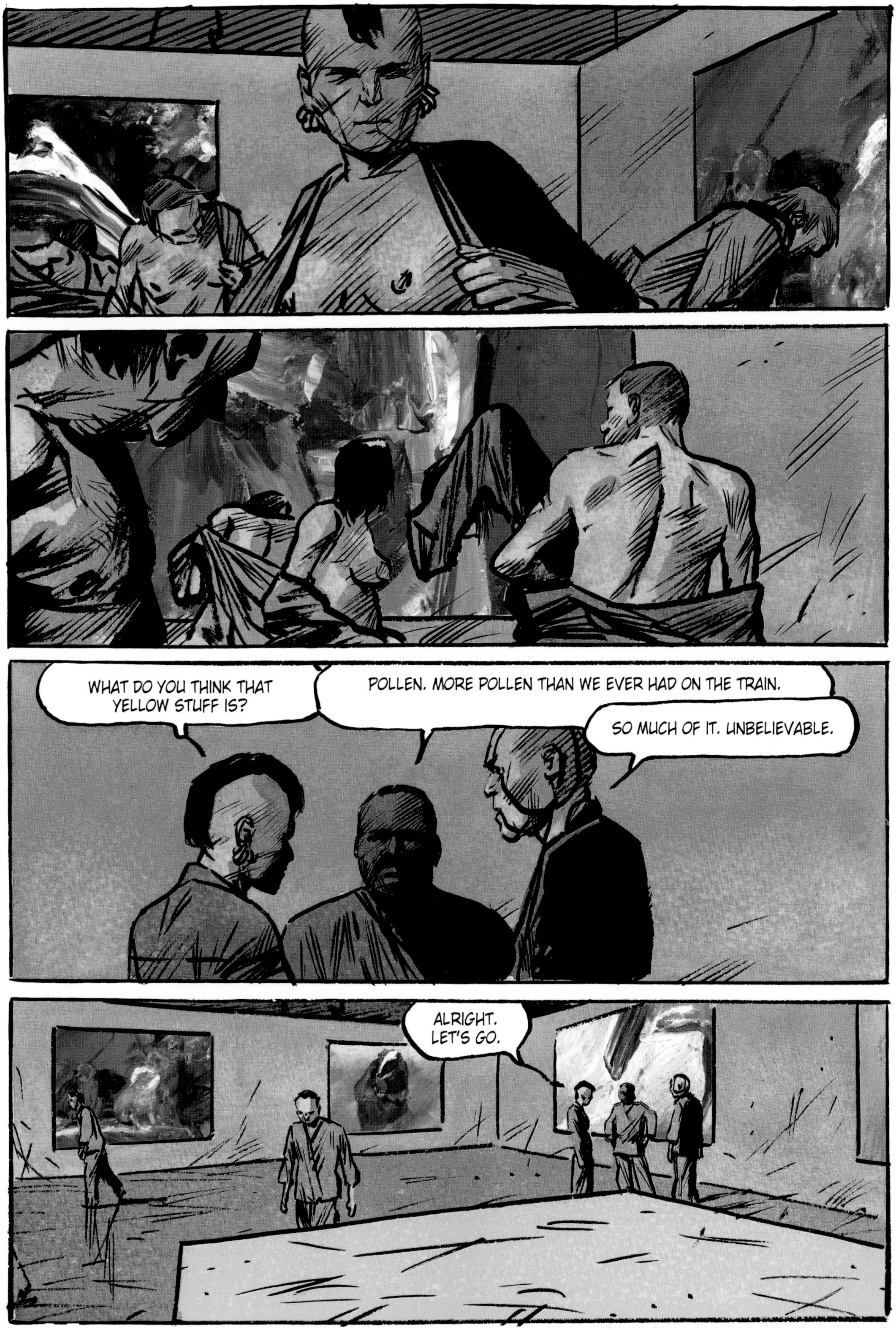
WHAT DO YOU THINK THAT YELLOW STUFF IS?
POLLEN. MORE POLLEN THAN WE EVER HAD ON THE TRAIN.
SO MUCH OF IT. UNBELIEVABLE.
ALRIGHT. LET'S GO.

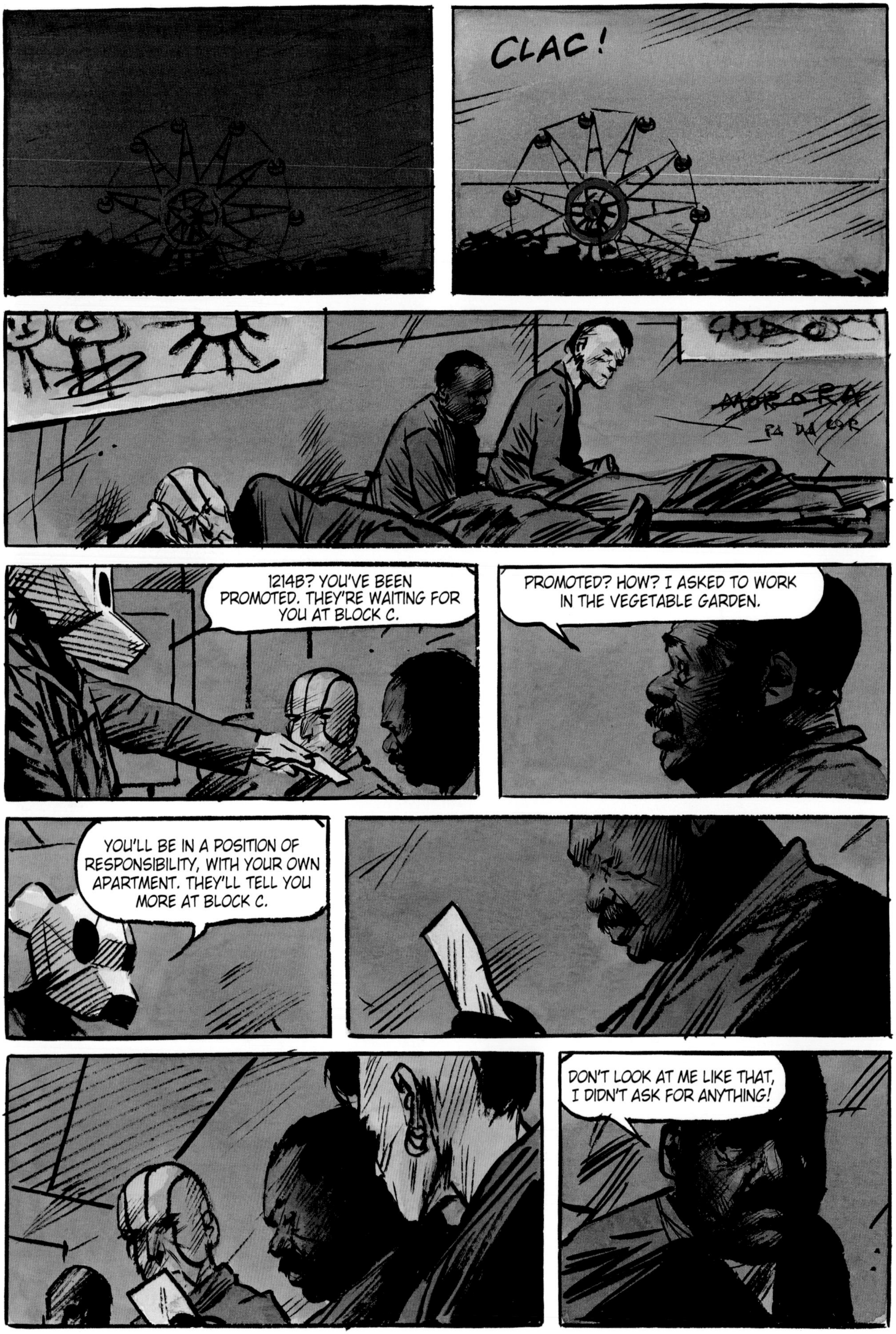
CLAC!
1214B? YOU'VE BEEN PROMOTED. THEY'RE WAITING FOR YOU AT BLOCK C.
PROMOTED? HOW? I ASKED TO WORK IN THE VEGETABLE GARDEN.
YOU'LL BE IN A POSITION OF RESPONSIBILITY, WITH YOUR OWN APARTMENT. THEY'LL TELL YOU MORE AT BLOCK C.
DON'T LOOK AT ME LIKE THAT, I DIDN'T ASK FOR ANYTHING!

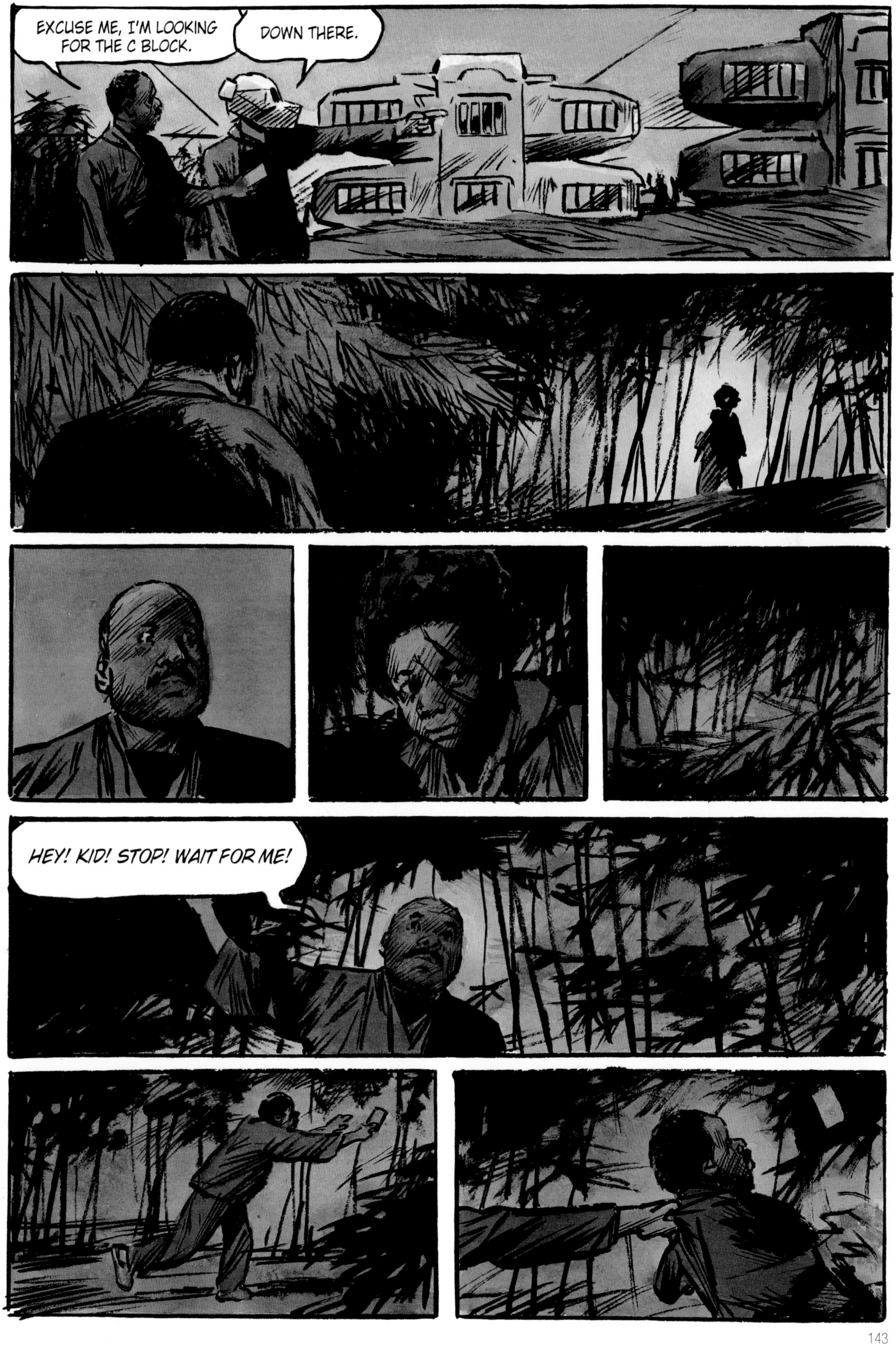
EXCUSE ME, I'M LOOKING FOR THE C BLOCK.
DOWN THERE.
HEY! KID! STOP! WAIT FOR ME!

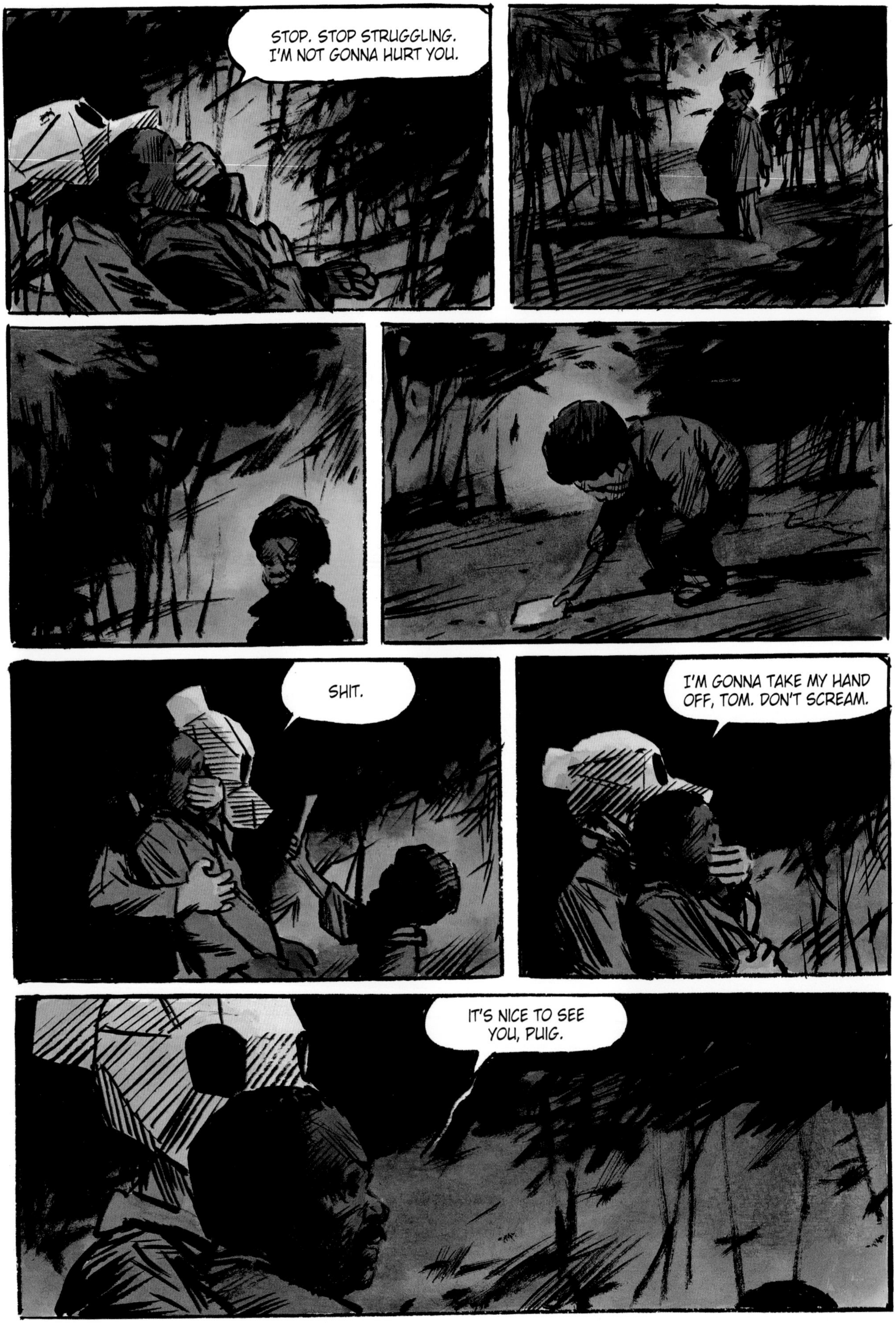
STOP. STOP STRUGGLING. I'M NOT GONNA HURT YOU.
SHIT.
I'M GONNA TAKE MY HAND OFF, TOM. DON'T SCREAM.
IT'S NICE TO SEE YOU, PUIG.

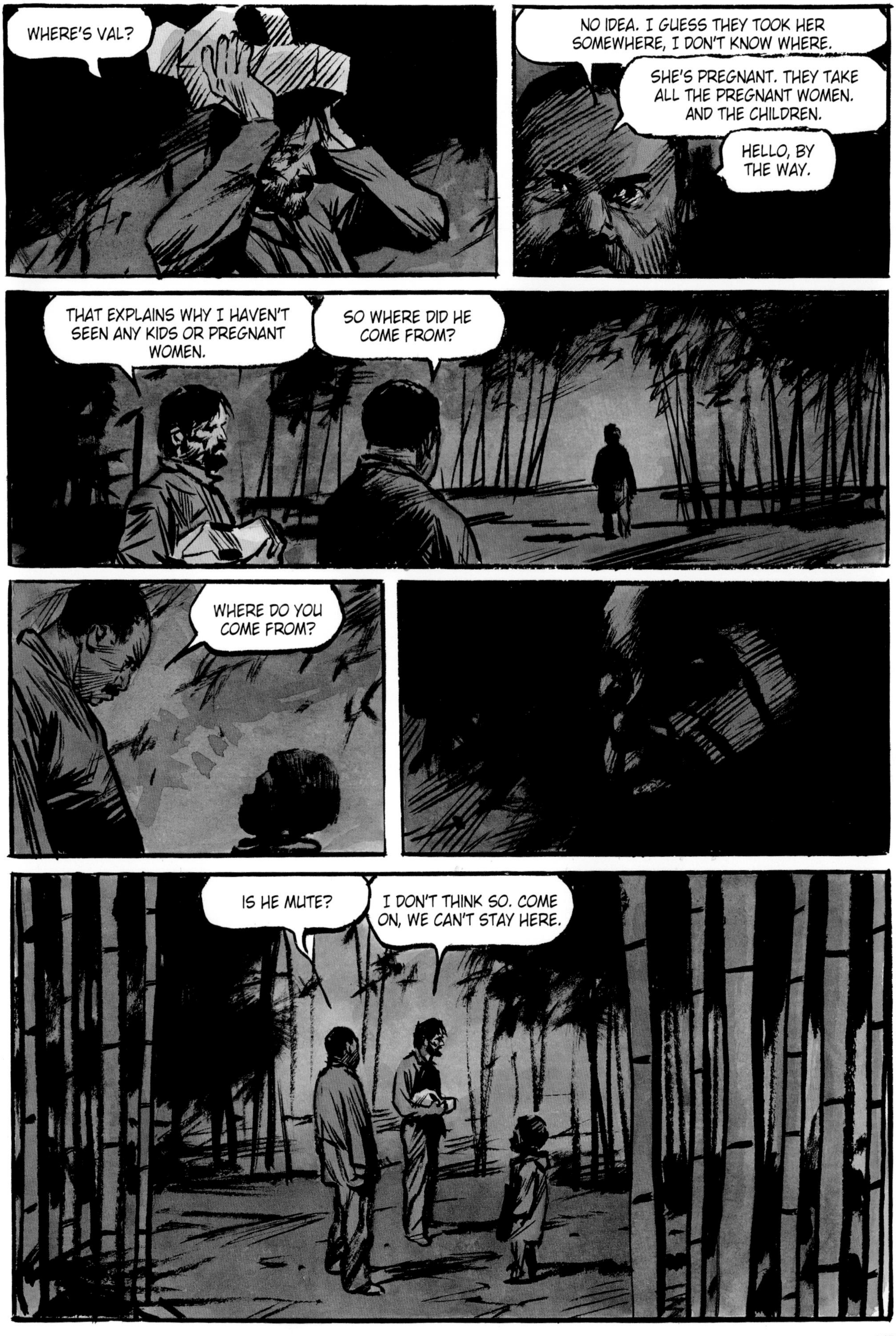
WHERE'S VAL?
NO IDEA. I GUESS THEY TOOK HER SOMEWHERE, I DON'T KNOW WHERE.
SHE'S PREGNANT. THEY TAKE ALL THE PREGNANT WOMEN. AND THE CHILDREN.
HELLO, BY THE WAY.
THAT EXPLAINS WHY I HAVEN'T SEEN ANY KIDS OR PREGNANT WOMEN.
SO WHERE DID HE COME FROM?
WHERE DO YOU COME FROM?
IS HE MUTE?
I DON'T THINK SO. COME ON, WE CAN'T STAY HERE.

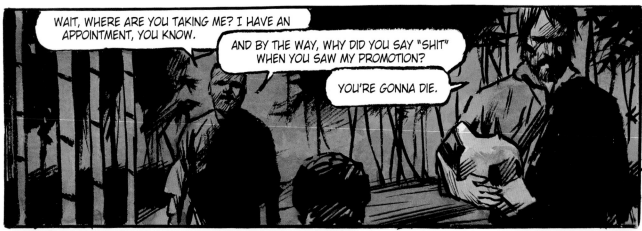

WAIT, WHERE ARE YOU TAKING ME? I HAVE AN APPOINTMENT, YOU KNOW.

AND BY THE WAY, WHY DID YOU SAY "SHIT" WHEN YOU SAW MY PROMOTION?

YOU'RE GONNA DIE.

I'M GONNA DIE?

WHAT DO YOU MEAN, "I'M GONNA DIE?" TELL ME!

I DON'T KNOW ALL THE PARTICULARS. COME WITH ME, I'LL SHOW YOU.

WELL, THAT'S A RELIEF. IF YOU DON'T KNOW ALL THE DETAILS, YOU MIGHT BE WRONG.

WHERE ARE WE GOING?

REMEMBER WE WERE LOOKING FOR THE POWER SOURCE? WELL, I FOUND IT.

LOOK. THE PROMOTED ONES.

FROM WHAT I UNDERSTAND, WHEN YOU GET PROMOTED, THIS IS WHERE YOU GO TO WORK.

WORK ON WHAT?

ON REPAIRING THE NUCLEAR PLANT.

WE'RE NEXT TO A NUCLEAR PLANT?

NOT NEXT TO IT. UNDER IT. LOOK AT THE VAULT.

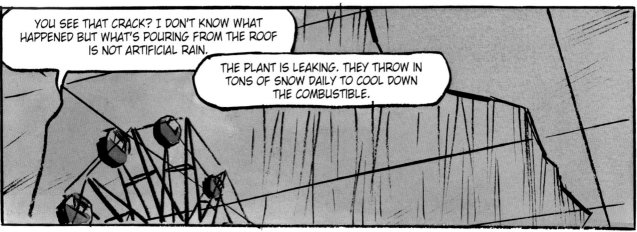

YOU SEE THAT CRACK? I DON'T KNOW WHAT HAPPENED BUT WHAT'S POURING FROM THE ROOF IS NOT ARTIFICIAL RAIN.

THE PLANT IS LEAKING. THEY THROW IN TONS OF SNOW DAILY TO COOL DOWN THE COMBUSTIBLE.

THAT RAIN IS MELTED SNOW. AND I BET ANYTHING YOU WANT THAT IT IS HIGHLY RADIOACTIVE.

I'VE SEEN THEM WORKING. THEY'RE TRYING TO SEAL THE CRACK AND TO REPAIR EVERYTHING THAT'S BROKEN.

BUT THERE'S ONLY SO MUCH YOU CAN DO WITH BAMBOO.

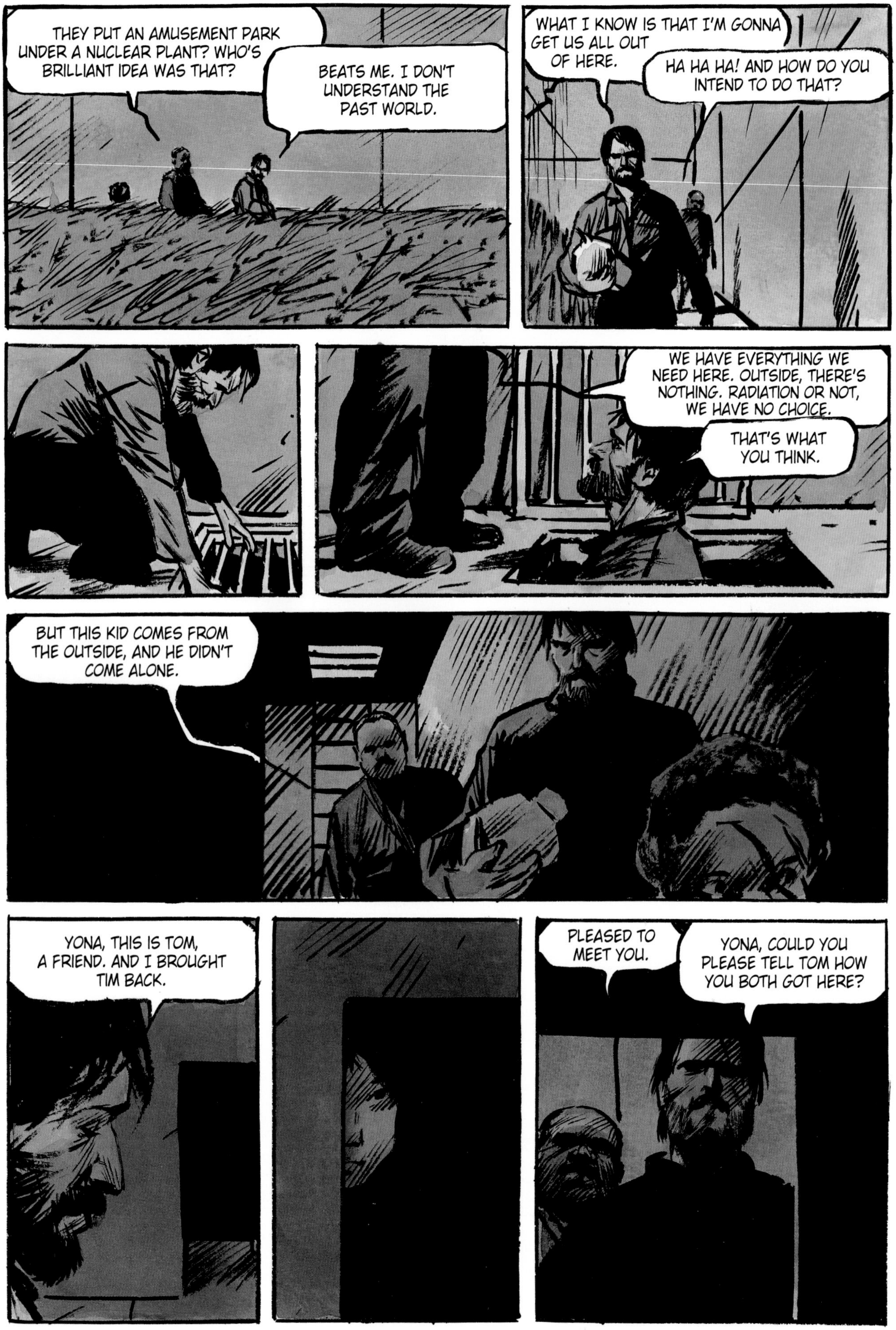
THEY PUT AN AMUSEMENT PARK UNDER A NUCLEAR PLANT? WHO'S BRILLIANT IDEA WAS THAT?
BEATS ME. I DON'T UNDERSTAND THE PAST WORLD.
WHAT I KNOW IS THAT I'M GONNA GET US ALL OUT OF HERE.
HA HA HA! AND HOW DO YOU INTEND TO DO THAT?
WE HAVE EVERYTHING WE NEED HERE. OUTSIDE, THERE'S NOTHING. RADIATION OR NOT, WE HAVE NO CHOICE.
THAT'S WHAT YOU THINK.
BUT THIS KID COMES FROM THE OUTSIDE, AND HE DIDN'T COME ALONE.
YONA, THIS IS TOM, A FRIEND. AND I BROUGHT TIM BACK.
PLEASED TO MEET YOU.
YONA, COULD YOU PLEASE TELL TOM HOW YOU BOTH GOT HERE?

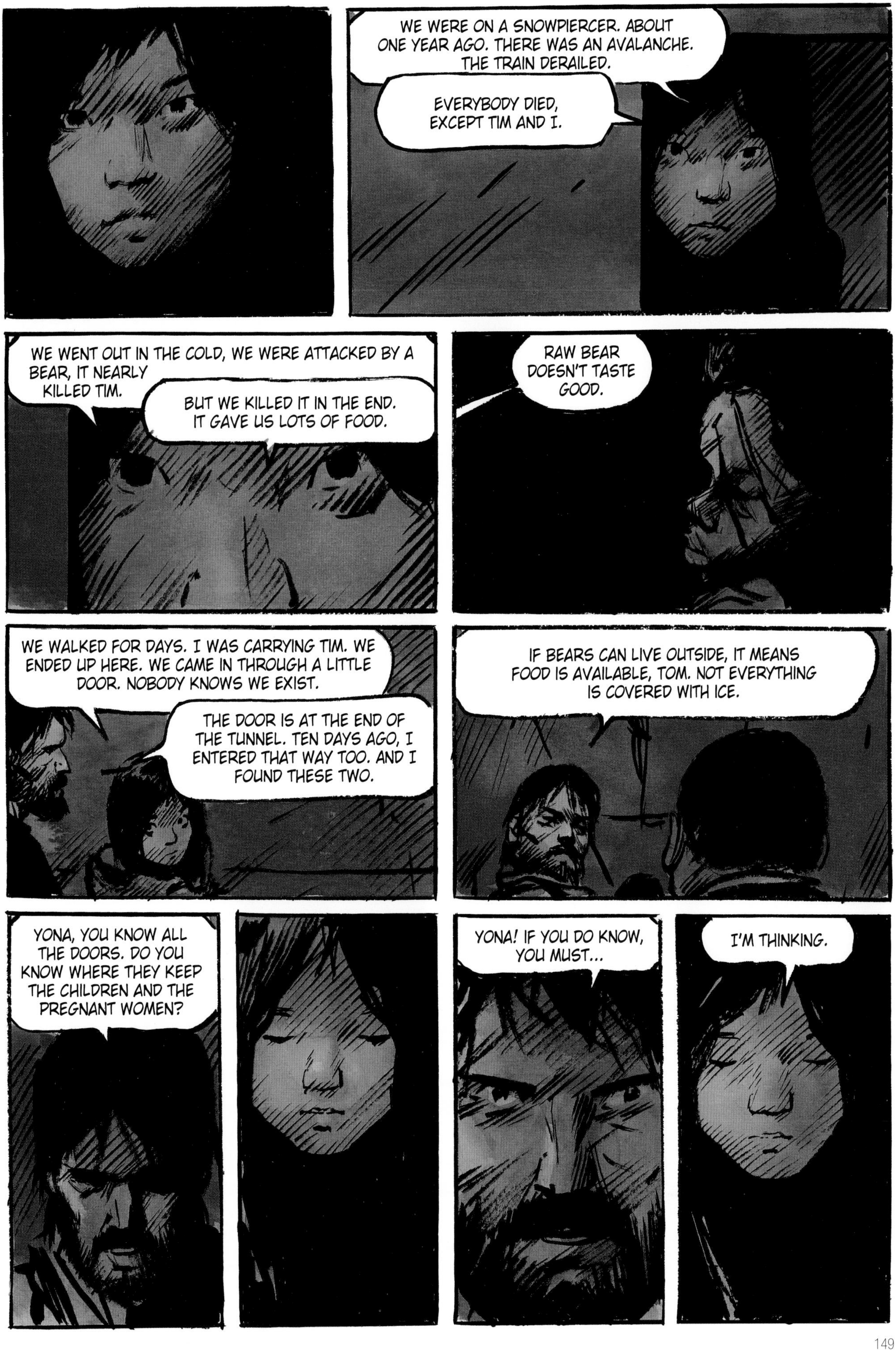
WE WERE ON A SNOWPIERCER. ABOUT ONE YEAR AGO. THERE WAS AN AVALANCHE. THE TRAIN DERAILED.
EVERYBODY DIED, EXCEPT TIM AND I.
WE WENT OUT IN THE COLD, WE WERE ATTACKED BY A BEAR, IT NEARLY KILLED TIM.
BUT WE KILLED IT IN THE END. IT GAVE US LOTS OF FOOD.
RAW BEAR DOESN'T TASTE GOOD.
WE WALKED FOR DAYS. I WAS CARRYING TIM. WE ENDED UP HERE. WE CAME IN THROUGH A LITTLE DOOR. NOBODY KNOWS WE EXIST.
THE DOOR IS AT THE END OF THE TUNNEL. TEN DAYS AGO, I ENTERED THAT WAY TOO. AND I FOUND THESE TWO.
IF BEARS CAN LIVE OUTSIDE, IT MEANS FOOD IS AVAILABLE, TOM. NOT EVERYTHING IS COVERED WITH ICE.
YONA, YOU KNOW ALL THE DOORS. DO YOU KNOW WHERE THEY KEEP THE CHILDREN AND THE PREGNANT WOMEN?
YONA! IF YOU DO KNOW, YOU MUST...
I'M THINKING.

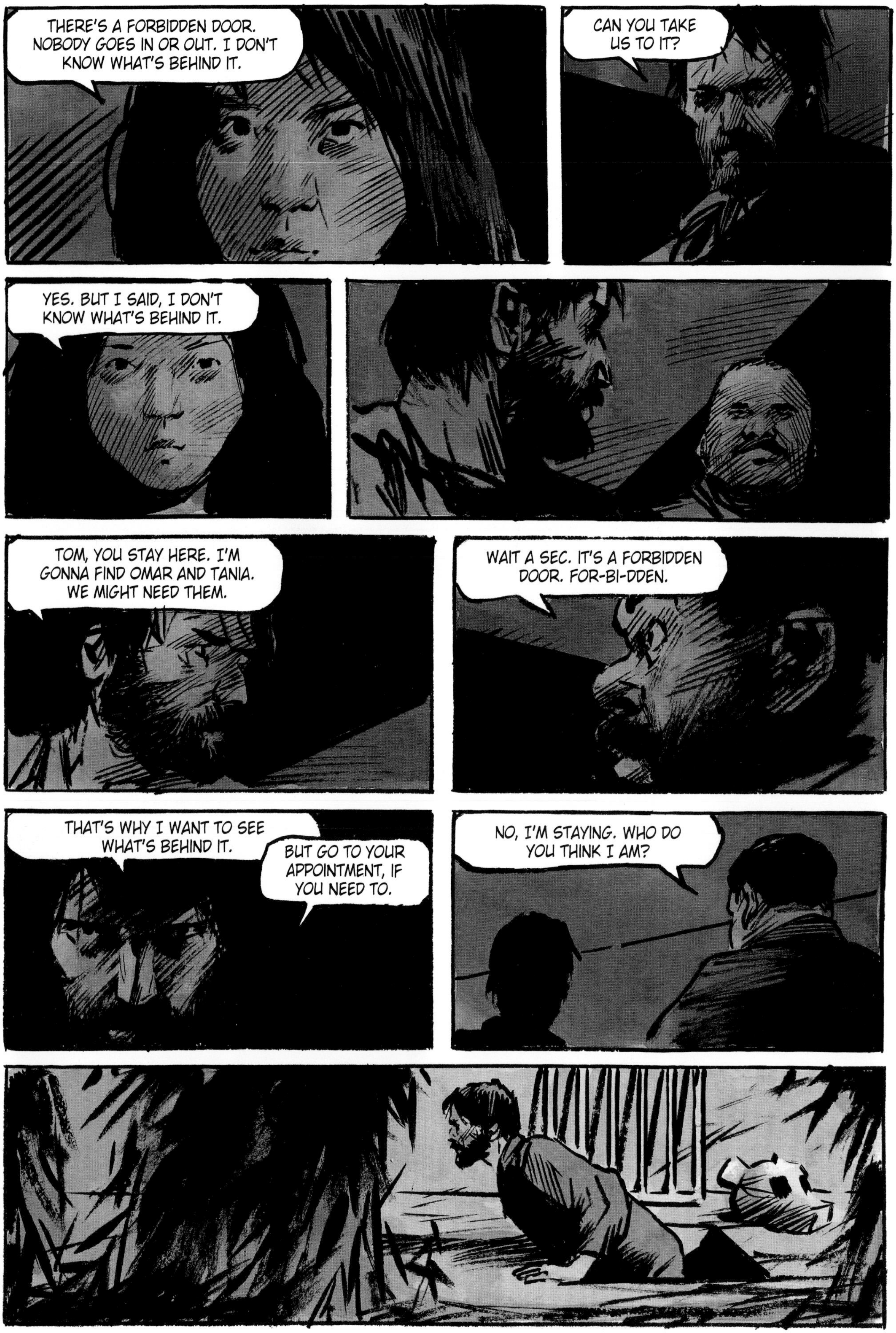
THERE'S A FORBIDDEN DOOR. NOBODY GOES IN OR OUT. I DON'T KNOW WHAT'S BEHIND IT.
CAN YOU TAKE US TO IT?
YES. BUT I SAID, I DON'T KNOW WHAT'S BEHIND IT.
TOM, YOU STAY HERE. I'M GONNA FIND OMAR AND TANIA. WE MIGHT NEED THEM.
WAIT A SEC. IT'S A FORBIDDEN DOOR. FOR-BI-DDEN.
THAT'S WHY I WANT TO SEE WHAT'S BEHIND IT.
BUT GO TO YOUR APPOINTMENT, IF YOU NEED TO.
NO, I'M STAYING. WHO DO YOU THINK I AM?

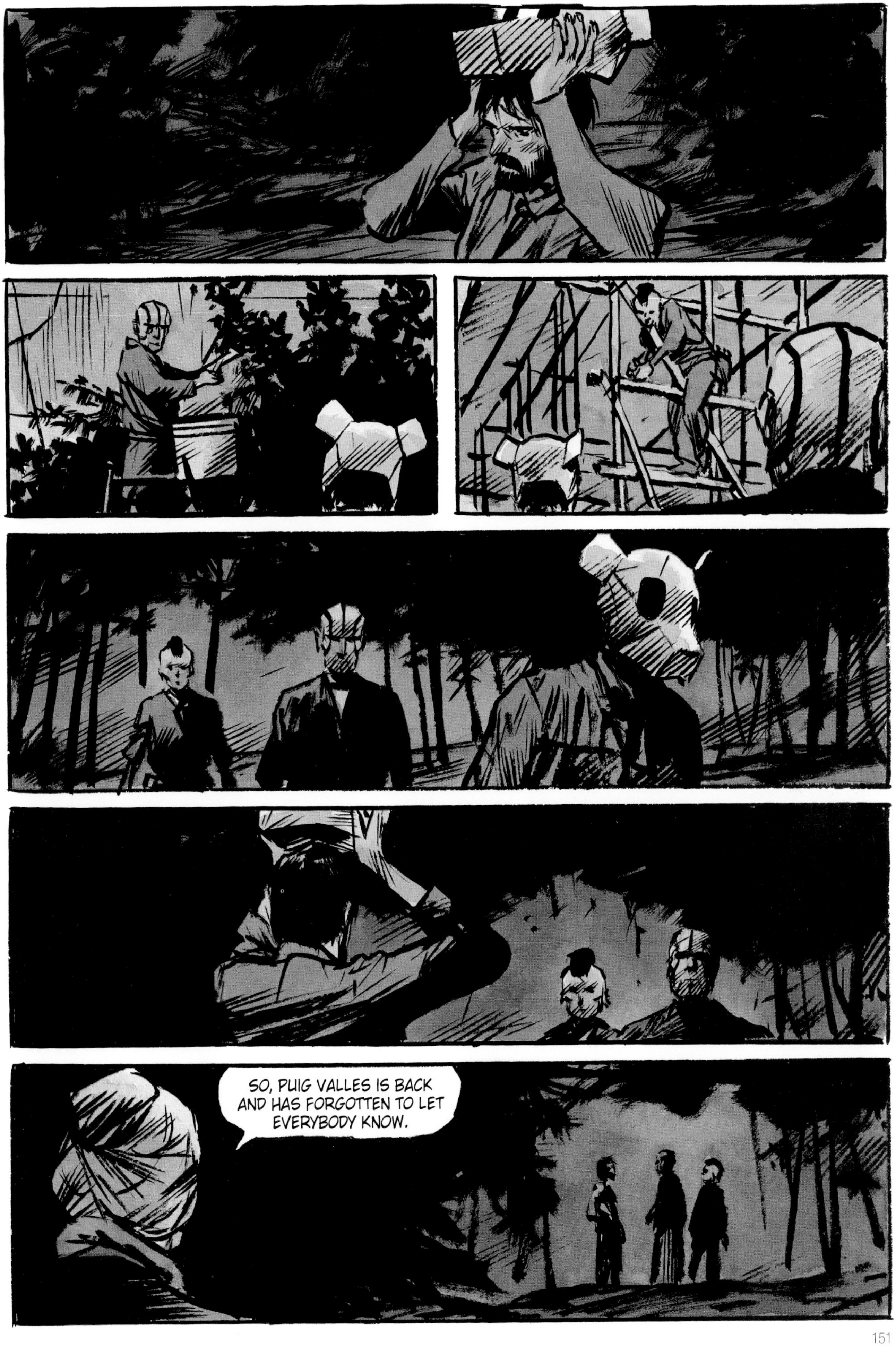
SO, PUIG VALLES IS BACK AND HAS FORGOTTEN TO LET EVERYBODY KNOW.

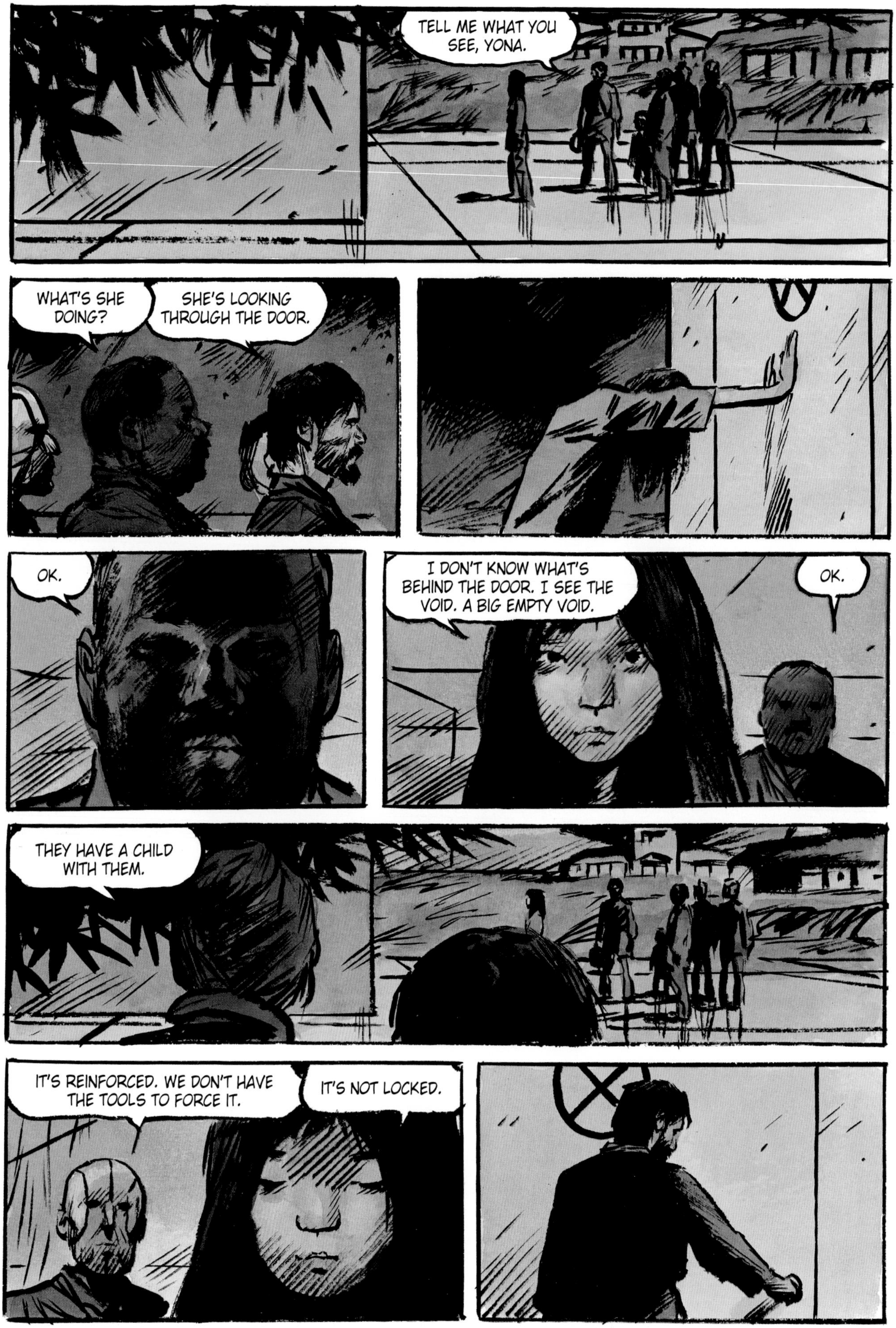
TELL ME WHAT YOU SEE, YONA.
WHAT'S SHE DOING?
SHE'S LOOKING THROUGH THE DOOR.
OK.
I DON'T KNOW WHAT'S BEHIND THE DOOR. I SEE THE VOID. A BIG EMPTY VOID.
OK.
THEY HAVE A CHILD WITH THEM.
IT'S REINFORCED. WE DON'T HAVE THE TOOLS TO FORCE IT.
IT'S NOT LOCKED.

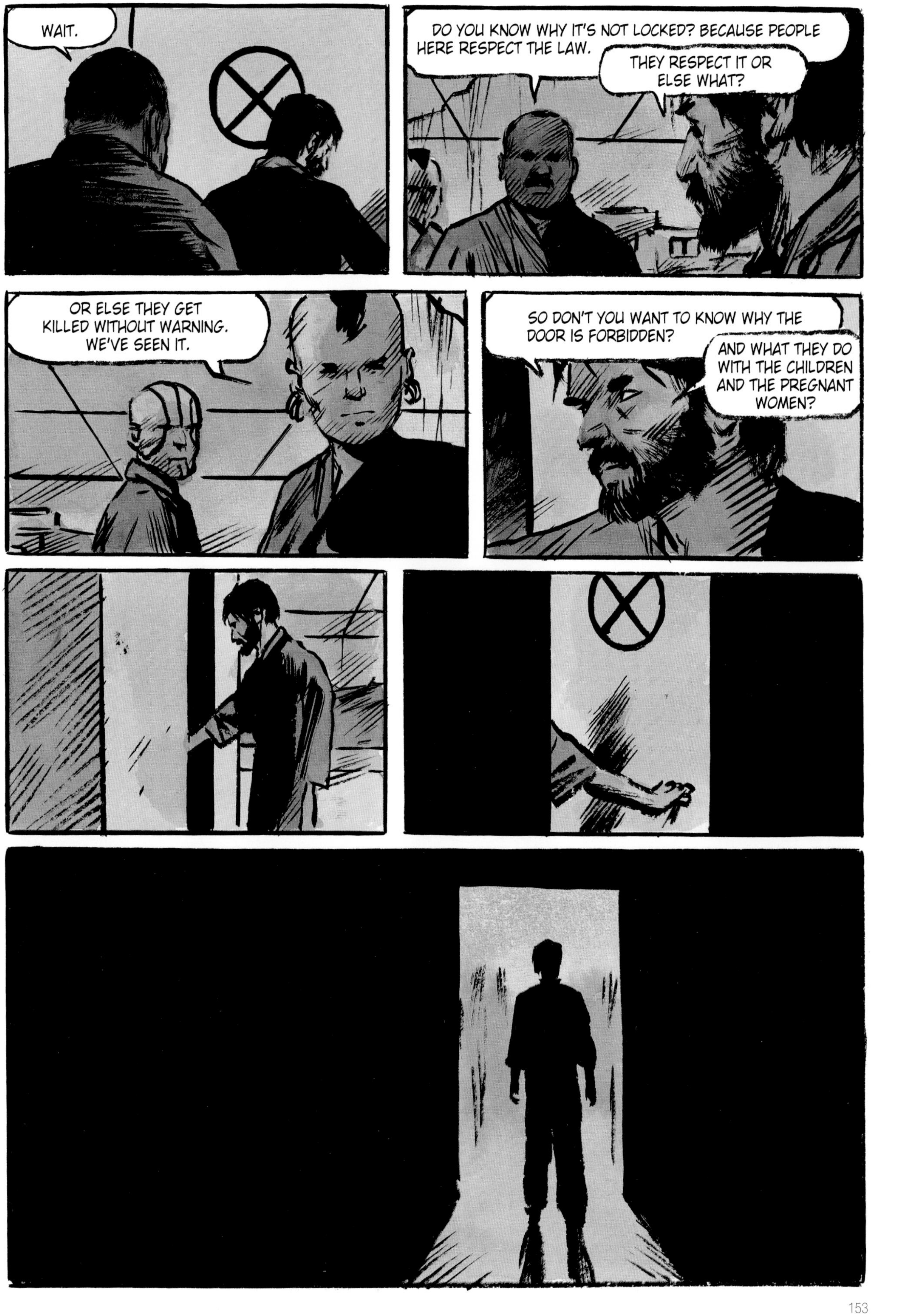

WAIT.
DO YOU KNOW WHY IT'S NOT LOCKED? BECAUSE PEOPLE HERE RESPECT THE LAW.
THEY RESPECT IT OR ELSE WHAT?
OR ELSE THEY GET KILLED WITHOUT WARNING. WE'VE SEEN IT.
SO DON'T YOU WANT TO KNOW WHY THE DOOR IS FORBIDDEN?
AND WHAT THEY DO WITH THE CHILDREN AND THE PREGNANT WOMEN?

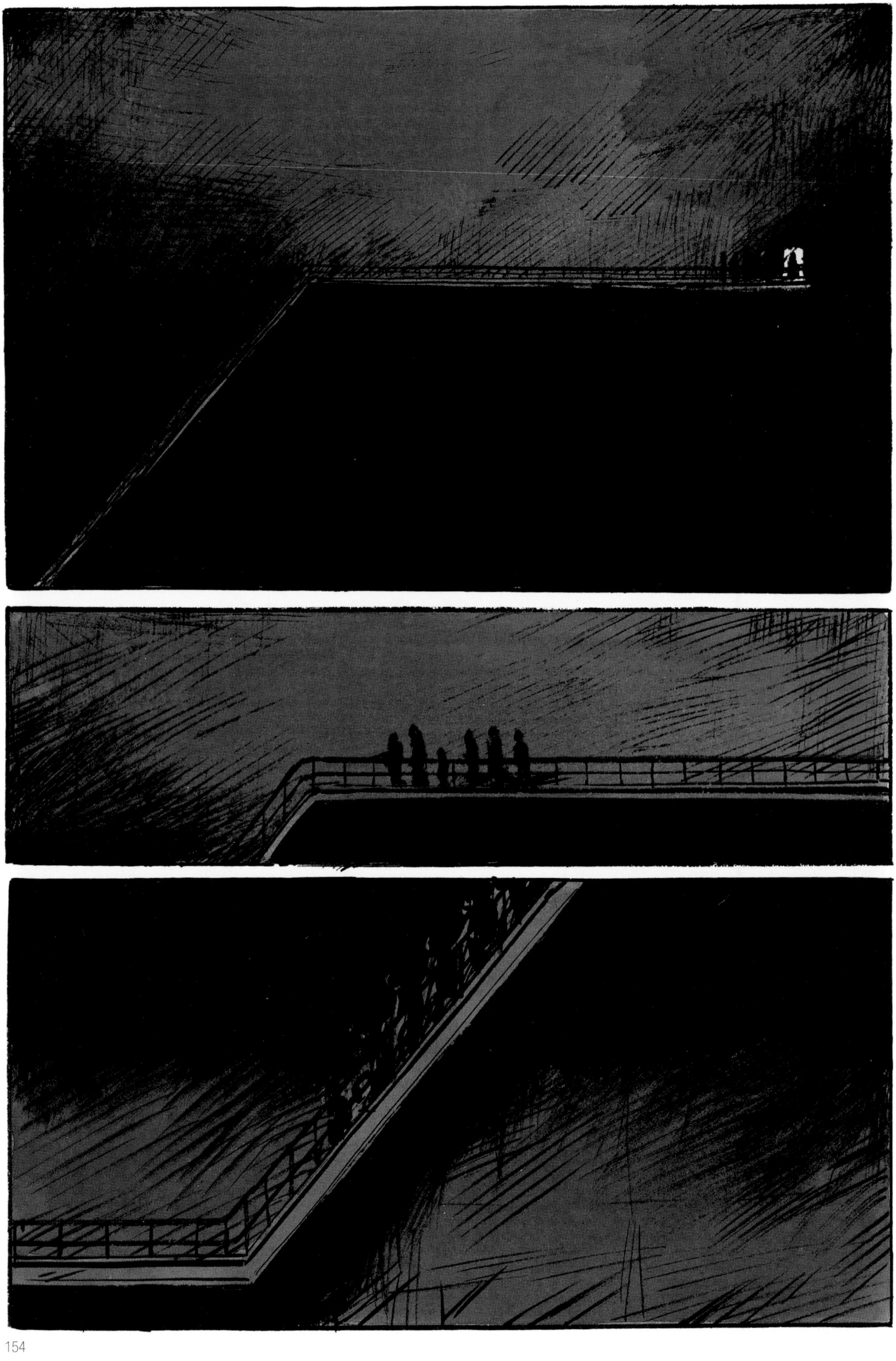

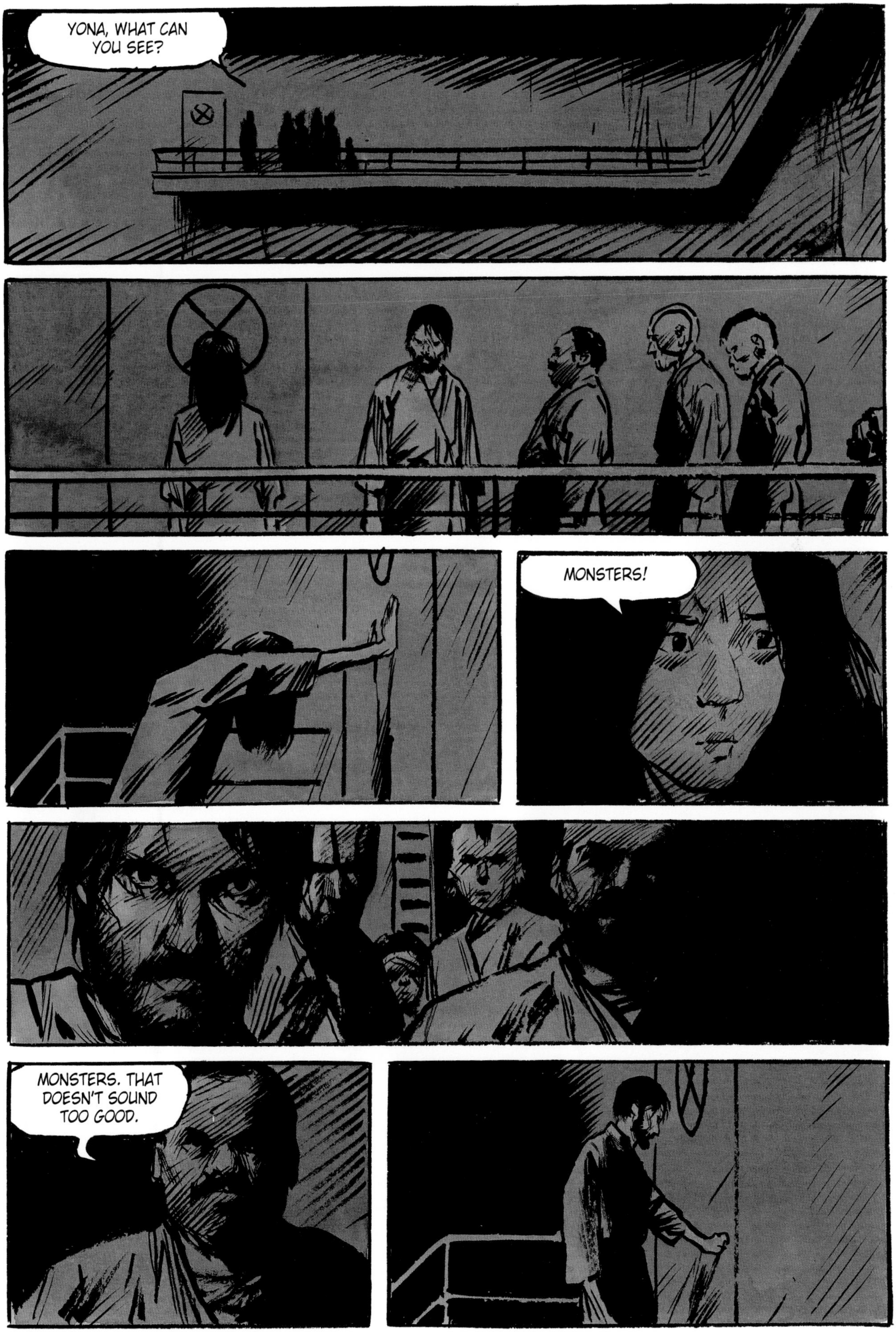
YONA, WHAT CAN YOU SEE?
MONSTERS!
MONSTERS. THAT DOESN'T SOUND TOO GOOD.

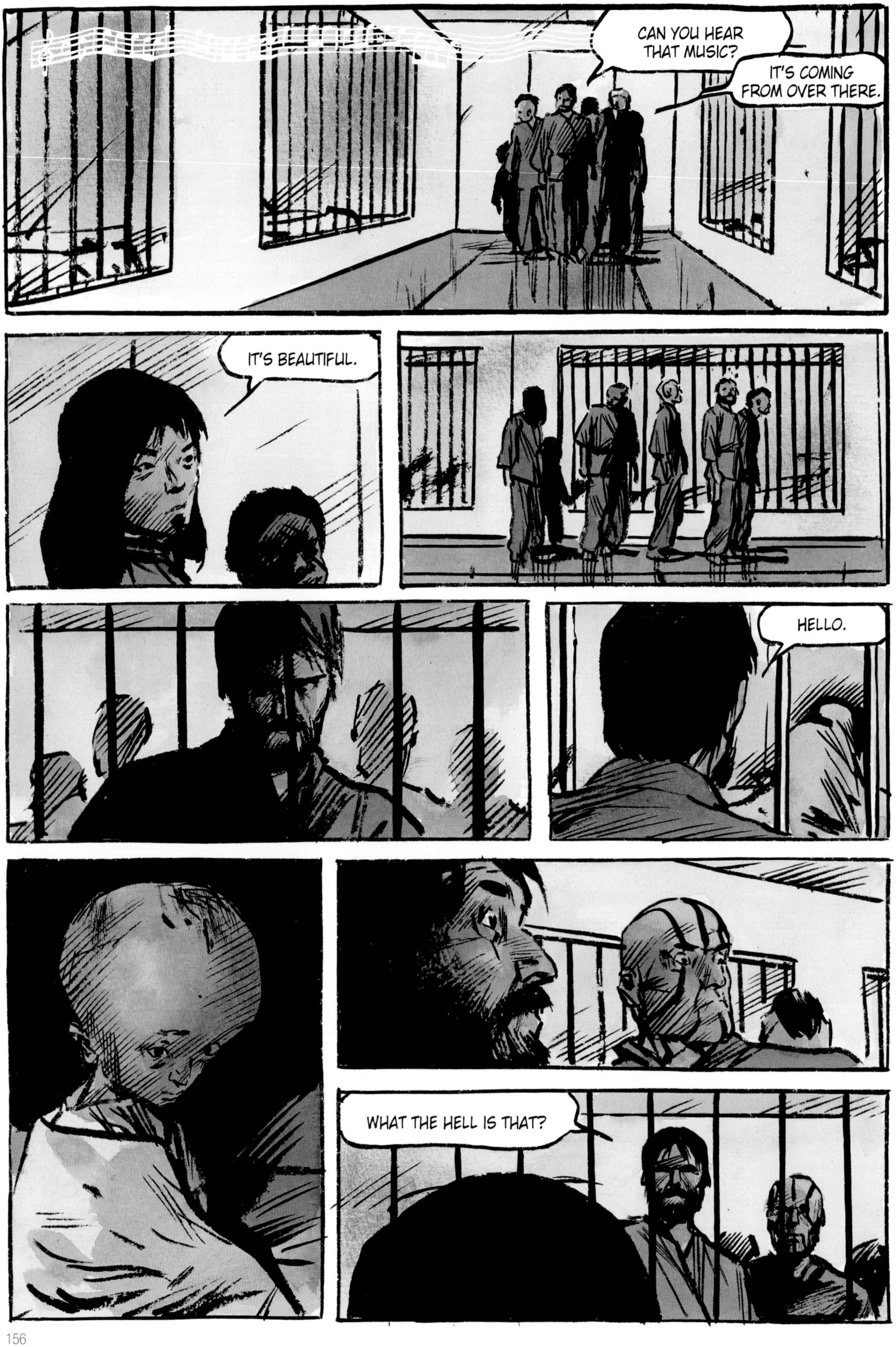
CAN YOU HEAR THAT MUSIC?
IT'S COMING FROM OVER THERE.
IT'S BEAUTIFUL.
HELLO.
WHAT THE HELL IS THAT?

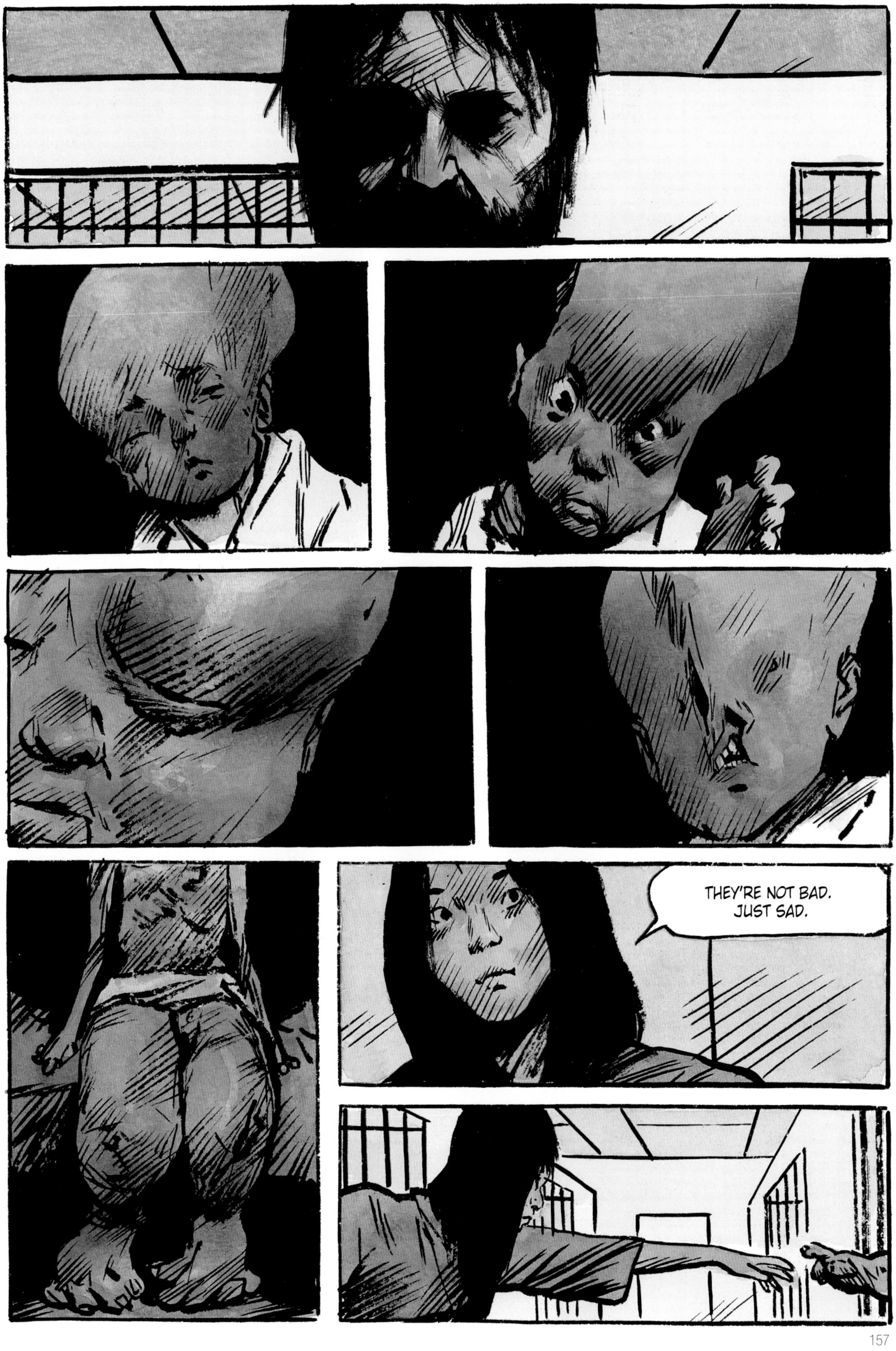
THEY'RE NOT BAD.
JUST SAD.

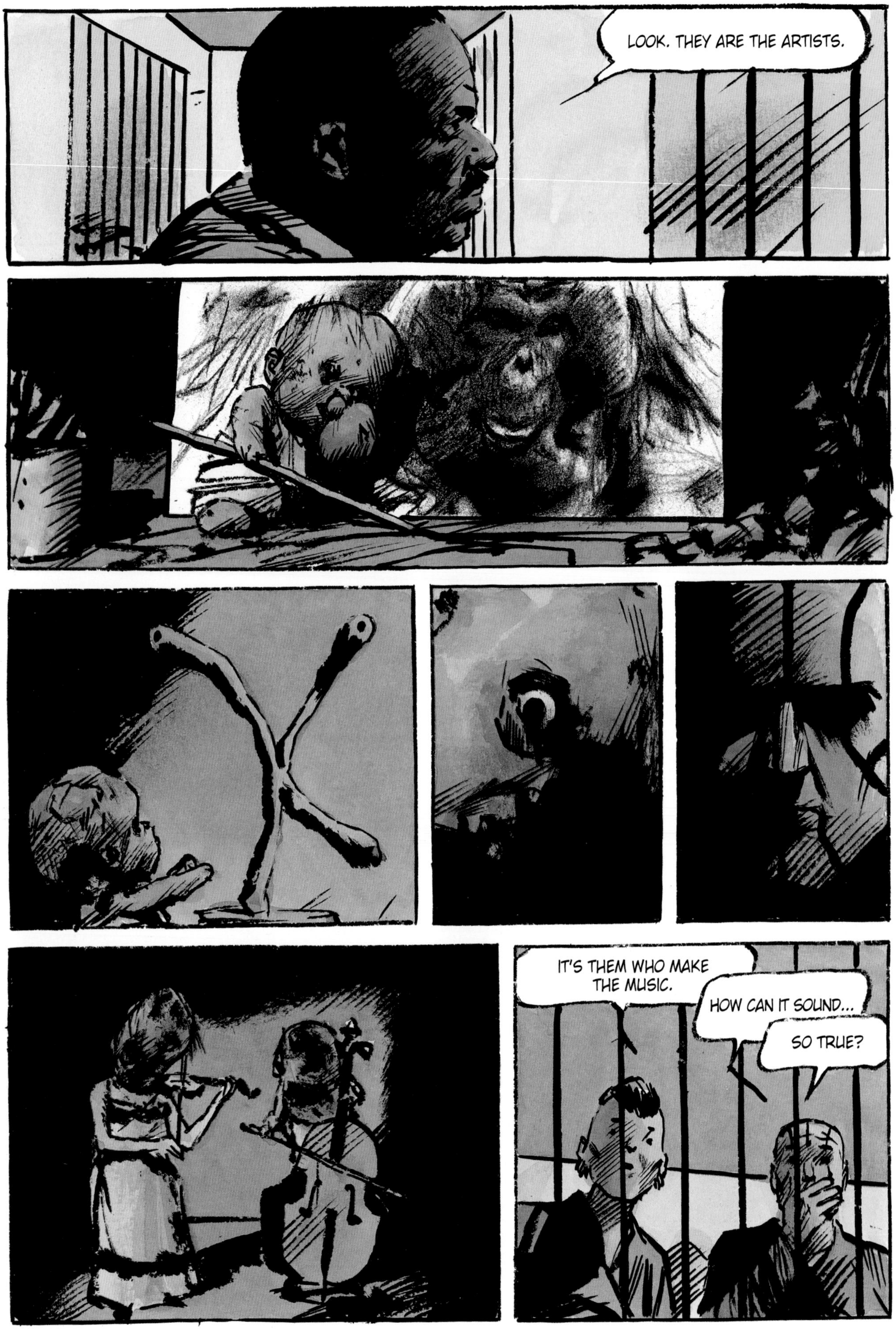
LOOK. THEY ARE THE ARTISTS.
IT'S THEM WHO MAKE THE MUSIC.
HOW CAN IT SOUND...
SO TRUE?

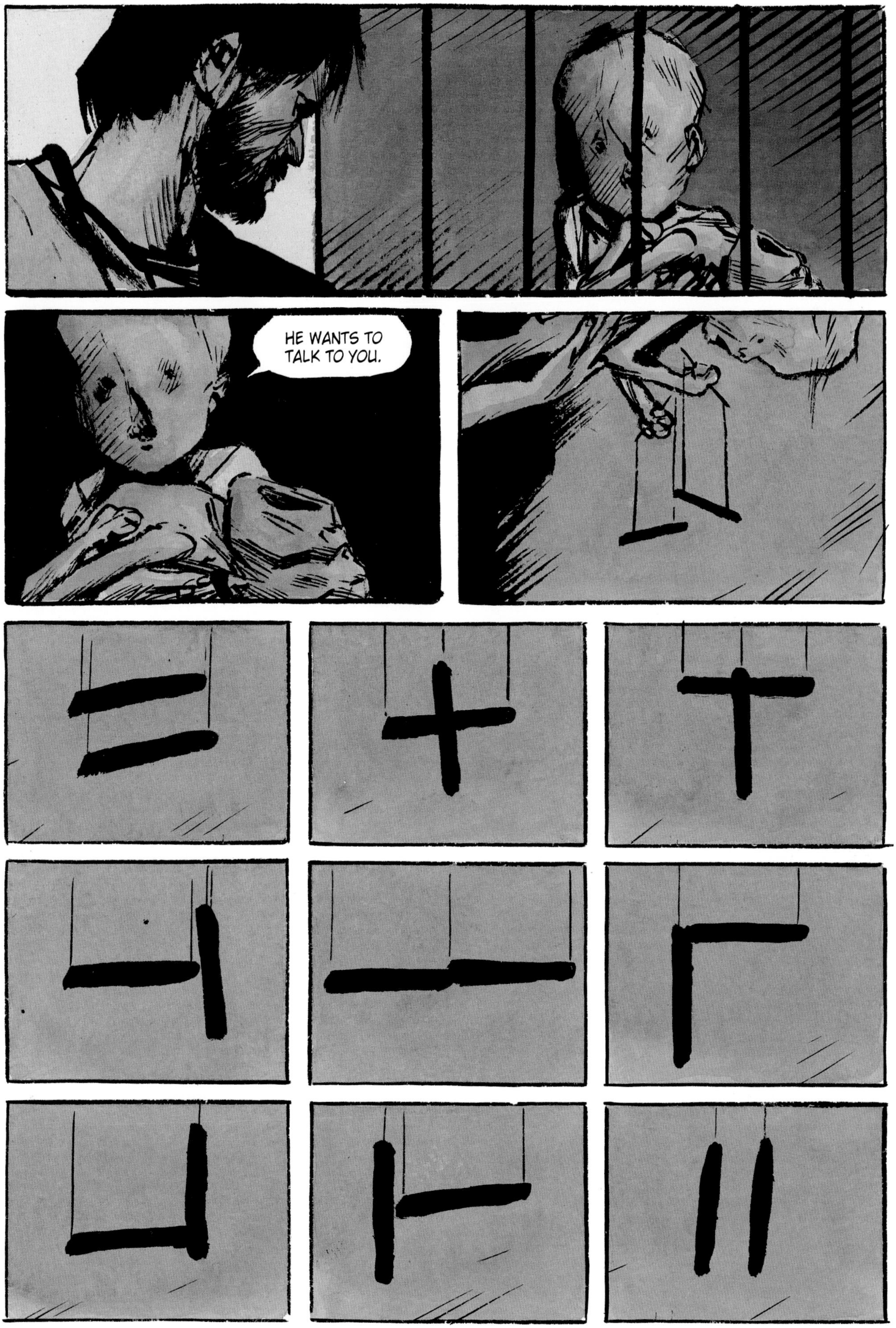
HE WANTS TO TALK TO YOU.

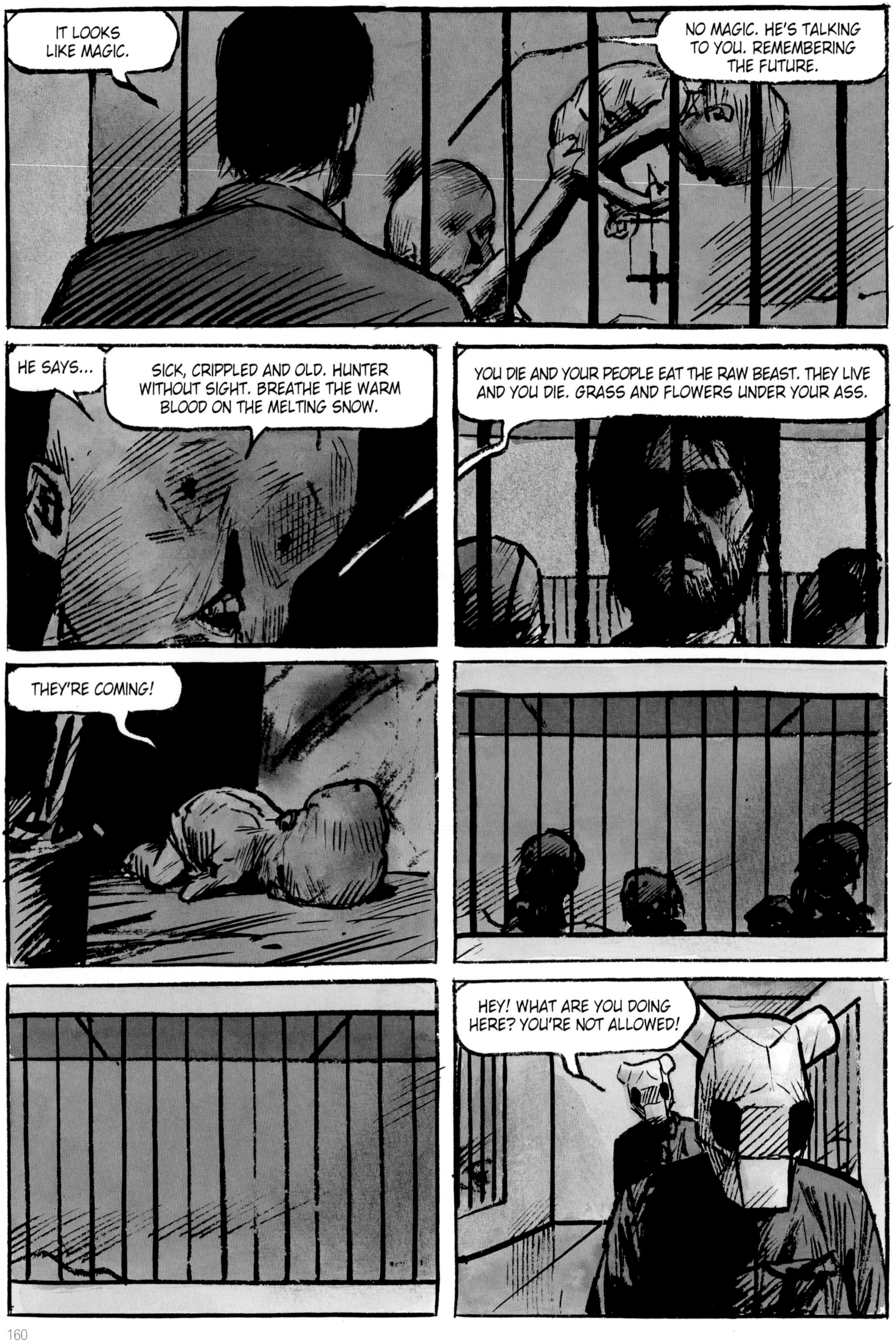
IT LOOKS LIKE MAGIC.
NO MAGIC. HE'S TALKING TO YOU. REMEMBERING THE FUTURE.
HE SAYS...
SICK, CRIPPLED AND OLD. HUNTER WITHOUT SIGHT. BREATHE THE WARM BLOOD ON THE MELTING SNOW.
YOU DIE AND YOUR PEOPLE EAT THE RAW BEAST. THEY LIVE AND YOU DIE. GRASS AND FLOWERS UNDER YOUR ASS.
THEY'RE COMING!
HEY! WHAT ARE YOU DOING HERE? YOU'RE NOT ALLOWED!

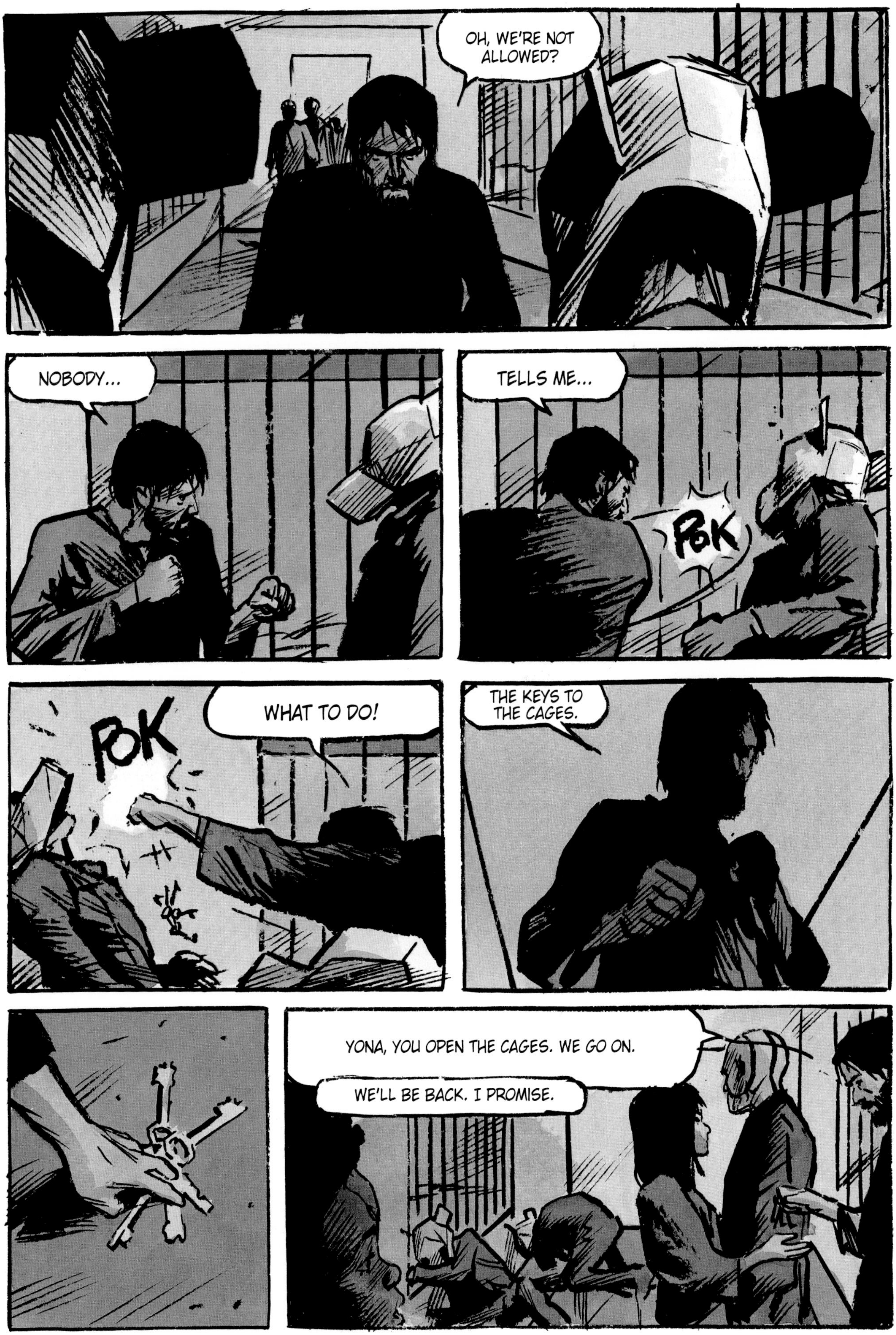
OH, WE'RE NOT ALLOWED?
NOBODY...
TELLS ME...
POK
POK
WHAT TO DO!
THE KEYS TO THE CAGES.
YONA, YOU OPEN THE CAGES. WE GO ON.
WE'LL BE BACK. I PROMISE.

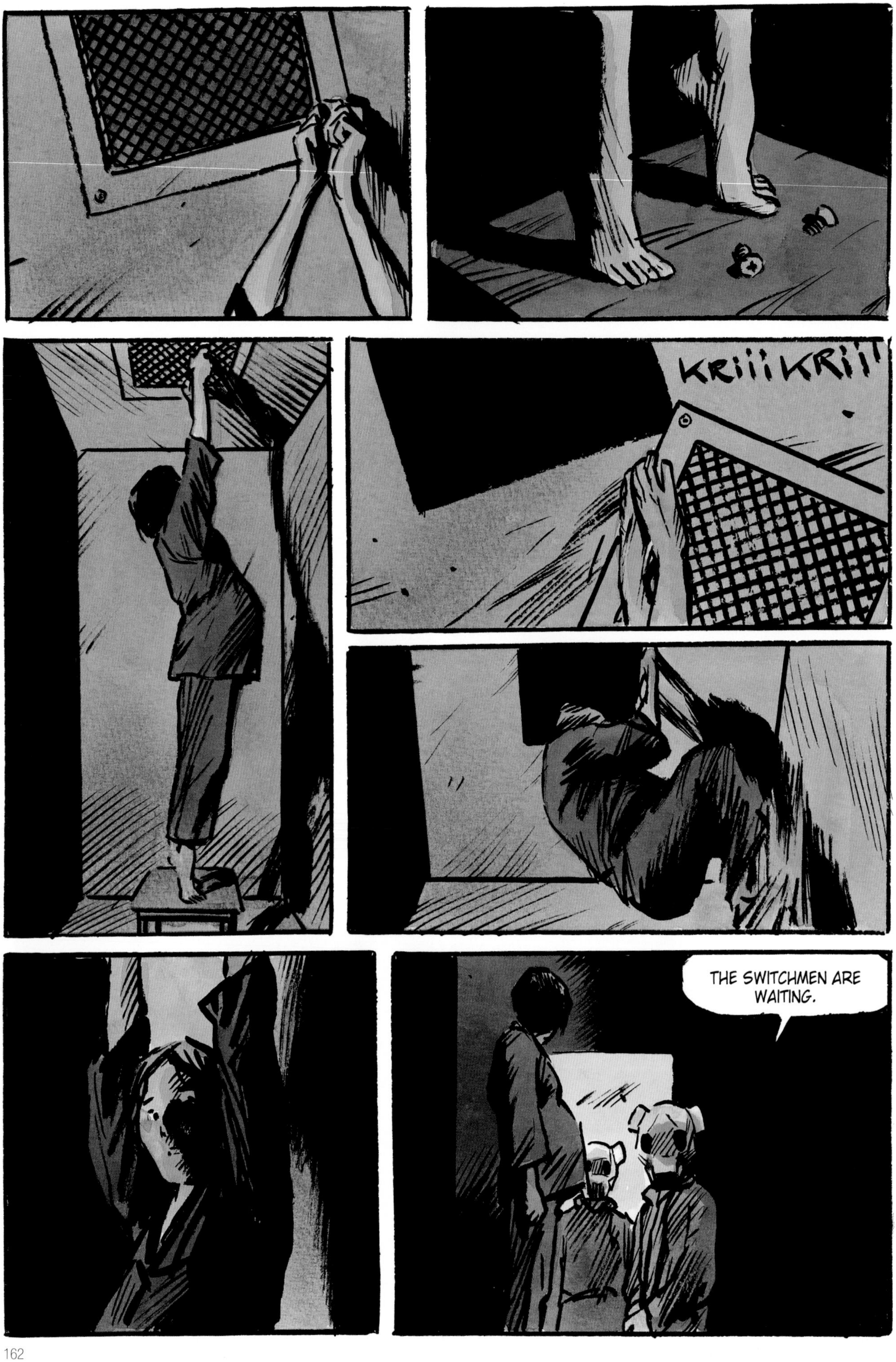
KRIIIKRIII
THE SWITCHMEN ARE WAITING.

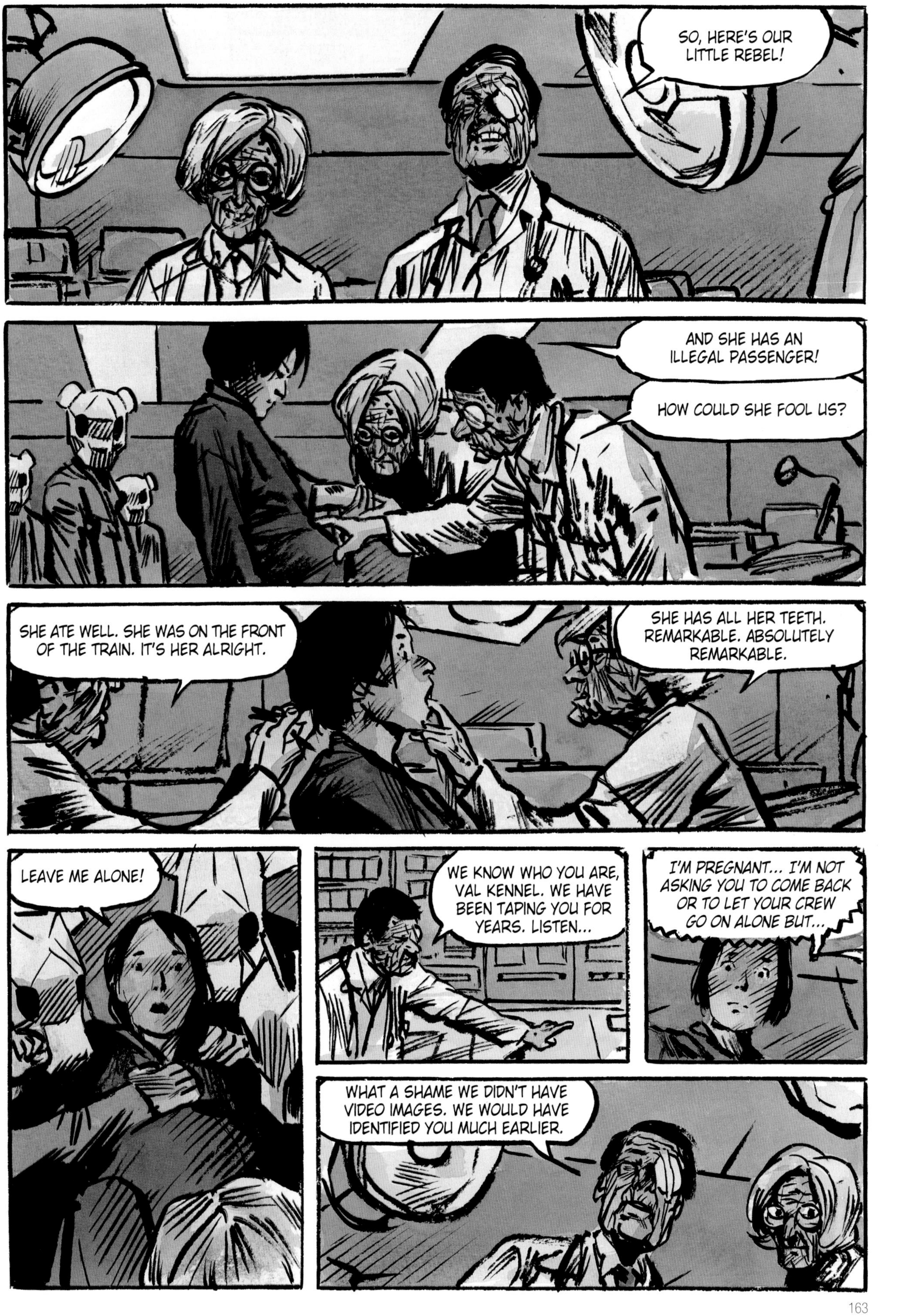
SO, HERE'S OUR LITTLE REBEL!
AND SHE HAS AN ILLEGAL PASSENGER!
HOW COULD SHE FOOL US?
SHE ATE WELL. SHE WAS ON THE FRONT OF THE TRAIN. IT'S HER ALRIGHT.
SHE HAS ALL HER TEETH. REMARKABLE. ABSOLUTELY REMARKABLE.
LEAVE ME ALONE!
WE KNOW WHO YOU ARE, VAL KENNEL. WE HAVE BEEN TAPING YOU FOR YEARS. LISTEN...
I'M PREGNANT... I'M NOT ASKING YOU TO COME BACK OR TO LET YOUR CREW GO ON ALONE BUT...
WHAT A SHAME WE DIDN'T HAVE VIDEO IMAGES. WE WOULD HAVE IDENTIFIED YOU MUCH EARLIER.

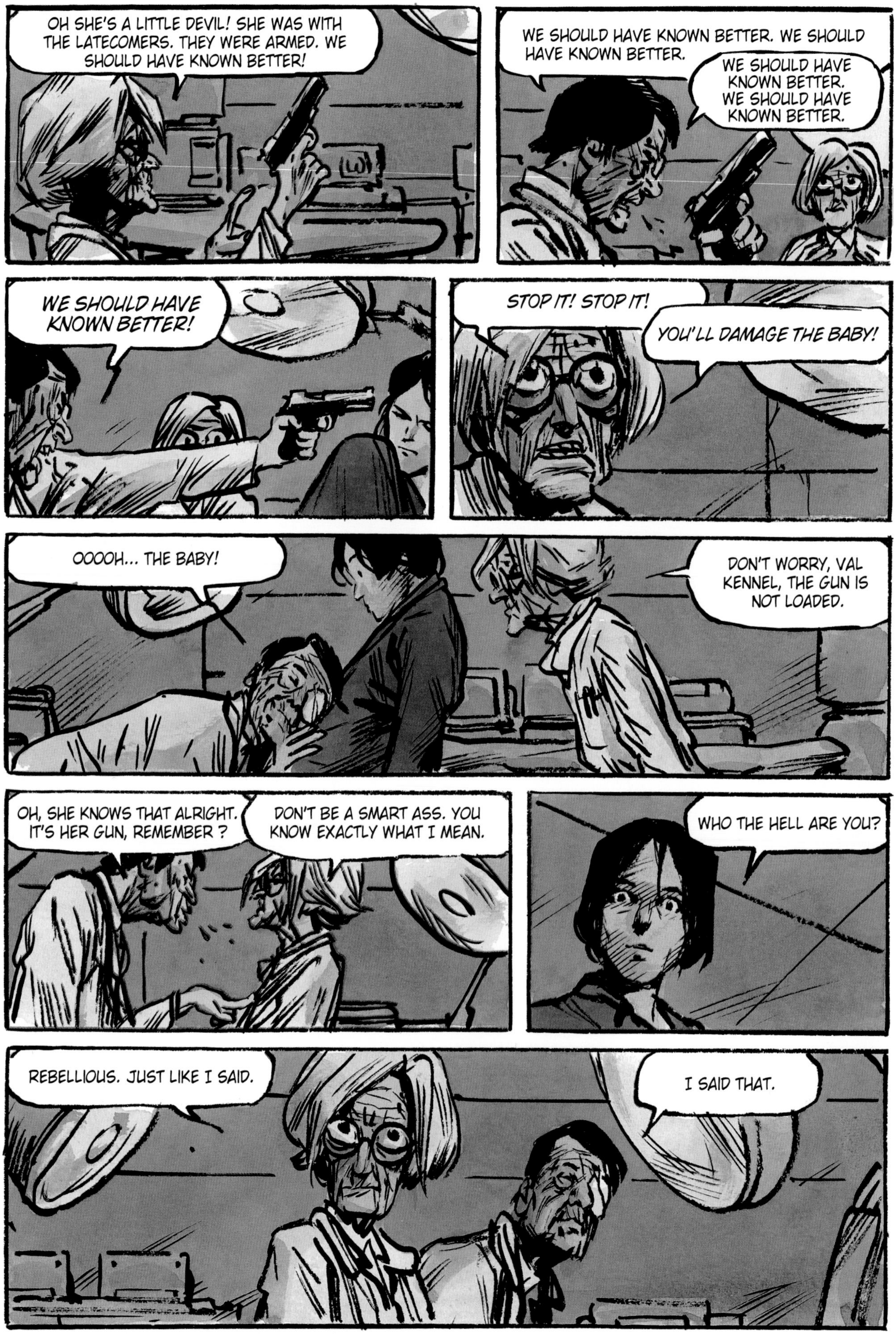
OH SHE'S A LITTLE DEVIL! SHE WAS WITH THE LATECOMERS. THEY WERE ARMED. WE SHOULD HAVE KNOWN BETTER!
WE SHOULD HAVE KNOWN BETTER. WE SHOULD HAVE KNOWN BETTER.
WE SHOULD HAVE KNOWN BETTER. WE SHOULD HAVE KNOWN BETTER.
WE SHOULD HAVE KNOWN BETTER!
STOP IT! STOP IT!
YOU'LL DAMAGE THE BABY!
OOOOH... THE BABY!
DON'T WORRY, VAL KENNEL, THE GUN IS NOT LOADED.
OH, SHE KNOWS THAT ALRIGHT. IT'S HER GUN, REMEMBER ?
DON'T BE A SMART ASS. YOU KNOW EXACTLY WHAT I MEAN.
WHO THE HELL ARE YOU?
REBELLIOUS. JUST LIKE I SAID.
I SAID THAT.

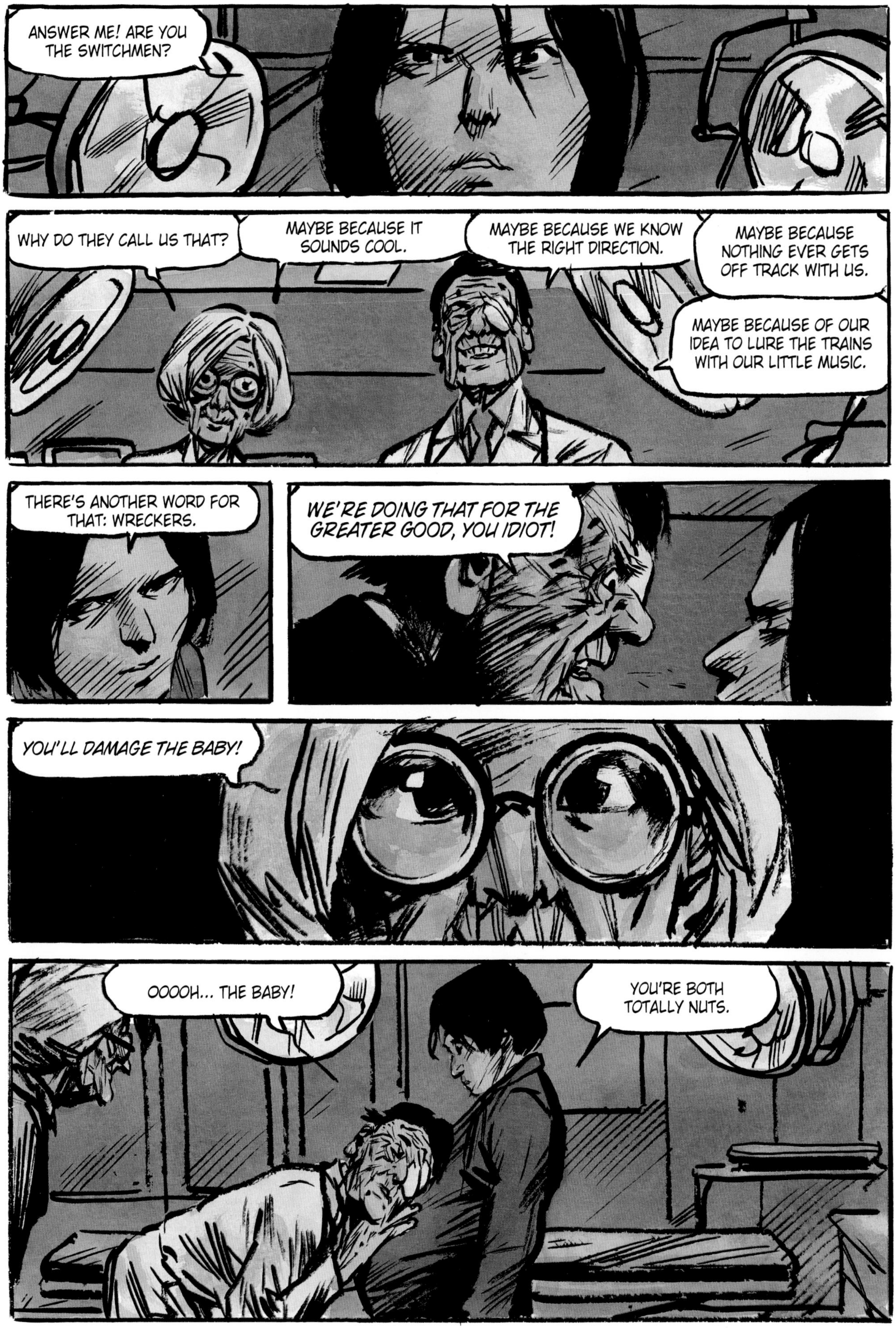
ANSWER ME! ARE YOU THE SWITCHMEN?
WHY DO THEY CALL US THAT?
MAYBE BECAUSE IT SOUNDS COOL.
MAYBE BECAUSE WE KNOW THE RIGHT DIRECTION.
MAYBE BECAUSE NOTHING EVER GETS OFF TRACK WITH US.
MAYBE BECAUSE OF OUR IDEA TO LURE THE TRAINS WITH OUR LITTLE MUSIC.
THERE'S ANOTHER WORD FOR THAT: WRECKERS.
WE'RE DOING THAT FOR THE GREATER GOOD, YOU IDIOT!
YOU'LL DAMAGE THE BABY!
OOOOH... THE BABY!
YOU'RE BOTH TOTALLY NUTS.

WE ARE NOT NUTS. WE ARE WILFRID AND NORA HEADWOOD, FOUNDERS OF THIS PARK. WE ARE SCIENTISTS, RESEARCHERS, AND BY THE WAY, SAVIORS OF MANKIND.

SO, SHOW SOME RESPECT, VAL KENNEL.

IT'S NOT THAT EASY TO SAVE THE WORLD, YOUNG LADY. BUT WE'RE DOING OK, CONSIDERING THE EARTHQUAKE.

AH, YES. THE EARTHQUAKE. THE TREACHEROUS BLOW. THE LEAK OF THE PLANT.

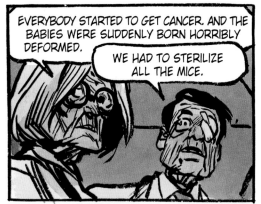

EVERYBODY STARTED TO GET CANCER. AND THE BABIES WERE SUDDENLY BORN HORRIBLY DEFORMED.

WE HAD TO STERILIZE ALL THE MICE.

ALL THE MICE? YOU MEAN THE PEOPLE, RIGHT?

WE HAD NO CHOICE!

STOP! THE BABY!

WE HAD NO CHOICE. WE HAD NO CHOICE. WE HAD NO CHOICE. WE HAD NO CHOICE.

DID WE HAVE ANY CHOICE?

NO. WE HAD NO CHOICE.

OF COURSE WE HAD NO CHOICE. CALM DOWN.

THEY'RE ESCAPING. I CAN SEE THEM.

CALM DOWN!

HAHAHAHAHA! ESCAPING TO WHERE?

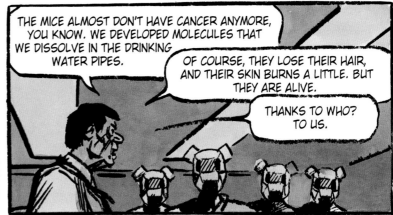

THE MICE ALMOST DON'T HAVE CANCER ANYMORE, YOU KNOW. WE DEVELOPED MOLECULES THAT WE DISSOLVE IN THE DRINKING WATER PIPES.

OF COURSE, THEY LOSE THEIR HAIR, AND THEIR SKIN BURNS A LITTLE. BUT THEY ARE ALIVE.

THANKS TO WHO? TO US.

YOU CAN'T SAVE MANKIND BY STERILIZING IT. IT'S ABSURD.

HAHAHA! HOW STUPID SHE IS!

WHY DO YOU THINK WE MADE ALL THESE TRAINS COME HERE? TO GET NEW BLOOD, OF COURSE! OOCYTES FULL OF BEANS, DASHING SPERM!

RADIATION-FREE EMBRYOS!

HENCE THE FERTILITY FEAST. YOU MISSED SOMETHING. IT WAS BEAUTIFUL.

IT WAS.

YOU WANT TO KNOW HOW TO ORGANIZE A FERTILITY FEAST? I'M GONNA TELL YOU HOW TO ORGANIZE A FERTILITY FEAST.

OH, PLEASE NO! THIS IS SO BORING!

LET ME TELL THE STORY, YOU OLD FART!

167

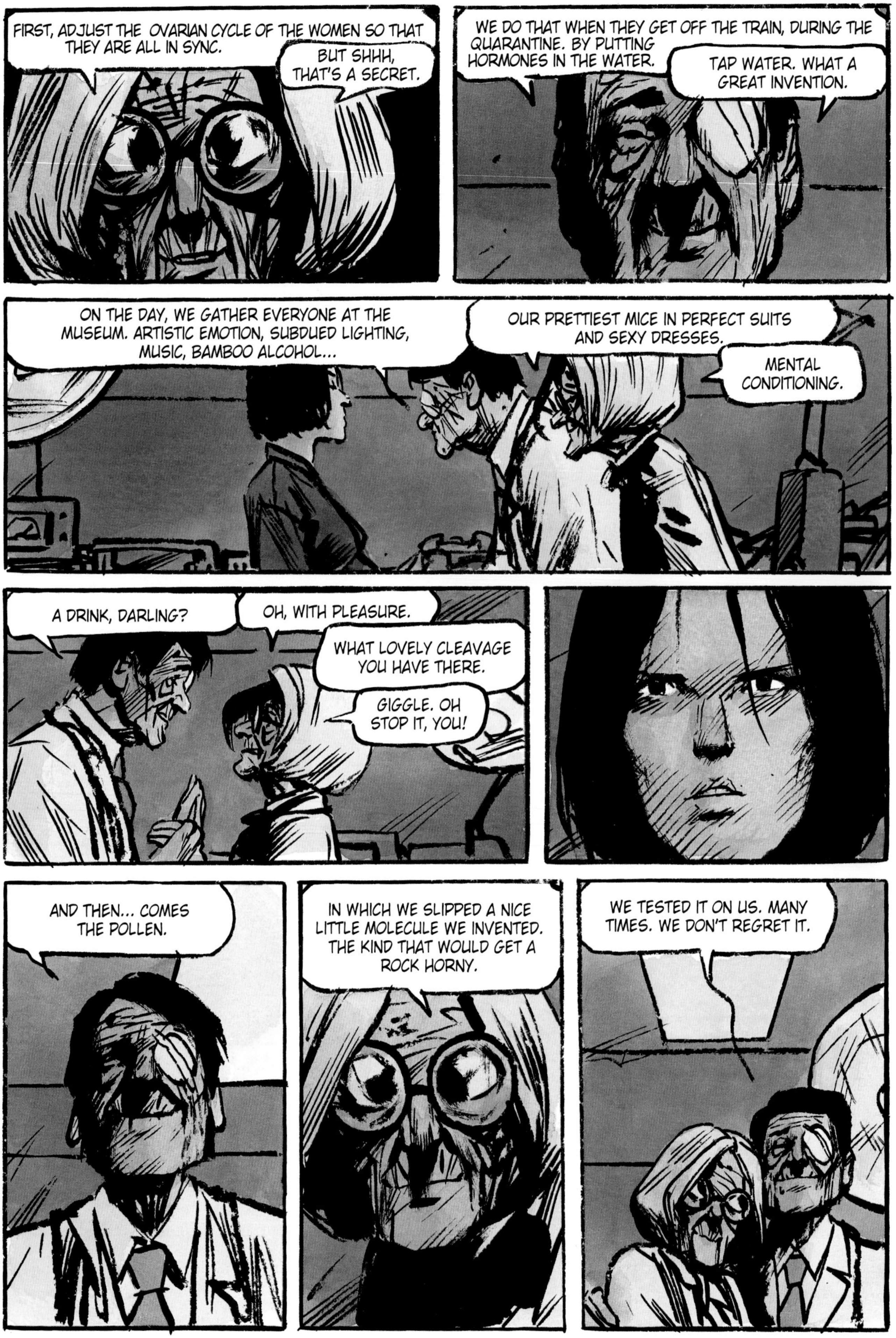
FIRST, ADJUST THE OVARIAN CYCLE OF THE WOMEN SO THAT THEY ARE ALL IN SYNC.
BUT SHHH, THAT'S A SECRET.
WE DO THAT WHEN THEY GET OFF THE TRAIN, DURING THE QUARANTINE. BY PUTTING HORMONES IN THE WATER.
TAP WATER. WHAT A GREAT INVENTION.
ON THE DAY, WE GATHER EVERYONE AT THE MUSEUM. ARTISTIC EMOTION, SUBDUED LIGHTING, MUSIC, BAMBOO ALCOHOL...
OUR PRETTIEST MICE IN PERFECT SUITS AND SEXY DRESSES.
MENTAL CONDITIONING.
A DRINK, DARLING?
OH, WITH PLEASURE.
WHAT LOVELY CLEAVAGE YOU HAVE THERE.
GIGGLE. OH STOP IT, YOU!
AND THEN... COMES THE POLLEN.
IN WHICH WE SLIPPED A NICE LITTLE MOLECULE WE INVENTED. THE KIND THAT WOULD GET A ROCK HORNY.
WE TESTED IT ON US. MANY TIMES. WE DON'T REGRET IT.

THEN, YOU JUST LET NATURE DO ITS BUSINESS.

OF COURSE, MICE DO NOT TAKE PART. WE WOULDN'T WANT THE SEMEN OF HEALTHY MALES TO END UP IN INFERTILE WOMBS.

NOW GET UNDRESSED AND CLIMB ON THE OPERATING TABLE.

WHAT? BUT...

NO. OUT OF THE QUESTION.

DO YOU THINK WE MADE YOU COME DOWN HERE TO CHITCHAT? GET ON THIS TABLE!

NO!

LEAVE ME THE FUCK ALONE!

REBELLIOUS. JUST LIKE I SAID.

SEE IT THROUGH OUR EYES. DO YOU THINK WE CAN WAIT FOR BABIES TO BE BORN? AFTER NINE MONTHS IN UTERO, THEY'RE ALREADY WAY TOO OLD.

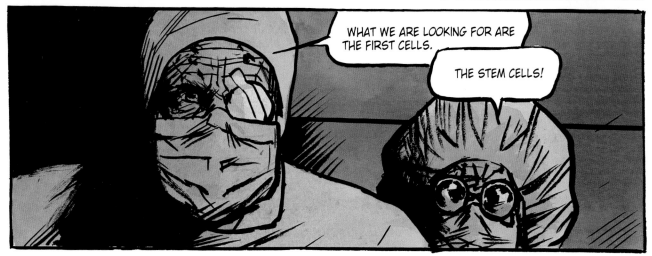

WHAT WE ARE LOOKING FOR ARE THE FIRST CELLS.

THE STEM CELLS!

OF COURSE, THE STEM CELLS! DO YOU THINK I DON'T KNOW THAT? I'M JUST MAKING SURE THAT SHE UNDERSTANDS ME!
DO YOU KNOW WHAT A STEM CELL IS?
GO FUCK YOURSELF.
I KNEW IT! SHE DOESN'T KNOW! SO STUPID!
SHE SAID GO FUCK YOURSELF, IT DOESN'T PROVE ANYTHING.
STEM CELLS ARE CELLS THAT AREN'T SPECIALIZED. THEY CAN BECOME WHATEVER WE WANT: MUSCLE, BLOOD, SKIN, BRAIN, BONE, ORGANS...
IF YOU MULTIPLY THEM ENOUGH, YOU GET A WHOLE HUMAN BODY!
GET THE FUCK OFF ME!
BUT THESE KIND OF CELLS ONLY EXIST ON THE FOUR DAYS FOLLOWING IMPREGNATION. AFTER THAT, THEY ARE LESS COOPERATIVE.
THAT IS WHY, IN THREE DAYS, WE WILL HARVEST THE WOMEN FROM...
STOP WRIGGLING! LISTEN TO ME WHEN I TALK!
TIE HER DOWN, DAMMIT!

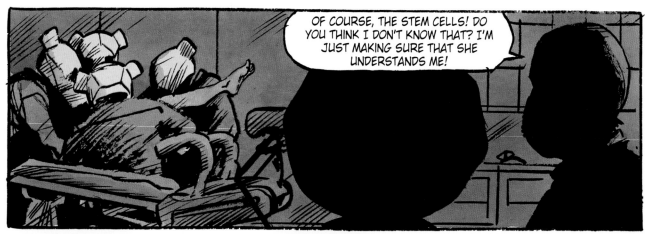

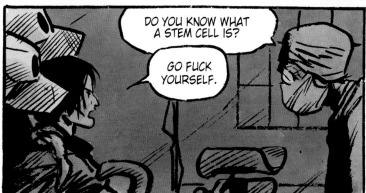

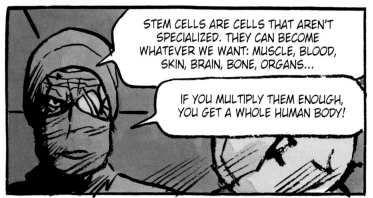

WHERE WAS I?

WHO CARES? LET'S TAKE HER BABY AND GET IT OVER.

WAIT, I HAD A LIST...

I'M TELLING YOU: NOBODY CARES !

AH, HERE.

NOBODY CARES!

AND THAT?

NOBODY CARES!

THAT?

NOBODY CARES!

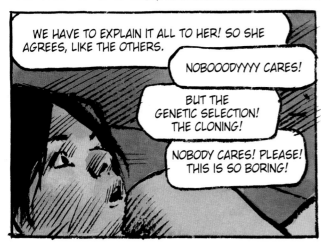

WE HAVE TO EXPLAIN IT ALL TO HER! SO SHE AGREES, LIKE THE OTHERS.

NOBOOODYYYY CARES!

BUT THE GENETIC SELECTION! THE CLONING!

NOBODY CARES! PLEASE! THIS IS SO BORING!

WHAT ABOUT WHAT WE'RE GONNA DO WITH HER BABY? SHE OUGHT TO KNOW!

LISTEN TO ME, HONEY BUNNY. YOU STARTED THIS CONVERSATION BY POINTING A GUN AT HER FACE. HOW DO YOU EXPECT HER TO LISTEN TO US NOW?

SHE DOESN'T CARE ABOUT SAVING HUMANITY! ALL SHE CARES ABOUT IS THAT AN OLD MAN IS WAVING A PISTOL AT HER!

DO YOU THINK SHE FINDS ME OLD?

HOW OLD DO YOU THINK I AM? SEVENTY? EIGHTY?

I AM 107 YEARS OLD, HAHAHA! WHAT DO YOU THINK ABOUT THAT?

AND I'M 109! HAHAHAHA!

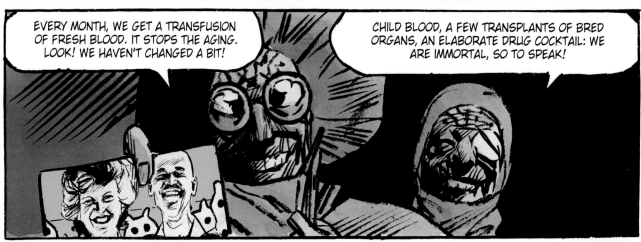

EVERY MONTH, WE GET A TRANSFUSION OF FRESH BLOOD. IT STOPS THE AGING. LOOK! WE HAVEN'T CHANGED A BIT!

CHILD BLOOD, A FEW TRANSPLANTS OF BRED ORGANS, AN ELABORATE DRUG COCKTAIL: WE ARE IMMORTAL, SO TO SPEAK!

CHILD BLOOD? IS THAT WHY YOU WANT TO TAKE MY BABY FROM ME?

SEE? SHE'S NOT THAT STUPID AFTER ALL.

I HAVE TO SAY, I'M SURPRISED.

MAKE NO MISTAKE, WE'RE NOT BEING SELFISH, HERE. WE'RE DOING THIS TO SAVE HUMANITY.

NOBODY ELSE HAS THE SKILLS TO CREATE THE NEW MAN. WE HAVE TO LIVE LONG ENOUGH TO FINISH THE PROJECT.

AND IN ORDER TO REPOPULATE EARTH, WE CAN'T COUNT ON THE TRADITIONAL WAY. TOO MANY GENETIC UNCERTAINTIES. TOO MANY FLAWS.

THANKS, MICE. YOU CAN LEAVE US, NOW.

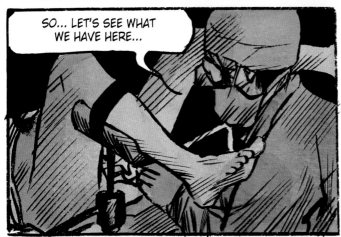

SO... LET'S SEE WHAT WE HAVE HERE...

I FORBID YOU...

WHAT... WHAT IS THAT?

IS THERE A PROBLEM?

SOMETHING'S STUCK. I'M TAKING IT OUT.

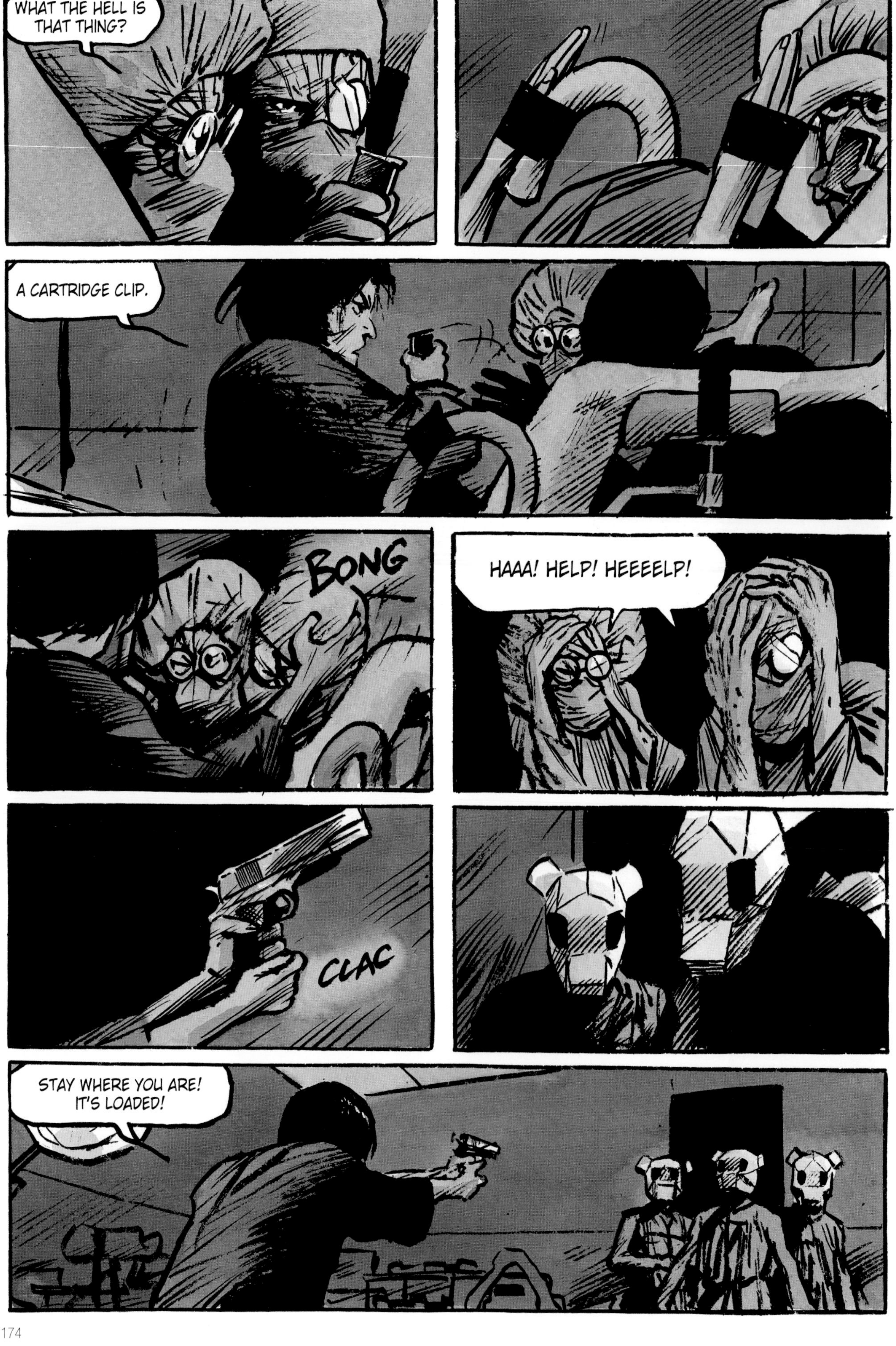
WHAT THE HELL IS THAT THING?
A CARTRIDGE CLIP.
BONG
HAAA! HELP! HEEEELP!
CLAC
STAY WHERE YOU ARE! IT'S LOADED!

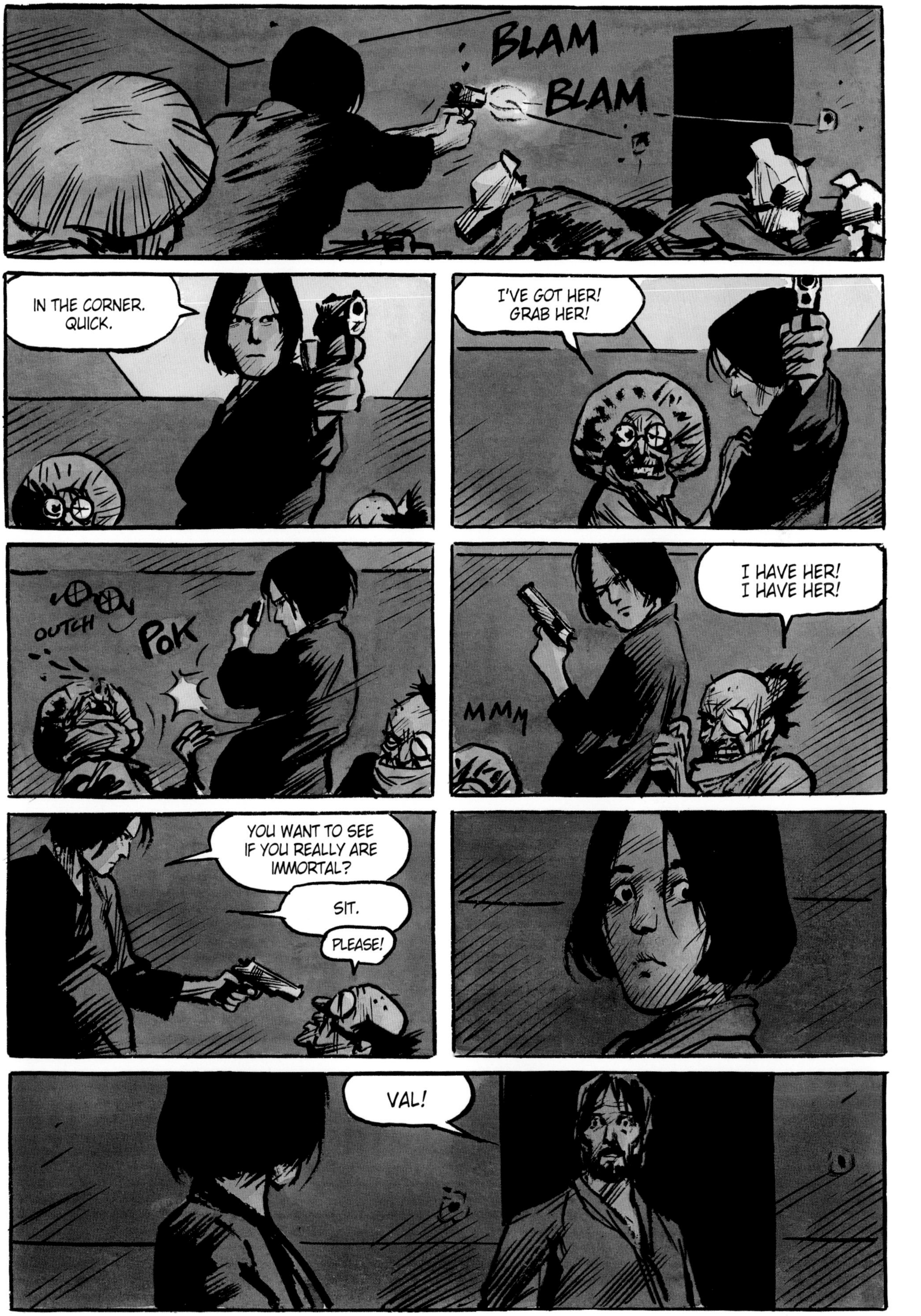
BLAM
BLAM
IN THE CORNER. QUICK.
I'VE GOT HER! GRAB HER!
OUTCH
POK
I HAVE HER! I HAVE HER!
MMM
YOU WANT TO SEE IF YOU REALLY ARE IMMORTAL?
SIT.
PLEASE!
VAL!

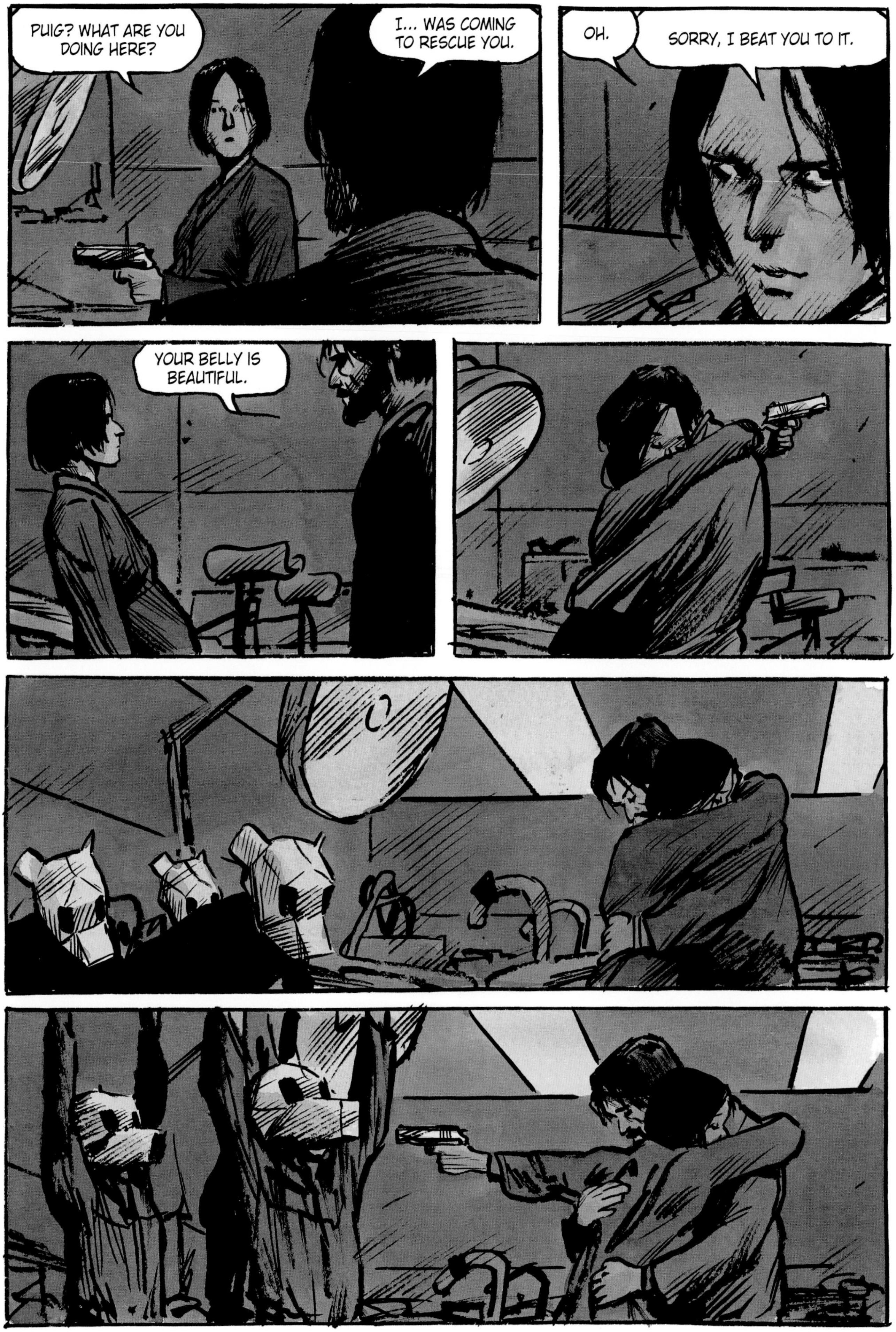
PUIG? WHAT ARE YOU DOING HERE?
I... WAS COMING TO RESCUE YOU.
OH.
SORRY, I BEAT YOU TO IT.
YOUR BELLY IS BEAUTIFUL.

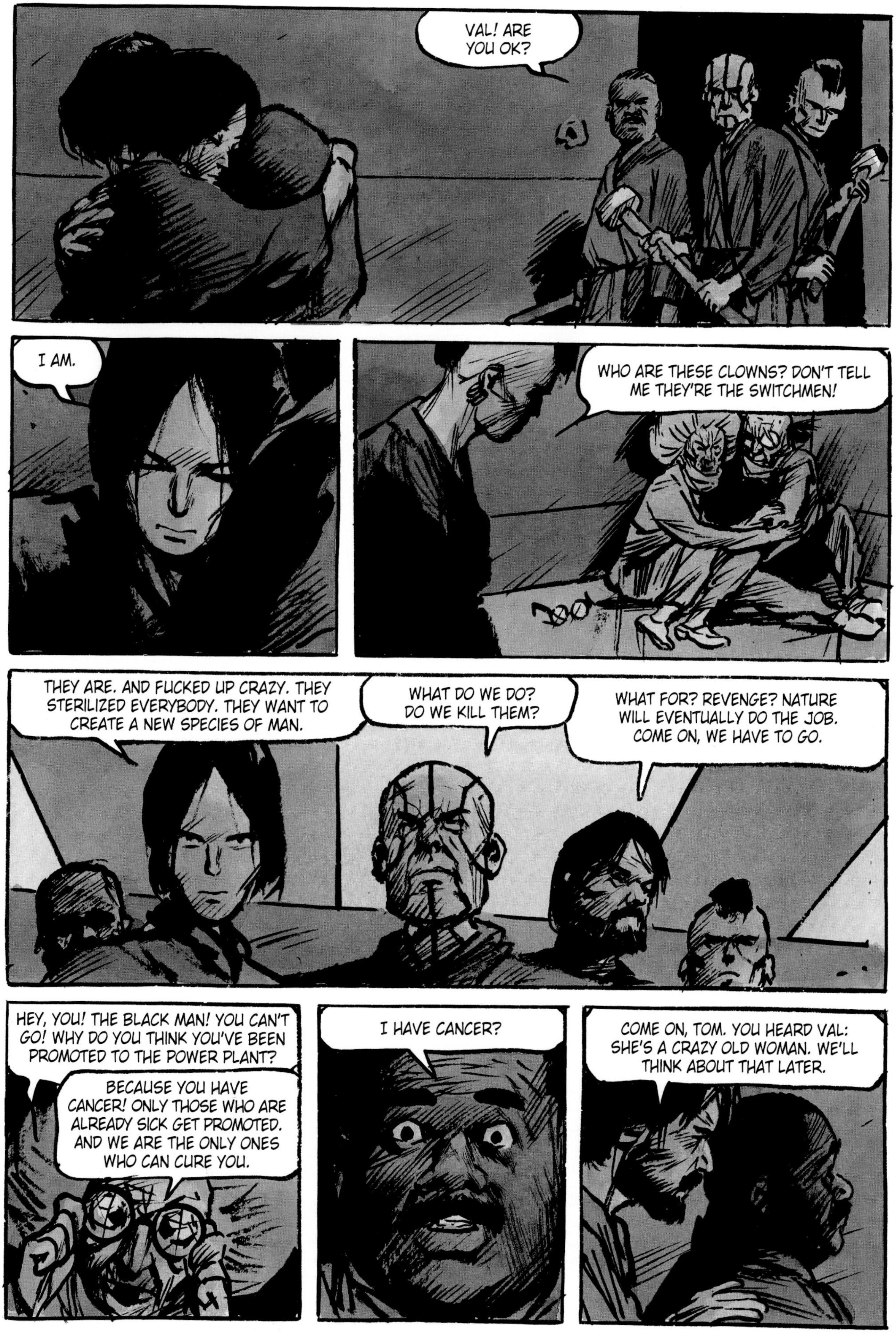
VAL! ARE YOU OK?
I AM.
WHO ARE THESE CLOWNS? DON'T TELL ME THEY'RE THE SWITCHMEN!
THEY ARE. AND FUCKED UP CRAZY. THEY STERILIZED EVERYBODY. THEY WANT TO CREATE A NEW SPECIES OF MAN.
WHAT DO WE DO? DO WE KILL THEM?
WHAT FOR? REVENGE? NATURE WILL EVENTUALLY DO THE JOB. COME ON, WE HAVE TO GO.
HEY, YOU! THE BLACK MAN! YOU CAN'T GO! WHY DO YOU THINK YOU'VE BEEN PROMOTED TO THE POWER PLANT?
BECAUSE YOU HAVE CANCER! ONLY THOSE WHO ARE ALREADY SICK GET PROMOTED. AND WE ARE THE ONLY ONES WHO CAN CURE YOU.
I HAVE CANCER?
COME ON, TOM. YOU HEARD VAL: SHE'S A CRAZY OLD WOMAN. WE'LL THINK ABOUT THAT LATER.

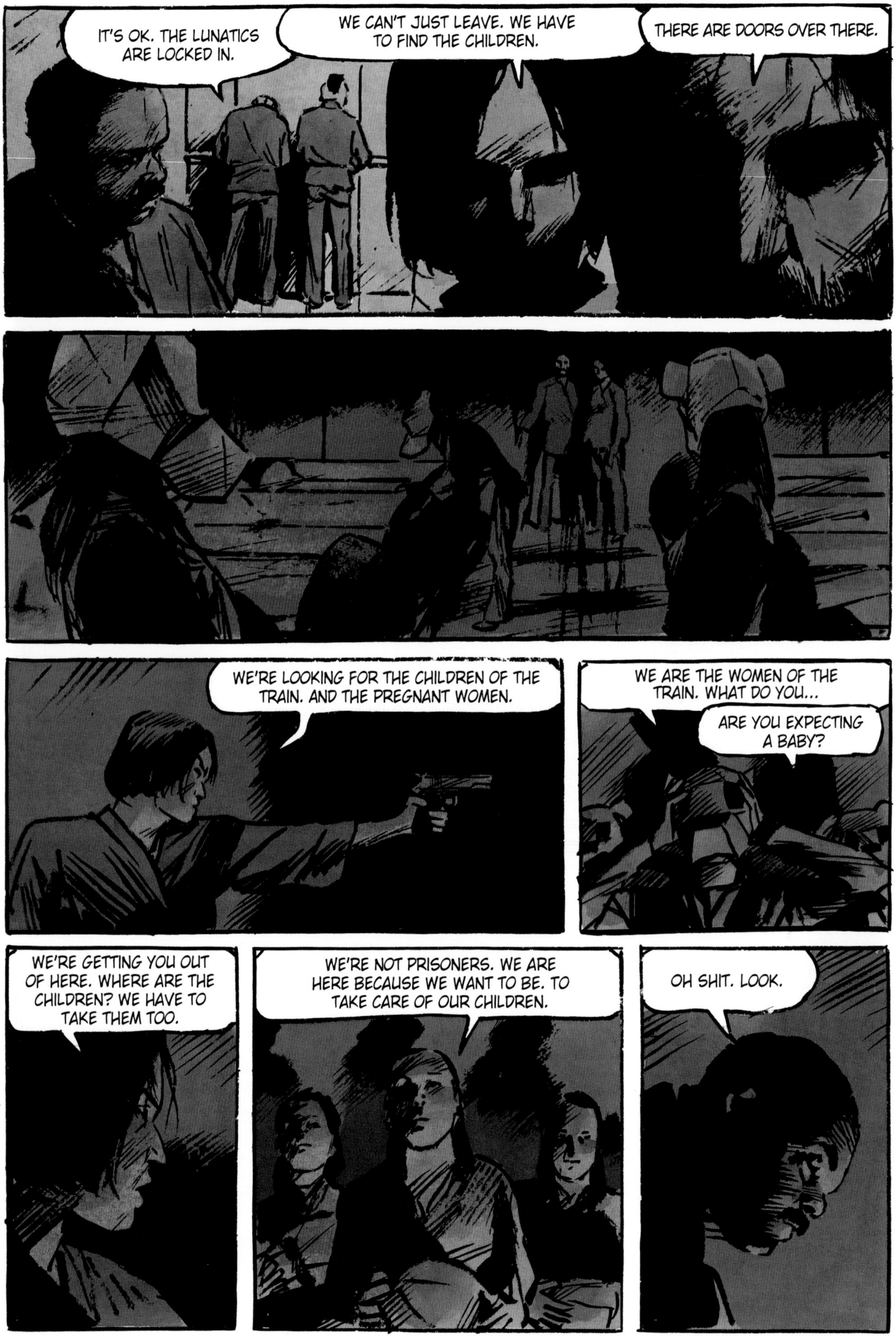
IT'S OK. THE LUNATICS ARE LOCKED IN.
WE CAN'T JUST LEAVE. WE HAVE TO FIND THE CHILDREN.
THERE ARE DOORS OVER THERE.
WE'RE LOOKING FOR THE CHILDREN OF THE TRAIN. AND THE PREGNANT WOMEN.
WE ARE THE WOMEN OF THE TRAIN. WHAT DO YOU...
ARE YOU EXPECTING A BABY?
WE'RE GETTING YOU OUT OF HERE. WHERE ARE THE CHILDREN? WE HAVE TO TAKE THEM TOO.
WE'RE NOT PRISONERS. WE ARE HERE BECAUSE WE WANT TO BE. TO TAKE CARE OF OUR CHILDREN.
OH SHIT. LOOK.

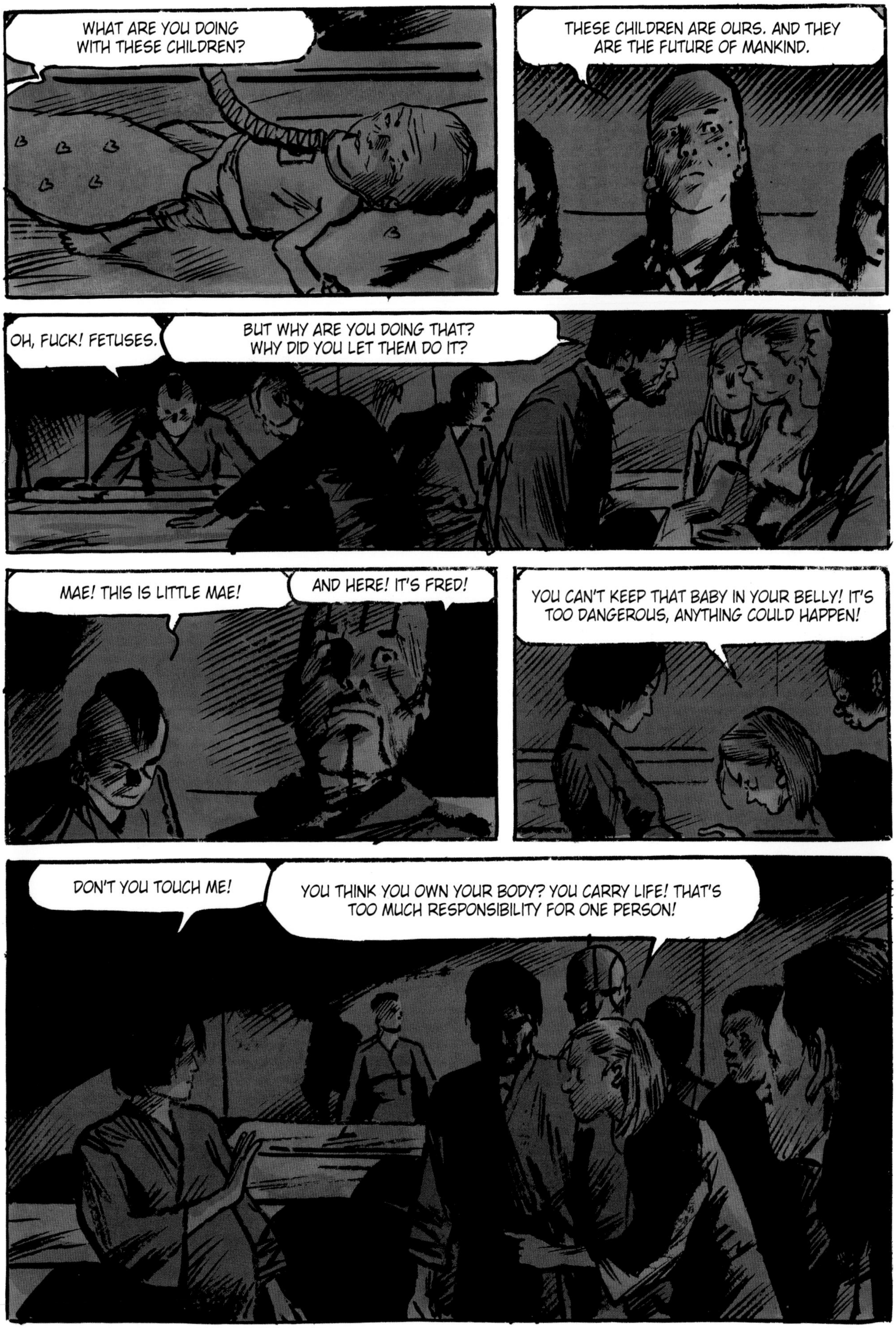
WHAT ARE YOU DOING WITH THESE CHILDREN?
THESE CHILDREN ARE OURS. AND THEY ARE THE FUTURE OF MANKIND.
OH, FUCK! FETUSES.
BUT WHY ARE YOU DOING THAT? WHY DID YOU LET THEM DO IT?
MAE! THIS IS LITTLE MAE!
AND HERE! IT'S FRED!
YOU CAN'T KEEP THAT BABY IN YOUR BELLY! IT'S TOO DANGEROUS, ANYTHING COULD HAPPEN!
DON'T YOU TOUCH ME!
YOU THINK YOU OWN YOUR BODY? YOU CARRY LIFE! THAT'S TOO MUCH RESPONSIBILITY FOR ONE PERSON!

YOU'RE ALL TOTALLY FUCKING CRAZY

YOU LET THEM TAKE YOUR CHILDREN BEFORE FULL TERM?

THEY DIDN'T TAKE THEM. THE CHILDREN ARE HERE, WITH US, ALWAYS BEFORE OUR EYES!

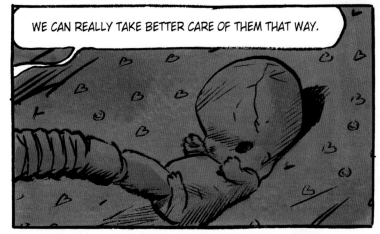

WE CAN REALLY TAKE BETTER CARE OF THEM THAT WAY.

TUMP TUMP TUN

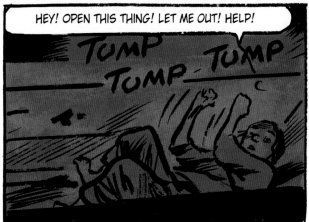

HEY! OPEN THIS THING! LET ME OUT! HELP!

TUMP TUMP-TUMP

IF YOU WANT TO STAY HERE, STAY. BUT WE'RE TAKING THE VIABLE CHILDREN.

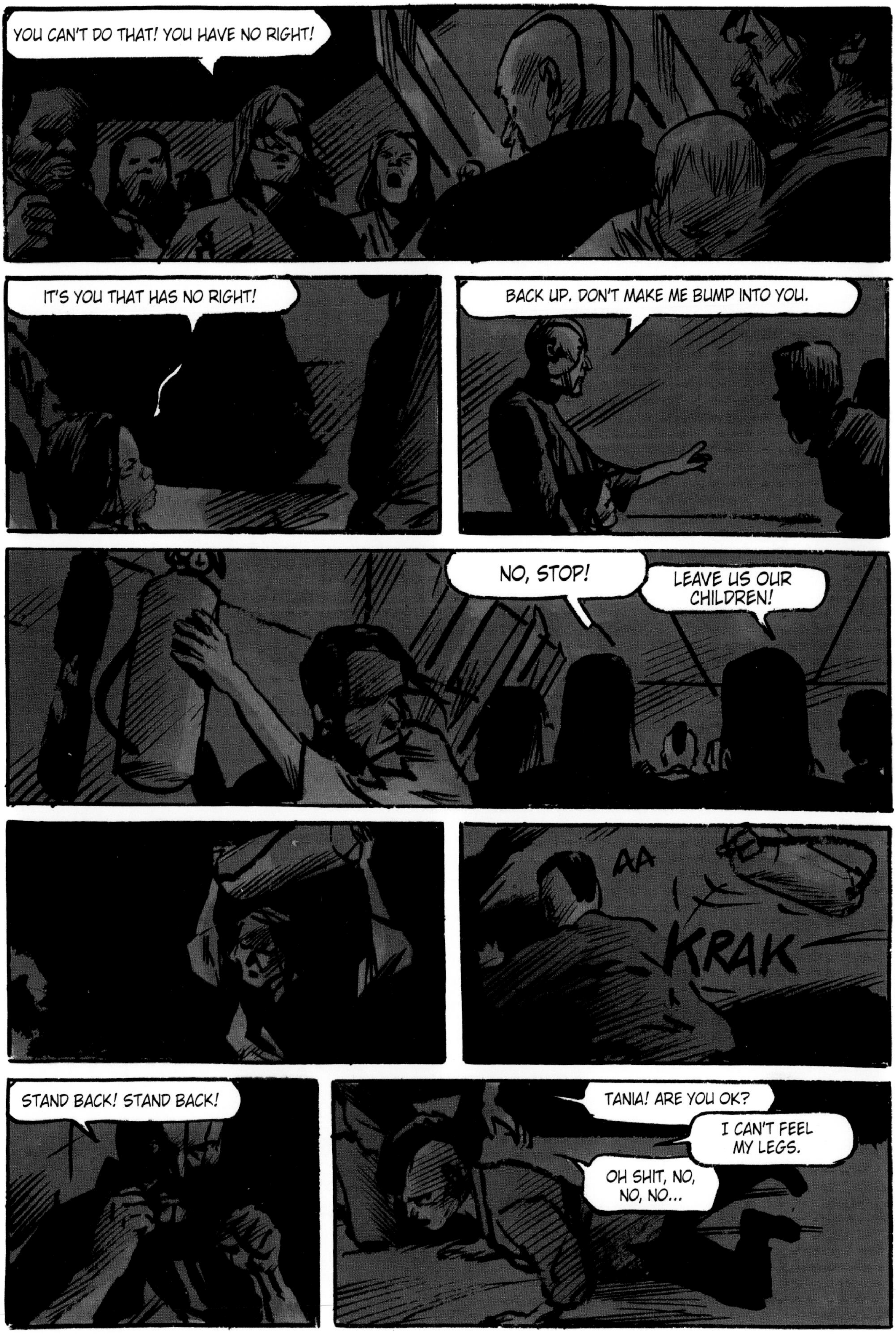
YOU CAN'T DO THAT! YOU HAVE NO RIGHT!
IT'S YOU THAT HAS NO RIGHT!
BACK UP. DON'T MAKE ME BUMP INTO YOU.
NO, STOP!
LEAVE US OUR CHILDREN!
AA
KRAK
STAND BACK! STAND BACK!
TANIA! ARE YOU OK?
I CAN'T FEEL MY LEGS.
OH SHIT, NO, NO, NO...

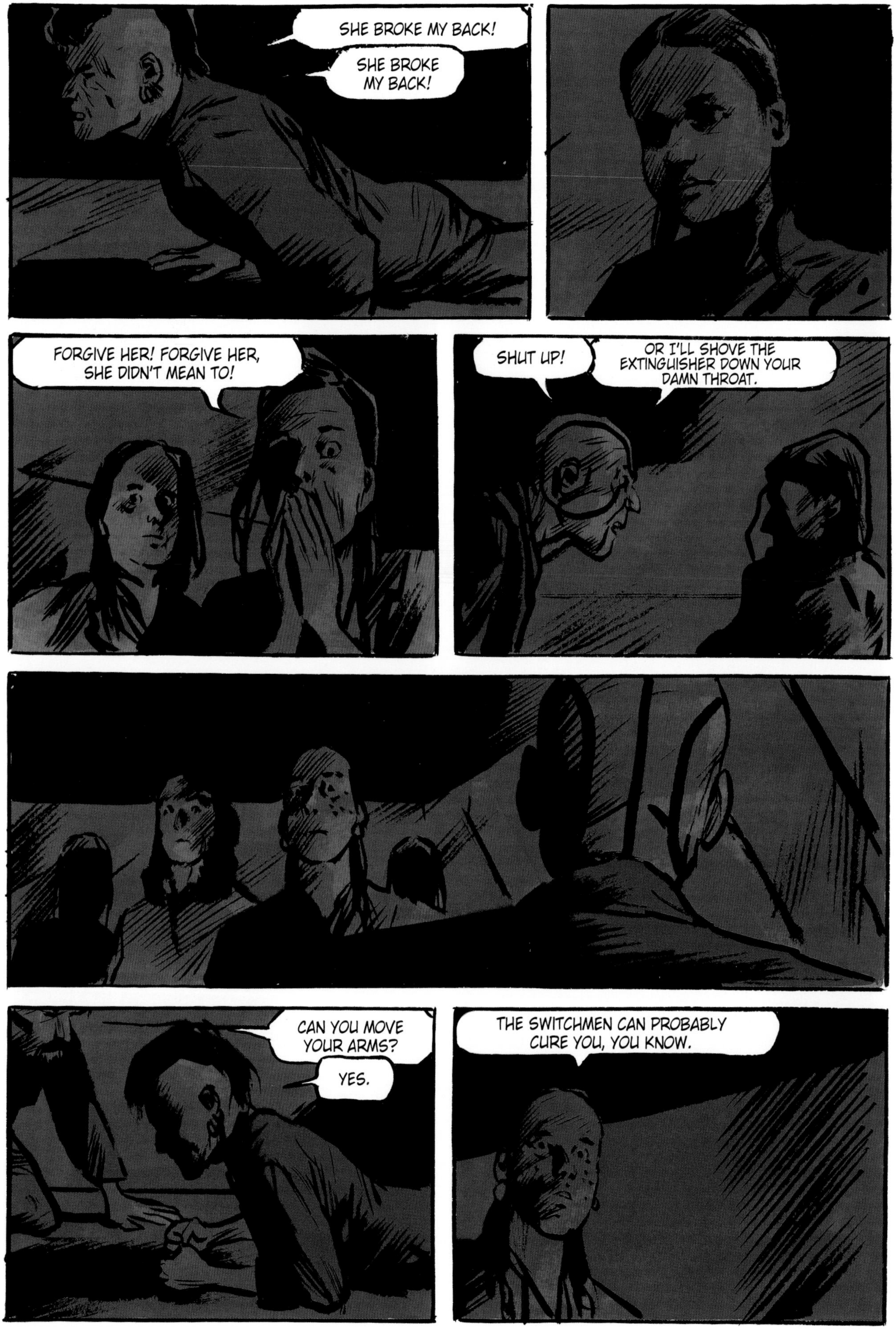
SHE BROKE MY BACK!
SHE BROKE MY BACK!
FORGIVE HER! FORGIVE HER, SHE DIDN'T MEAN TO!
SHUT UP!
OR I'LL SHOVE THE EXTINGUISHER DOWN YOUR DAMN THROAT.
CAN YOU MOVE YOUR ARMS?
YES.
THE SWITCHMEN CAN PROBABLY CURE YOU, YOU KNOW.

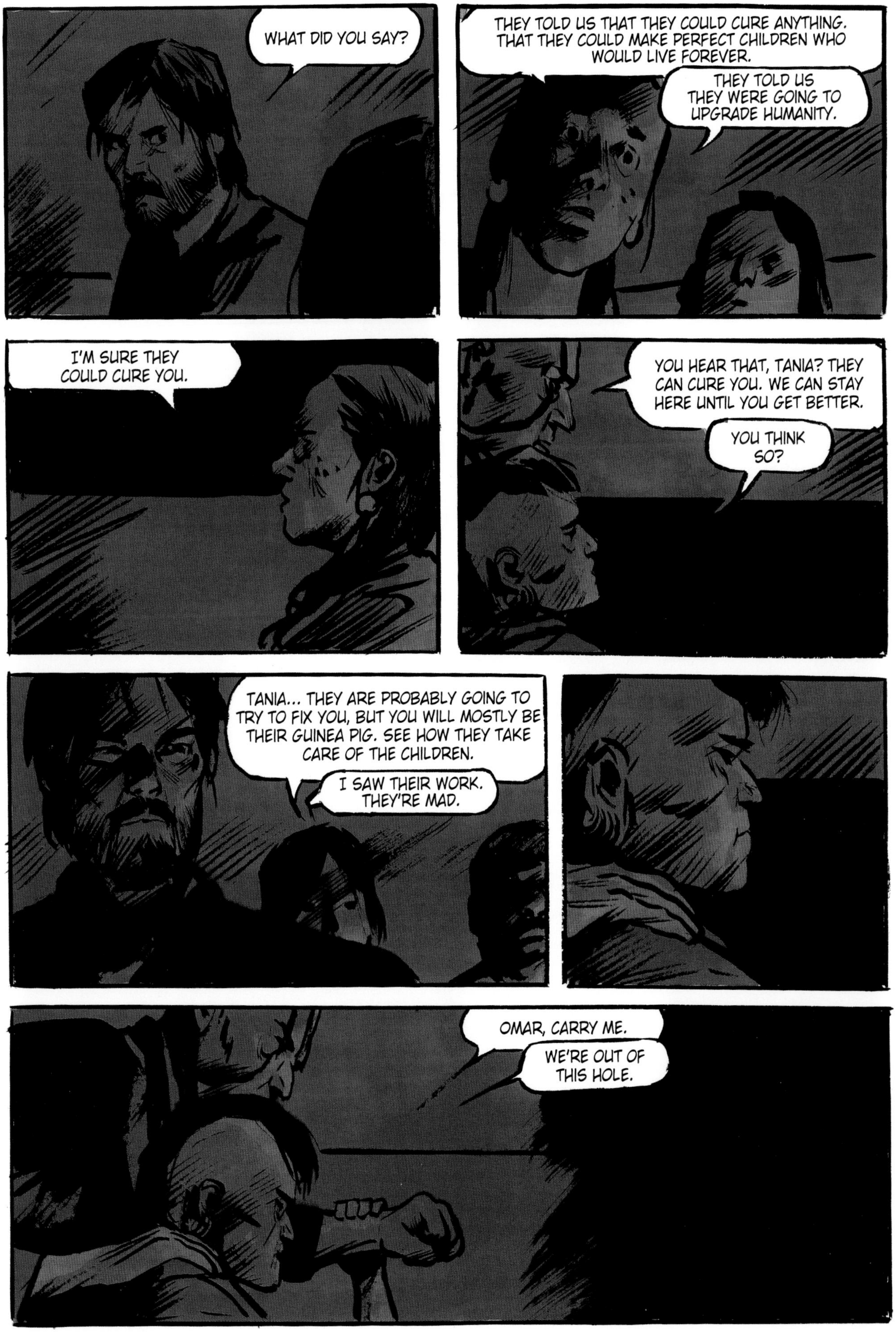
WHAT DID YOU SAY?
THEY TOLD US THAT THEY COULD CURE ANYTHING. THAT THEY COULD MAKE PERFECT CHILDREN WHO WOULD LIVE FOREVER.
THEY TOLD US THEY WERE GOING TO UPGRADE HUMANITY.
I'M SURE THEY COULD CURE YOU.
YOU HEAR THAT, TANIA? THEY CAN CURE YOU. WE CAN STAY HERE UNTIL YOU GET BETTER.
YOU THINK SO?
TANIA... THEY ARE PROBABLY GOING TO TRY TO FIX YOU, BUT YOU WILL MOSTLY BE THEIR GUINEA PIG. SEE HOW THEY TAKE CARE OF THE CHILDREN.
I SAW THEIR WORK. THEY'RE MAD.
OMAR, CARRY ME.
WE'RE OUT OF THIS HOLE.

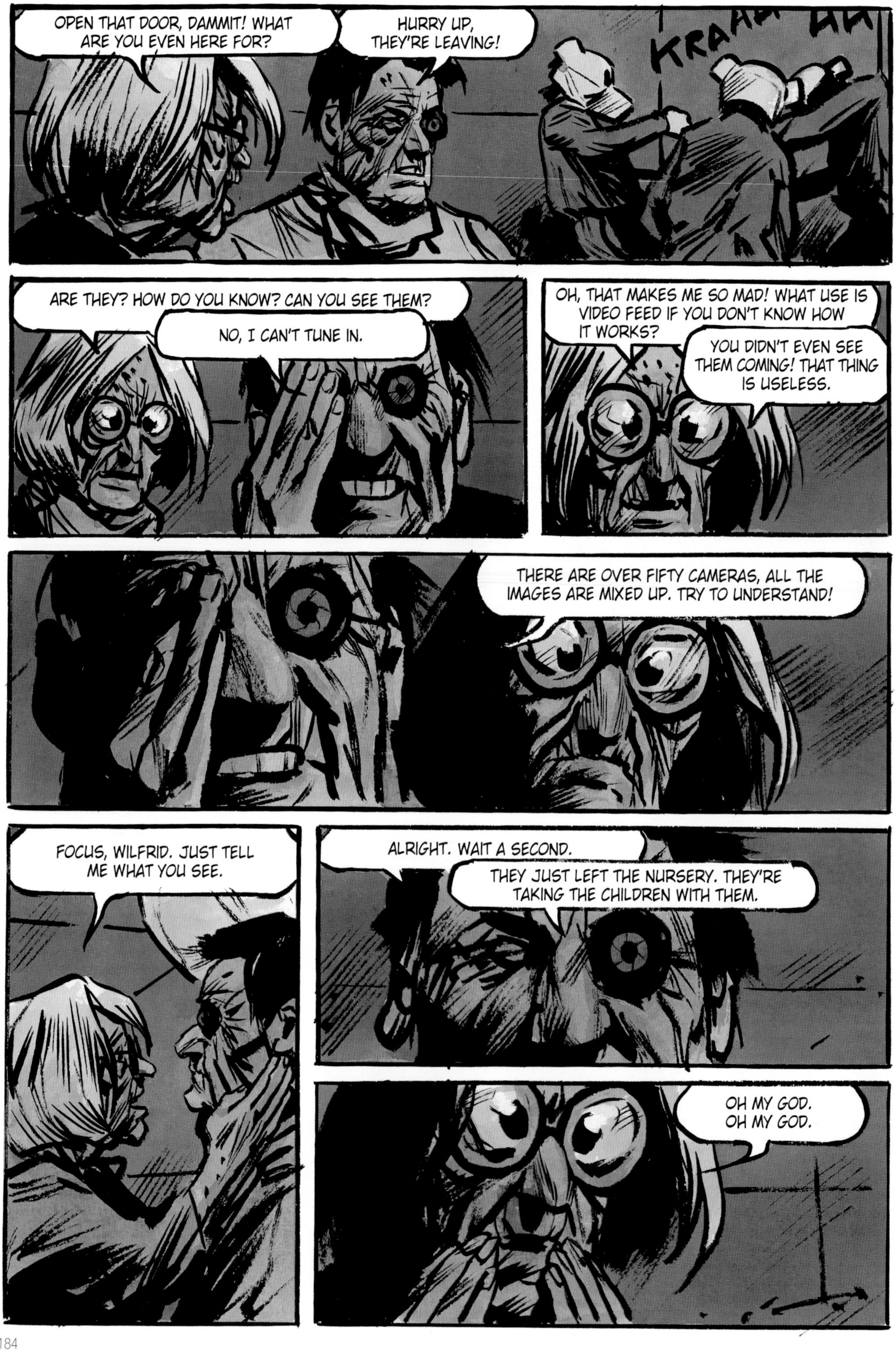
OPEN THAT DOOR, DAMMIT! WHAT ARE YOU EVEN HERE FOR?
HURRY UP, THEY'RE LEAVING!
ARE THEY? HOW DO YOU KNOW? CAN YOU SEE THEM?
NO, I CAN'T TUNE IN.
OH, THAT MAKES ME SO MAD! WHAT USE IS VIDEO FEED IF YOU DON'T KNOW HOW IT WORKS?
YOU DIDN'T EVEN SEE THEM COMING! THAT THING IS USELESS.
THERE ARE OVER FIFTY CAMERAS, ALL THE IMAGES ARE MIXED UP. TRY TO UNDERSTAND!
FOCUS, WILFRID. JUST TELL ME WHAT YOU SEE.
ALRIGHT. WAIT A SECOND.
THEY JUST LEFT THE NURSERY. THEY'RE TAKING THE CHILDREN WITH THEM.
OH MY GOD. OH MY GOD.

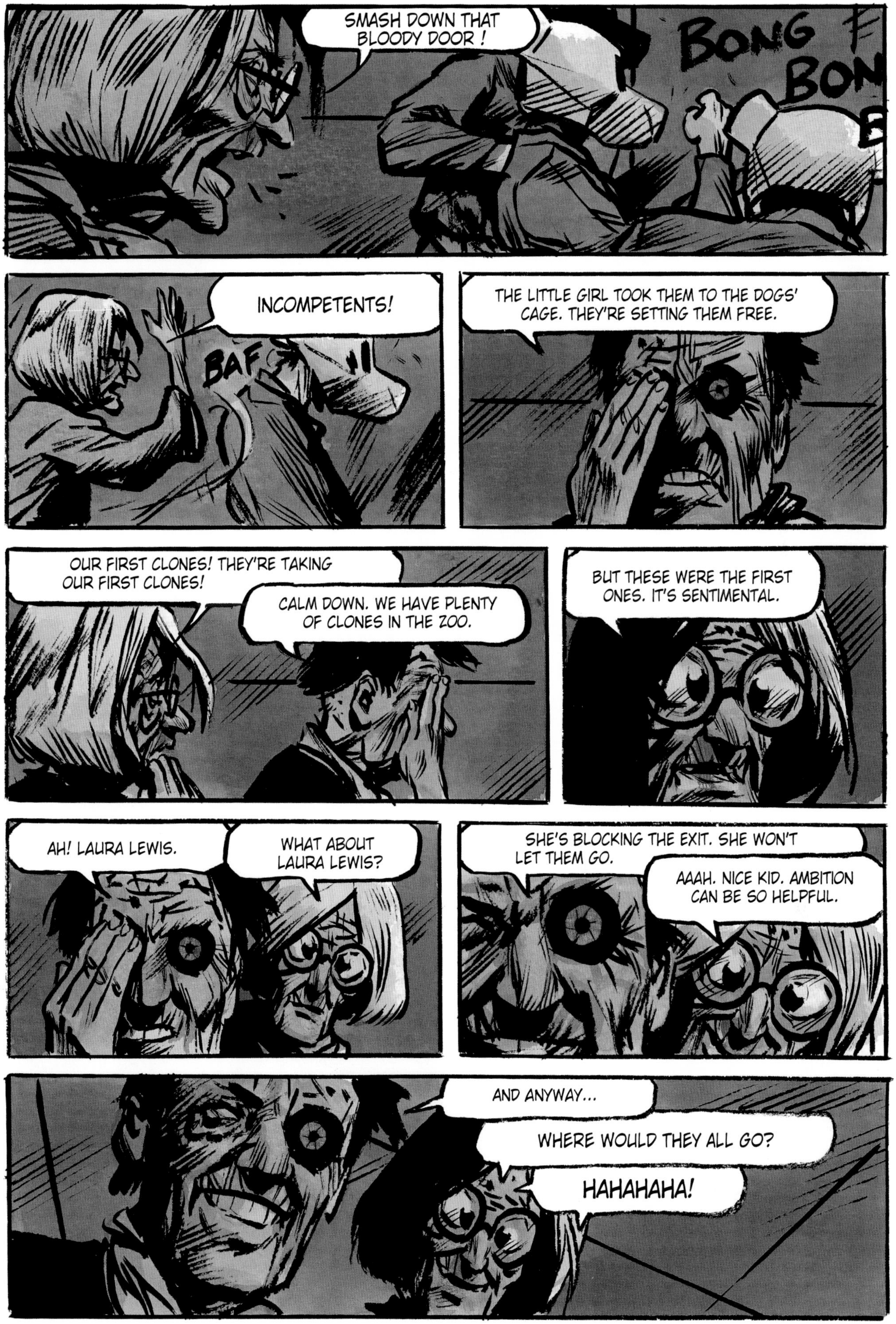
SMASH DOWN THAT BLOODY DOOR !
BONG
BON
B
INCOMPETENTS!
BAF
THE LITTLE GIRL TOOK THEM TO THE DOGS' CAGE. THEY'RE SETTING THEM FREE.
OUR FIRST CLONES! THEY'RE TAKING OUR FIRST CLONES!
CALM DOWN. WE HAVE PLENTY OF CLONES IN THE ZOO.
BUT THESE WERE THE FIRST ONES. IT'S SENTIMENTAL.
AH! LAURA LEWIS.
WHAT ABOUT LAURA LEWIS?
SHE'S BLOCKING THE EXIT. SHE WON'T LET THEM GO.
AAAH. NICE KID. AMBITION CAN BE SO HELPFUL.
AND ANYWAY...
WHERE WOULD THEY ALL GO?
HAHAHAHA!

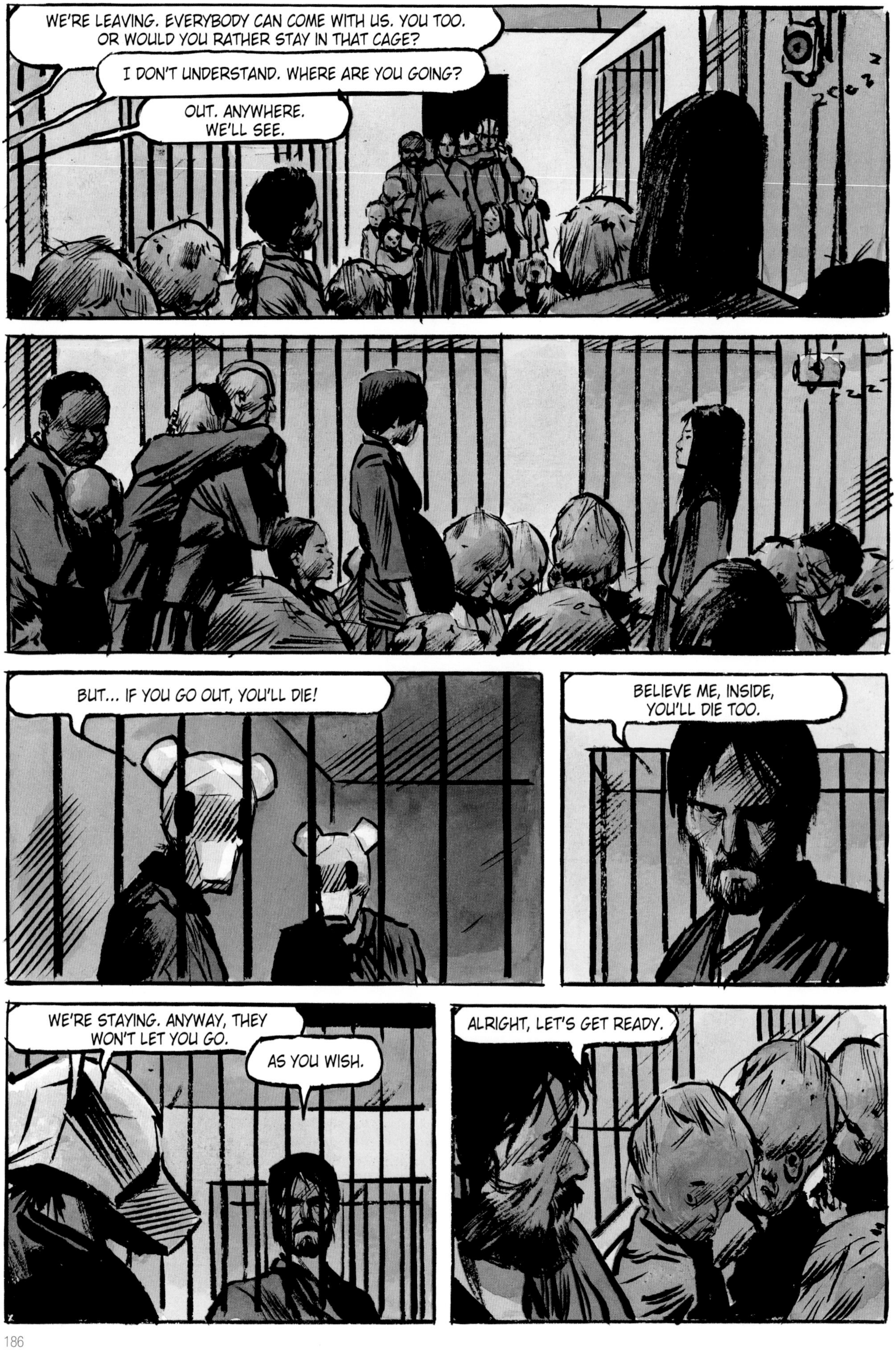
WE'RE LEAVING. EVERYBODY CAN COME WITH US. YOU TOO. OR WOULD YOU RATHER STAY IN THAT CAGE?
I DON'T UNDERSTAND. WHERE ARE YOU GOING?
OUT. ANYWHERE. WE'LL SEE.
BUT... IF YOU GO OUT, YOU'LL DIE!
BELIEVE ME, INSIDE, YOU'LL DIE TOO.
WE'RE STAYING. ANYWAY, THEY WON'T LET YOU GO.
AS YOU WISH.
ALRIGHT, LET'S GET READY.

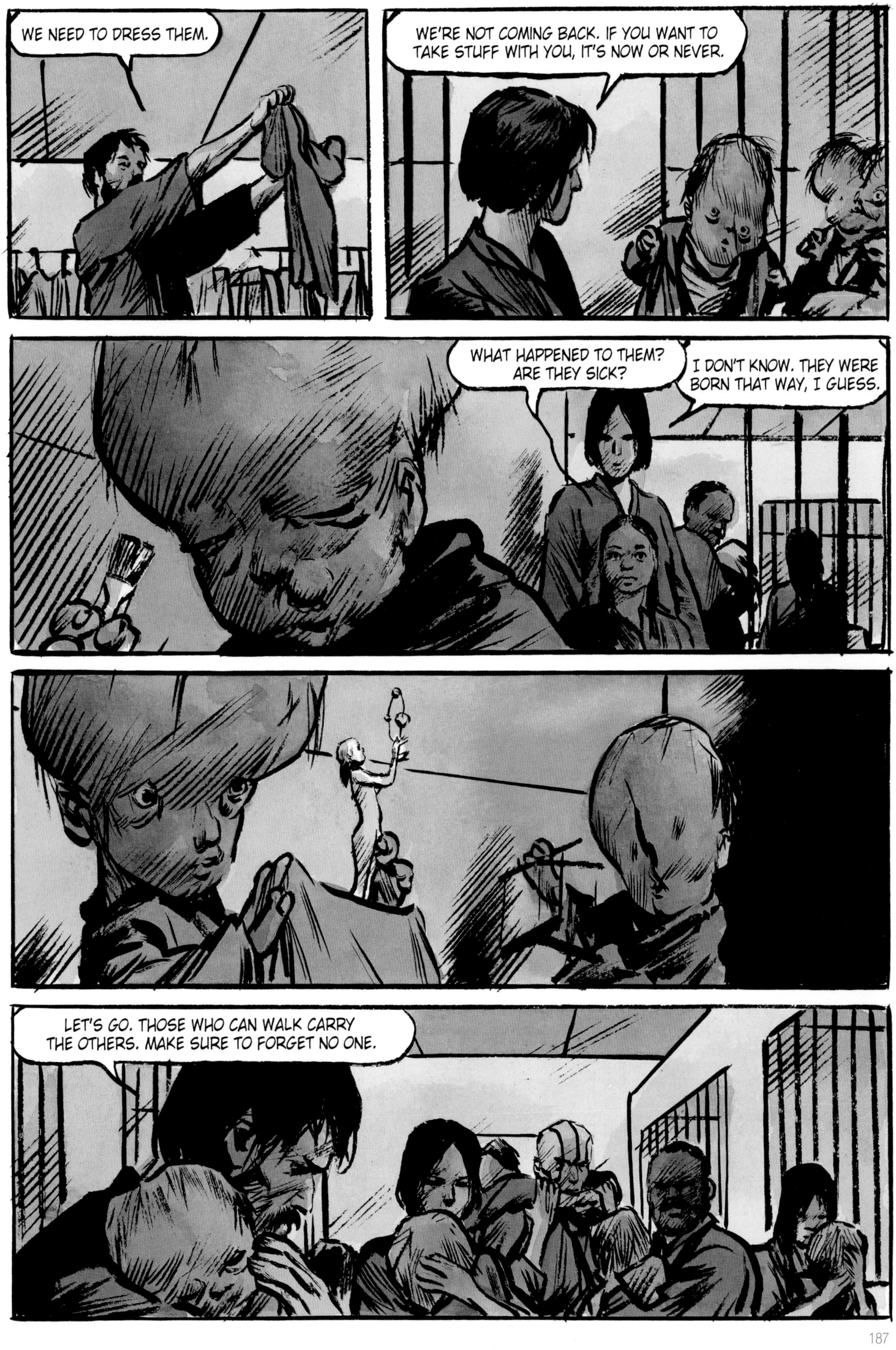
WE NEED TO DRESS THEM.
WE'RE NOT COMING BACK. IF YOU WANT TO TAKE STUFF WITH YOU, IT'S NOW OR NEVER.
WHAT HAPPENED TO THEM? ARE THEY SICK?
I DON'T KNOW. THEY WERE BORN THAT WAY, I GUESS.
LET'S GO. THOSE WHO CAN WALK CARRY THE OTHERS. MAKE SURE TO FORGET NO ONE.

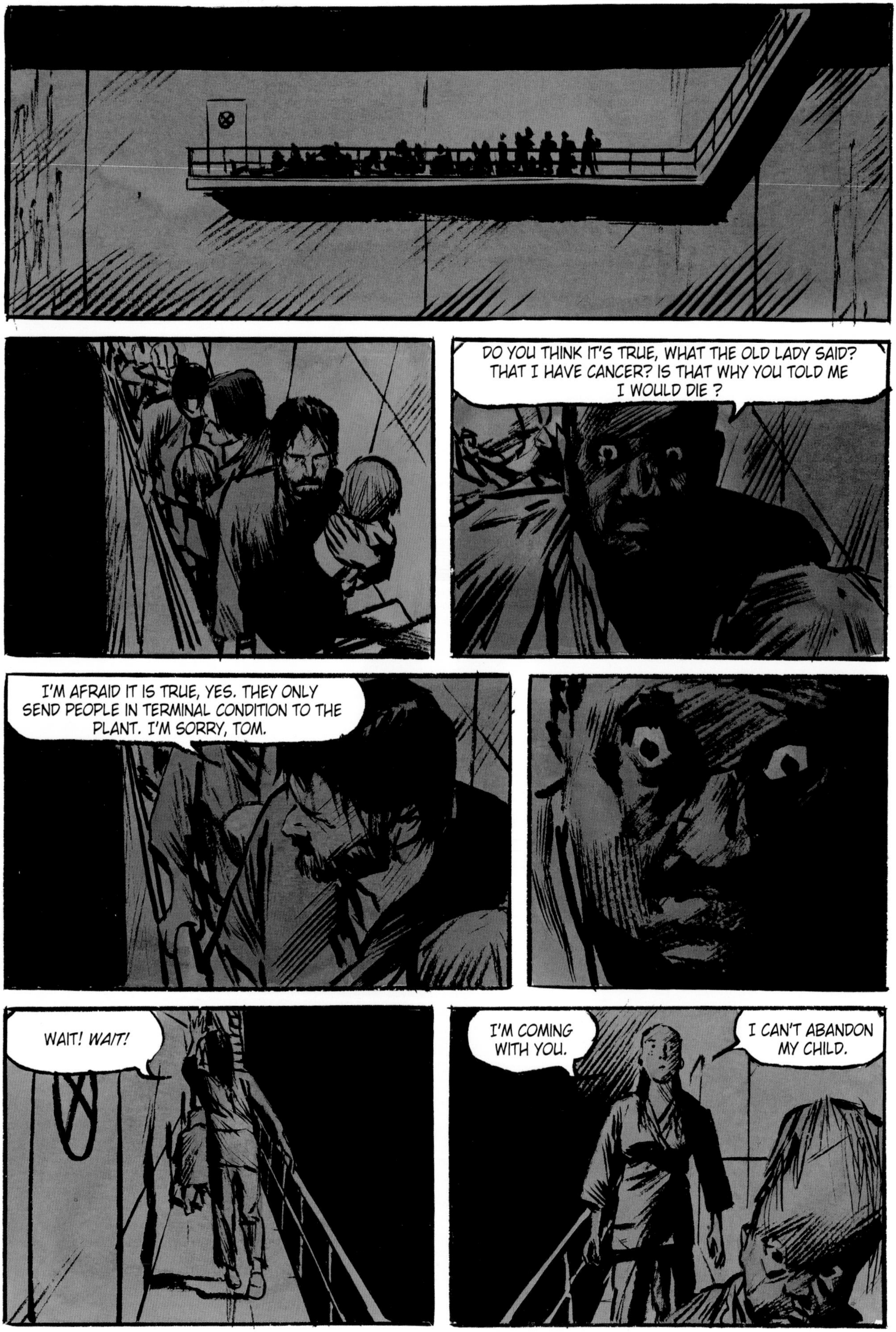
DO YOU THINK IT'S TRUE, WHAT THE OLD LADY SAID? THAT I HAVE CANCER? IS THAT WHY YOU TOLD ME I WOULD DIE ?
I'M AFRAID IT IS TRUE, YES. THEY ONLY SEND PEOPLE IN TERMINAL CONDITION TO THE PLANT. I'M SORRY, TOM.
WAIT! *WAIT!*
I'M COMING WITH YOU.
I CAN'T ABANDON MY CHILD.

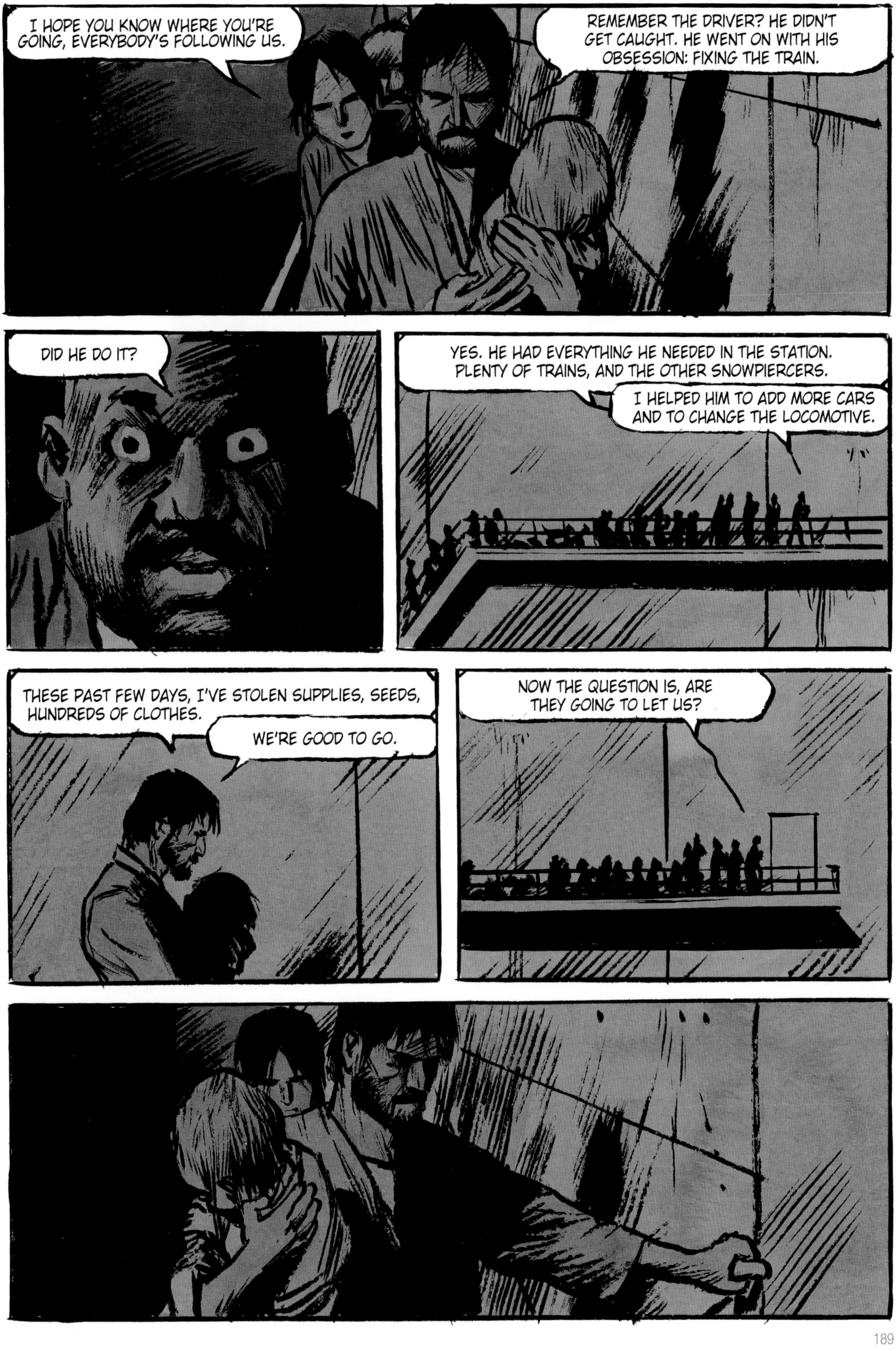
I HOPE YOU KNOW WHERE YOU'RE GOING, EVERYBODY'S FOLLOWING US.
REMEMBER THE DRIVER? HE DIDN'T GET CAUGHT. HE WENT ON WITH HIS OBSESSION: FIXING THE TRAIN.
DID HE DO IT?
YES. HE HAD EVERYTHING HE NEEDED IN THE STATION. PLENTY OF TRAINS, AND THE OTHER SNOWPIERCERS.
I HELPED HIM TO ADD MORE CARS AND TO CHANGE THE LOCOMOTIVE.
THESE PAST FEW DAYS, I'VE STOLEN SUPPLIES, SEEDS, HUNDREDS OF CLOTHES.
WE'RE GOOD TO GO.
NOW THE QUESTION IS, ARE THEY GOING TO LET US?

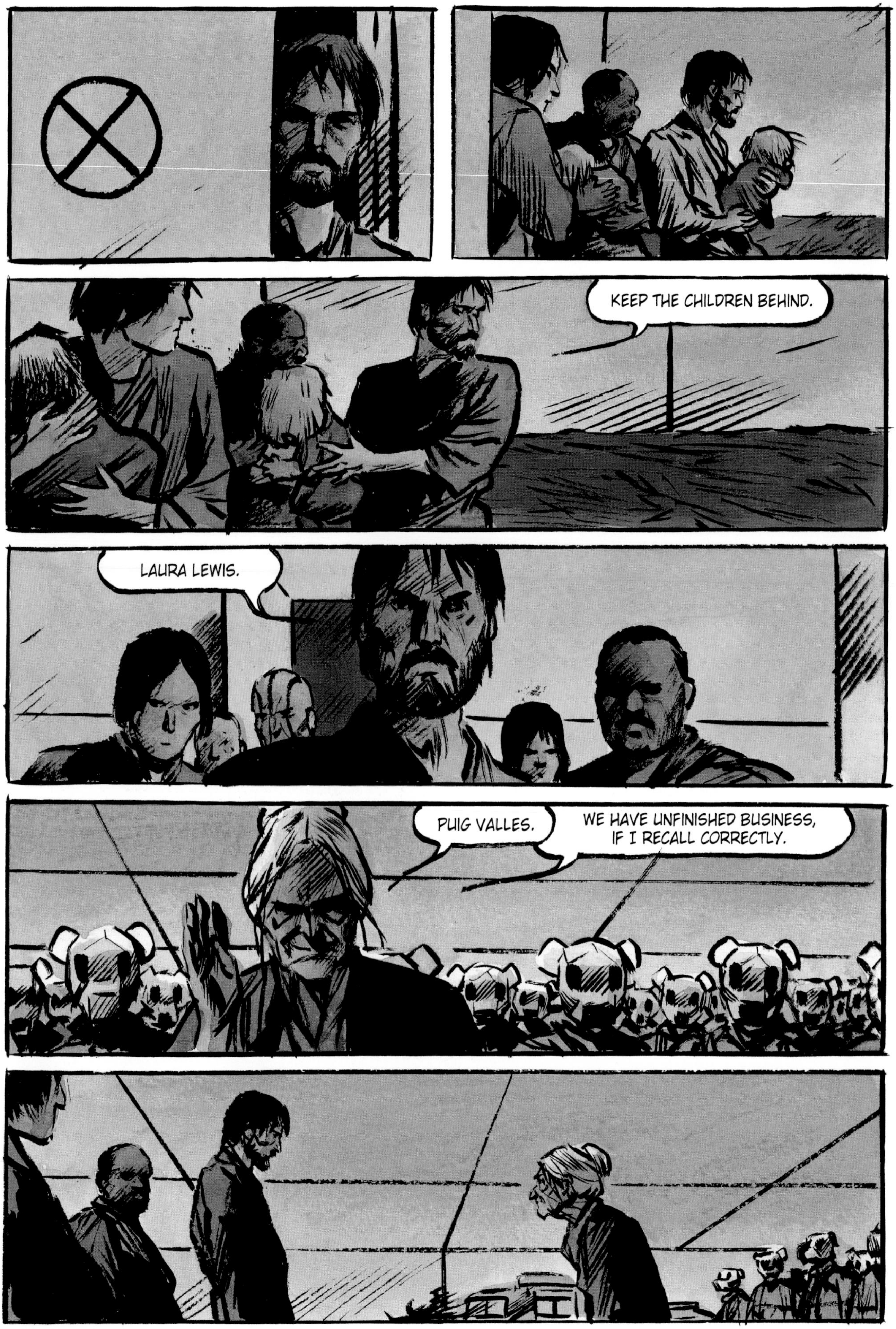
KEEP THE CHILDREN BEHIND.
LAURA LEWIS.
PUIG VALLES.
WE HAVE UNFINISHED BUSINESS, IF I RECALL CORRECTLY.

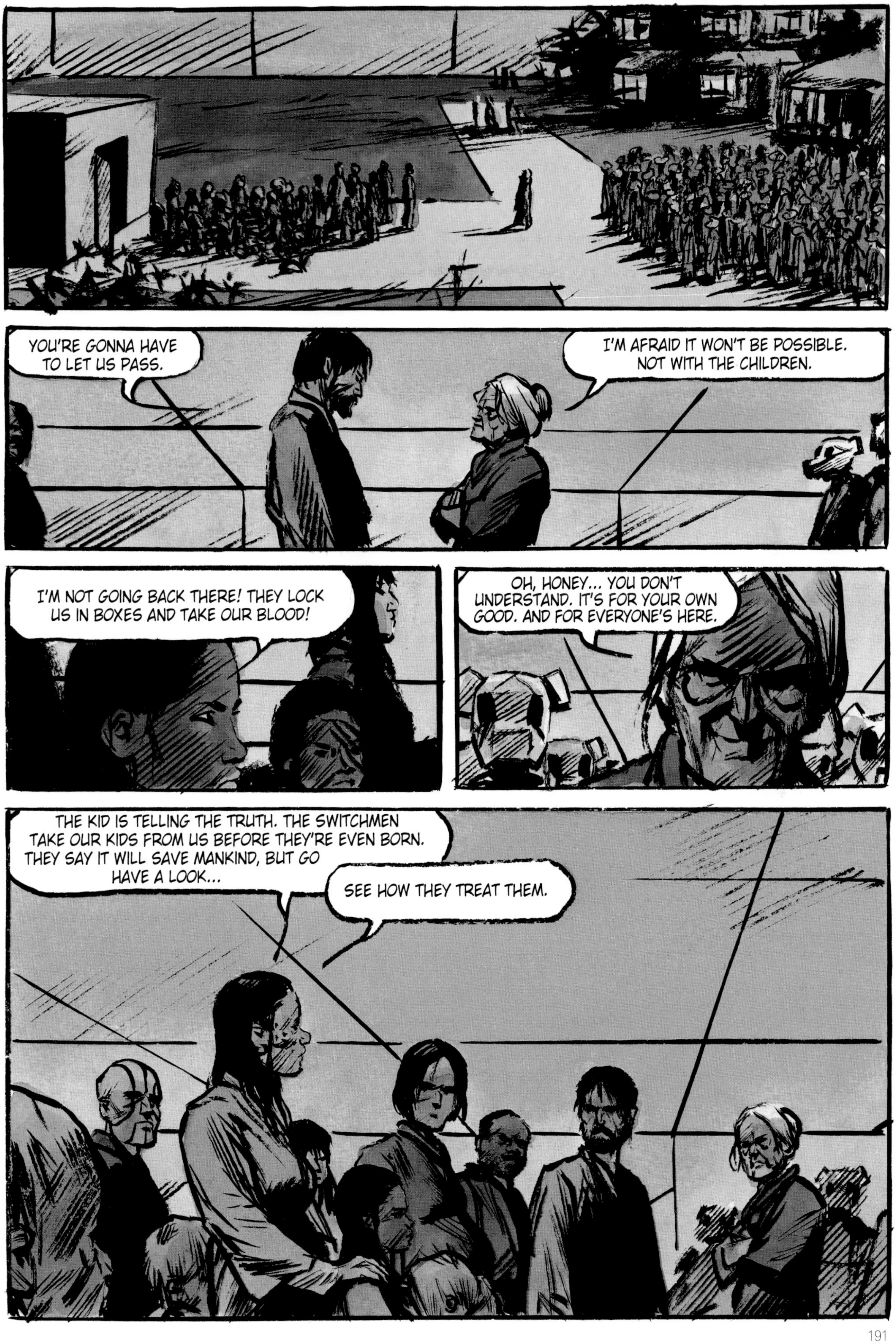
YOU'RE GONNA HAVE TO LET US PASS.
I'M AFRAID IT WON'T BE POSSIBLE. NOT WITH THE CHILDREN.
I'M NOT GOING BACK THERE! THEY LOCK US IN BOXES AND TAKE OUR BLOOD!
OH, HONEY... YOU DON'T UNDERSTAND. IT'S FOR YOUR OWN GOOD. AND FOR EVERYONE'S HERE.
THE KID IS TELLING THE TRUTH. THE SWITCHMEN TAKE OUR KIDS FROM US BEFORE THEY'RE EVEN BORN. THEY SAY IT WILL SAVE MANKIND, BUT GO HAVE A LOOK...
SEE HOW THEY TREAT THEM.

I SAW. YOU THINK THEY DO THAT FOR FUN? LOOK AT WHAT HAPPENS TO THE CHILDREN WHEN WE LEAVE NATURE IN CHARGE.

IS THIS THE FUTURE OF MANKIND? IS THIS WHAT YOU WANT? MONSTERS?

WHAT NATURE? THIS CITY IS UNDER A LEAKING NUCLEAR PLANT. AIR, WATER, FOOD... EVERYTHING IS POLLUTED, HERE. YOU ARE ALL GOING TO DIE.

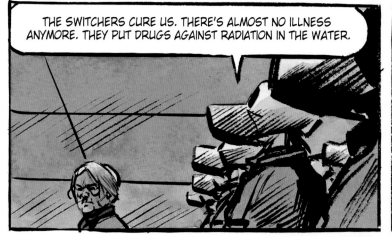

THE SWITCHERS CURE US. THERE'S ALMOST NO ILLNESS ANYMORE. THEY PUT DRUGS AGAINST RADIATION IN THE WATER.

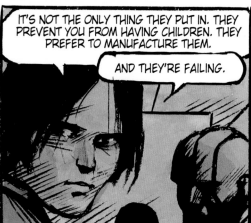

IT'S NOT THE ONLY THING THEY PUT IN. THEY PREVENT YOU FROM HAVING CHILDREN. THEY PREFER TO MANUFACTURE THEM.

AND THEY'RE FAILING.

YEAH, BUT LOOK! WE HAVE NO CHOICE! LOOK AT WHAT HAPPENS WHEN WE MAKE BABIES THE NATURAL WAY!

YOU DON'T WANT THEM? FINE! WE'LL TAKE THEM WITH US.

192

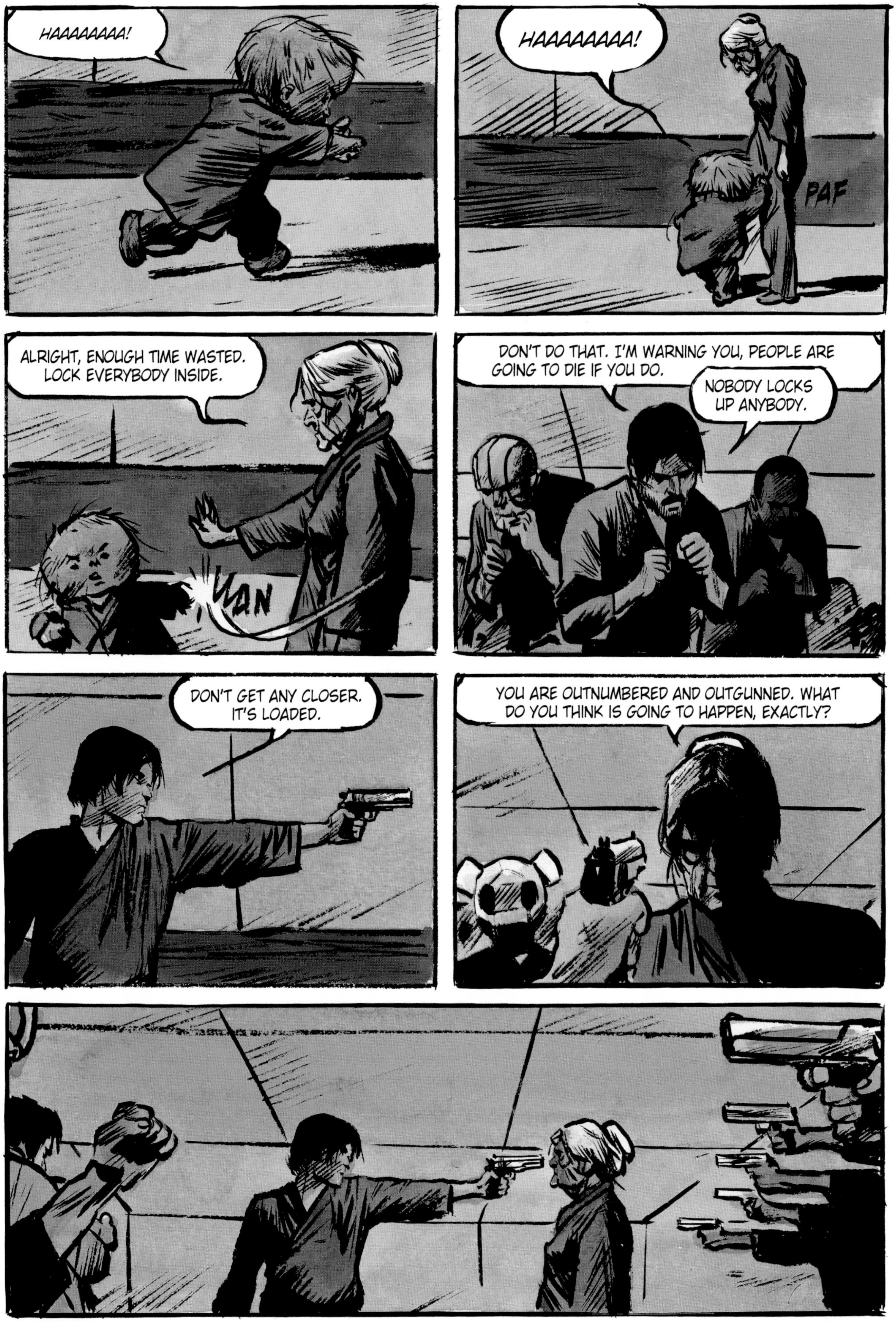
HAAAAAAAA!
HAAAAAAAA!
PAF
ALRIGHT, ENOUGH TIME WASTED. LOCK EVERYBODY INSIDE.
WAN
DON'T DO THAT. I'M WARNING YOU, PEOPLE ARE GOING TO DIE IF YOU DO.
NOBODY LOCKS UP ANYBODY.
DON'T GET ANY CLOSER. IT'S LOADED.
YOU ARE OUTNUMBERED AND OUTGUNNED. WHAT DO YOU THINK IS GOING TO HAPPEN, EXACTLY?

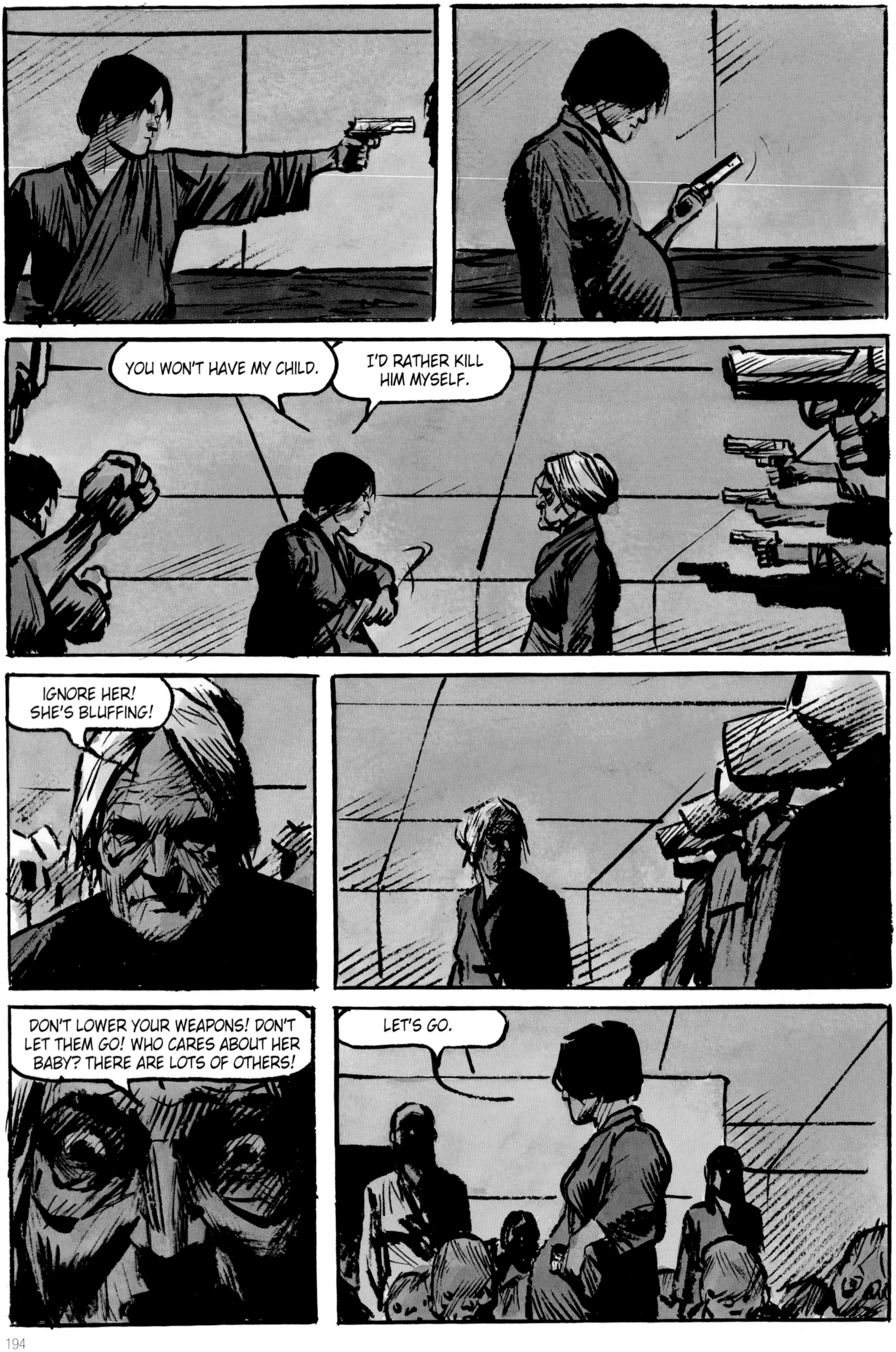
YOU WON'T HAVE MY CHILD.
I'D RATHER KILL HIM MYSELF.
IGNORE HER! SHE'S BLUFFING!
DON'T LOWER YOUR WEAPONS! DON'T LET THEM GO! WHO CARES ABOUT HER BABY? THERE ARE LOTS OF OTHERS!
LET'S GO.

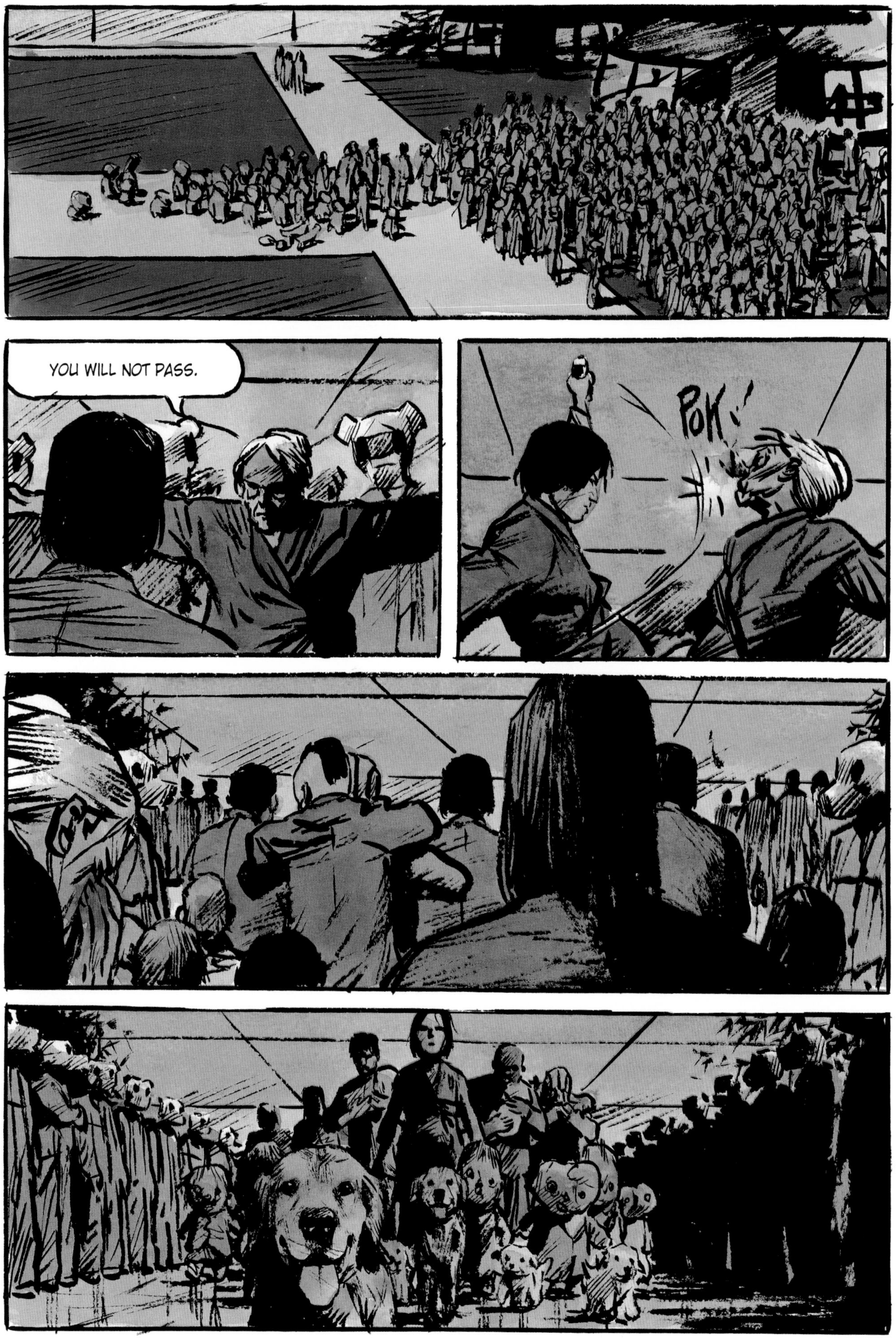
YOU WILL NOT PASS.
POK

WHAT ARE THEY DOING? WHAT ARE THEY DOING? WHY DOESN'T SHE STOP THEM?
I DON'T KNOW! I'M STUCK ON THIS CAMERA THAT'S FILMING THE WHEAT FIELD.
KRA
ARGH! THIS IS DRIVING ME CRAZY!
USELESS MORONS! OPEN THAT DOOR!
AH! I GOT IT! I CAN SEE THEM!
WHAT ARE THEY UP TO?
OH MY GOD!
WHAT? WHAT'S HAPPENING!?
I THINK THEY WANT TO LEAVE BY TRAIN.
WHAT TRAIN? IT'S OUT OF ORDER AND THE TUNNEL COLLAPSED BEHIND IT!
THEY REOPENED THE LITTLE STATION IN THE PARK. THEY REOPENED THE DOORS. AND THE BELL IS RINGING.
OH MY GOD!

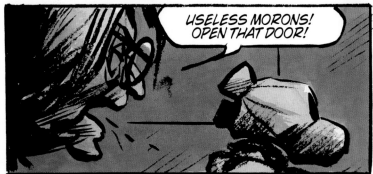

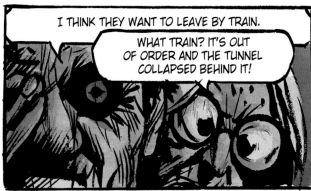

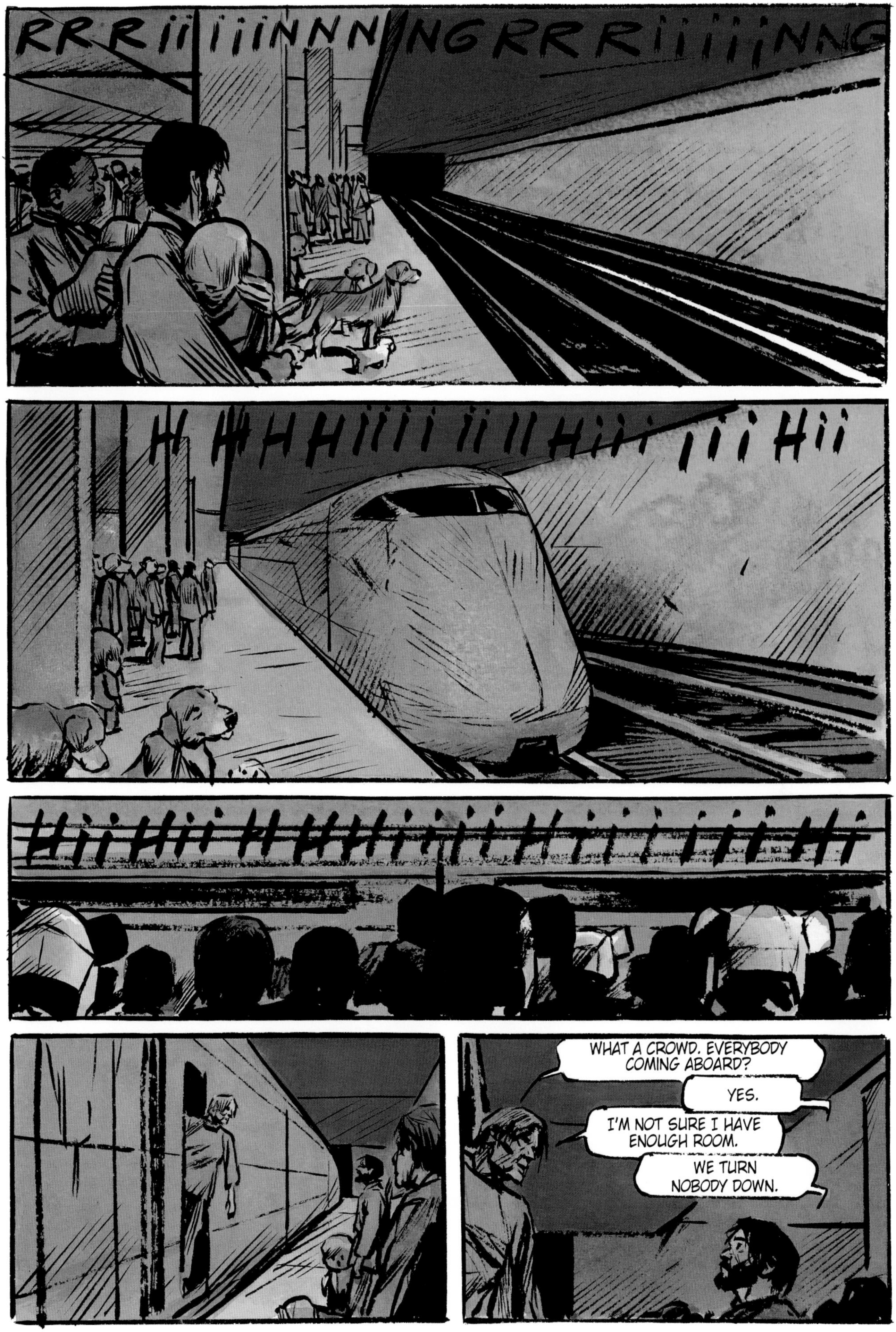
RRRii iiiNNNNGRRRRiiiiiiNNG
HHHHiiii iill Hiii iii Hii
HiiHii H HHHiiiii Hiiiii iii Hi
WHAT A CROWD. EVERYBODY COMING ABOARD?
YES.
I'M NOT SURE I HAVE ENOUGH ROOM.
WE TURN NOBODY DOWN.

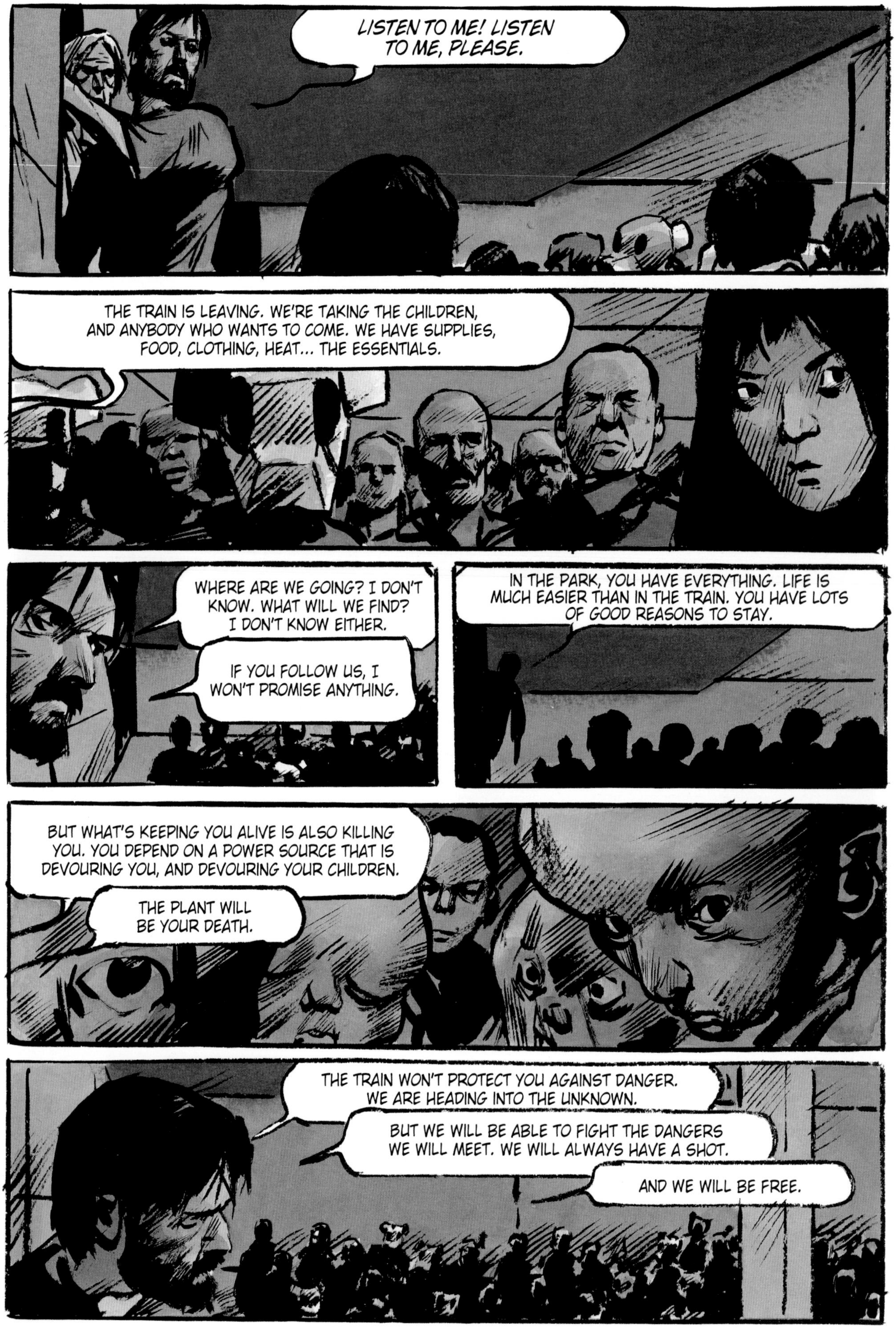
LISTEN TO ME! LISTEN TO ME, PLEASE.
THE TRAIN IS LEAVING. WE'RE TAKING THE CHILDREN, AND ANYBODY WHO WANTS TO COME. WE HAVE SUPPLIES, FOOD, CLOTHING, HEAT... THE ESSENTIALS.
WHERE ARE WE GOING? I DON'T KNOW. WHAT WILL WE FIND? I DON'T KNOW EITHER.
IF YOU FOLLOW US, I WON'T PROMISE ANYTHING.
IN THE PARK, YOU HAVE EVERYTHING. LIFE IS MUCH EASIER THAN IN THE TRAIN. YOU HAVE LOTS OF GOOD REASONS TO STAY.
BUT WHAT'S KEEPING YOU ALIVE IS ALSO KILLING YOU. YOU DEPEND ON A POWER SOURCE THAT IS DEVOURING YOU, AND DEVOURING YOUR CHILDREN.
THE PLANT WILL BE YOUR DEATH.
THE TRAIN WON'T PROTECT YOU AGAINST DANGER. WE ARE HEADING INTO THE UNKNOWN.
BUT WE WILL BE ABLE TO FIGHT THE DANGERS WE WILL MEET. WE WILL ALWAYS HAVE A SHOT.
AND WE WILL BE FREE.

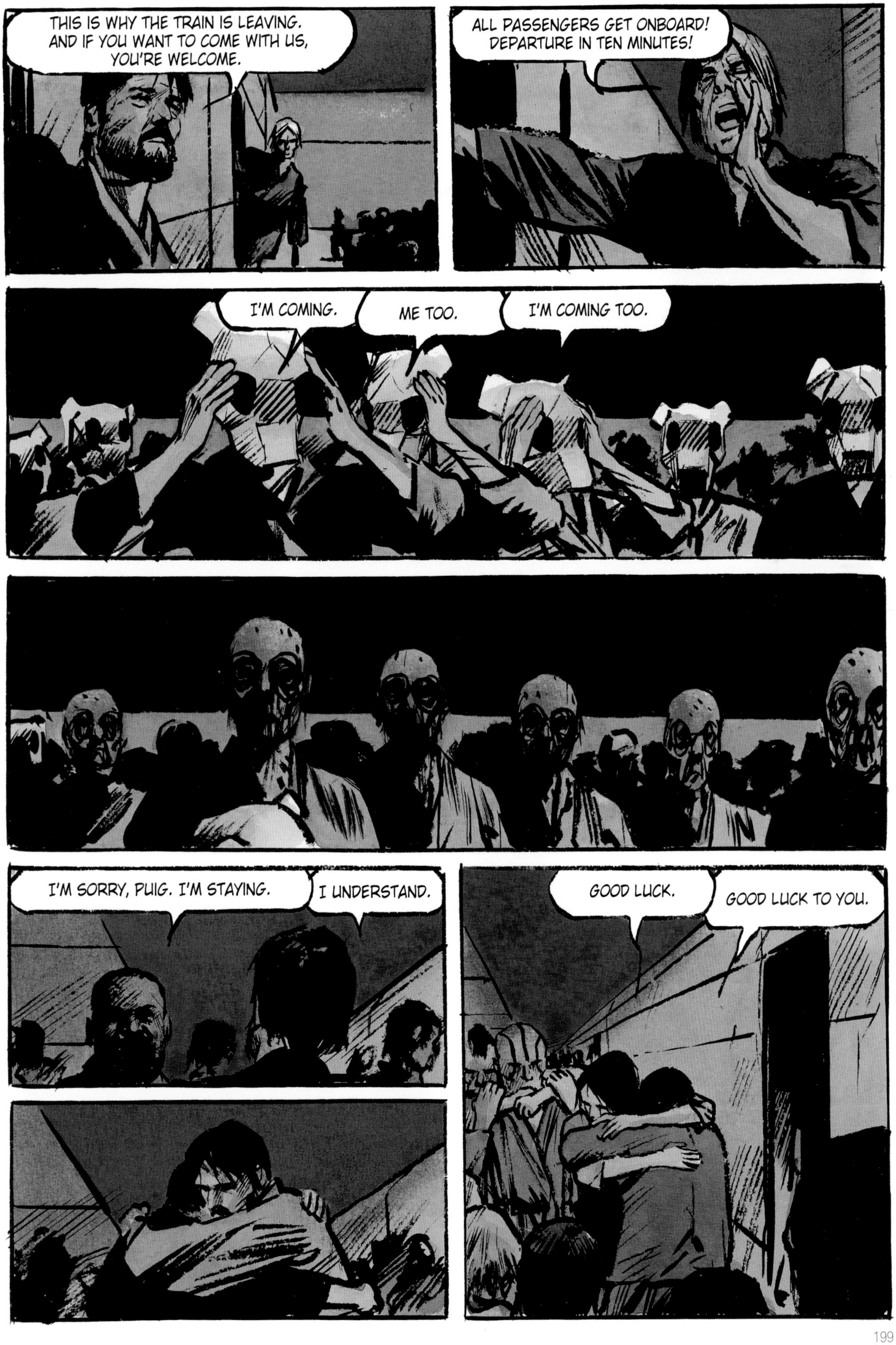
THIS IS WHY THE TRAIN IS LEAVING. AND IF YOU WANT TO COME WITH US, YOU'RE WELCOME.
ALL PASSENGERS GET ONBOARD! DEPARTURE IN TEN MINUTES!
I'M COMING.
ME TOO.
I'M COMING TOO.
I'M SORRY, PUIG. I'M STAYING.
I UNDERSTAND.
GOOD LUCK.
GOOD LUCK TO YOU.

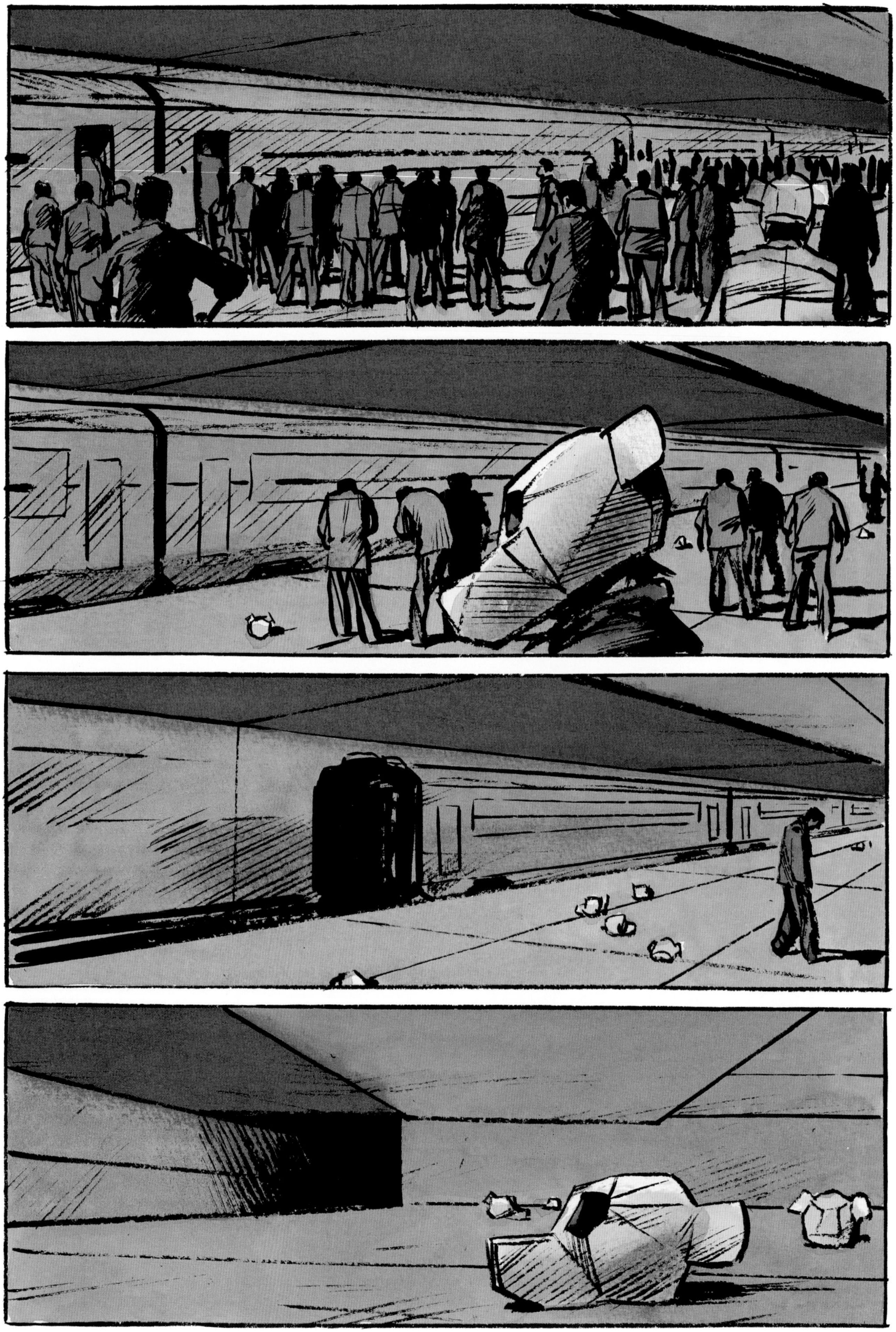

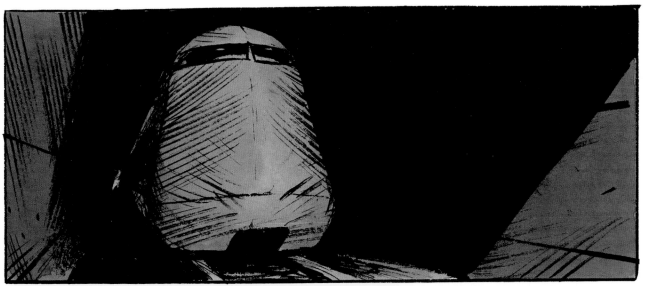

STOP! YOU ARE NOT AUTHORIZED! STOP!

BLAM BLAM BLAM BLA
BLAM BLA

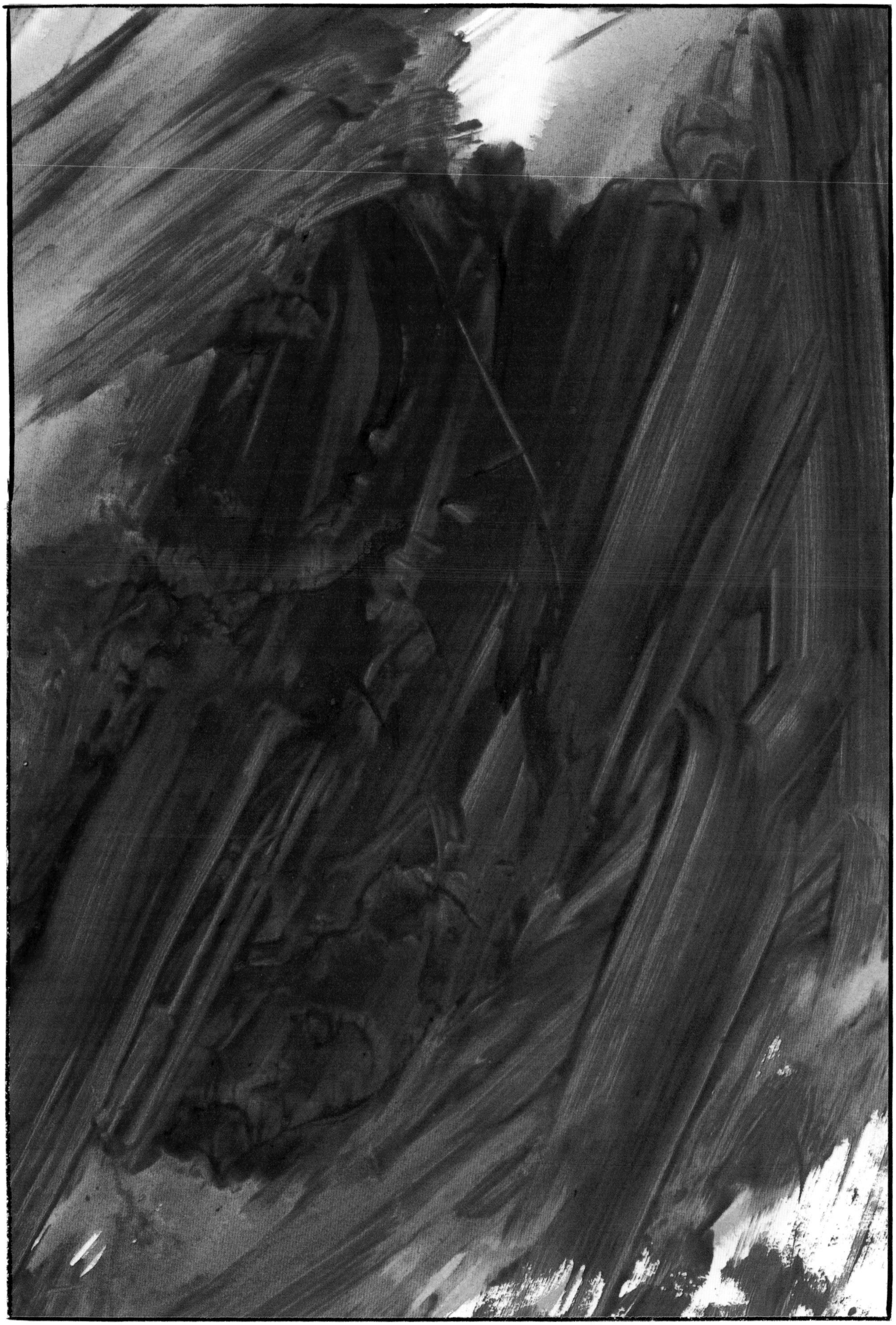

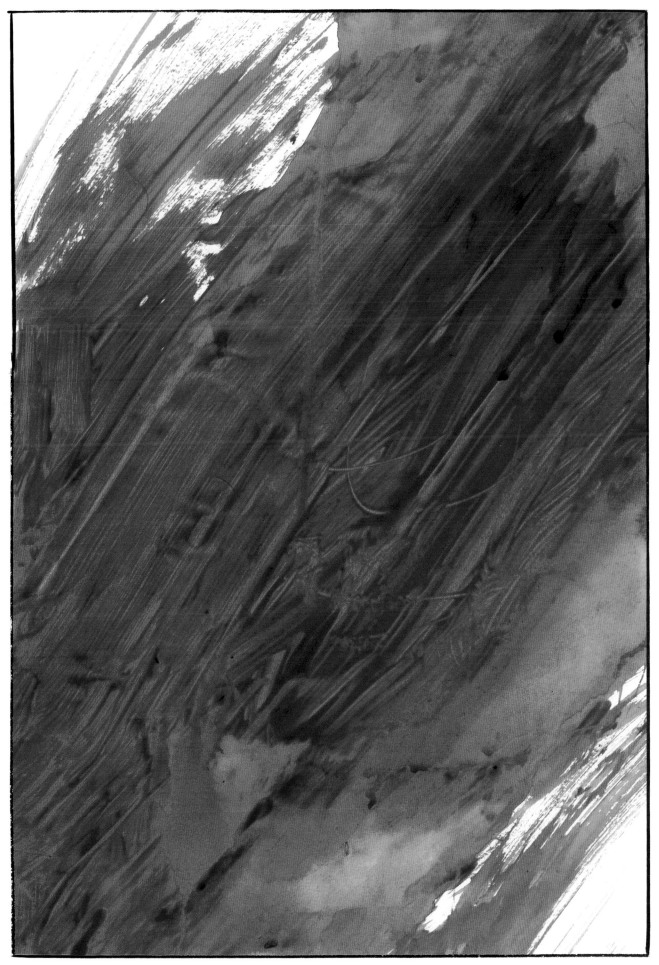

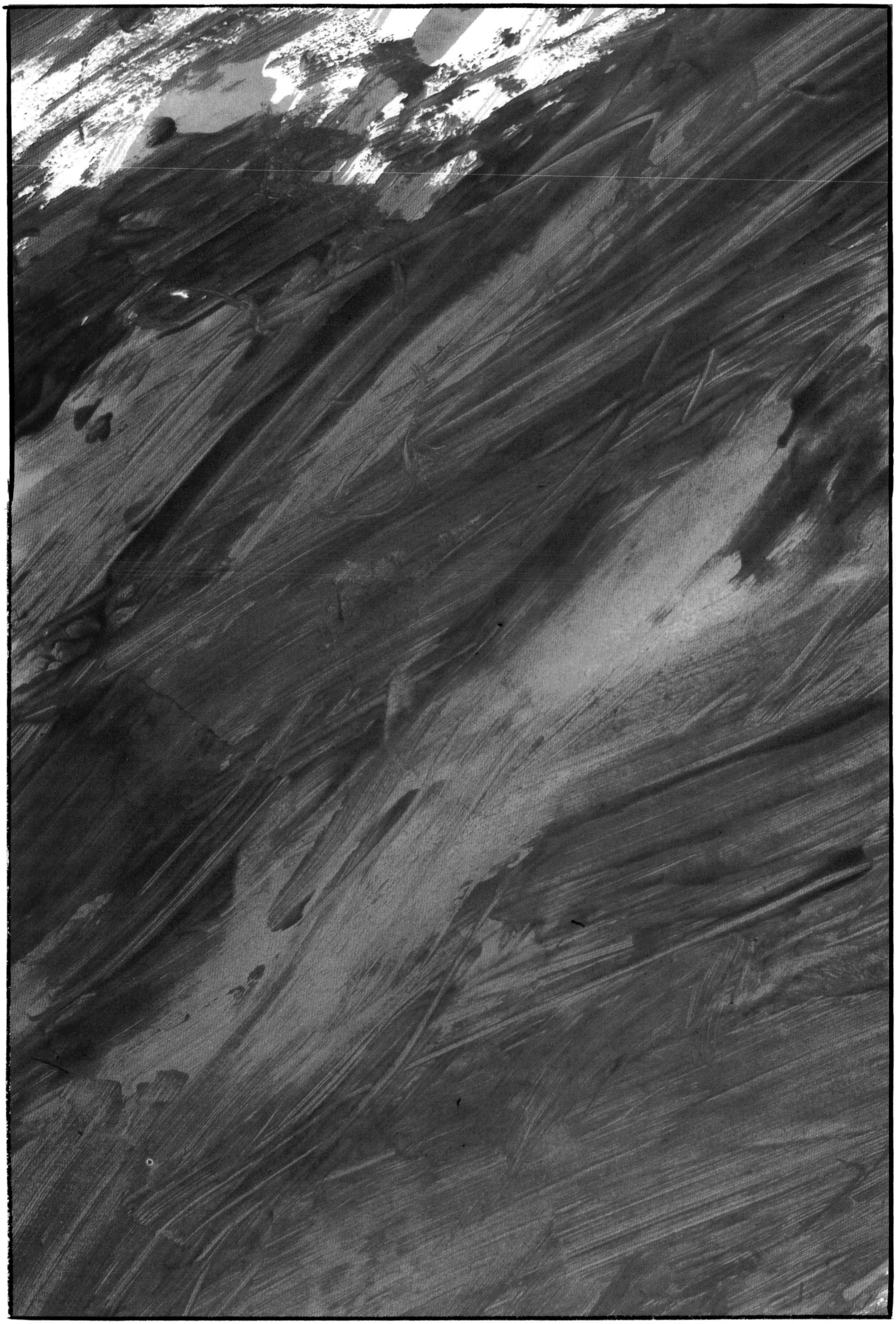

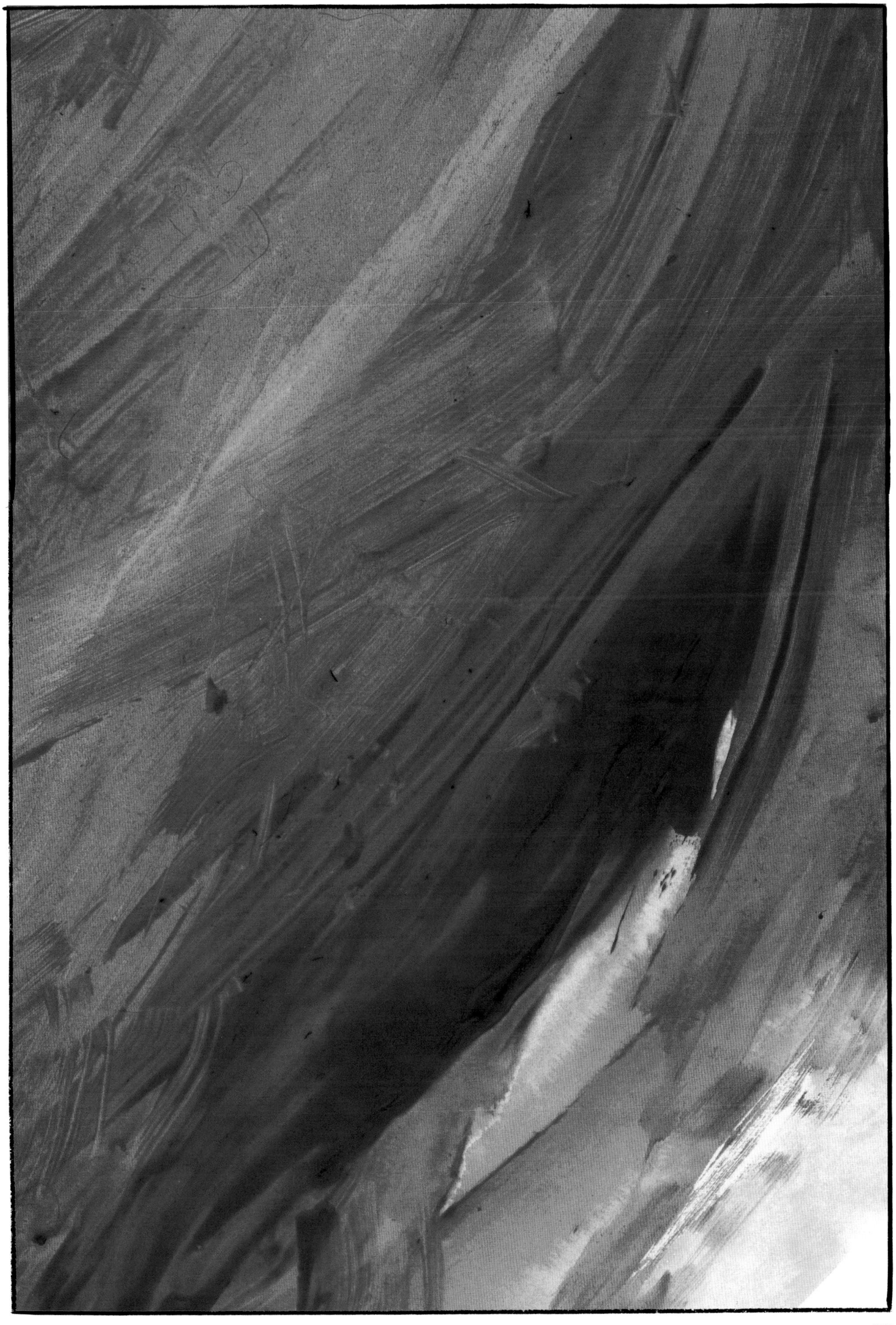

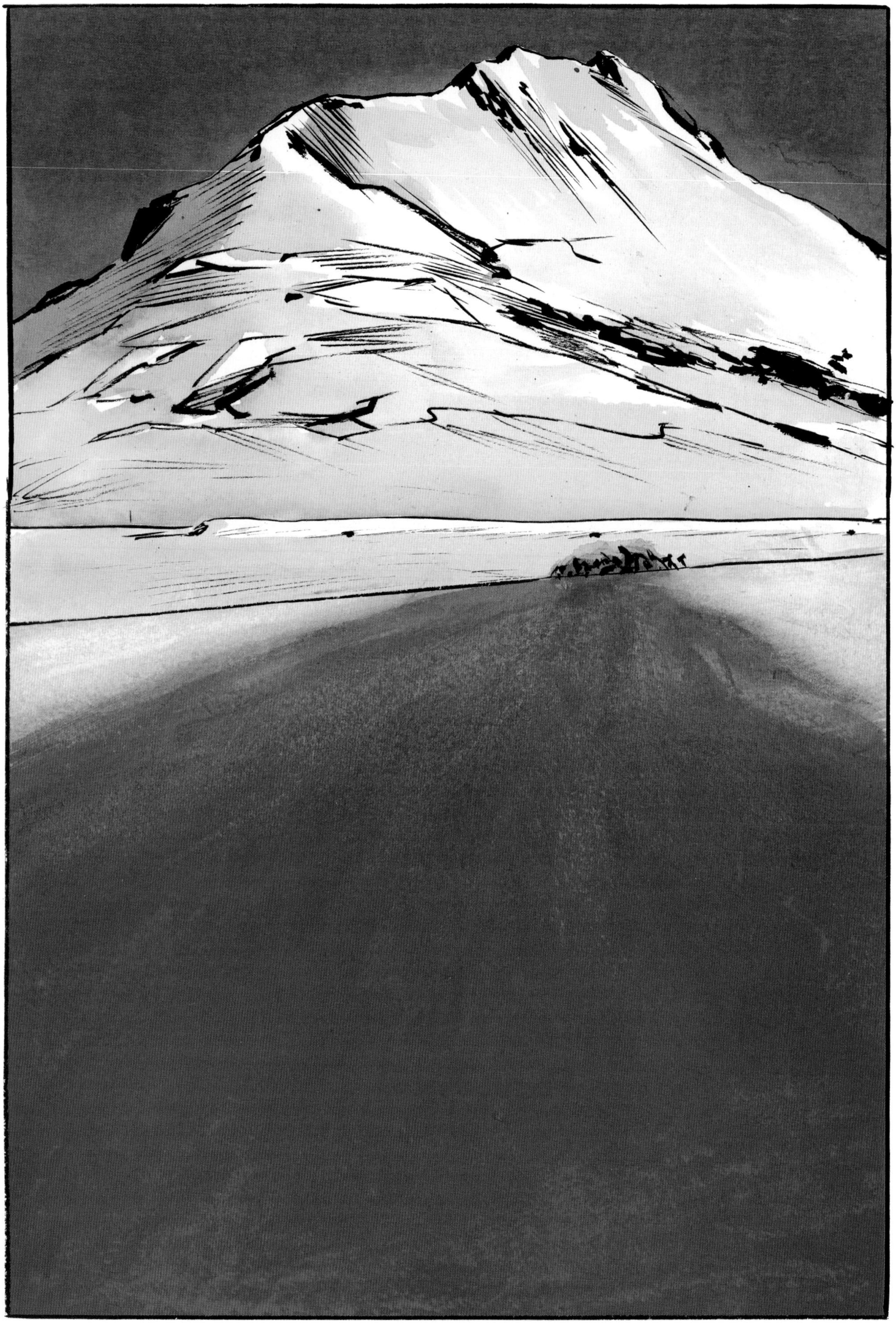

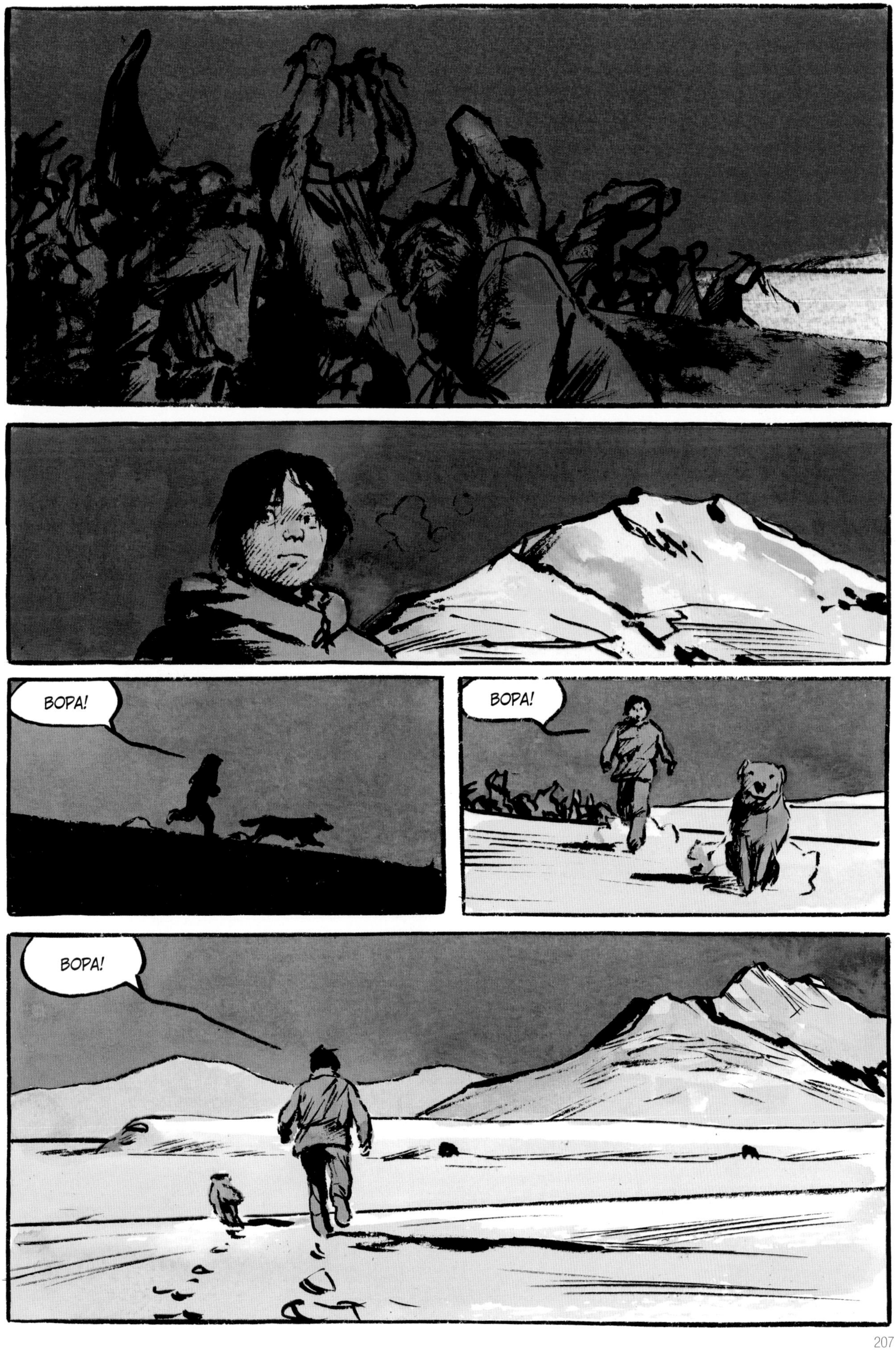
BOPA!
BOPA!
BOPA!

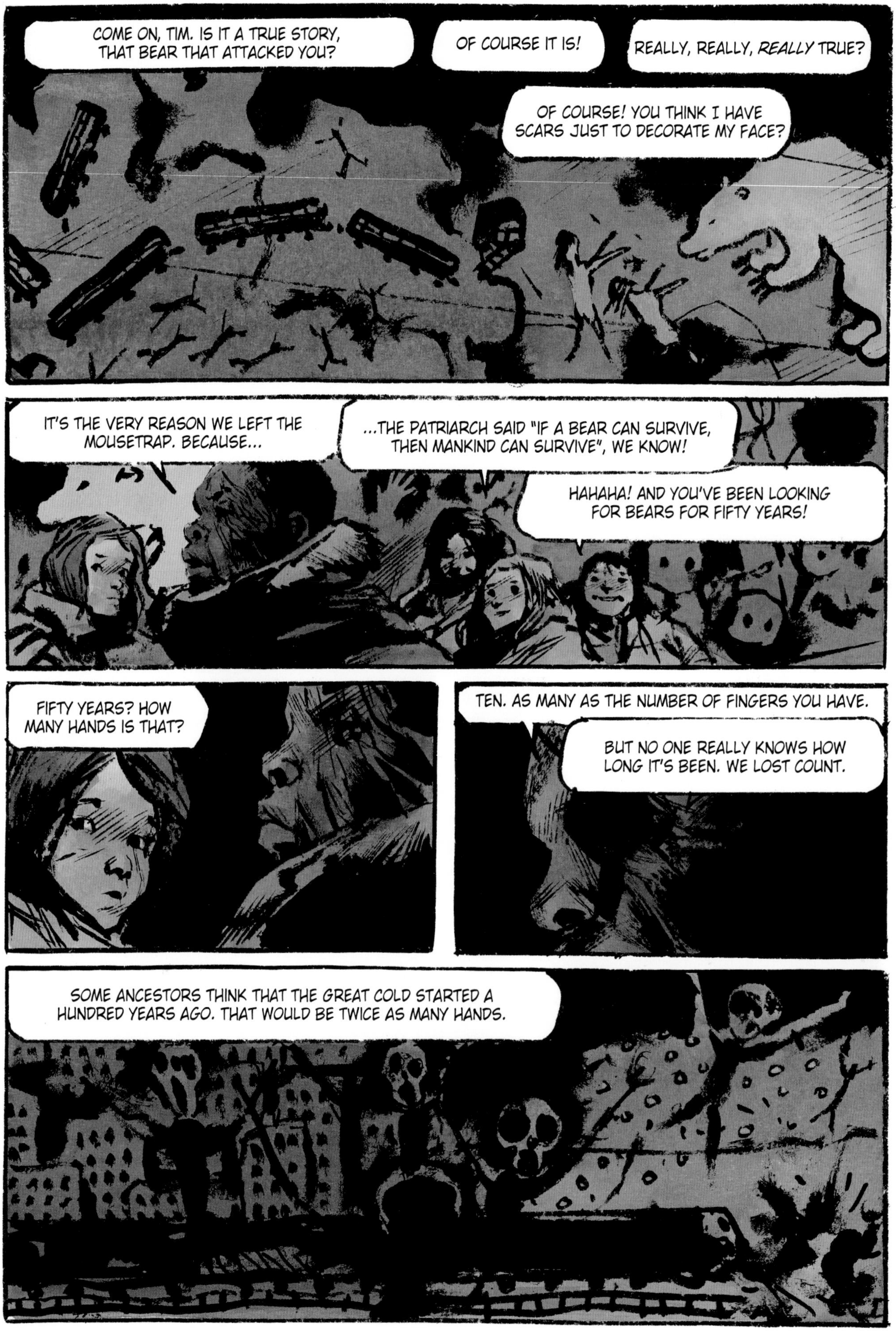
COME ON, TIM. IS IT A TRUE STORY, THAT BEAR THAT ATTACKED YOU?
OF COURSE IT IS!
REALLY, REALLY, *REALLY* TRUE?
OF COURSE! YOU THINK I HAVE SCARS JUST TO DECORATE MY FACE?
IT'S THE VERY REASON WE LEFT THE MOUSETRAP. BECAUSE...
...THE PATRIARCH SAID "IF A BEAR CAN SURVIVE, THEN MANKIND CAN SURVIVE", WE KNOW!
HAHAHA! AND YOU'VE BEEN LOOKING FOR BEARS FOR FIFTY YEARS!
FIFTY YEARS? HOW MANY HANDS IS THAT?
TEN. AS MANY AS THE NUMBER OF FINGERS YOU HAVE.
BUT NO ONE REALLY KNOWS HOW LONG IT'S BEEN. WE LOST COUNT.
SOME ANCESTORS THINK THAT THE GREAT COLD STARTED A HUNDRED YEARS AGO. THAT WOULD BE TWICE AS MANY HANDS.

WHAT IS THAT?

YOU KNOW EXACTLY WHAT IT IS.

HAHAHA! YEAH! IT'S THE FIRST HUNTING! YOU CAME BACK WITH JUST A BABY PENGUIN!

HA-HA HA. HA-HA

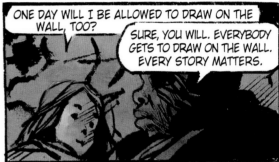

ONE DAY WILL I BE ALLOWED TO DRAW ON THE WALL, TOO?

SURE, YOU WILL. EVERYBODY GETS TO DRAW ON THE WALL. EVERY STORY MATTERS.

BIRTHS, LIVES, DEATHS. IT'S ALL THERE. EVEN SOME MADE UP STORIES.

BOPA!

BOPA!

HEY, CALM DOWN A LITTLE!

BOPA!

MAM! IS HE ASLEEP?

WITH ALL YOUR YELLING, I'D BE SURPRISED IF HE WAS.

WHAT'S THE MATTER, NOW? CAN'T ONE EVEN HAVE A MOMENT'S PEACE?

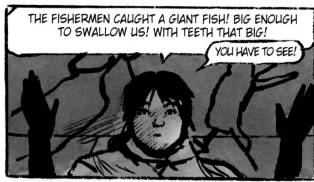

THE FISHERMEN CAUGHT A GIANT FISH! BIG ENOUGH TO SWALLOW US! WITH TEETH THAT BIG!

YOU HAVE TO SEE!

HELP ME UP.

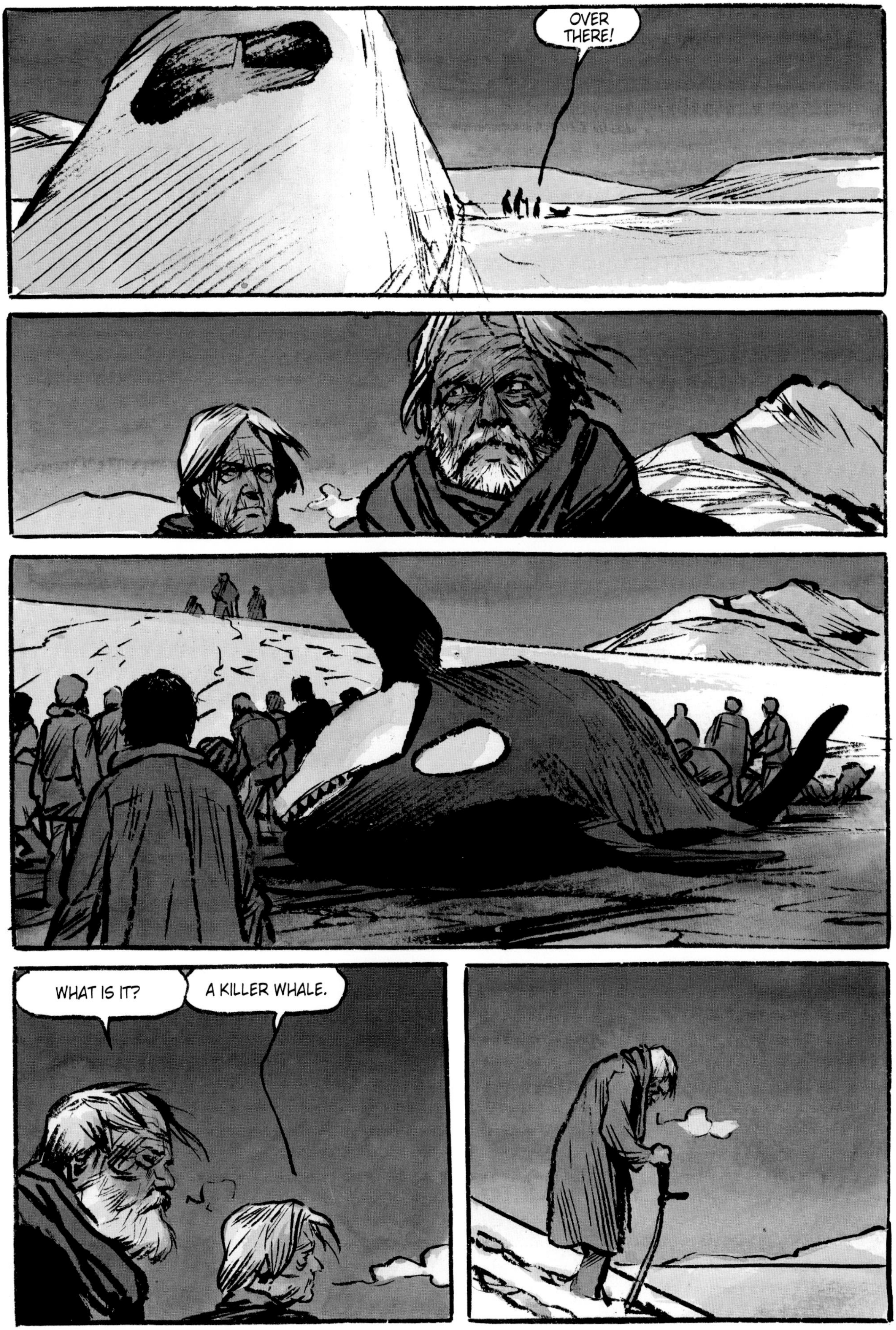
OVER THERE!
WHAT IS IT?
A KILLER WHALE.

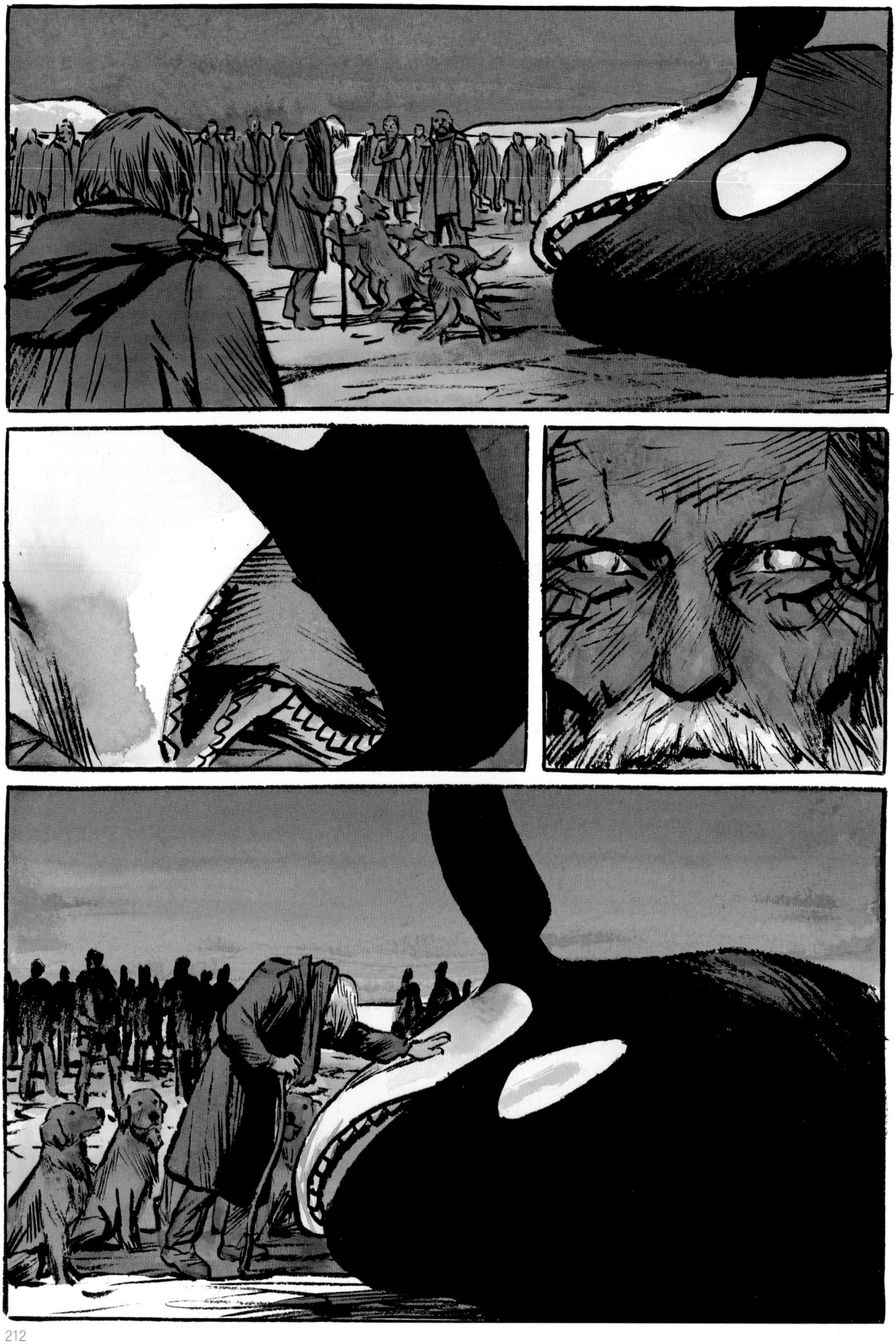

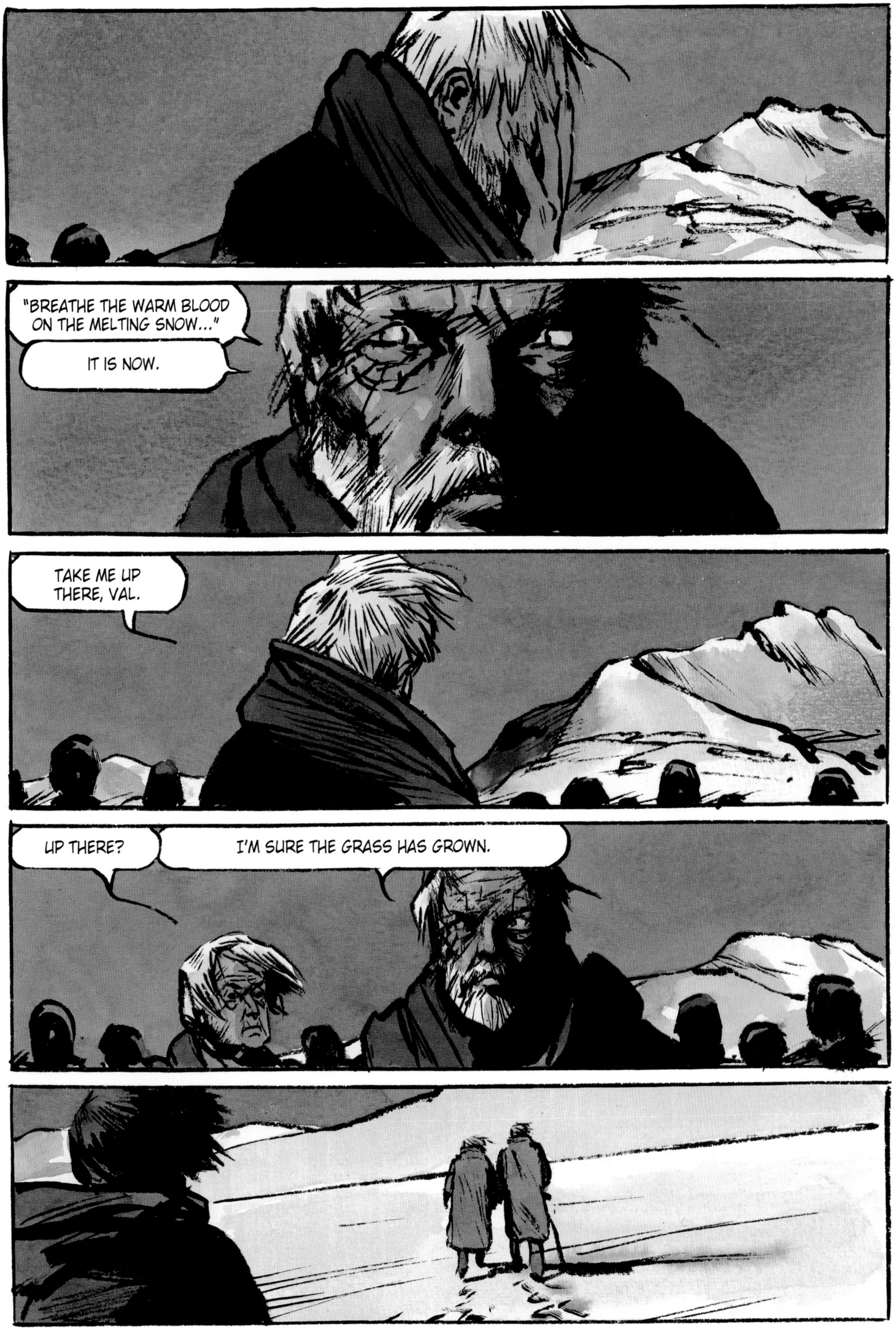
"BREATHE THE WARM BLOOD ON THE MELTING SNOW..."
IT IS NOW.
TAKE ME UP THERE, VAL.
UP THERE?
I'M SURE THE GRASS HAS GROWN.

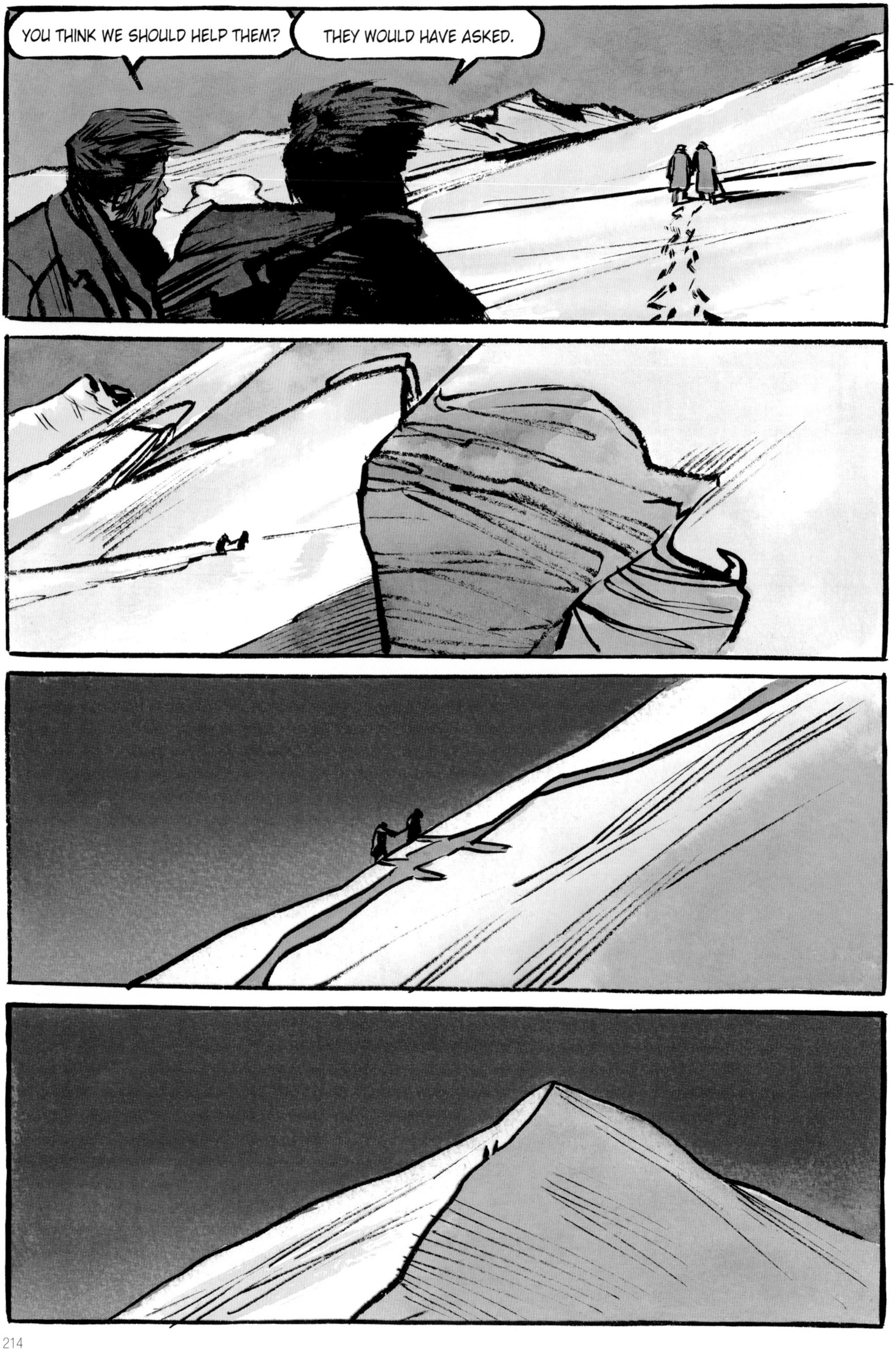
YOU THINK WE SHOULD HELP THEM?
THEY WOULD HAVE ASKED.

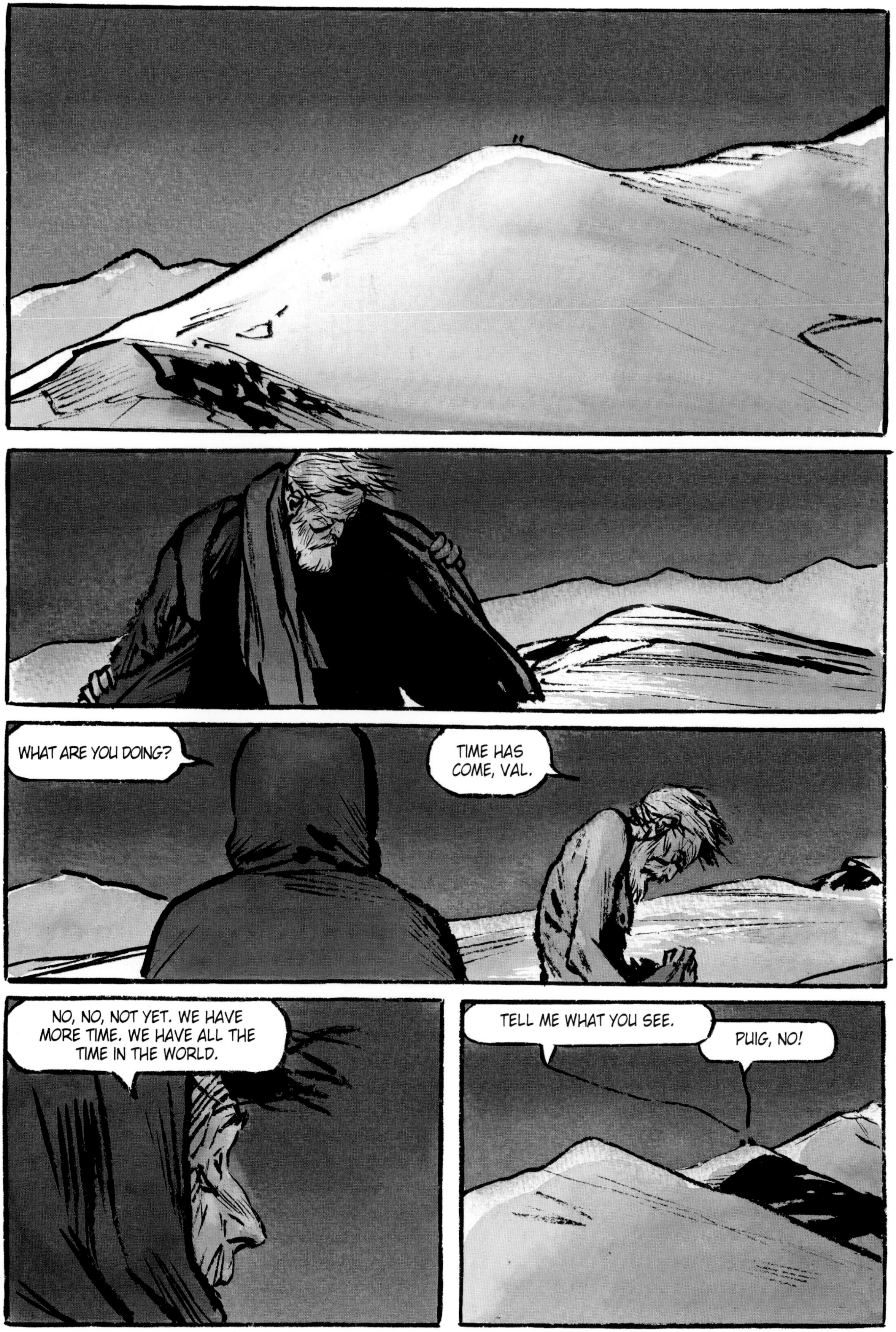
WHAT ARE YOU DOING?
TIME HAS COME, VAL.
NO, NO, NOT YET. WE HAVE MORE TIME. WE HAVE ALL THE TIME IN THE WORLD.
TELL ME WHAT YOU SEE.
PUIG, NO!

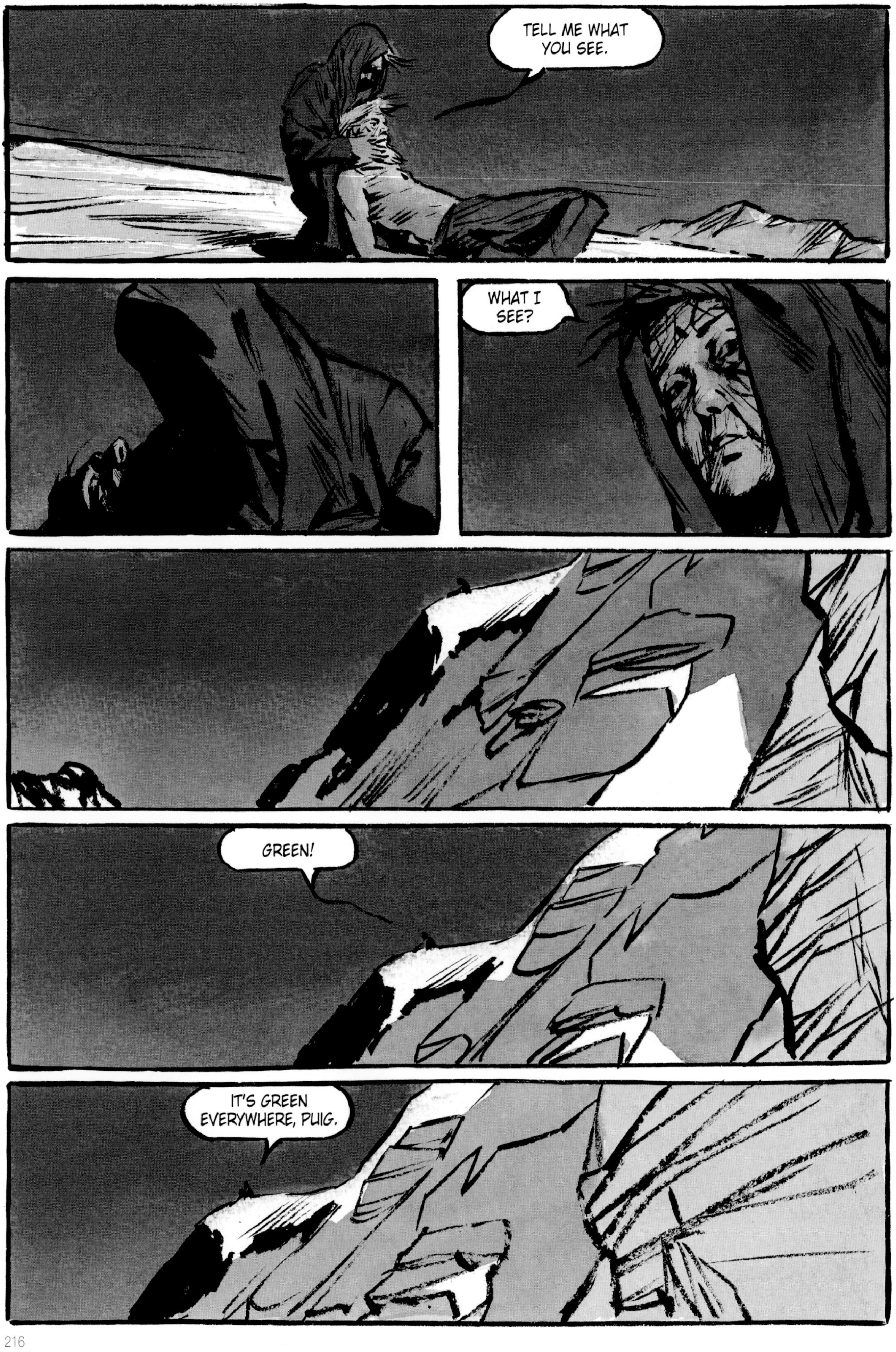
TELL ME WHAT YOU SEE.
WHAT I SEE?
GREEN!
IT'S GREEN EVERYWHERE, PUIG.

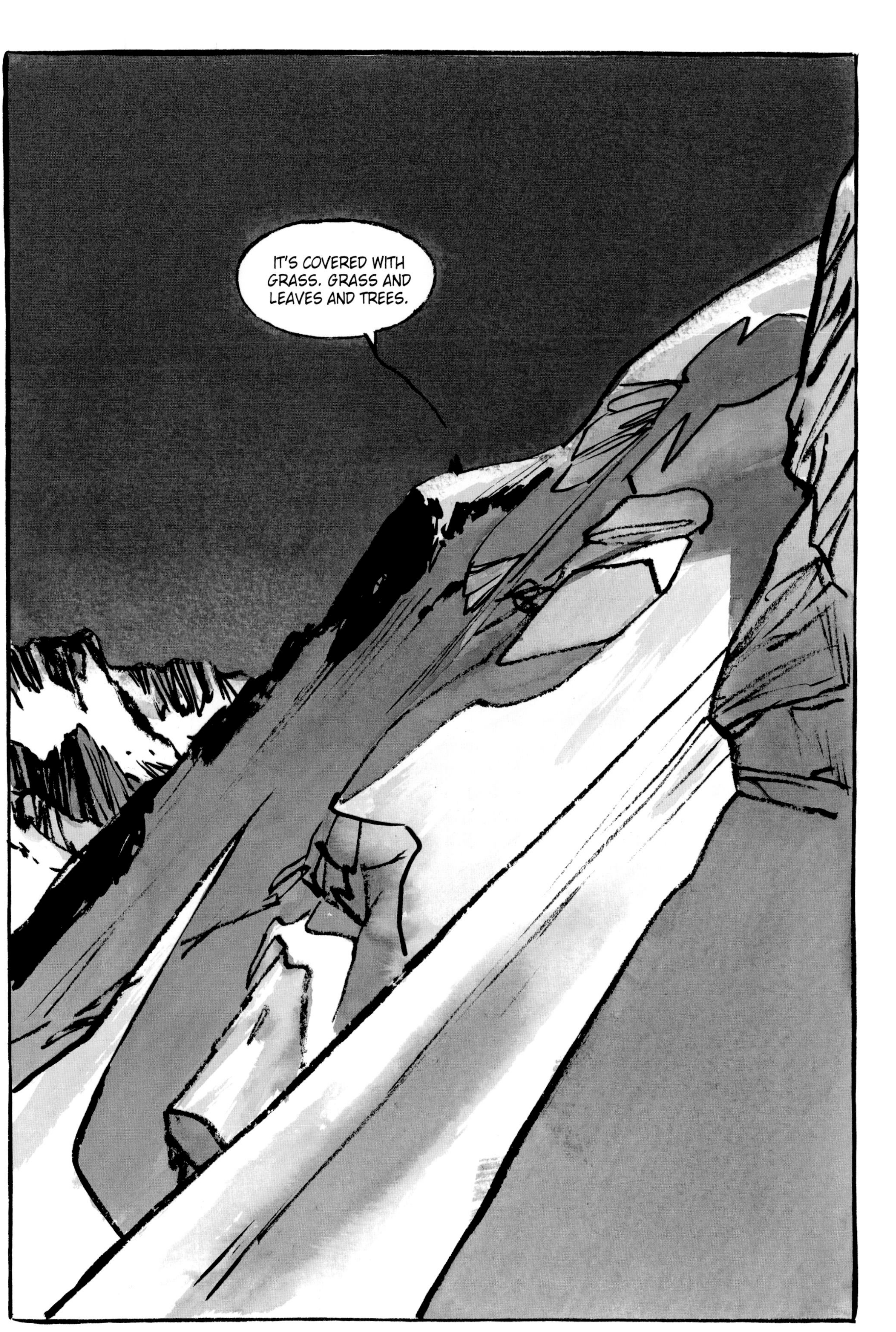
IT'S COVERED WITH GRASS. GRASS AND LEAVES AND TREES.

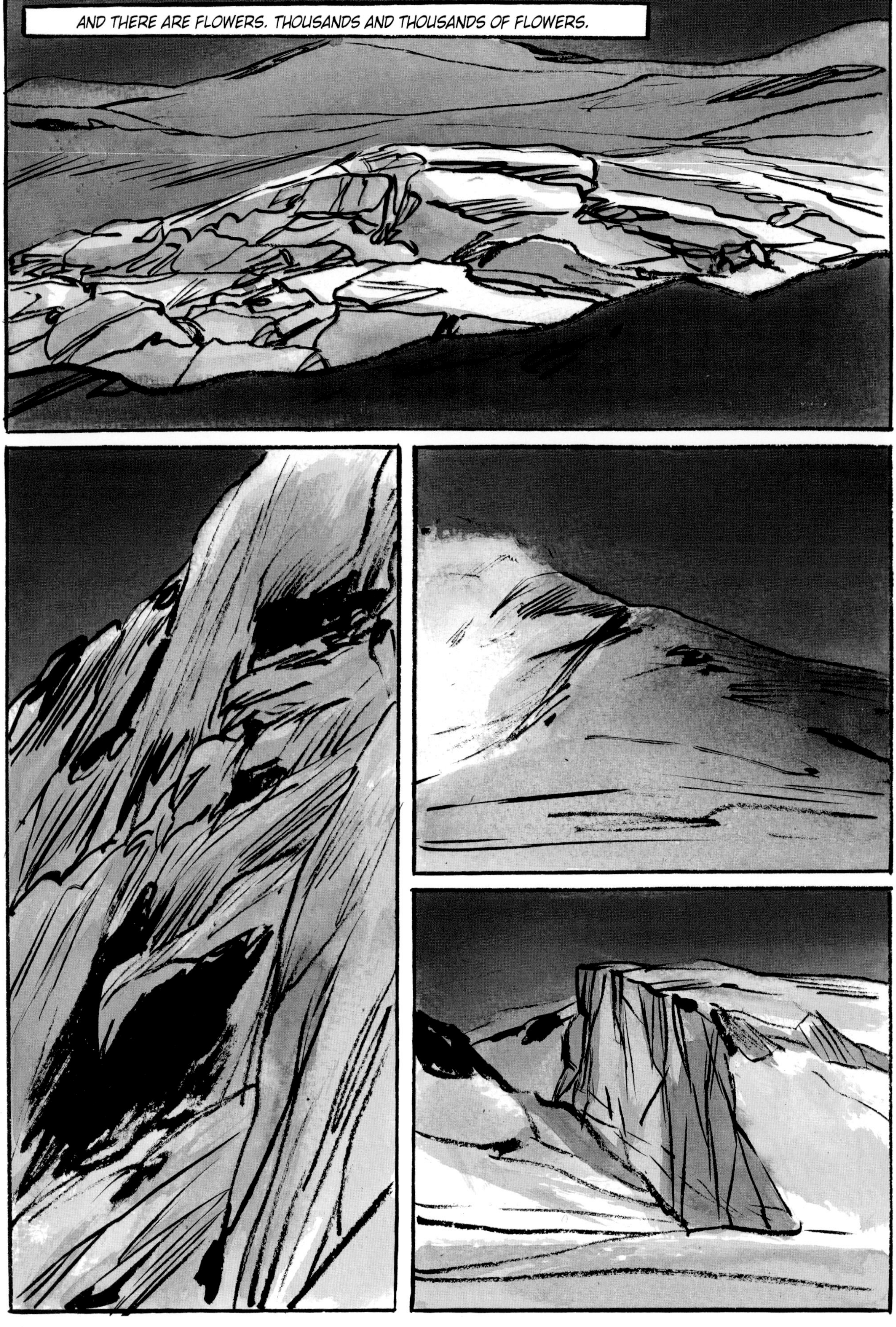
AND THERE ARE FLOWERS. THOUSANDS AND THOUSANDS OF FLOWERS.

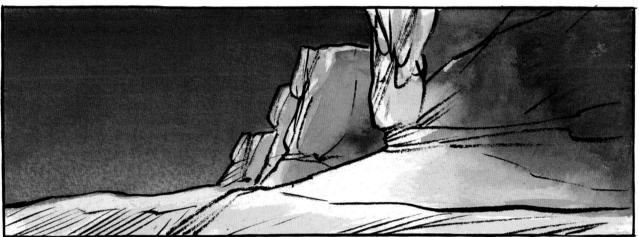

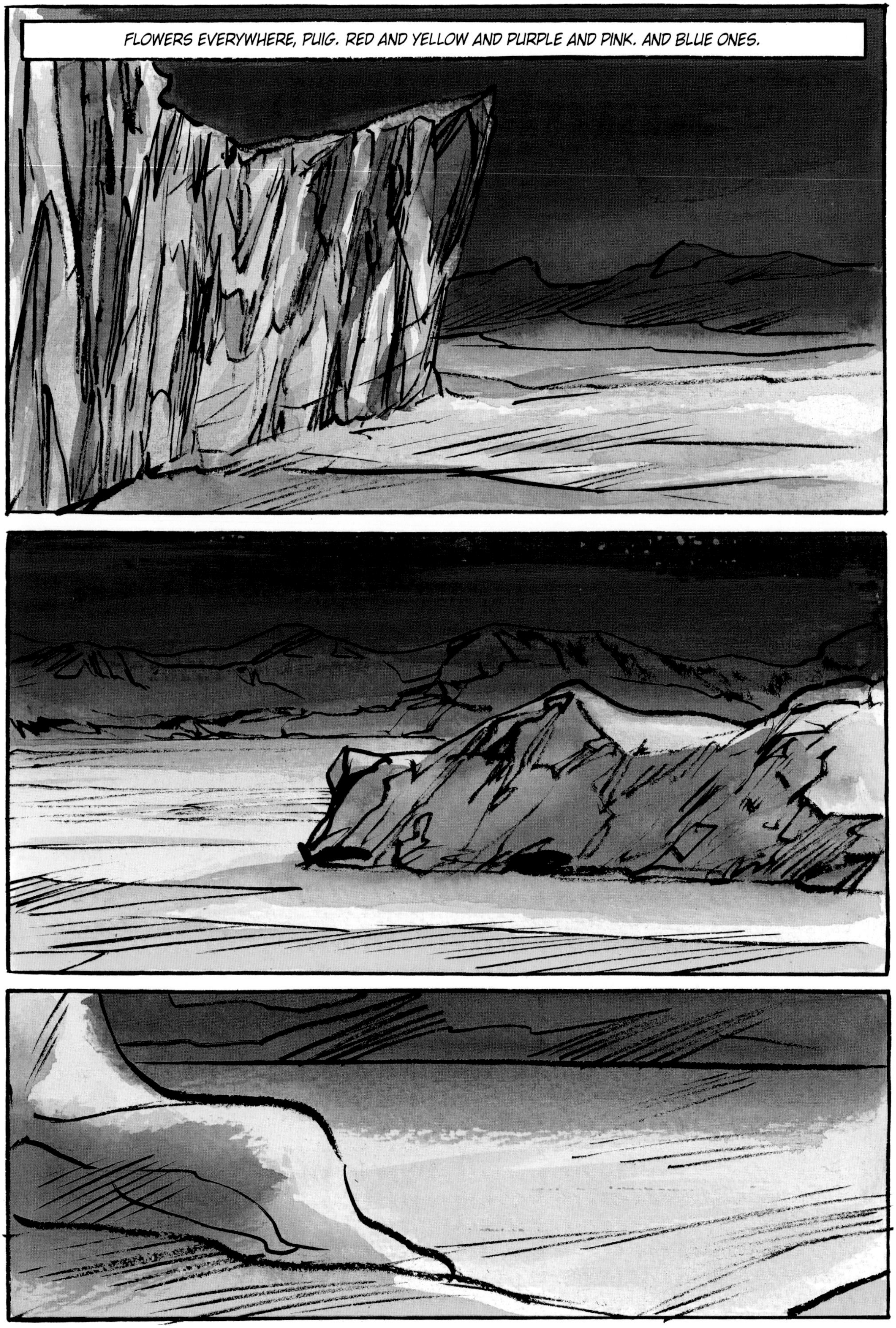
FLOWERS EVERYWHERE, PUIG. RED AND YELLOW AND PURPLE AND PINK. AND BLUE ONES.

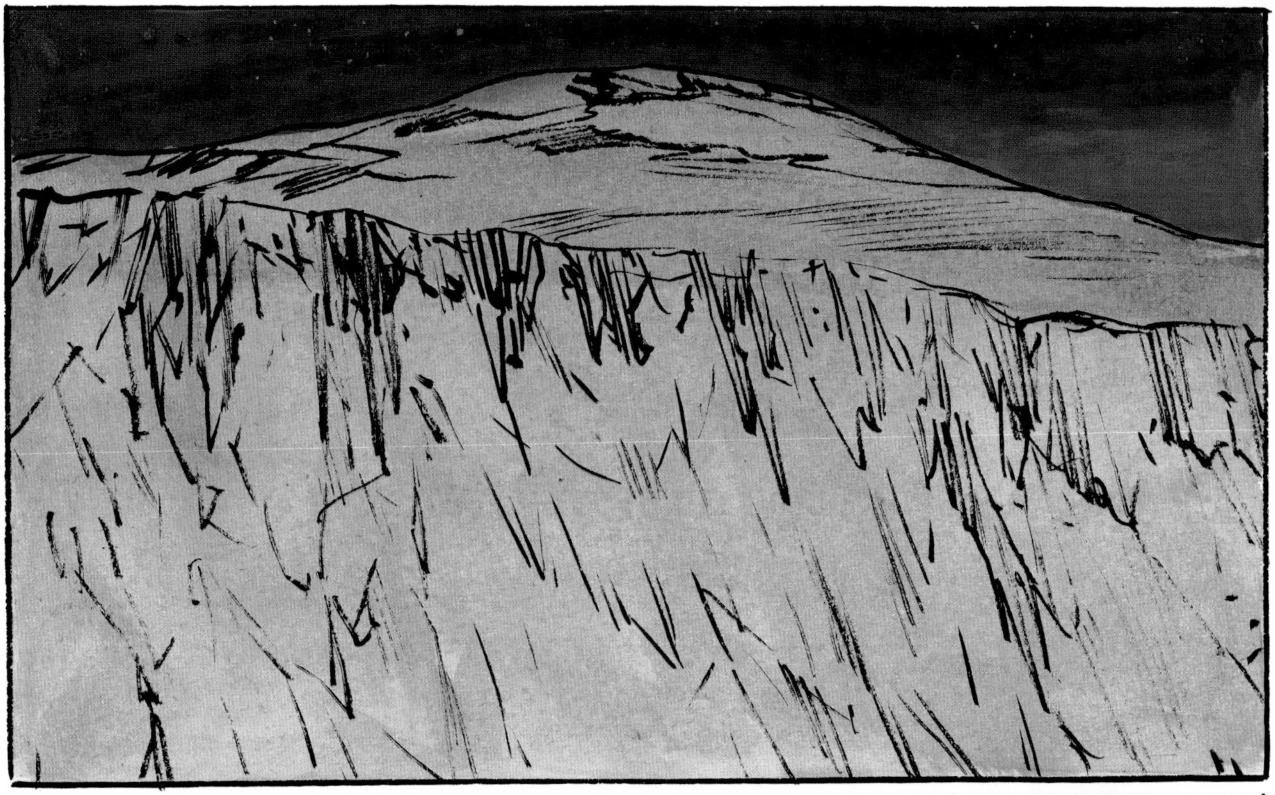

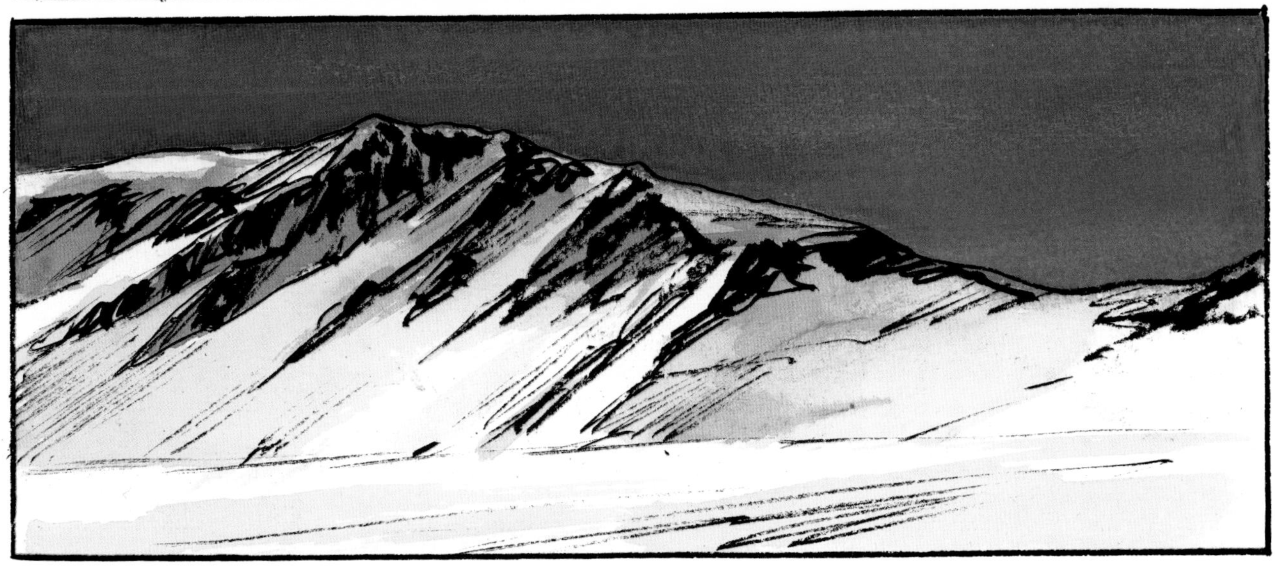

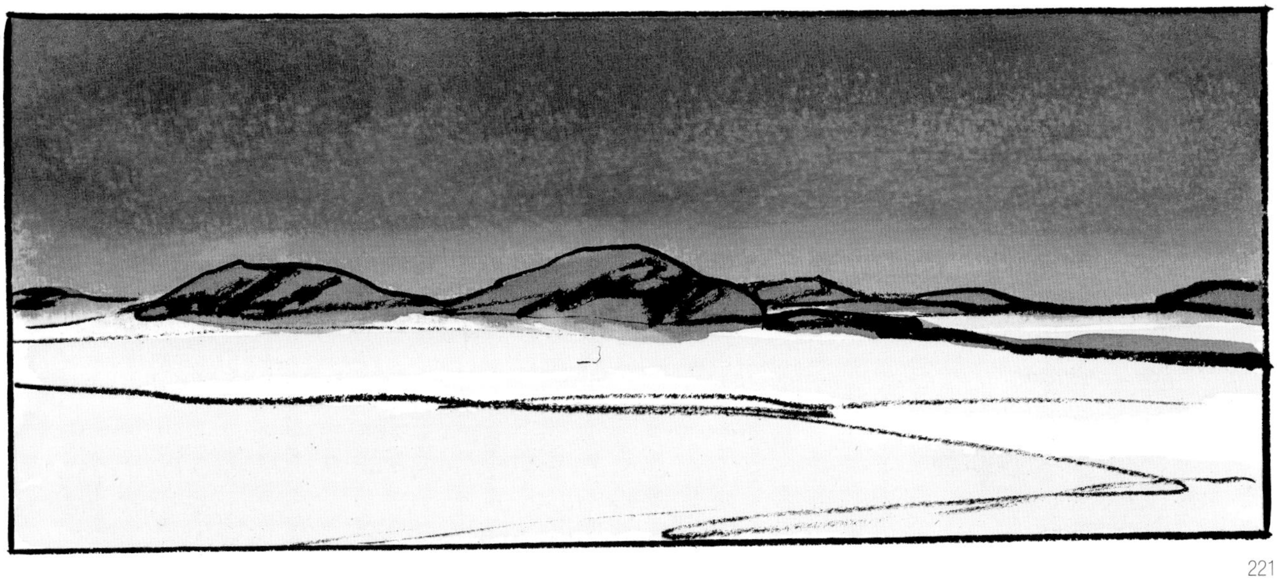

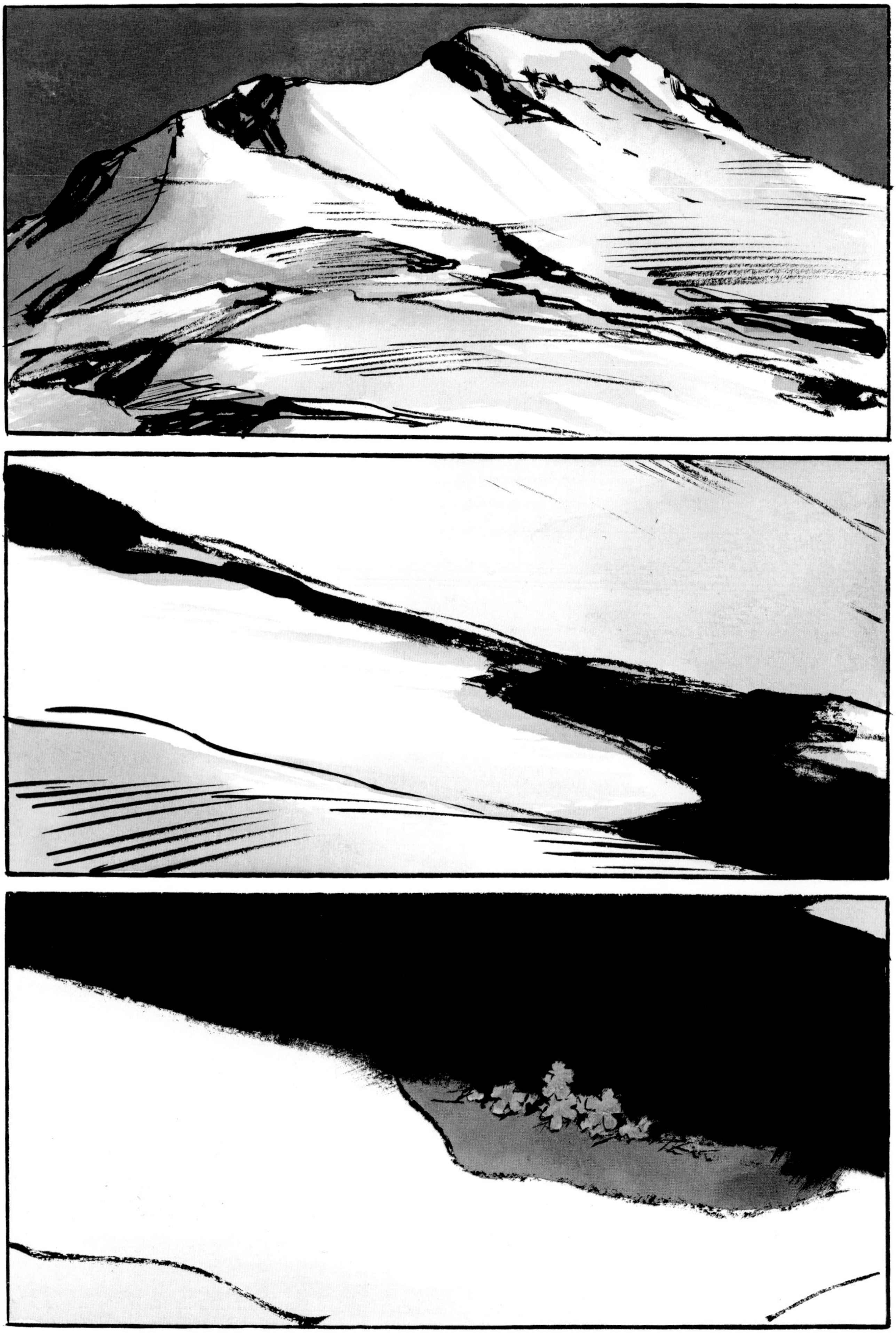

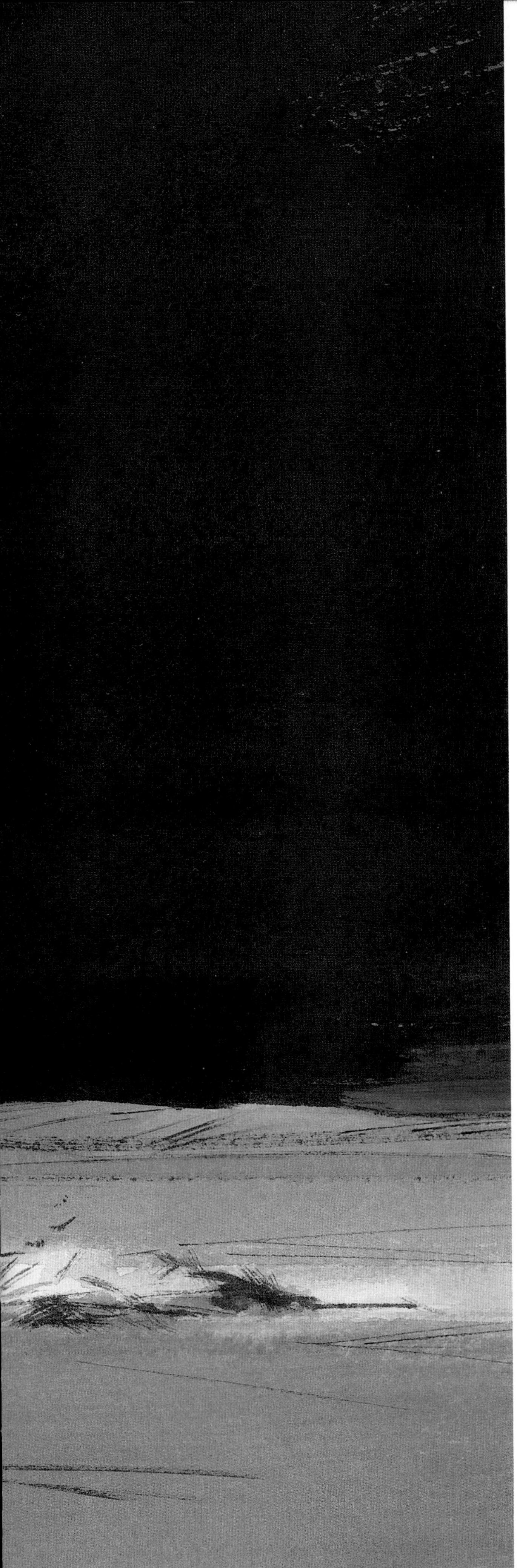

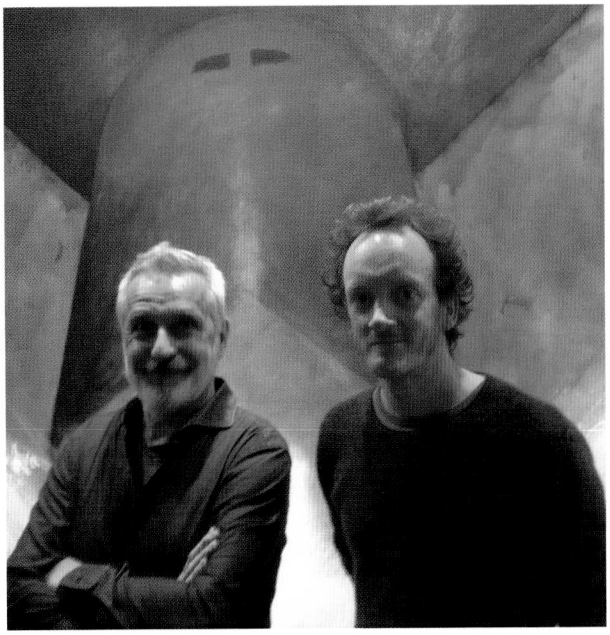

"A sudden ice age has wiped out life on Earth. What's left of humanity have gathered together on an endlessly moving train."

Read this *Snowpiercer* summary to anyone, and you'll see their face light up: they're already onboard the train, completely taken in by the adventure. They already feel the clattering of the tracks, and can sense the fight for survival, the heroes, the cowards, the poetry, the violence, a society laid bare. This is the genius of Jacques Lob: to find such a strong story, one that is so obvious, and yet is both new and familiar to the point where you don't need to know anything about it to love it.

Like all who have heard of it, I've imagined this story a hundred times over. I finally saw it, before reading, in November 2013, when *Snowpiercer* was released in cinemas. Of course, it wasn't at all what I expected. The film was by Bong Joon-Ho; crazy, explosive, stupendous, poetic and extravagant. I knew I'd have to see it twice to be able to completely understand, even to completely love it, just like with all Bong Joon-Ho's films. It progressed in total metaphor, with no attempt at realism; deviating from the usual Hollywood style. Each train carriage was overtly a representation of every facet of society. As a result, the film contained no abstract concepts; it's an examination of life. On the first level, we simply follow the stories of the different characters, who could have been any Hollywood blockbuster characters, but who, as is always the case with Bong

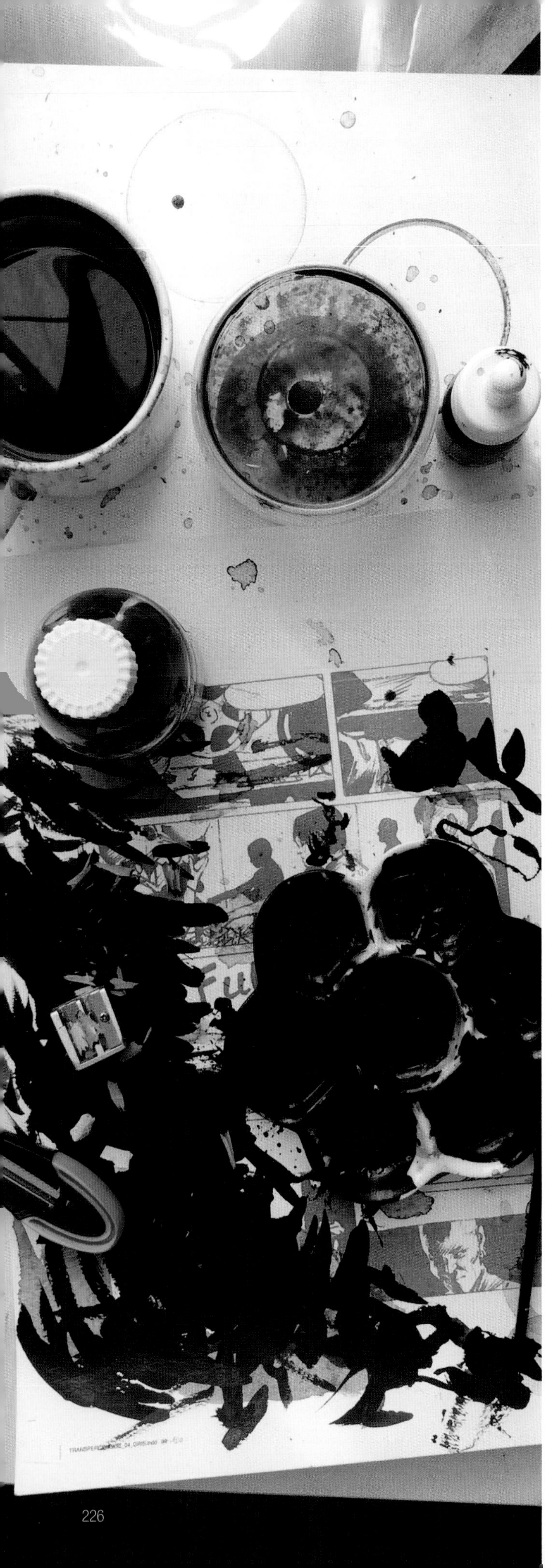

Joon-Ho, were completely deconstructed. A film you definitely have to see twice, in other words.

But even when you've digested the film, it still leaves many questions unanswered. It would have been so easy to imagine a sequel, or a prequel, or a remake... I could see myself working on a new version, but I'd have a better chance of winning the lottery, I thought.

Except this time, I did win the lottery. On June 20 2014, Christine Cam, my editor at Casterman, asked me : "How would you feel about working on *Snowpiercer*?"

Rochette had been a key player in creating the film and had produced the art which appeared in it. He had been involved in the concept art, discovered the global status surrounding this story... All of this convinced him that *Snowpiercer* had much more to be unveiled. And Rochette had plenty more to say.

His idea according to Christine's email was: "Describe the descent of the damned into a subterranean world. The fleeting joy of survivors who think they've finally managed to escape their fate, only to find that they've fallen into the very worst possibilities today's world could produce. But with a happy ending of a new model of society. Underlying criticism of contemporary society: migration, detention centers, nuclear power, the dangers of eugenics and transhumanism. Don't lose sight of what's at its heart: a hard-hitting action adventure."

In short, a story I'd love to get my teeth into.

......

Before I met with Jean-Marc Rochette, I (finally) read the comics. And of course, it was nothing like I'd imagined. Jacques Lob created an almost realistic *Snowpiercer*, firmly anchored in the 1970s and 80s. Rochette drew up a train for him with realistic controls and cab, SNCF seats and compartments of the time, and even a bar car!

The dialogue could be heard anywhere on the streets of Paris; but the army uniform had a flavor of the Soviet. This was not only a realistic *Snowpiercer,* but also an organic one. It addressed the practicalities; the meat-making machine, the engine they name Olga (who they have to take care of like a human being), and the disease that sweeps through the train.

Lob brought the organic realism. Fifteen years later, Benjamin Legrand, along with Rochette, imagined a more dreamlike *Snowpiercer*. The limits of the train were redefined, its boundaries widened until not even the tracks could stand in its way. Men in snowsuits exited the train and flew around in machines, the passengers were drugged into a virtual reality, avoiding life by gorging on dreamed images. We all escaped the train. Foreshadowing the fifteen years to come, by the year 2000 everyone was transfixed by screens, the threat to humanity coming not from an epidemic, but from totalitarianism, terrorism and fanaticism.

Another thirteen years passed, and Bong Joon-Ho delivered his version. And every time it's the same story, just told in a different way. Is there not just one Snowpiercer? Ten? Five? There are three. Three trains, so why not a fourth?

This is how I decided to treat *Terminus*: with the idea that all of these stories coexisted, and that they could all form one final communal ending.

Rochette had written up a dense synopsis, filled with striking images: abseiling down an elevator shaft, escalators moving by themselves in an abandoned train station, a meeting with a dog, an underground wheat field. He also painted a picture of perfect happiness, 'like in all the ads'. There was obligatory vaccination; sterility; an entombed city - a 'Fukushima in a glass dome'; children deformed by radiation; and a couple trying to save their people…

Plenty of material for a script.

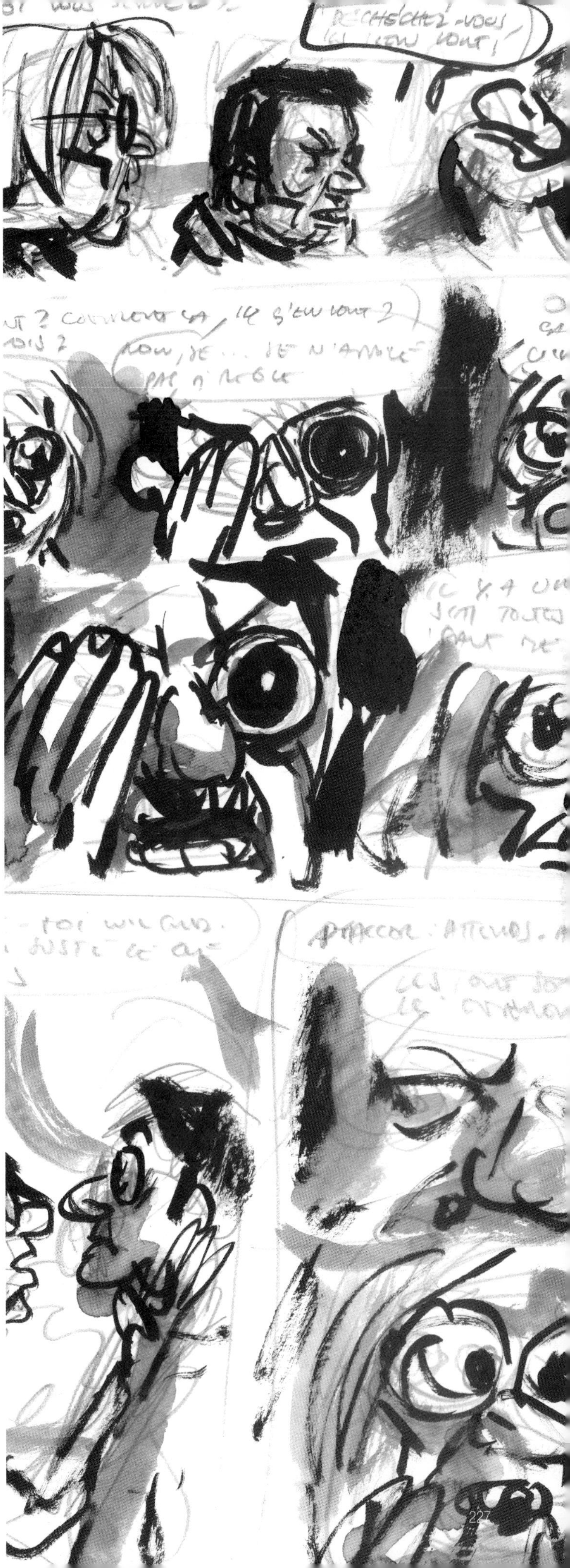

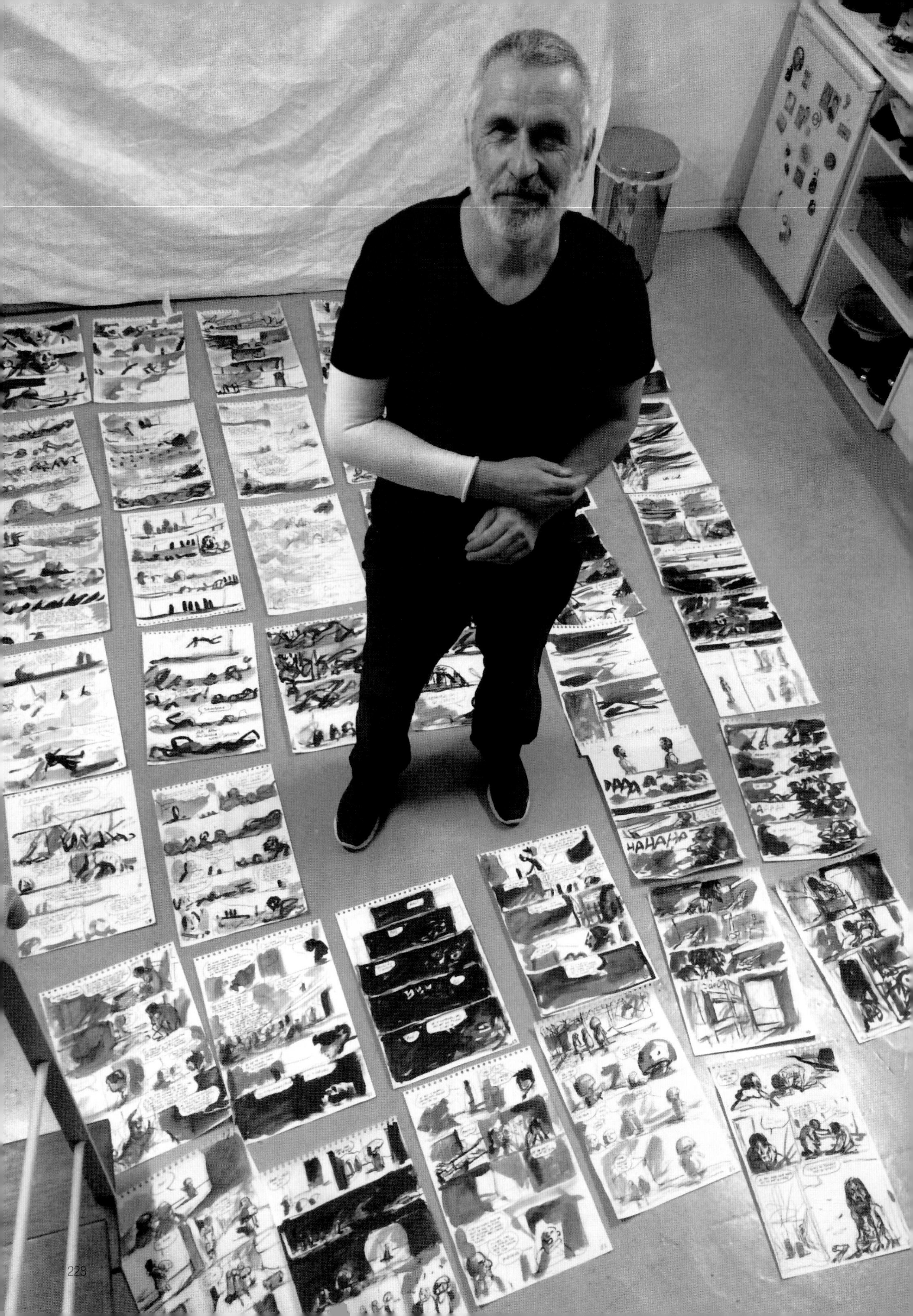
HAHAHA

We met up, and we both felt like we wanted to tell the same story. Two days later, I sent him the synopsis for the first forty pages. Ten days later, the breakdown. Two days after that, we started working on the storyboard at his place… the train was set in motion. We were on fire. Every time we saw each other, we had new ideas; I wrote, he drew, he would give me solutions to script problems, and I would do the same for his drawings. Everything was on track, nothing could stop us… until Jean-Marc had a fall. Double fracture to his right elbow. At first, he refused to believe it. He wrapped up his arm, put ice on it and carried on drawing. The twenty-second page of the book (the one with the three kids on the train roof and Brady asking who they are) was drawn in the hours straight after the accident, before he even decided to go to the hospital. The following two pages were drawn the next day.

He refused the metal plate and the operation. All he did was strap up his arm, loosely enough to keep the flexibility to draw. Just like Puig Valles who breaks his arm at the beginning of the book, he carried on regardless.

There isn't much to report on the rest of the process – like in all comic book production. Have ideas, organize them, problem-solve… We talked, I wrote, we worked on the storyboard, he drew. At each stage, the story was refined, became more precise. There were moments of euphoria, hard times, and times where you can't think anymore, you're just getting it done.

Working on this book was a real insight into Rochette's methods, trying to bring a twelve-page scene about a guy in a drawer to life. It was listening to Rochette tell me 'it needs sex,' but resisting for two months before realising that actually, yes, it needs sex and it would be vital to the story. It was making a mouse mask out of cardboard to convince Rochette that this crazy idea would work. It was taking advantage of the visual sense of the artist to make a script: the pool, the zoo, the museum, the pollen, the puppeteer, the red pages, the whale, the cave paintings, the blind hero… all were down to him.

It also meant braving a territory laden with clichés, and trying to do better. To not blow up the nuclear reactor at the end. Or create an ultramodern futuristic city, nor a completely decadent one. To not have everyone in battle armor. No big bad guy. To not solve all their problems with violence… How many people get killed by our heroes in the book? Zero.

Therefore, the script became on one hand the themes running through it, but on the other, related to the lasting decisions made by the characters on their journey, the backgrounds and the costumes. The goal was simply to link it all up in a way to make it a good story.

The background, for example, could appear secondary. A subterranean city. Classic science-fiction trope, shouldn't be too much of an issue. It was a no-brainer, and shouldn't need too much thought. However, I got complete writer's block over it. How would I justify this city's existence? It'd be unbelievable that people would have had the time and the means to build in the midst of the catastrophe. It would have had to have existed before, but why build something for the end of the world? And who would have had the funds to do it? The practical idea of a survivalist cult was the first that came to mind. But with that idea came a lot of other associations: religious societies preparing for the apocalypse, dictatorship leaders, probably crazy and surrounded by harems, human sacrifice, grandiose ceremonies, a people who have seen the light, those who resist, etc.

So, I needed to find the best way to tell a story that had been told thousands of times. I needed to find something else.

Then I thought of one of the places in Disneyland that had existed in nearly all the parks since 1955: Tomorrowland. This was a place created as a demonstration for what the future could be. It was an interesting concept, and one that hadn't been explored too much: that the post-apocalyptic underground world would be, in fact, a theme park. In contrast, 'a window' into what would be an autonomous city. Of course, in order to remain the happy place usually associated with theme parks, it would not exist to prepare for the end of the world, but the journey into Space.

MADAME ET MONSIEUR

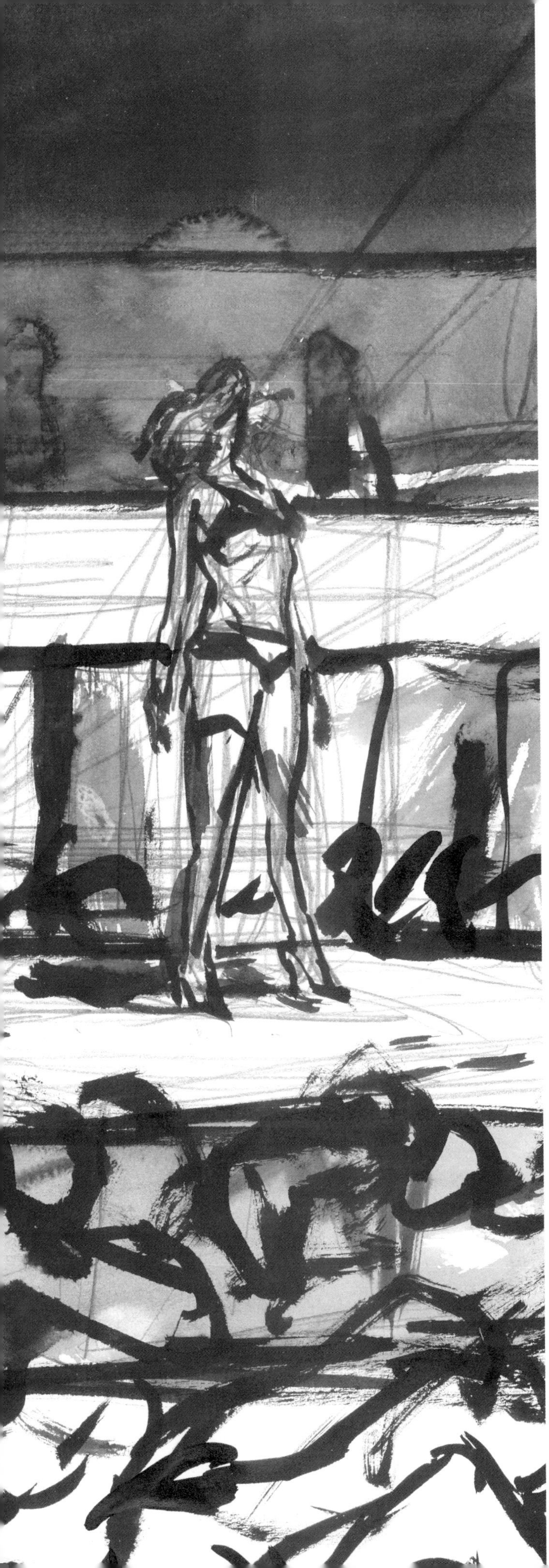

And if this theme park had been envisaged as a means of funding research, then the scientists would be on-site. After weeks of scratching our heads, finding this solution was like switching on a lightbulb: everything all just fell into place.

- If the research being carried out in this city focused on space travel, then it was only one more step toward prolonging human life, and another to consider the omnipotence of pharmaceuticals, genetic manipulation or transhumanism, the great fanaticism of the 21st century. The search for the perfect human, the perfect child. The takeover of our bodies by medicine and science, with or without our consent.

- The city was built underneath a nuclear power plant. Not next to, underneath. As Tom is shocked, Puig tells him: "I don't understand the past world." What world? The one that accepted living with nuclear power despite its dangers. Our world. Is your environment making you sick? Cancers multiplying? That's progress! But there's no reason to leave, we'll find a way to heal you.

- Before the disaster, tourists went willingly to the park, for fun. They wore mouse masks and found it 'nice, funny and convivial.' Then after the Great Freeze, when the radiation and their medication started eroding their skin, the tourists (now inhabitants) became slaves to the masks to hide the truth. To hide it from others like themselves. The dictatorship of fun and appearances right through to during the apocalypse. Uniformity up until death.

Bonus: the mouse masks also allow for a very distinct graphic style for the book, and plunge it into mystery: *Unheimliche*, 'worrying strangeness'.

What began as just a science-fiction setting became the framework on which we could hang the main themes of the book. Future Land doesn't show the future; it is a vision of the present. This city ended up being the spine of the whole book.

– Olivier Bocquet, 2015

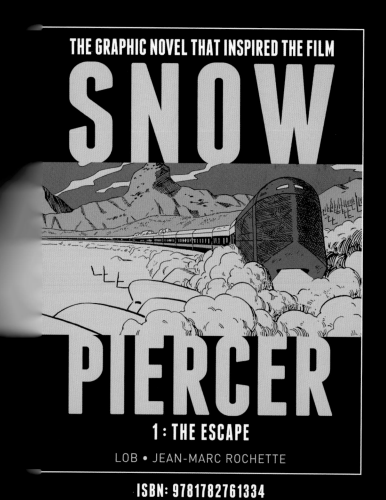

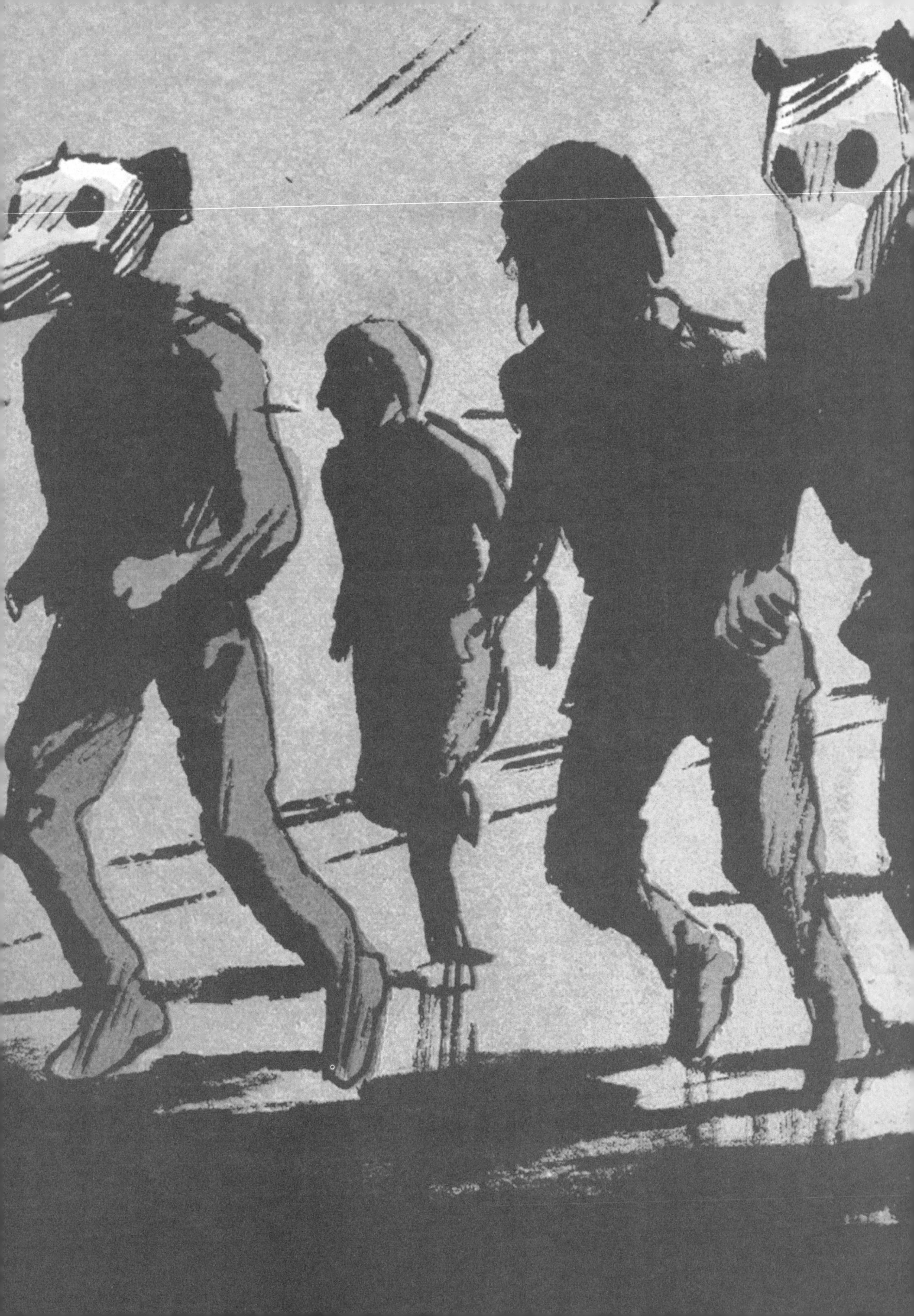